# THE ALA
# BOOK OF
# LIBRARY
# GRANT
# MONEY

# THE ALA BOOK OF LIBRARY GRANT MONEY

## EIGHTH EDITION

Edited by Ann Kepler

AMERICAN LIBRARY ASSOCIATION
CHICAGO   2012

Printed in the United States of America

**3 1984 00304 6040**

16  15  14  13  12      5  4  3  2  1

Extensive effort has gone into ensuring the reliability of the information in this book; however, the publisher makes no warranty, express or implied, with respect to the material contained herein.

ISBNs: 978-0-8389-1058-0 (paper); 978-0-8389-9401-6 (PDF). For more information on digital formats, visit the ALA Store at alastore.ala.org and select eEditions.

Cover design by Casey Bayer. Text design by Karen Sheets de Gracia in Charis SIL.

♾ This paper meets the requirements of ANSI/NISO Z39.48-1992 (Permanence of Paper).

# CONTENTS

# INTRODUCTION

The *ALA Book of Library Grant Money*, eighth edition, provides detailed descriptive profiles of philanthropic programs in the United States—programs associated with private foundations, corporate foundations, and corporate direct givers. All of the funders in this directory have either made grants to libraries within the last few reporting periods or have listed libraries as a typical recipient category.

The *ALA Book of Library Grant Money* offers fund-raisers and researchers quick and convenient access to important information on the major U.S. funding organizations supporting libraries. The book includes data on the top private foundations, those with assets or grant distributions of at least $100,000. Interfiled with these major private foundations are corporate foundations and hard-to-find direct corporate givers.

The directory generally excludes funders that do not accept unsolicited requests for funds and those funders that give only to preselected recipients.

## Content and Arrangement

The funders are arranged alphabetically by the name of the foundation or by the name of the corporation sponsoring the foundation or direct giving program. Foundations named after family members are listed alphabetically by family name. For instance, the Theodore H. Barth Foundation appears alphabetically under "Barth." For corporation names and corporate foundations that are personal names, the user is advised to locate a company first by surname and, if unsuccessful, to try the first element in the name. Professional grants available from state library associations can be found alphabetically under the name of the state.

Giving profiles are as detailed as permitted by the information available. Contents of a profile can include

- foundation name or sponsoring company name and corporate foundation name, if applicable

- corporate and/or foundation contact information
- corporate profile information—year founded, operating locations, type of product or service, in-kind service or support, and corporate sponsorship
- foundation profile information— year founded, operating location, organization type, and grant types
- financial summary
- typical recipients
- past grant recipients
- requirements and restrictions
- application procedures, including submission guidelines and deadlines
- grant-specific website

## Method of Compilation

*The ALA Book of Library Grant Money* contains giving profiles that support libraries and library services. Foundation profiles are based on the most recent Form 990-PF available from the IRS, as well as the foundation's annual reports, grants lists, and guidelines. Profiles of corporate direct-giving programs are based on information provided directly by the companies in their annual reports and websites.

# USER'S GUIDE

## Arrangement of Giving Profiles

Giving profiles are arranged alphabetically by the name of the foundation or by the sponsoring company name in the case of corporate foundations and corporate direct-giving programs. If a giving profile is for a corporate foundation, such as Andersen Corp./Andersen Corporate Foundation, the profile has two headings—one for information on the corporation and another for information on the foundation. Giving profiles for private foundations and corporate direct-giving programs have only one profile heading.

## Information Elements

Information elements for each type of profile vary. The description of entry elements below explains the standard elements that a giving profile can contain, depending on the nature of the profile—private foundation, corporate foundation, or corporate direct-giving program.

## Description of Information Elements

**Company Name**

**Company Headquarters:** address, phone, fax, e-mail, and URL for the sponsoring corporation's headquarters location, when available

**Company Description:** general information to give a capsule look at the financial health and business interests of the profiled company

- year the company was founded
- operating locations—since company business typically revolves around corporate headquarters and operating locations, charitable giving information reflects this orientation
- types of products or services—a company's field of business or marketing slant often influences its charitable objectives
- in-kind or service support—these types and amounts of nonmonetary support include cause-related marketing and promotion, donated equipment, donated products,

in-kind services, loaned employees, and workplace orientation

- corporate sponsorship—information about the types of events or causes sponsored, such as art fairs or sports events

**Foundation Name**

**Foundation Headquarters:** address, phone, fax, e-mail, and URL for the foundation's headquarters location, when available

**Foundation Description:** general information about the foundation

- year the foundation was founded
- operating locations—a foundation's location may indicate its geographic preference for disbursing funds
- foundation information—type of foundation, such as family, private, or corporate

**Financial Summary:** the most current figures of market value of a foundation's assets, along with figures for overall giving for the most recent years available

**Grants Information:** detailed information about available grants and how to apply for them

- grant types—awards, general support, scholarship, operating support, project, multiyear continuing support, employee matching, and so forth
- typical recipients—For corporate

and foundation profiles, this includes an inventory of the types of nonprofit causes that a corporation or foundation has supported in recent years, using 215 standard recipient subcategories under nine broad categories: Arts & Humanities, Civic & Public Affairs, Education, Environment, Health, International, Religion, Science, and Social Services. This section is designed to catalog the kinds of activities supported, rather than indicate priority. A complete list of the 215 recipient organization types, arranged under the nine major categories, is available on page 0000. For profiles of professional library organizations, this includes more library-specific information about recipients.

- grant values—an analytical section that includes total dollar amount of grants, number of grants, average grant, highest grant, lowest grant, and typical range in the most current time period available
- past grant recipients—when available, provides a listing of the top library- and school-related grants and a general listing of the top recently awarded grants from the nine broad categories (Arts & Humanities, Civic & Public Affairs, Education, Environment, Health, International, Religion, Science, and Social Services)
- requirements and restrictions—a brief description of restrictions on

eligibility (for example, an applicant must have tax-exempt status) or on types of programs, campaigns, or organizations that are not funded
- application procedures—preferred methods of contacting the company or foundation, meeting requirements for proposals, and sending requests within specific time frames. When available, the decision notification time frame and procedure are included.

- contact information—name and specific contact information of person to contact when applying for a grant, when available
- grant-specific website—access information for a website focused on the grant process adopted by the company or foundation

# NONPROFIT RECIPIENT CATEGORIES AND ORGANIZATION TYPES

## Arts & Humanities

Art History, Arts Appreciation, Arts Associations & Councils, Arts Centers, Arts Festivals, Arts Funds, Arts Institutes, Arts Outreach, Ballet, Community Arts, Dance, Ethnic & Folk Art, Film & Video, Historic Preservation, History & Archeology, Libraries, Literary Arts, Museums/Galleries, Music, Opera, Performing Arts, Public Broadcasting, Theater, Visual Arts

## Civic & Public Affairs

African American Affairs, Asian American Affairs, Botanical Gardens/ Parks, Business/Free Enterprise, Chambers of Commerce, Civil Rights, Clubs, Community Foundations, Economic Development, Economic Policy, Employment/Job Training, Ethnic Organizations, First Amendment Issues, Gay/Lesbian Issues, Hispanic Affairs, Housing, Inner-City Development, Law & Justice, Legal Aid, Minority Business, Municipalities/ Towns, Native American Affairs, Nonprofit Management, Parades/

Festivals, Philanthropic Organizations, Professional/Trade Associations, Public Policy, Rural Affairs, Safety, Urban/ Community Affairs, Women's Affairs, Zoos/Aquariums

## Education

After-School Enrichment Programs, Agricultural Education, Arts/Humanities Education, Business Education, Business-School Partnerships, Colleges & Universities, Community/Junior Colleges, Continuing Education, Economic Education, Education Associations, Education Funds, Education Reform, Elementary Education (private), Elementary Education (public), Engineering Education, Environmental Education, Faculty Development, Gifted & Talented Programs, Health & Physical Education, International Exchange, International Studies, Journalism/Media Education, Leadership Training, Legal Education, Literacy, Medical Education, Minority Education, Preschool Education, Private Education (precollege), Public Education (precollege), Religious Education, School

Volunteerism, Science/Mathematics Education, Secondary Education (private), Secondary Education (public), Social Sciences Education, Special Education, Student Aid, Vocational/Technical Education

# Environment

Air/Water Quality, Energy, Forestry, Protection, Research, Resource Conservation, Sanitary Systems, Watershed, Wildlife Protection

# Health

Adolescent Health Issues, AIDS/HIV, Alzheimer's Disease, Arthritis, Cancer, Children's Health/Hospitals, Clinics/Medical Centers, Diabetes, Emergency/Ambulance Services, Eyes/Blindness, Geriatric Health, Health Funds, Health Organizations, Health Policy/Cost Containment, Heart, Home-Care Services, Hospices, Hospitals, Hospitals (university affiliated), Kidney, Long-Term Care, Medical Rehabilitation, Medical Research, Medical Training, Mental Health, Multiple Sclerosis, Nursing Services, Nutrition, Outpatient Health Care, Prenatal Health Issues, Preventive Medicine/Wellness Organizations, Public Health, Research/Studies Institutes, Respiratory, Single-Disease Health Associations, Speech & Hearing, Transplant Networks/Donor Banks, Trauma Treatment

# International

Foreign Arts Organizations, Foreign Education Institutions, Health Care/Hospitals, Human Rights, International Affairs, International Development, International Environmental Issues, International Law, International Organizations, International Peace & Security Issues, International Relations, International Relief Efforts, Missionary/Religious Activities, Trade

# Religion

Bible Study/Translation, Churches, Dioceses, Jewish Causes, Ministries, Missionary Activities (domestic), Religious Organizations, Religious Welfare, Seminaries, Social/Policy Issues, Synagogues/Temples

# Science

Observatories/Planetariums, Science Exhibits/Fairs, Science Museums, Scientific Centers/Institutes, Scientific Labs, Scientific Organizations, Scientific Research

# Social Services

Animal Protection, At-Risk Youth, Big Brother/Big Sister, Camps, Child Abuse, Child Welfare, Community Centers, Community Service Organizations, Counseling, Crime Prevention, Day Care,

Delinquency/Criminal Rehabilitation, Domestic Violence, Emergency Relief, Family Planning, Family Services, Food & Clothing Distribution, Homes, People with Disabilities, Recreation & Athletics, Refugee Assistance, Scouts, Senior Services, Sexual Abuse, Shelters/Homeless, Special Olympics, Substance Abuse, United Funds/United Way, Veterans, Volunteer Services, YMCA/YMHA/YWCA/YWHA, Youth Organizations

# PROFILES

## Abbott Laboratories

### Headquarters

100 Abbott Park Rd.
Abbott Park, IL 60064
Phone: 847-937-6100
www.abbott.com

### Description

**Founded:** 1900

**Operating Locations:** Illinois

**Type of Product/Service:**
Pharmaceuticals/biological, surgical/
medical instruments

**In-Kind or Service Support:**
Donated products to overseas health
care programs and disaster relief
efforts

**Corporate Sponsorship:**
Arts, cultural, music, entertainment
events

## ABBOTT FUND

100 Abbott Park Rd., Dept. 379, Bldg.
6D
Abbott Park, IL 60064
www.abbottfund.org
**Foundation Information:** Corporate
foundation of Abbott Laboratories

### Financial Summary

Assets: $191,987,250
Total Giving: $22,840,194

### Grants Information

**GRANT TYPES**
Continuing support, general support,
operating support, scholarship, research,
employee matching

**TYPICAL RECIPIENTS**
Arts and humanities, education, health,
international, science, social services

**GRANT VALUES**
Total Dollar Amount of Grants:
$22,840,194

Highest Grant: $11,045,000
Lowest Grant: $25
Typical Range of Grants:
$5,000–$20,000

## PAST GRANT RECIPIENTS

### Library or School Related

- Columbus Literacy Council (OH), general support, $10,000
- Columbus Metropolitan Library (OH), general support, $25,000
- Franklin University Library (OH), general support, $50,000
- Rocky Mount Senior High School (NC), general support, $5,000
- St. Labre Indian School (MT), general support, $1,526
- Weber State University Foundation (UT), general support, $6,000

### General

- American Society of Health-System Pharmacists Research & Educational Foundation (MD), general support, $50,000
- Baltimore Children's Museum (MD), general support, $20,000
- Ivinson Memorial Hospital Foundation (WY), general support, $5,000
- National Association of People with AIDS (DC), general support, $10,000
- Society for Women's Health Research (DC), general support, $10,000
- Utah Federation for Youth (UT), general support, $1,000

## REQUIREMENTS AND RESTRICTIONS

Abbott Fund is interested in headquarters (Illinois) and operating communities and disadvantaged communities worldwide; 33 percent of grants go to Illinois, 25 percent to Ohio, and the rest to the other 40 states and overseas communities. Criteria of successful applications include promoting science and medical innovation and strengthening community organizations. The fund has a special interest in children and youth and children in poverty. Abbott Fund is shifting much of its funding to international causes, especially health care education. The fund does not award grants to individuals, political or lobbying groups, religious organizations for sectarian purposes, advertising symposia, conferences, or meetings. Applicants must pass an eligibility test.

## APPLICATION PROCEDURES

**Submission Guidelines:** Abbott Fund accepts only online applications. See the website for eligibility test and submission guidelines. Grant requests must include

- description of organization's mission
- confirmation of current 501(c)(3) status
- geographic area served
- description of project/program for which support is requested
- amount of money requested

- budget information
- list of corporations and foundations supporting the organization

**Decisions:** Decisions are delivered by e-mail within 6–8 weeks.

## CONTACT
Cindy Schwab
Phone: 847-937-7075
Fax: 847-935-5051
E-mail: cindy.schwab@abbott.com

## GRANT-SPECIFIC WEBSITE
www.abbottfund.org
Application information: www.
abbottfund.org/pdfs/fund_
guidelines.pdf

# ADC Telecommunications

## Headquarters

13625 Technology Dr.
Eden Prairie, MN 55344-2252
Phone: 800-366-3889
www.adc.com

## Description

**Founded:** 1935

**Operates in:** United States, Mexico, Australia, India

**Type of Product/Service:**
Communications services and products

**In-Kind or Service Support:** Donated products, in-kind services, employee gift matches; supports employee community volunteerism

**Support Contact:** Community Connections Committee; Phone: 800-366-3889

# ADC FOUNDATION

PO Box 1101
Minneapolis, MN 55440-1101
**Foundation Information:** Corporate foundation of ADC Telecommunications

## Financial Summary

Assets: $8,046,997
Total Giving: $1,625,983

## Grants Information

### GRANT TYPES
General support, operating support, scholarship, endowment in mathematics and science education, nonprofit access to technology, STEM (science, technology, engineering, mathematics)

### TYPICAL RECIPIENTS
Arts and humanities, civic affairs, education, health, science, social services

## GRANT VALUES

Total Dollar Amount of Grants:
   $1,625,983

Highest Grant: $75,000

Lowest Grant: $500

Typical Range of Grants: $2,000–$5,000

## PAST GRANT RECIPIENTS

*Library or School Related*

- Bakken Library and Museum (MN), science education program, $5,000
- MATHCOUNTS Foundation (VA), nationwide middle school mathematics competitions, $75,000
- Minnesota High Technology Foundation (MN), Bakken Library's participation in Wonders of Technology, $5,000
- Puerto Rican Cultural Center (IL), library technology, $2,500
- University of St. Thomas (MN), STEPS (Science, Technology, and Engineering Preview Summer Camp for Girls) Program, $5,000

*General*

- Society of Women Engineers (IL), scholarships in engineering, $5,000
- Girl Scouts of Rio Grande (TX), mobile computer lab, $5,000
- Grantmakers for Education (OR), general operating support, $1,000
- International Engineering Consortium (IEC) (IL), tuition for IEC's forums, $25,000
- African-American AIDS Task Force (MN), technology upgrade, $2,000

- Center for Homicide Research (MN), technology grant, $2,000
- Crisis Connection (MN), call center upgrade, $10,000

## REQUIREMENTS AND RESTRICTIONS

Applications must fit ADC focus. The foundation does not support political or lobbying groups or religious organizations for sectarian purposes.

## APPLICATION PROCEDURES

**Submission Guidelines:** Letter of inquiry form from website. Applications must include

- description of organization
- amount requested
- purpose of funds sought
- recently audited financial statement
- proof of tax-exempt status
- list of board of directors

**Decisions:** Funding decisions are made quarterly (FY Nov. 1 to Oct. 31).

## CONTACT

Bill Linder-Scholer

Phone: 952-917-0580

E-mail: bill.linder-scholer@adc.com

## GRANT-SPECIFIC WEBSITE

www.adc.com/philanthropy/
Application information:
   www.adc.com/aboutadc/
   adcfoundation/
   letterofinquiryform/

# Adobe Systems

## Headquarters

345 Park Ave.
San Jose, CA 95110-2704
Phone: 408-538-6000
www.adobe.com

## Description

**Founded:** 1982

**Operating Locations:** California

**Type of Product/Service:** Business and mobile software and equipment

**In-Kind or Service Support:** Donated software; employee matching gift program; provides employee volunteer teams to offer services and training to nonprofit and educational organizations

**Support Contact:** Phone: 408-536-6000

**Corporate Sponsorship:** Organization events

# ADOBE FOUNDATION

625 Townsend
San Francisco, CA 94103
Phone: 408-536-3993
www.adobe.com/aboutadobe/
philanthropy/commgivingprgm.html

**Foundation Information:** Corporate foundation of Adobe Systems

## Financial Summary

Assets: $9,452,758
Gifts Received: $9,500,000
Total Giving: $7,429,248

## Grants Information

### GRANT TYPES
Operating support, education, reduction of hunger and homelessness

### TYPICAL RECIPIENTS
Arts and humanities, civic affairs, education, environment, social services

### GRANT VALUES
Total Dollar Amount of Grants:
$7,429,248
Highest Grant: $90,000
Lowest Grant: $5,000
Typical Range of Grants: $10,000–40,000

### PAST GRANT RECIPIENTS

*Library or School Related*
- Alliance for Education (WA), Nathan Hale High School Adobe Youth Voices Project, $5,000
- Arts Engine (NY), general and unrestricted, $5,000
- Galileo Academy Science Technology Alumni Association (CA), Adobe

Youth Voices Project, $5,000
- Peter Burnett Academy (CA), Adobe Youth Voices Project, $5,000
- Newcomer's High School (NY), Adobe Youth Voices Project, $5,000
- Aki Kurose Middle School Academy (WA), Adobe Youth Voices Project, $5,000
- Bridges to Understanding (WA), Adobe Youth Voices Project, $5,000

### REQUIREMENTS AND RESTRICTIONS

The foundation concentrates on northern California and Washington but donates at national and international locations. The foundation does not support individuals, religious organizations for sectarian purposes, political or lobbying groups, or organizations that unlawfully discriminate against any kind of person. Community Investment Grants provide multiyear support, but recipients must wait one year after grant ends before reapplying.

### APPLICATION PROCEDURES

**Submission Guidelines:** Send a postcard, call, or visit website.

**Deadlines:** Round 1, June 1; Round 2, June 30

**Decisions:** Round 1, February 18; Round 2, August 31

### CONTACT

Phone: 408-536-3993

### GRANT-SPECIFIC WEBSITE

www.adobe.com/aboutadobe/ philanthropy/commgivingprgm.html

# Air Products and Chemicals, Inc.

## Headquarters

7201 Hamilton Blvd.
Allentown, PA 18195
Phone: 610-481-4911
www.airproducts.com

## Description

**Founded:** 1940

**Operating Locations:** 35 locations worldwide

**Type of Product/Service:** Industrial gases and chemicals, fabricated plate work, coatings and adhesives

**In-Kind or Service Support:** Donated products and equipment, loaned employees; employee volunteerism encouraged; matching gifts program

**Support Contact:** Marta Boulos Gabriel; E-mail: gabrielmb@apci.com

**Corporate Sponsorship:** Art and cultural events, festivals, musical events

# AIR PRODUCTS FOUNDATION

7201 Hamilton Blvd.
Allentown, PA 18195
Phone: 610-481-4911
www.airproducts.com/social_
    responsibilities/
**Foundation Information:** Corporate
foundation of Air Products and
Chemicals, Inc.

## Financial Summary

Assets: $53,635,948
Total Giving: $3,329,057

## Grants Information

### GRANT TYPES
General support, operating support,
project, matching

### TYPICAL RECIPIENTS
Arts and humanities, civic affairs,
education, environment, health, international, religion, science, social services

### GRANT VALUES
Total Dollar Amount of Grants:
    $3,329,057

### PAST GRANT RECIPIENTS
*Library or School Related*
- Allentown Public Library (PA),
  general support, $6,000
- Adult Literacy Center (PA), general
  support, $2,500
- Allentown School District (PA),
  general support, $25,500
- Bucknell University (PA), general
  support, $13,000
- Carnegie Mellon University (PA),
  general support, $10,000
- Cornell University (NY), general
  support, $47,500
- Georgia Tech (GA), general support,
  $69,000

*General*
- Lehigh Gap Nature Center (PA),
  general support, $15,000
- Boys and Girls Club of Allentown
  (PA), general support, $10,000

### REQUIREMENTS AND RESTRICTIONS
Applicants must have tax-exempt
status. Grants will not be made to
individuals, sectarian or denominational
organizations, political organizations,
veterans organizations, service clubs, or
labor groups.

### APPLICATION PROCEDURES

**Submission Guidelines:** Send a
letter accompanied by a copy of the
organization's tax-exempt determination
letter from the IRS. The letter should
include

- amount of funding sought
- description of community need
- project description

- metrics for measuring success
- current project budget
- complete contact information for the applicant
- list of board of directors and their terms
- most recent IRS Form 990

### CONTACT
Laurie Gostlely-Hackett
Phone: 610-481-6118
E-mail: gostlelj@airproducts.com

### GRANT-SPECIFIC WEBSITE
www.airproducts.com/social_
    responsibilities/

# AKC Fund

## Headquarters

6 W. 48th St., 10th fl.
New York, NY 10038
Phone: 212-812-4362
Fax: 212-812-4395

## Description

**Founded:** 1955

**Operating Locations:** New York

**Foundation Information:** Private foundation

## Financial Summary

Assets: $6,545,772
Gifts Received: $484,682
Total Giving: $264,000

## Grants Information

### GRANT TYPES
Capital, general support, multiyear continuing support, professorship

### TYPICAL RECIPIENTS
Arts and humanities, civic affairs, education, environment, health, international, religion, science, social services

### GRANT VALUES
Total Dollar Amount of Grants: $264,000
Number of Grants: 44
Average Grant: $6,000
Highest Grant: $30,000
Lowest Grant: $1,000

### PAST GRANT RECIPIENTS

*Library or School Related*
- Norfolk Library (CT), general support, $1,000
- Skidmore College (NY), general support, $1,000
- Miss Porter's School (CT), faculty development program, $10,000
- Cornell School of Agriculture and Life Sciences (NY), general support, $2,000

- Shady Hill School (MA), capital campaign, $15,000
- Alameda Education Foundation (CA), Kids Chalk Art Program, $1,000

*General*
- The Montpelier Foundation (VA), permanent stand-alone exhibit on African American experience, $20,000
- National Public Radio (DC), general support, $1,000
- Forest History Society (NC), general support, $10,000
- Nature Conservancy of Montana (MT), protect lands in Blackfoot Valley, $30,000
- Susan B. Anthony Project (CT), support shelters, counseling, advocacy programs, $10,000
- I Have a Dream Foundation (VA), train mentors of Dream Program, $10,000

**REQUIREMENTS AND RESTRICTIONS**
Applicants must be located in the northeastern United States.

**APPLICATION PROCEDURES**
**Submission Guidelines:** The foundation does not accept unsolicited applications.

**CONTACT**
Ann Brownell Sloane
c/o Sloane & Hinshaw
67A E. 77th St.
New York, NY 10021
Phone: 212-737-1011

**GRANT-SPECIFIC WEBSITE**
NA

# Alaska State Library

## Headquarters

PO Box 110571
Juneau, AK 99811-0571
www.library.state.ak.us

## Description

**Founded:** 1900

**Operating Locations:** Alaska

The Alaska State Library promotes and coordinates library services to the community of Alaskan libraries; serves as the primary research library for state government; and collects, preserves, and makes accessible Alaska-related materials.

## Grants Information

**GRANT TYPES**
General support, continuing education, operating support

**TYPICAL RECIPIENTS**
Alaska libraries

**GRANT VALUES**
Highest Grant: $7,000

## NAMED GRANTS

### CONTINUING EDUCATION GRANT

The purpose of these noncompetitive Continuing Education grants is to provide funding for continuing education for Alaska public library personnel in order to provide improved library services. These grants will also help public library directors meet their biennial continuing education requirement for the annual Alaska public library assistance grant. Actual costs, not to exceed $1,000 for in-state training and $1,500 for out-of-state training, will be reimbursed.

Grant funds can be used for workshops or conferences held by the Alaska Library Association, the Pacific Northwest Library Association, the American Library Association, or the Public Library Association; distance education online classes; technical training events; or for travel and fees paid to a trainer to provide a workshop on-site for public library staff.

**Typical Recipients:** Library directors and individual staff members in all public or combined school/public library outlets in Alaska

**Grant Values:** Highest Grant, $1,500

**Requirements and Restrictions:** DirLead library directors may not apply for continuing education grants, since continuing education for these individuals is provided through the annual DirLead workshop. However, one individual staff member working in each DirLead library is eligible to apply for a grant every fiscal year.

**Deadlines:** Submit the application and pertinent documentation well in advance of the event to be assured of approval in time for the event.

### PUBLIC LIBRARY ASSISTANCE GRANT

Public Library Assistance Grant funds may be used to pay staff, purchase library materials, or pay for any other daily operating costs of the library. Alaska public libraries and combined school/public libraries are eligible. The grant will match local funds one-to-one up to a maximum of $7,000.

### INTERLIBRARY COOPERATION GRANT

Interlibrary Cooperation Grants are competitive and project oriented. Projects should have a direct impact on library users. Funds are available for a wide variety of projects, such as reading incentive programs, automation projects, computers and printers for public use, and the development of special programs for patrons.

### REQUIREMENTS AND RESTRICTIONS
Vary by grant

### APPLICATION PROCEDURES
**Submission Guidelines:** Applicants

should download and print an application from the grant website. Completed applications should be mailed to the address below.

**Deadlines:** April

**CONTACT**
Grants Administrator
Alaska State Library
344 W. Third Ave., Suite 125
Anchorage, AK 99501
Phone: 800-776-6566 or 907-269-6566
Fax: 907-269-6580

**GRANT-SPECIFIC WEBSITE**
www.library.state.ak.us/dev/grants.html

# Alcoa, Inc.

## Headquarters

Alcoa Corporate Center
201 Isabella St.
Pittsburgh, PA 15212-5858
www.alcoa.com

## Description

**Founded:** 1888

**Operating Locations:** More than 200 locations in 31 countries worldwide

**Type of Product/Service:** Aluminum products

# ALCOA FOUNDATION

201 Isabella St.
Pittsburgh, PA 15212
Phone: 412-553-2348
www.alcoa.com/global/en/community/
    foundation.asp
**Foundation Information:** Corporate foundation of Alcoa, Inc.

## Financial Summary

Assets: $329,033,495
Total Giving: $26,193,332

## Grants Information

**GRANT TYPES**
General support, capital, research, multiyear continuing support, challenge, emergency, matching, seed money

**TYPICAL RECIPIENTS**
Arts and humanities, civic affairs, education, environment, health, international, religion, science, social services

**GRANT VALUES**
Total Dollar Amount of Grants:
    $26,193,332

**PAST GRANT RECIPIENTS**
*Library or School Related*
• Carnegie Library of Pittsburgh

(PA), Libraries for Life programs for children, $200,000
- New York Public Library (NY), central and digital library projects, $250,000
- Frontier College Foundation (Ontario, Canada), Learning for Life family literacy program, $30,000
- Connecticut Regional School District (CT), development of environmental studies program, $10,000
- Temple University (PA), judicial education program for Chinese judges, $56,160
- University of Detroit (MI), engineering career program, $5,000

*General*
- August Wilson Center for African American Culture (PA), educational curriculum development, $120,000
- Texarkana Historical Society and Museum (TX), exhibit and historical educational program, $7,500
- Northern Area Health Education Center (MI), virtual science and technology career center, $22,000
- St. Luke's Community House (TN), child development program, $15,000
- Three Rivers Youth (PA), educational support services and life skills program, $35,000

## REQUIREMENTS AND RESTRICTIONS
Applicants must have tax-exempt status. The foundation does not fund individuals, programs that influence legislation or public office candidates, religious organizations, funds directed to deficit reduction, fund-raising events, videos or documentaries, overhead costs, or trust funds.

## APPLICATION PROCEDURES
**Submission Guidelines:** Send a two-page letter of inquiry through the closest Alcoa facility. The letter should include

- complete contact information
- proof of tax-exempt status
- name of project
- description of project including purpose, population groups being addressed, and anticipated results
- total amount requested
- annual operating revenue

**Deadlines:** Directors usually meet bimonthly.

**Decisions:** Requests acknowledged upon receipt

## CONTACT
Requests for foundation funding should be directed to your local Alcoa office.

## GRANT-SPECIFIC WEBSITE
www.alcoa.com/global/en/community/ foundation.asp

# Tom S. and Marye Kate Aldridge Charitable and Educational Trust

## Headquarters

3035 NW 63rd St., Suite 207N
Oklahoma City, OK 73116
Phone: 405-840-9916

## Description

**Founded:** 1996

**Operating Locations:** Oklahoma

**Foundation Information:** Private foundation

## Financial Summary

Assets: $3,692,253
Total Giving: $91,800

## Grants Information

### GRANT TYPES
General support

### TYPICAL RECIPIENTS
Arts and humanities, civic affairs, education, international, religion, social services

## GRANT VALUES
Total Dollar Amount of Grants: $91,800
Number of Grants: 17
Average Grant: $5,400
Highest Grant: $20,000
Lowest Grant: $2,000

## PAST GRANT RECIPIENTS

*Library or School Related*
- Lone Oak Public Library (TX), general support, $1,900
- Oklahoma State University (OK), general support, $9,000
- University of Central Oklahoma (OK), general support, $13,400
- Rogers State University (OK), general support, $6,000
- University of Oklahoma Price (OK), general support, $11,000
- Gulf Breeze High School (FL), general support, $200

*General*
- National Institute on Developmental Delays (OK), general support, $20,000
- Gulf Breeze Sports Association (FL), general support, $400
- Lone United Methodist Church (TX), general support, $200

## REQUIREMENTS AND RESTRICTIONS
Applicants must have tax-exempt status. The trust does not make grants for facility construction or repair, retirement of debt, funding of day-to-day operating costs, or fund-raising activities.

## APPLICATION PROCEDURES

**Submission Guidelines:** Send a brief letter of inquiry, including

- description of the organization
- proof of tax-exempt status
- name and qualifications of person responsible for funds
- statement of goals and purposes of the program
- staff required and their qualifications
- itemized budget
- amount requested
- other sources of funding

## CONTACT

Robert S. Aldridge
3035 NW 63rd St., Suite 207N
Oklahoma City, OK 73116
Phone: 405-840-9916

**GRANT-SPECIFIC WEBSITE:** NA

# Joseph Alexander Foundation

## Headquarters

400 Madison Ave., Suite 906
New York, NY 10017
Phone: 212-355-3688

## Description

**Founded:** 1960

**Operating Locations:** New York

**Foundation Information:** Private foundation established by Joseph Alexander

## Financial Summary

Assets: $19,141,999
Total Giving: $673,300

## Grants Information

### GRANT TYPES
Research, educational, charitable, religious

### TYPICAL RECIPIENTS
Arts and humanities, civic affairs, education, environment, health, international, religion, science, social services

### GRANT VALUES
Total Dollar Amount of Grants: $673,300
Number of Grants: 63
Average Grant: $10,600
Highest Grant: $50,000
Lowest Grant: $1,500
Typical Range of Grants: $2,500–
    $20,000

### PAST GRANT RECIPIENTS

*Library or School Related*
- Reading Reform Foundation (NY), unrestricted, $10,000

- Delaware Valley Reading Association (PA), unrestricted, $5,000
- Yeshiva University (NY), science education, $50,000
- Pace University (NY), scholarships, $10,000
- Upper Dublin Education Foundation (PA), unrestricted, $3,500
- University of Pennsylvania (PA), School of Engineering, $50,000

*General*
- Salk Institute for Biological Studies (CA), optic nerve research, $25,000
- American-Israel Friendship League (NY), youth exchange program, $10,000
- Brooklyn Museum (NY), unrestricted, $5,000
- Guiding Eyes for the Blind (NY), unrestricted, $1,500
- International Center of Photography (NY), unrestricted, $5,000
- Museum of the City of New York (NY), unrestricted, $2,500

**REQUIREMENTS AND RESTRICTIONS**
There are no restrictions or limitations on awards, such as by type, location, charitable field, endeavor, applying institution, or any other type of factor. Accordingly, as there are no restrictions or limitations in the process, the Joseph Alexander Foundation can affirm that there is no discrimination of any kind relating to the decisions made by the foundation regarding the approval process for the granting of awards, grants, or contributions.

**APPLICATION PROCEDURES**

**Submission Guidelines:** Contact the foundation to obtain the details that relate to the specific required content of the application.

**Deadlines:** The board meets on a regular basis.

**CONTACT**
Phone: 212-355-3688

**GRANT-SPECIFIC WEBSITE**
NA

# Allegheny Foundation

## Headquarters

One Oxford Center
301 Grant St., Suite 3900
Pittsburgh, PA 15219
Phone: 412-392-2900
www.scaife.com/alleghen.html

## Description

**Founded:** NA

**Operating Locations:** Pennsylvania

**Foundation Information:** Private foundation established by Richard Mellon Scaife

# Financial Summary

Assets: $54,990,394
Gifts Received: $3,000,000
Total Giving: $3,195,500

# Grants Information

**GRANT TYPES**
General support, project

**TYPICAL RECIPIENTS**
Arts and humanities, civic affairs, education, environment, health, international, religion, science, social services

**GRANT VALUES**
Total Dollar Amount of Grants:
    $3,195,500

**PAST GRANT RECIPIENTS**

*Library or School Related*
- Andrew Carnegie Free Library (PA), general support, $100,000
- Carnegie Library of Homestead (PA), project support, $30,000
- Carnegie Library of McKeesport (PA), project support, $25,000
- Imani Christian Academy (PA), operation support, $595,000
- The Glen Montessori School (PA), program support, $10,000

- Seton Hill University (PA), project support, $300,000

*General*
- Doctors Without Borders (NY), general support, $10,000
- Cleveland Police Historical Society (OH), project support, $36,000
- Fayette County Community Actions (PA), food bank, $25,000
- Guiding Eyes for the Blind (NY), program support, $10,000
- David Horowitz Freedom Center (CA), general support, $50,000
- Tutwiler Community Education (MS), program support, $15,000

**REQUIREMENTS AND RESTRICTIONS**
Applicants must have tax-exempt status. The Allegheny Foundation concentrates its giving in the Western Pennsylvania area and confines most of its grant awards to programs for historic preservation, civic development, and education. The foundation does not make grants to individuals, and generally does not fund events, endowments, capital campaigns, renovations, or government agencies.

**APPLICATION PROCEDURES**
**Submission Guidelines:** Send a letter signed by an authorized board member and approved by the organization's board. The letter should include
- concise description of the specific program for which funds are requested

- budget for the program and for the organization
- latest audited financial statement and annual report
- copy of the organization's current ruling letter evidencing tax exemption under Section 501(c)(3) of the Internal Revenue Service Code

Grant application letters should be mailed to the address below. Additional information may be requested if needed for further evaluation.

**Deadlines:** The foundation normally considers grants at an annual meeting held in November. However, requests may be submitted at any time and will be acted upon as expeditiously as possible.

**CONTACT**
Matthew A. Groll, Executive Director
Allegheny Foundation
One Oxford Centre
301 Grant Street, Suite 3900
Pittsburgh, Pennsylvania 15219-6401
Phone: 412-392-2900

**GRANT-SPECIFIC WEBSITE**
www.scaife.com/alleghen.html

# Alliant Energy Corp.

## Headquarters

4902 N. Biltmore La.
Madison, WI 53718
www.alliant-energy.com

## Description

**Founded:** NA

**Operating Locations:** Wisconsin

**Type of Product/Service:**
Electric services

# ALLIANT ENERGY FOUNDATION, INC.

4902 N. Biltmore La.
Madison, WI 53718
Phone: 608-458-4483
Fax: 608-458-4820
www.alliantenergy.com/Community
**Foundation Information:** Corporate foundation of Alliant Energy Corp.

## Financial Summary

Assets: $25,643,652
Total Giving: $2,821,694

# Grants Information

## GRANT TYPES
General support, capital

## TYPICAL RECIPIENTS
Arts and humanities, civic affairs, education, environment, health, science, social services

## GRANT VALUES
Total Dollar Amount of Grants:
$2,821,694

## PAST GRANT RECIPIENTS

*Library or School Related*
- Herbert Hoover Presidential Library Association (IA), Herbert Hoover documentary, $7,500
- Friends of the Marshalltown Iowa Public Library (IA), computer purchase, $5,000
- Horicon Public Library (WI), teen space and after-school programs, $1,000
- Keck Memorial Library (IA), book and returns video project, $1,000
- Albert Lea Public Library Foundation (MN), support drive to equip expanded space, $1,500
- Blakesburg Public Library (IA), library improvement, $1,000
- Johnson Elementary School of the Arts (IA), SHAPE program, $4,000
- University of Wisconsin (WI), fine arts budget, $20,000

*General*
- Iowa Public Television Foundation (IA), funding for George Washington Carver video, $10,000
- Madison Children's Museum (WI), support for Family Access program, $3,500
- Opera for the Young (WI), fall tour, $2,500
- Overture Center for the Arts (WI), support for cultural heritage series, $5,000

## REQUIREMENTS AND RESTRICTIONS
Applicants must have tax-exempt status. The foundation does not accept proposals for capital projects. The foundation does not provide grants for individuals, ads in programs, door prizes, organized sports teams or activities, religious or social clubs, or fund-raising events.

## APPLICATION PROCEDURES
**Submission Guidelines:** Contact the foundation for an application form or download it from the website.

**Deadlines:** December 1 for funding in the following year

**Decisions:** Grant notification letters are sent in the first quarter of each year.

## CONTACT
Marthea A. Fox or JoAnn Healy (for Hometown Challenge)
Phone: 608-458-4483

**GRANT-SPECIFIC WEBSITE**
www.alliantenergy.com/Community

# Maurice Amado Foundation

## Headquarters

3940 Laurel Canyon Blvd., no. 809
Studio City, CA 91604
Phone: 818-980-9190
www.mauriceamadofdn.org

## Description

**Founded:** NA

**Operating Locations:** California

**Foundation Information:** Private
foundation. Maurice Amado was a
descendent of Sephardic Jews who
settled in the Ottoman Empire after their
expulsion from Spain in 1492.

## Financial Summary

Assets: $36,300,479
Total Giving: $1,374,800

## Grants Information

**GRANT TYPES**
General support, project

**TYPICAL RECIPIENTS**
Arts and humanities, civic affairs,
education, health, international, religion,
social services

**GRANT VALUES**
Total Dollar Amount of Grants:
    $1,374,800
Highest Grant: $415,000
Lowest Grant: $1,000

**PAST GRANT RECIPIENTS**

*Library or School Related*
- Blue Hill Public Library (ME),
  operating expenses, $5,000
- UCLA Foundation (CA), operating
  expenses, $26,000
- Brooklyn Kindergarten Society (NY),
  operating expenses, $10,000
- Institute of Jewish Education (CA),
  operating expenses, $1,000
- Pacific Hills School (CA), operating
  expenses, $1,000
- Stanford University Library (CA),
  purchase of the Rifat Bali collection
  of 20th century Sephardic Judaica
  published in Turkey, consisting of 700
  monographic and serial titles mostly
  in Turkish but also in French, English,
  Hebrew, and Judeo-Spanish

*General*
- River Performing and Visual Arts
  Center (TX), operating expenses,
  $5,000
- Jewish Community Foundation (CA),
  operating expenses, $415,000

- Conservation International (DC), operating expenses, $5,000
- Children's Hospital of Philadelphia (PA), operating expenses, $5,000
- Delaware Symphony Orchestra (DE), operating expenses, $14,000

**REQUIREMENTS AND RESTRICTIONS**

Applicants must have tax-exempt status. The foundation does not make grants to individuals.

**APPLICATION PROCEDURES**

**Submission Guidelines:** Send an e-mail letter of inquiry to inquiry@ mauriceamadofdn.org with the subject line "Grant Inquiry." The letter should include

- background and purpose of organization
- description of specific program or project
- dollar amount of request

If the foundation is interested, the applicant will be sent instructions on how to submit a grant proposal.

**Deadlines:** For spring board meeting, March 15; for fall board meeting, August 31

**CONTACT**

Pam Kaizer
E-mail: pkaizer@mauriceamandofdn.org

**GRANT-SPECIFIC WEBSITE**

www.mauriceamadofdn.org

# American Association of Law Libraries (AALL)

## Headquarters

105 W. Adams St., Suite 3300
Chicago, IL 60603
Phone: 312-939-4764
www.aallnet.org

## Description

**Founded:** 1906

**Operating Locations:** Illinois

The American Association of Law Libraries (AALL) was founded in 1906 to promote and enhance the value of law libraries to the legal and public communities, to foster the profession of law librarianship, and to provide leadership in the field of legal information. Today, with more than 5,000 members, the association represents law librarians and related professionals who are affiliated with a wide range of institutions: law firms; law schools; corporate legal departments; courts; and local, state, and federal government agencies.

There are 31 chapters of AALL throughout the United States. Many grants are administered by each individual chapter and by the individual divisions of AALL. Please visit the AALL's grant website, which lists links to each chapter's grant website and each division's grant website. Most of the chapter/division grants are for traveling expenses to AALL's annual conference or for continuing education.

## Financial Summary

Assets: $4,423,680
Gifts Received: $352,666
Total Giving: $88,120

## Grants Information

### GRANT TYPES
Conference attendance, continuing education, leadership development

### TYPICAL RECIPIENTS
Law librarians

### GRANT VALUES
Total Dollar Amount of Grants: $15,707
Number of Grants: 33
Average Grant: $476
Highest Grant: $2,000
Lowest Grant: $100

### NAMED GRANTS

### AALL ANNUAL MEETING/ WORKSHOP GRANT
The AALL Annual Meeting/Workshop Grant provides financial assistance to law librarians or graduate students who hold promise of future involvement in AALL and the law library profession. Funds are provided by vendors, AALL, and AALL individual members. Grants cover registration costs at either the annual meeting or workshops. Preference is given to newer, active members of AALL or of its chapters.

### MINORITY LEADERSHIP DEVELOPMENT AWARD
The Minority Leadership Development Award was created in 2001 to nurture leaders for the future and to introduce minority law librarians to leadership opportunities within the association. The award consists of travel, lodging, and registration expenses for one recipient to attend the annual meeting of AALL; an experienced AALL leader to serve as the recipient's mentor for at least one year; and an opportunity to serve on an AALL committee during the year following the monetary award.

### FCIL SCHAFFER GRANT FOR FOREIGN LAW LIBRARIANS
The purpose of the FCIL Schaffer Grant for Foreign Law Librarians is to provide financial assistance to ensure the presence and participation of a foreign librarian at the AALL annual meeting. Foreign attendees enrich AALL events by sharing global perspectives for the benefit of all participants. The FCIL Schaffer Grant for Foreign Law Librarians consists of a waiver of the AALL annual meeting full registration fee and a grant of a minimum

US$2,000 to assist with accommodations and travel costs.

An applicant must be a law librarian or other professional working in the legal information field, who is currently employed in a country other than the United States. An applicant must be in a position of significant responsibility for the dissemination, preservation, or organization of legal information. An applicant may be from any type of law library (public, law firm, corporate, academic, court, etc.). An applicant who would not otherwise have the opportunity to attend the AALL annual meeting is invited and encouraged to apply. The Grant Committee will not consider applications from individuals who have previously received the FCIL Schaffer Grant for Foreign Law Librarians.

## ALAN HOLOCH MEMORIAL GRANT

The Alan Holoch Memorial Grant helps members of the AALL Social Responsibilities Special Interest Section defray the cost of travel or registration for the AALL annual meeting. The $500 grant is funded by a generous bequest made by Alan Holoch. Individuals chosen to receive the grant have the potential to make significant contributions to law librarianship through their involvement with AALL and the SR-SIS Standing Committee on Lesbian and Gay Issues: Embracing the Diversity of Sexual Orientations and Gender Identities.

## VERONICA MACLAY GRANT

The Veronica Maclay Grant financially assists a student currently enrolled in an ALA-accredited library and information studies master's program in attending the AALL annual meeting and Conference of Newer Law Librarians. Preference is given to those individuals interested in government information and a career in law libraries. The grant may be applied toward student registration costs and for associated travel and lodging costs, up to a maximum of $1,000.

## REQUIREMENTS AND RESTRICTIONS

Applicants must be law librarians in the United States, except for grants specifically meant for foreign law librarians. Eligibility usually also requires AALL or AALL chapter membership.

## APPLICATION PROCEDURES

**Submission Guidelines:** Visit website for application information.

## CONTACT

Anne McDonald, AALL Grants
    Committee Chair
Phone: 401-274-4400
Fax: 401-222-2995
E-mail: amcdonald@riag.ri.gov

## GRANT-SPECIFIC WEBSITE

www.aallnet.org/committee/grants/
    grants.asp

# American Association of School Librarians (AASL)

## Headquarters

50 E. Huron St.
Chicago, IL 60611
Phone: 800-545-2433, ext. 1396
www.aasl.org OR www.ala.org/ala/
mgrps/divs/aasl/

## Description

**Founded:** 1951

**Operating Locations:** Illinois

The American Association of School Librarians (AASL), a division of the American Library Association since 1951, promotes the improvement and extension of library media services in elementary and secondary schools as a means of strengthening the total education program. Its mission is to advocate excellence, facilitate change, and develop leaders in the school library media field.

## Grants Information

### GRANT TYPES

Leadership development, disaster relief, conference attendance, project, awards

### TYPICAL RECIPIENTS

School libraries and librarians within the United States

### GRANT VALUES

Number of Grants: 11
Average Grant: $2,500
Highest Grant: $10,000
Lowest Grant: $1,250
Typical Range of Grants: $1,000–$3,000

### NAMED GRANTS

#### ABC-CLIO LEADERSHIP GRANT

The ABC-CLIO Leadership Grant, sponsored by ABC-CLIO, a publisher of educational and reference products, was established in 1986. The grant of up to $1,750 is given to school library associations affiliated with AASL in planning and implementing leadership programs at the state, regional, or local levels.

#### BEYOND WORDS GRANT

The Beyond Words grant program, which is a collaboration of Dollar General, AASL, and the National Education Association (NEA), provides funds to public schools whose school library program has been affected by a disaster. Grants are to replace or supplement books, media, and library equipment in the school library setting. Grants are awarded to public school libraries that have incurred substantial damage or hardship due to a natural disaster (tornado, earthquake, hurricane, flood, avalanche, mudslide), fire, or an act recognized by the federal government as terrorism.

**Requirements and Restrictions:** Recipient must be a public school library (pre-K–12) and must be located within 20 miles of a Dollar General store, distribution center, or corporate office. Recipient must have (1) lost its building or incurred substantial damage or hardship due to a natural disaster (tornado, earthquake, hurricane, flood, avalanche, mudslide), fire, or an act recognized by the federal government as terrorism; or (2) absorbed a significant number (more than 10 percent enrollment) of displaced/evacuee students. Schools may request grants in the range of $5,000 to $15,000. Funds granted by Beyond Words are in addition to any federal, state or local assistance received. Grants may not be used to supplant money normally budgeted for the school library program. Funds must be expended within 180 days of the awarding of the grant. Within one year, grant recipients will be required to complete a report briefly describing how this grant impacted their school library program.

**Submission Guidelines:** Only the online application found at http://beyondwords.ala.org will be accepted. No faxed, e-mailed, or printed forms will be accepted.

**Deadlines:** Grant applications are accepted on an ongoing basis.

**Decisions:** Applications are reviewed on the first of each month. Applicants will be notified by mail and e-mail within 8 weeks of submission.

**Contact:** Phone: 800-545-2433, ext. 1396; E-mail: beyondwords@ala.org

## FRANCES HENNE AWARD

AASL's Frances Henne Award, sponsored by Greenwood Publishing Group, was established in 1986. The $1,250 award recognizes a school library media specialist with no more than five years of experience who demonstrates leadership qualities with students, teachers, and administrators. Award recipients have the opportunity to attend an AASL conference or ALA Annual Conference for the first time and must be AASL personal members.

## INNOVATIVE READING GRANT

The AASL Innovative Reading Grant is sponsored by Capstone Publishers (Capstone Press, Compass Point Books, Picture Window Books, Stone Arch Books, and Red Brick Learning). Established in 2006, the $2,500 grant supports the planning and implementation of a unique and innovative program for children that motivates and encourages reading, especially with struggling readers.

## COLLABORATIVE SCHOOL LIBRARY AWARD

Established in 2000 and sponsored by Highsmith, Inc., the AASL Collaborative School Library Media Award recognizes and encourages collaboration and partnerships between school library media specialists and teachers in meeting goals outlined in Empowering Learners: Guidelines for School Library Programs through joint planning of a program, unit, or event in support of the curriculum and using media center resources. A cash award of $2,500 will be given to the recipient's school library. It is recommended that a portion of the cash award be used to provide opportunities for the recipients to share their project at a state association conference. Recipients may also use a portion of the award toward travel expenses to attend the American Library Association conference to accept the award. Applicants must be AASL personal members.

## INTELLECTUAL FREEDOM AWARD

Established in 1982, the Intellectual Freedom Award consists of $2,000 to the recipient and $1,000 to the media center of the recipient's choice. The award is given for upholding the principles of intellectual freedom as set forth by AASL and ALA. Applicants must be AASL personal members.

## RESEARCH GRANT

Research grants of $2,500—sponsored by Heinemann-Raintree—are given to up to two school library media specialists, library educators, or library information science or education professors to conduct innovative research aimed at measuring and evaluating the impact of school library media programs on learning and education. Special consideration will be given to pilot research studies that employ experimental methodologies. Winners of AASL Research Grants will be expected to present the results of their projects at the ALA Annual Conference in the year following the year of their grant. Applicants must be AASL personal members.

## REQUIREMENTS AND RESTRICTIONS

All grants and awards, except for the ABC-CLIO Leadership Grant, the Innovative Reading Grant, and the Beyond Words Grant, require applicants to be AASL members.

## APPLICATION PROCEDURES

**Submission Guidelines:** Application online

**Deadlines:** Beyond Words Grant applications are accepted on an ongoing basis. All other applications are due in February of each year, with applications available at the end of the preceding June.

**Decisions:** Beyond Words Grant applications are reviewed monthly. Recipients of all other grants are announced at the ALA Annual Conference.

**CONTACT**
Melissa Jacobsen
Phone: 800-545-2433, ext. 4381, or 312-
280-4381
E-mail: mjacobsen@ala.org

**GRANT-SPECIFIC WEBSITE**
www.ala.org/aasl/awards/

# American Library Association (ALA)

## Headquarters

50 E. Huron St.
Chicago, IL 60611
Phone: 800-545-2433
www.ala.org

## Description

**Founded:** 1876

**Operating Locations:** Illinois, District of Columbia

The mission of the American Library Association (ALA) is to provide leadership for the development, promotion, and improvement of library and information services and the profession of librarianship in order to enhance learning and ensure access to information for all.

ALA and its member units offer a variety of grants that provide funding or material support for present or future activities. Grants may be offered to support the planning and implementation of programs, to aid in the preparation of a dissertation or other publications, and to promote research in library and information science. Grants are also given to support travel to conferences or other events that can broaden an individual's experience or education in librarianship. Grants are administered by the ALA Awards Program, as well as by ALA divisions, offices, and round tables. These individual divisions, offices, and round tables should be contacted for specific grant information.

A list of all the grants offered by all of the different divisions and offices is available here: www.ala.org/ala/awardsgrants/grants/index.cfm.

Monetary awards for recognition are also given by ALA and can be found here: www.ala.org/ala/awardsgrants/awardgov/index.cfm.

## Financial Summary

Assets: $68,275,480
Total Giving: $1,602,570

## Grants Information

**GRANT TYPES**
Project, research, publication, conference attendance, scholarship, staff development, awards

## TYPICAL RECIPIENTS

Individual librarians, library school students, high schools, elementary schools, library districts, library systems, and university and public libraries

## GRANT VALUES

Total Dollar Amount of Grants:
$1,602,570
Number of Grants: 324
Average Grant: $4,946
Highest Grant: $15,000
Lowest Grant: $2,500

## NAMED GRANTS

### LITA/CHRISTIAN LAREW MEMORIAL SCHOLARSHIP

The LITA/Christian Larew Memorial scholarships are for master's-level study, with an emphasis on library technology or automation, at a library school accredited by the ALA. The Library and Information Technology Association (LITA), a division of the ALA, sponsors these $3,000 scholarships jointly with three other organizations: Informata.com, LSSI, and OCLC, Inc.

**Grant-Specific Website:** www.ala.org/ala/mgrps/divs/lita/awards/larew/

### H. W. WILSON LIBRARY STAFF DEVELOPMENT GRANT

The H. W. Wilson Library Staff Development Grant is an annual award consisting of $3,500 and a 24 karat gold–framed citation given to a library organization whose application demonstrates greatest merit for a program of staff development designed to further the goals and objectives of the library organization. Staff development is defined as "a program of learning activities that is developed by the library organization and develops the on-the-job staff capability and improves the abilities of personnel to contribute to the overall effectiveness of the library organization." The award is donated by H. W. Wilson Co. For the purposes of this award, a library organization is defined as an individual library; a library system; a group of cooperating libraries; a state governmental agency; or a local, state, or regional association.

**Contact:** Cheryl Malden, Program Officer, Governance, American Library Association, 50 E. Huron St., Chicago, IL 60611-2788; Phone: 312-280-3247; E-mail: cmalden@ala.org

**Grant-Specific Website:** www.ala.org/template.cfm?template = / CFApps/awards_info/award_detail_info.cfm&FilePublishTitle = Awards,%20 Grants%20and%20Scholarships&uid = 3 897605B70D78A2D

### SPECTRUM SCHOLARSHIP

The Spectrum Scholarship program's primary goal is to recruit applicants and award scholarships to American Indian/Alaska Native, Asian, black/African American, Hispanic/Latino, and Native Hawaiian/other Pacific Islander students for graduate programs in library and information studies. Its mission is to improve service at the local level through the development of a representative workforce that reflects the communities served by all libraries in the new millennium. Since 1997, the ALA has awarded a total of 495 Spectrum Scholarships. Nearly 70 percent of past Spectrum Scholars remain active in the ALA three years after graduation. Spectrum provides a one-time, nonrenewable $5,000 scholarship award paid in two installments directly to the recipient. Recipients must begin a program by the fall semester following the award; funds will be forfeited if enrollment is delayed. Recipients must be enrolled at the time of the second installment, or they will forfeit this portion of the award.

**Grant-Specific Website:** www.ala. org/ala/aboutala/offices/diversity/ spectrum/index.cfm

**REQUIREMENTS AND RESTRICTIONS**
Vary by grant

**APPLICATION PROCEDURES**
**Submission Guidelines:** Visit website for application information.

**CONTACT**
Varies by grant

**GRANT-SPECIFIC WEBSITE**
www.ala.org/ala/awardsgrants/

# American Library Association, Federal and Armed Forces Libraries Round Table (FAFLRT)

## Headquarters

50 E. Huron St.
Chicago, IL 60611
www.ala.org/ala/mgrps/rts/faflrt/

## Description

**Founded:** NA

**Operating Locations:** Illinois, District of Columbia

The Federal and Armed Forces Libraries Round Table (FAFLRT) exists as an official round table under the American Library Association to promote library and information service and the library and information profession in the federal and armed forces communities; to promote appropriate utilization of federal and armed forces library and information resources and facilities; and to provide an environment for the stimulation of research and development relating to the planning, development, and operation of federal and armed forces libraries.

# Financial Summary

Total Giving: $2,500

# Grants Information

### GRANT TYPES
Conference attendance

### TYPICAL RECIPIENTS
Library school students

### GRANT VALUES
Total Dollar Amount of Grants: $1,000
Number of Grants: 1

### NAMED GRANTS

### THE FEDERAL LIBRARIANS ADELAIDE DEL FRATE CONFERENCE SPONSORSHIP
Award is given to a library school student who has an interest in working in a federal library. The student will receive an award of $1,000 for the annual conference registration fee, transportation, and other expenses related to attendance at the next ALA Annual Conference. Students who are currently enrolled in any ALA-accredited library school, who do not already have an ALA-accredited degree, and who have expressed an interest in some aspect of federal librarianship are eligible. Applicants must be full- or part-time students at the time of application. Students nominate themselves for this award; a letter of reference from a federal librarian, a library school professor, or the like may be sent to the awards committee chair in support of an application.

### REQUIREMENTS AND RESTRICTIONS
Must be a student enrolled in an ALA-accredited library school but does not yet have an ALA-accredited degree; applicant must express an interest in some aspect of federal librarianship.

### APPLICATION PROCEDURES

**Submission Guidelines:** Nomination form online

**Deadlines:** Mid-April

### CONTACT
Rosalind (Ros) Reynolds
Phone: 800-941-8478 or 202-628-8410
Fax: 202-628-8419
E-mail: rreynolds@alawash.org

### GRANT-SPECIFIC WEBSITE
www.ala.org/ala/mgrps/rts/faflrt/
initiatives/awards/conference-
sponsorship.cfm

# American Library Association, International Relations Office (IRO)

## Headquarters

50 E. Huron St.
Chicago, IL 60611
Phone: 800-545-2433, ext. 3201
www.ala.org/iro/

## Description

**Founded:** NA

**Operating Locations:** Illinois

The mission of the International Relations Office (IRO) is to increase ALA's presence in the global library community, to implement ALA policies concerning international librarianship, to promote greater understanding of international librarianship and international library issues within ALA, and to manage international library activities on behalf of the ALA.

To accomplish its mission the IRO coordinates ALA activities in support of official ALA delegations to international events such as book fairs and congresses; promotes international library exchanges and partnerships; recruits international librarians to become members of ALA and attend ALA conferences; responds to international inquiries concerning library issues and activities in the United States; serves as a point of contact for ALA's routine communication with international organizations to which ALA belongs, including IFLA; and provides support for the ALA International Relations Committee (IRC) and the International Relations Round Table (IRRT).

## Grants Information

**GRANT TYPES**
Conference attendance

**TYPICAL RECIPIENTS**
Librarians interested in building up a foreign collection

**GRANT VALUES**
Total Dollar Amount of Grants: $16,000
Number of Grants: 3

**NAMED GRANTS**

**BOGLE PRATT INTERNATIONAL LIBRARY TRAVEL FUND**
The Bogle Pratt International Library Travel Fund, sponsored by the Bogle Memorial Fund and the Pratt Institute School of Information and Library Science, consists of an award of $1,000 given to an ALA personal member to attend his or her first international

conference. An international conference may be defined as a conference sponsored by an international organization or a conference held in a country other than the applicant's home country. The award is in recognition of Sarah Comly Norris Bogle, a prominent U.S. librarian who made notable contributions to international library service.

**Deadlines:** January 1

**Decisions:** Winners will be announced after the ALA Midwinter Meeting.

## Hong Kong Book Fair Free Pass Program for Librarians

The Hong Kong Book Fair offers the Free Pass Program for Librarians. The fair will provide selected librarians from the United States and Canada who collect Chinese language materials four nights of hotel accommodation, free book fair registration, and an invitation to a cocktail reception. Those eligible to participate in the program must be personal members of ALA who work in the area of Chinese language acquisitions or are working to build their Chinese language collections to better serve their community of users.

The Hong Kong Book Fair features

- 400 exhibitors from Hong Kong, China, and Taiwan
- firsthand access to the latest publications for public and academic libraries

- the latest in music, software, and electronic publishing, and more
- an opportunity to purchase materials at large discounts

**Deadlines:** June

**Decisions:** Applicants will be notified of their selection within 5–7 business days after the application form is received.

## ALA/FIL Free Pass Program

ALA and the Guadalajara International Book Fair partner to provide support for ALA members to attend the Guadalajara International Book Fair (FIL). The ALA-FIL FREE PASS Program provides three nights of hotel accommodation (six nights if applicant shares a room with a colleague who is also part of the program), three continental breakfasts, FIL 2007 registration (courtesy of FIL), and $100 toward the cost of airfare (courtesy of ALA). Free Passes will be awarded to 150 librarians who work in the area of Spanish language acquisitions or are working to build their Spanish language collection to better serve their community and users.

FIL, the most important exhibit of Spanish-language books in the world, features

- firsthand access to the latest publications in Spanish
- an exhibit of more than 300,000 titles
- access to the complete catalogs of more than 1,500 publishers from more than 35 countries

- networking opportunities with 15,000 book professionals
- literary programming with Latin American authors
- lectures on Mexican culture delivered by experts in the field

**Deadlines:** August

### REQUIREMENTS AND RESTRICTIONS

Some grants require applicants to be from the United States or Canada. Applicants must be personal ALA members.

### APPLICATION PROCEDURES

**Submission Guidelines:** Application online

### CONTACT

Delin R. Guerra

Phone: 800-545-2433, ext. 3201, or 312-280-3201

E-mail: dguerra@ala.org

### GRANT-SPECIFIC WEBSITE

www.ala.org/ala/aboutala/offices/iro/
awardsactivities/awardsgrants.cfm

# American Library Association, Library Research Round Table (LRRT)

## Headquarters

50 E. Huron St.
Chicago, IL 60611
Phone: 800-545-2433, ext. 4283
www.ala.org/ala/mgrps/rts/lrrt

## Description

**Founded:** NA

**Operating Locations:** Illinois

The mission of the Library Research Round Table (LRRT) is to contribute toward the extension and improvement of library research; to provide public program opportunities for describing and evaluating library research projects and for disseminating their findings; to inform and educate ALA members concerning research techniques and their usefulness in obtaining information with which to reach administrative decisions and solve problems; and to expand the theoretical base of the field. LRRT also serves as a forum for discussion and action on issues related to the literature and information needs for the field of library and information science.

# Grants Information

## GRANT TYPES
Research

## TYPICAL RECIPIENTS
Practicing librarians, faculty, and students at schools of library and information science; independent scholars

## GRANT VALUES
Total Dollar Amount of Grants: $7,000
Number of Grants: 1

## NAMED GRANTS

### INGENTA RESEARCH AWARD
The Ingenta Research Award is a grant that consists of up to $6,000 for research and up to $1,000 for travel to a national or international conference to present the results of the research. Expenditures must directly support research; the award does not cover indirect costs or overhead. Half of the research amount will be paid within 1 month of the selection of the awardee; the remaining half will be provided approximately 6 months later upon the receipt of a satisfactory progress report as determined by the Ingenta Award Jury Chair and the ALA staff liaison to the Ingenta Award Jury.

## REQUIREMENTS AND RESTRICTIONS
The Ingenta Award Jury will evaluate applications on the basis of the following criteria:

- appropriateness of the proposed project to understanding of seeking and use of digital information
- significance of the problem
- design of the study
- qualifications of the investigator(s)
- realism of the timetable

## APPLICATION PROCEDURES

**Submission Guidelines:** Application should include

- a proposal of no more than six double-spaced pages that provides an overall statement of the project, relation of the project to previous research, research questions, method/plan of investigation, timetable for the work, significance of the project, and plan to disseminate the results
- budget (1 page)
- curriculum vitae (2 pages)

**Deadlines:** January

## CONTACT
Norman Rose
Phone: 800-545-2433, ext. 4283, or 312-280-4283
Fax: 312-280-4392
E-mail: nrose@ala.org

## GRANT-SPECIFIC WEBSITE
www.ala.org/ala/mgrps/rts/lrrt/popularresources/awardsabc/lrrtawards.cfm

# American Library Association, New Members Round Table (NMRT)

## Headquarters

50 E. Huron St.
Chicago, IL 60611
Phone: 800-545-2433, ext. 4279
www.ala.org/ala/mgrps/rts/nmrt

## Description

**Founded:** NA

**Operating Locations:** Illinois

The New Members Round Table (NMRT) is an organization for people with fewer than ten years of membership in ALA. The group has close to 2,000 members representing every aspect of librarianship, from nearly every state and even some foreign countries. Its mission is to help those who have been association members fewer than ten years become actively involved in the association and the profession. The goals are fourfold: (1) to structure formal opportunities for involvement and training for professional association committee experiences on the national, state, and local levels; (2) to provide a wide variety of programs to assist, encourage, and educate those new to the association and the profession; (3) to offer a variety of leadership training and opportunities to help those approaching the end of their NMRT eligibility make the transition to future positions in the association and the profession; and (4) to develop and implement ongoing programs for library school students that encourage professional involvement and networking.

## Grants Information

**GRANT TYPES**
Conference attendance

**TYPICAL RECIPIENTS**
Members of ALA and NMRT

**GRANT VALUES**
Number of Grants: 2

**NAMED GRANTS**

**3M/NMRT PROFESSIONAL DEVELOPMENT GRANT**
The 3M/NMRT Professional Development Grant, sponsored by 3M Library Systems, covers round-trip airfare, lodging, and conference registration fees for attendance at the ALA Annual Conference.

**SHIRLEY OLOFSON MEMORIAL AWARD**
The Shirley Olofson Memorial Award is presented annually in honor of Shirley

Olofson, a well-respected former NMRT president who died during her term in office. The award, which is intended to help defray costs to attend the ALA Annual Conference, is presented in the form of a check for $1,000 during ALA Annual Conference. The winner is chosen in January before the ALA Midwinter Meeting. All applicants are notified in March.

## REQUIREMENTS AND RESTRICTIONS

Applicants must be working in the territorial United States and must be personal ALA and NMRT members who are able to attend ALA Annual Conference.

## APPLICATION PROCEDURES

**Submission Guidelines:**
Application online

**Deadlines:** Usually by mid-December

**Decisions:** Usually by mid-March

## CONTACT

Kimberly Sanders
Phone: 800-545-2433, ext. 4279, or 312-280-4279
E-mail: ksanders@ala.org

## GRANT-SPECIFIC WEBSITE

www.ala.org/ala/mgrps/rts/nmrt/
initiatives/applyforfunds/
applyfunds.cfm

# American Library Association, Office for Diversity

## Headquarters

50 E. Huron St.
Chicago, IL 60611
Phone: 800-545-2433, ext. 5295
www.ala.org/ala/aboutala/offices/
diversity/

## Description

**Founded:** 2000

**Operating Locations:** Illinois

The Office for Diversity serves as a clearinghouse for diversity resources and a focal point for administering and fostering diversity as a value and key action area of the association.

## Grants Information

**GRANT TYPES**
Research

**TYPICAL RECIPIENTS**
Library researchers

**GRANT VALUES**
Total Dollar Amount of Grants: $7,500
Number of Grants: 3
Average Grant: $2,500

## NAMED GRANTS

### DIVERSITY RESEARCH GRANT

The Diversity Research Grant program is intended to address critical gaps in the knowledge of diversity issues within library and information science. Each year the Office for Diversity and the Diversity Research Grant Jury identify three areas of scholarship where research is needed. One of the three topics must be addressed in the applicant's proposal. The grant consists of a one-time $2,000 annual award for original research and a $500 travel grant to attend and present at ALA Annual Conference. Three grants are awarded each year. Projects that have been funded in the past include "Library and Information Center Accessibility: The Differently-Able Patron's Perspective," "Bringing the Library to the People: Addressing the Job-Related Information Needs of Day Laborers," and "ICT Readiness Index: Measuring the Preparedness of Libraries to Serve Patrons with Disabilities in the Context of Economic Challenge."

### REQUIREMENTS AND RESTRICTIONS

Applicants must be current ALA members.

### APPLICATION PROCEDURES

**Submission Guidelines:** Electronic submissions are preferred. All proposal elements should be collated and submitted in a single Word document attachment via e-mail to the address below. Mailed submissions should be sent to the ALA Office for Diversity at the address above.

A complete proposal must include the following:

- a cover letter
- a one-page curriculum vitae for each of the researchers involved
- a concise abstract of the project
- a description of the project detailing the justification and needs for the research, research objectives, expected outcomes, and benefits
- a budget plan
- a time line

**Deadlines:** The call for proposals is announced at the ALA Midwinter Meeting in January. Applications are due in April.

**Decisions:** Recipients are announced in June.

### CONTACT

Phone: 800-545-2433, ext. 5295, or 312-280-5295
E-mail: diversity@ala.org

### GRANT-SPECIFIC WEBSITE

www.ala.org/ala/aboutala/offices/diversity/divresearchgrants/diversityresearch.cfm

# American Library Association, Office for Research and Statistics (ORS)

## Headquarters

50 E. Huron St.
Chicago, IL 60611
Phone: 800-545-2433, ext. 4283
www.ala.org/ala/aboutala/offices/ors/

## Description

**Founded:** 1970

**Operating Locations:** Illinois

The mission of the Office for Research and Statistics (ORS) is to provide leadership and expert advice to ALA staff, members, and the public on all matters related to research and statistics about libraries, librarians, and other library staff; to represent the association to federal agencies on these issues; and to initiate projects needed to expand the knowledge base of the field through research and the collection of useful statistics.

## Grants Information

### GRANT TYPES
Research, library improvement

### TYPICAL RECIPIENTS
Local, regional, or state libraries; associations or organizations; units within ALA; library schools; individual ALA members

### GRANT VALUES
Total Dollar Amount of Grants: $13,000
Number of Grants: 2
Highest Grant: $5,000
Lowest Grant: $3,000

### NAMED GRANTS

#### CARROLL PRESTON BABER RESEARCH GRANT
The Carroll Preston Baber Research Grant consists of an amount of up to $3,000 given annually, pending available funds, to one or more librarians or library educators who will conduct innovative research that could lead to an improvement in services to any specified group(s) of people. The project should aim to answer a question that is of vital importance to the library community and the researchers should plan to provide documentation of the results of their work. The jury welcomes proposals that involve innovative uses of technology and proposals that involve cooperation between libraries, between libraries and other agencies, or between librarians and persons in other disciplines. Any ALA member is eligible to apply. Half of the grant amount is paid within 1 month of the ALA Annual

Conference. Recipients receive the remaining half approximately 6 months later upon the receipt of a satisfactory progress report.

**Grant-Specific Website:** www.ala.org/ala/aboutala/offices/ors/orsawards/baberresearchgrant/babercarroll.cfm

### LOLETA D. FYAN GRANT

Loleta D. Fyan, 1951–52 ALA president, bequeathed funds to ALA to "be used for the development and improvement of public libraries and the services they provide." The grant provides up to $5,000 for projects that have the potential for broader impact and application beyond meeting a specific local need, are designed to effect changes in public library services that are innovative and responsive to the future, and are capable of completion within one year. Applicants can include but are not limited to local, regional, or state libraries; associations or organizations, including ALA units; library schools; or individuals. A check for half the total amount of the grant (up to $2,500) is paid within 1 month of the ALA Annual Conference. The remaining amount is released after the winner submits a 6-month report and the report is approved by chair of the Fyan Jury and Staff Liaison to the Jury.

**Grant-Specific Website:** www.ala.org/ala/aboutala/offices/ors/orsawards/fyanloletad/fyanloletad.cfm

**REQUIREMENTS AND RESTRICTIONS**
Vary by grant

**APPLICATION PROCEDURES**
**Submission Guidelines:** Applicants should send via e-mail one completed application cover sheet and proposal with budget to the ORS staff liaison. File formats accepted are MS Word 2003 or newer, and PDF. Applications should not be mailed or faxed.

**CONTACT**
Cathleen Bourdon
Phone: 800-545-2433, ext. 3217, or 312-280-3217
E-mail: cbourdon@ala.org

**GRANT-SPECIFIC WEBSITE**
www.ala.org/ala/aboutala/offices/ors/orsawards/awards.cfm

# American Library Association, Public Information Office (PIO)

## Headquarters

50 E. Huron St.
Chicago, IL 60611
Phone: 800-545-2433, ext. 5041
www.ala.org/ala/aboutala/offices/pio

# Description

**Founded:** NA

**Operating Locations:** Illinois

The Public Information Office (PIO) manages the public awareness efforts of the association through the Campaign for America's Libraries, delivering key messages to external audiences about the value of libraries and librarians. PIO also communicates ALA's key messages through media relations and crisis communications and offers public relations counsel and editorial services. Tools are also developed and shared with librarians to help advance ALA's 2010 Key Action Areas.

# Grants Information

**GRANT TYPES**
Project

**TYPICAL RECIPIENTS**
Libraries

**GRANT VALUES**
Total Dollar Amount of Grants: $5,000
Number of Grants: 1

**NAMED GRANTS**

**SCHOLASTIC LIBRARY PUBLISHING NATIONAL LIBRARY WEEK GRANT**
The Scholastic Library Publishing National Library Week Grant, sponsored by Scholastic Library Publishing and administered by the ALA's Public Awareness Committee, is awarded annually for the best public awareness campaign in support of National Library Week. The $3,000 grant is to be used to support the winner's National Library Week promotional activities as outlined in the application and cannot be used for capital expenses, such as books or equipment.

**REQUIREMENTS AND RESTRICTIONS**
In addition to incorporating the annual theme, other factors are creativity, originality, clarity of planning, and potential for generating widespread public visibility and support for libraries. Commitment to ongoing public relations activities and allocation of resources (staff, materials, time) also are considered.

**APPLICATION PROCEDURES**

**Submission Guidelines:** Application online

**Deadlines:** November

**Decisions:** After ALA Midwinter Meeting in January

**CONTACT**
Megan McFarlane
Phone: 800-545-2433, ext. 2148, or 312-280-2148
E-mail: mmcfarlane@ala.org

**GRANT-SPECIFIC WEBSITE**
www.ala.org/nlwgrant/

# American Library Association, Public Programs Office (PPO)

## Headquarters

50 E. Huron St.
Chicago, IL 60611
Phone: 800-545-2433, ext. 5045
www.ala.org/publicprograms/

## Description

**Founded:** NA

**Operating Locations:** Illinois

The mission of the Public Programs Office (PPO) is to foster cultural programming as an integral part of library service.

## Grants Information

### GRANT TYPES
Library improvement

### TYPICAL RECIPIENTS
Public libraries and school libraries (K–12) in the United States, including public, private, parochial, and charter schools; libraries with collections that circulate to the general public and offer reading-based programs for the general public.

### GRANT VALUES
Number of Grants: 4,000

### NAMED GRANTS

#### WE THE PEOPLE BOOKSHELF GRANT
The We the People Bookshelf, a collection of classic books for young readers, is a project of the National Endowment for the Humanities' (NEH) We the People program, conducted in cooperation with the ALA's Public Programs Office. Grants aim to encourage and strengthen the teaching, study, and understanding of American history and culture through libraries, schools, colleges, universities, and cultural institutions. Grant recipients will receive a We the People Bookshelf (a set of classic hardcover books based on a yearly theme) and will be required to use selections from the bookshelf in programs for young readers in their communities.

#### REQUIREMENTS AND RESTRICTIONS
In return for receiving a bookshelf, libraries are required to organize programs that introduce the books and theme to the library's students, young patrons, or intergenerational audiences. Programs should take place within the recipient school or library, although programs may also extend beyond the library walls through collaboration with other school or public libraries. The central office of a school district or

library system may apply on behalf of all of its member libraries, up to a total of one hundred. Winners will be chosen based on the strength of their project narratives explaining how the bookshelf would be used in their library or libraries. This narrative must not exceed 3,200 characters (approximately 425 words), and should address the following questions:

- What programs will the library use to promote the We the People Bookshelf?
- How will the programs encourage young people to read the books on the bookshelf?
- How will the programs engage library patrons in exploring the theme?
- Is the program being planned in collaboration with other libraries or other community organizations?
- What strategies will the library use to encourage long-term use of the bookshelf?

**APPLICATION PROCEDURES**

**Submission Guidelines:** Applications must be prepared and submitted through an online application system on the ALA Public Programs Office grant website.

**Deadlines:** January

**CONTACT**
Phone: 800-545-2433, ext. 5045 (ALA), or 202-606-8337 (NEH)

E-mail: publicprograms@ala.org or wethepeople@neh.gov

**GRANT-SPECIFIC WEBSITE**
http://publicprograms.ala.org/bookshelf/

# American Library Association, Publishing Department

## Headquarters

50 E. Huron St.
Chicago, IL 60611
Phone: 800-545-2433, ext. 5416
www.ala.org/ala/aboutala/offices/publishing/index.cfm

## Description

**Founded:** NA

**Operating Locations:** Illinois

The ALA's Publishing Department provides all librarians a comprehensive, one-stop resource for print and digital materials dedicated to professional development, improving library services, and the promotion of libraries, literacy, and reading.

# Grants Information

## GRANT TYPES

Publication, continuing education

## TYPICAL RECIPIENTS

Individuals; local, regional, or state libraries; associations and organizations, including ALA units, affiliates, and committees; and programs of information and library studies/science

## GRANT VALUES

Total Dollar Amount of Grants: $5,750
Number of Grants: 2

## NAMED GRANTS

### CARNEGIE-WHITNEY GRANT

The Carnegie-Whitney Grant has been established to provide funding for the preparation and publication of popular or scholarly reading lists, indexes, and other guides to library resources that will be useful to users of all types of libraries. The $5,000 grant may be used for print and electronic projects of varying lengths. The grant is intended to cover preparation costs appropriate to the development of a useful product, including the cost of research, compilation, and production exclusive of printing. This award is given out annually. Grants are awarded to individuals; local, regional, or state libraries; associations and organizations, including ALA units, affiliates,

and committees; and programs of information and library studies/science. International applicants welcome.

**Grant-Specific Website:** www. ala.org/template.cfm?template = / CFApps/awards_info/award_detail_info. cfm&FilePublishTitle = Awards,%20 Grants%20and%20 Scholarships&uid = F87E802B11F8EAD8

### WOMEN'S NATIONAL BOOK ASSOCIATION/ANN HEIDBREDER EASTMAN GRANT

The purpose of the Women's National Book Association/Ann Heidbreder Eastman Grant is to help provide funds for a librarian to take a course or to participate in an intensive institute devoted to aspects of publishing as a profession. (This does not include courses, institutes, seminars, or workshops devoted to desktop publishing for the purposes of setting up a newsletter or an individual home office.) Librarians holding an MLS or its equivalent master's level credential and having at least two years of post-master's work experience in a library are eligible to apply. Criteria for selecting the winner include the assessment of the likelihood of career benefit to the person taking the course. One $750 grant is funded annually.

**Grant-Specific Website:** www. ala.org/template.cfm?template = / CFApps/awards_info/award_detail_info.

cfm&FilePublishTitle=Awards,%20
Grants%20and%20Scholarships&uid=F
D9BB42E6FA68B3F

## REQUIREMENTS AND RESTRICTIONS
Vary by grant

## APPLICATION PROCEDURES
**Submission Guidelines:** Visit website
for application information.

## CONTACT
Phone: 800-545-2433, ext. 5416, or 312-
280-5416

## GRANT-SPECIFIC WEBSITE
Varies by grant

# American Society for Information Science and Technology (ASIS&T)

## Headquarters

1320 Fenwick La., Suite 510
Silver Spring, MD 20910
Phone: 301-495-0900
www.asis.org

## Description

**Founded:** 1937

**Operating Locations:** Maryland

Since 1937, the American Society for Information Science and Technology (ASIS&T) has been the society for information professionals leading the search for new and better theories, techniques, and technologies to improve access to information. The society seeks to stimulate participation and interaction among its members by affording them an environment for substantive professional exchange. It encourages and supports personal and professional growth through opportunities for members to extend their knowledge and skills, develop and use professional networks, pursue career development goals and assume leadership roles in the society and in the information community. ASIS&T increases the influence of information professionals among decision makers by focusing attention on the importance of information as a vital resource in a high-technology age and promotes informed policy on national and international information issues by contributing to the formation of those policies. It supports the advancement of the state-of-the-art and -practice by taking a leadership position in the advocacy of research and development in basic and applied information science.

To accomplish these goals, ASIS&T edits, publishes, and disseminates publications concerning research and development; convenes annual meetings providing a forum for papers, discussions, and major policy statements; hosts an annual Information Architecture Summit; holds smaller chapter and special interest meetings, as well as special symposia; and acts as a sounding board for promotion of research and development and for the education of information professionals.

## Financial Summary

Assets: $1,625,466

## Grants Information

### GRANT TYPES
Research

### TYPICAL RECIPIENTS
Library researchers

### GRANT VALUES
Total Dollar Amount of Grants: $4,500
Number of Grants: 2
Highest Grant: $3,500
Lowest Grant: $1,000

### NAMED GRANTS

### HISTORY FUND RESEARCH GRANT
The History Fund Research Grant is for a maximum of $1,000 and is awarded for the best research support proposal. All topics relevant to the history of information science and technology may be proposed. The proposal should state the central topic or question to be researched, qualifications of the researcher (a brief curriculum vitae should be included), and how the funds will be expended. All funds must be expended by August 31.

**Deadlines:** September 1

### THOMSON REUTERS CITATION ANALYSIS RESEARCH GRANT
The Thomson Reuters Citation Analysis Research Grant consists of an award of $3,000 (donated by Thomson Reuters). Additionally, Thomson Reuters shall contribute $500 toward travel or other expenses to the grant recipient, contingent upon the recipient's attending the ASIS&T Annual Meeting, and $250 to ASIS&T Headquarters toward administrative fees. The purpose of this grant is to support research based on citation analysis by encouraging and assisting individuals in this area of study with their research. Citation analysis is broadly defined, including but not limited to analysis using resources developed by Thomson Reuters. Because of the limits proposed by timing considerations, the grant may be made for underway research as well as for newly proposed research. Proposals are sought globally and may be submitted by anyone. Proposals should be submitted electronically. The ASIS&T jury for this award will review all proposals, assessing technical feasibility only.

**Deadlines:** June 15

**REQUIREMENTS AND RESTRICTIONS**
Vary by grant

**APPLICATION PROCEDURES**
**Submission Guidelines:** Vary by grant but generally include an online application and research proposal submission.

**CONTACT**
Varies by grant

**GRANT-SPECIFIC WEBSITE**
www.asis.org/awards.html

# American Theological Library Association (ATLA)

## Headquarters

300 S. Wacker Dr., Suite 2100
Chicago, IL 60606-6701
Phone: 888-665-2852 or 312-454-5100
Fax: 312-454-5505
www.atla.com

## Description

**Founded:** 1946

**Operating Locations:** Illinois

Established in 1946, the American Theological Library Association (ATLA) is a professional association of more than 1,000 individual, institutional, and affiliate members providing programs, products, and services in support of theological and religious studies libraries and librarians. ATLA's ecumenical membership represents many religious traditions and denominations.

## Financial Summary

Assets: $4,588,418
Gifts Received: $252,370

## Grants Information

**GRANT TYPES**
Publication, library improvement, continuing education, conference attendance

**TYPICAL RECIPIENTS**
Librarians working in a theological information science setting

**GRANT VALUES**
Total Dollar Amount of Grants: $7,750
Number of Grants: 5
Average Grant: $1,937
Highest Grant: $4,000
Lowest Grant: $400

**NAMED GRANTS**

**PUBLICATION GRANT**
The ATLA Publications Committee awards publication grants each year to one or more recipients to aid in the

development of a scholarly work that advances some aspect of theological librarianship or provides bibliographic access to a significant body of literature within theological or religious studies. The committee especially encourages proposals from persons undertaking their first major project in this area. The goal of projects proposed should be peer-reviewed publication (e.g., in the ATLA journal, Theological Librarianship, or in one of the book series it publishes with Scarecrow Press). ATLA reserves first right of refusal of publication for all projects receiving grants. Grants consist of up to $4,000 for reimbursable expenses.

## CONSULTATION GRANT

As a service to its institutional member libraries, ATLA provides funds for library consultations. This service is designed to help theological libraries and their administrations assess library operations and facilitate planning. Through this program ATLA shares the expertise and experience of its members with schools contemplating improvements in library resources, operations, plans, and services. Librarians serving in this capacity have had extensive experience as consultants and as members of accreditation teams, as well as administrators of libraries. This service is intended to offer practical guidance to theological libraries anticipating building programs, reorganization of administration, assessment of personnel and resources, visits from accrediting agencies, acquisition and utilization of computer and newer technologies, or expansion of other library resources or services. The grant pays an honorarium to the consultant of $400 for a one-day visit or $800 for a two-day visit.

## CONTINUING EDUCATION GRANT

ATLA, in its commitment to support professional education opportunities, provides continuing education grants for programs. The Professional Development Committee invites both regional groups associated with ATLA and individual institutional libraries to create educational programming and apply for a grant. There are now two categories of grants available: (1) regional groups associated with ATLA, or (2) institutional members of ATLA, whether or not in a regional group. A maximum of $750 may be awarded in each category. Grant funds may be requested for all types of expenses related to speakers. Additional funding (up to $500) may also be requested to subsidize the costs of members travelling to the event. Please note that grants are not available for individuals' projects. Awarded funds should not be used for lunch/break expenses or parking fees. Suggested honoraria are $400–$450 for a full day, $200–$250 for a half day, $150–$250 for one- to two-hour workshops. Exceptions should be noted in the application.

## REQUIREMENTS AND RESTRICTIONS

Some grants require ATLA membership. Application requirements vary by grant.

## APPLICATION PROCEDURES

**Submission Guidelines:** Visit website for application information.

## CONTACT

Phone: 888-665-2852
Fax: 312-454-5505
E-mail: atla@atla.com

## GRANT-SPECIFIC WEBSITE

www.atla.com/Members/programs/
awards/Pages/default.aspx

# Ametek, Inc.

## Headquarters

1100 Cassatt Road
PO Box 1764
Berwyn, PA 19312
Phone: 610-647-2121
Fax: 215-323-9337
www.ametek.com

## Description

**Founded:** 1930

**Operating Locations:** Pennsylvania, Illinois, Ohio, Washington, Delaware, New York

**Type of Product/Service:** Electronic instruments and electromechanical devices

**In-Kind or Service Support:** Supports volunteers in Science Explorers program in schools

# AMETEK FOUNDATION

37 N. Valley Rd., Bldg. 4
Paoli, PA 19301
Phone: 610-647-2121
**Foundation Information:** Corporate foundation of Ametek, Inc.

## Financial Summary

Assets: $7,982,663
Gifts Received: $228,020,000
Total Giving: $1,211,414

## Grants Information

### GRANT TYPES

General support, research

### TYPICAL RECIPIENTS

Arts and humanities, civic affairs, education, environment, health, international, religion, science, social services

### GRANT VALUES

Total Dollar Amount of Grants:
$1,211,414

Number of Grants: 77
Average Grant: $15,700
Highest Grant: $100,873
Lowest Grant: $1,000

## PAST GRANT RECIPIENTS

*Library or School Related*
- Free Library of Philadelphia Foundation (PA), general support, $15,000
- New York Public Library (NY), general support, $10,000
- North Wales Library (PA), general support, $5,000
- Binghamton School District (NY), 100 Book Challenge, $37,490
- Panther Valley School District (PA), 100 Book Challenge, $100,873
- West Chicago School District (IL), 100 Book Challenge, $89,600
- Christina School District (DE), Science Explorer Program, $45,117
- Northeastern University (MA), Engineers Without Borders, $4,800

*General*
- Eagles Youth Partnership (PA), general support, $50,000
- Juvenile Diabetes Association (NY), general support, $15,000
- Central Park Conservancy (NY), general support, $25,000
- Children's Museum of Naples (FL), general support, $25,000

## REQUIREMENTS AND RESTRICTIONS

Applicants must have tax-exempt status. The foundation does not support political or lobbying groups.

## APPLICATION PROCEDURES

**Submission Guidelines:** Send a brief letter or proposal, including

- description of organization
- amount requested
- purpose of funds sought
- recently audited financial statement
- proof of tax-exempt status

## CONTACT

Kathryn E. Sena
Phone: 610-647-2121

## GRANT-SPECIFIC WEBSITE

NA

# Andersen Corp.

## Headquarters

PO Box 12
Bayport, MN 55003
Phone: 651-264-5150
www.andersenwindows.com

## Description

**Founded:** 1903

**Operating Locations:** Minnesota, Wisconsin, Iowa

**Type of Product/Service:** Wood doors and windows, millwork

# ANDERSEN CORPORATE FOUNDATION

342 Fifth Avenue North
Bayport, MN 55003
**Foundation Information:** Corporate foundation of Andersen Corp.

## Financial Summary

Assets: $817,604,041
Total Giving: $36,479,528

## Grants Information

### GRANT TYPES
Operating support, capital

### TYPICAL RECIPIENTS
Civic affairs, education, health, social services

### GRANT VALUES
Total Dollar Amount of Grants:
 $36,479,528

## PAST GRANT RECIPIENTS

*Library or School Related*
- Stillwater Public Library (MN), capital campaign, $100,000
- Luck Public Library (WI), capital campaign, $100,000
- Bayport Public Library (MN), operating expenses, $56,000
- Bayport Public Library Foundation (MN), operating expenses, $34,500
- Minnesota Literacy Council (MN), operating expenses, $5,000
- Asbury College (KY), general support, $250,000

*General*
- Afton Historical Society (NY), program support, $10,000
- Family Resource Center (MN), operating expenses, $50,000
- National Right to Work Legal Defense Foundation (VA), operating expenses, $75,000
- Prevent Blindness America (IL), program support, $10,000
- Minnesota Teen Challenge (MN), operating expenses, $10,000
- Community Homestead (WI), capital campaign, $16,000

## REQUIREMENTS AND RESTRICTIONS
The foundation focuses on organizations in communities where Andersen operates, including St. Paul/Minneapolis, Minnesota, and western Wisconsin. Applicants must have tax-exempt

status. The foundation does not fund individuals.

## APPLICATION PROCEDURES

**Submission Guidelines:** Application online or typewritten letter (foundation does not accept requests by e-mail or telephone). Application should include

- contact information for organization
- tax-exempt status letter from IRS
- purpose of grant
- goal of project
- amount of cash request
- other organizations contacted
- community served
- evaluation criteria to measure success
- current operating budget
- current project budget
- audited financial statement
- list of board of directors and affiliations

**Deadlines:** April 15, July 15, October 15, and December 15. When deadlines fall on a weekend or holiday, the deadline will be the following working day. Proposals must be received in the foundation's office (not postmarked) on or before the deadline date. Hand delivered applications must be received in the foundation's office by 5:00 p.m. on the day of the deadline.

**Decisions**: Board meets to consider applications in July, November, January, and April, respectively.

**CONTACT**
Chloette Haley, Program Officer
White Pine Bldg.
342 Fifth Avenue North
Bayport, MN 55003
Phone: 651-275-4450
Fax: 651-439-9480
E-mail: andersencorpfdn@srinc.biz

**GRANT-SPECIFIC WEBSITE**
https://www.srinc.biz/foundations/
andersen-corporate-foundation/

# Annenberg Foundation

## Headquarters

150 N. Radnor Chester Rd.
Radnor, PA 19087
Phone: 610-341-9066
Fax: 610-964-8688
E-mail: infor@annenbergfoundation.org
www.annenbergfoundation.org

## Description

**Founded:** 1989

**Operating Locations:** Pennsylvania

**Foundation Information:** Private foundation established by Walter H. Annenberg

# Financial Summary

Assets: $2,487,703,921
Gifts Received: $6,370
Total Giving: $266,898,723

# Grants Information

**GRANT TYPES**
General support, project, seed money

**TYPICAL RECIPIENTS**
Arts and humanities, civic affairs, education, environment, health, international, religion, science, social services

**GRANT VALUES**
Total Dollar Amount of Grants:
$266,898,723

**PAST GRANT RECIPIENTS**

*Library or School Related*
- Henry E. Huntington Library and Art Gallery (CA), general support, $1,070,000
- Library of Congress (DC), Center for the Book, $5,000
- Episcopal Academy (PA), funding for Roger Annenberg Library on new campus, $1,000,000
- Friends of Short Avenue (CA), library renovation, $79,800
- Library Foundation of Los Angeles (CA), Adult Literary Endowment Fund, $2,500

- Long Beach Nonprofit Partnership (CA), funding for Gale Writing Research Library, $12,000
- University of Pennsylvania (PA), funding for Annenberg Public Policy Center, $10,500,000
- University of Southern California (CA), funding for Annenberg School for Communication, $1,000,000

*General*
- National Constitution Center (PA), funding for seven major educational programs, $1,825,197
- Watts Cinema Education Center, Inc. (CA), support for Annenberg Education and Communications Center, $1,000,000
- Ventura County Community Foundation (CA), support for resource center for nonprofit management, $75,000

**REQUIREMENTS AND RESTRICTIONS**
The foundation does not support individuals, basic research, construction projects, capital campaigns, or operating expenses. The foundation does not support political candidates or those who influence legislation.

**APPLICATION PROCEDURES**
**Submission Guidelines:** Send a brief letter of inquiry before preparing a full proposal. Proposals should include

- a cover letter with a brief description of the organization, proposed program, amount of request, IRS number from exemption letters, and contact information

- background information, including history of organization and constituency served
- program description, including goals and objectives, evidence of need, method for achieving goals, evaluation plan, and sustainability statement
- information about personnel who will carry out the program and list of board of directors
- financial summary, including program budget, other sources of funding, most recent IRS form 990, recent audited financial statements, and organizational budget covering years during which the program will be carried out

The foundation does not open attachments; send letter of inquiry or proposal in the body of an e-mail as text.

**Decisions:** The foundation tries to answers all letters of inquiry within 6–8 weeks of receipt. Final decisions on proposals may take 6 months.

**CONTACT**
Wallis Annenberg
E-mail: lainfo@annenbergfoundation.org

**GRANT-SPECIFIC WEBSITE**
www.annenbergfoundation.org

# Aon Foundation

## Headquarters

200 E. Randolph St.
Chicago, IL 60601
Phone: 312-381-3551
www.aon.com/usa/about-aon/
community-involvement.jsp

## Description

**Founded:** NA

**Operating Locations:** Illinois

**Foundation Information:** Corporate foundation of Aon Corp.

## Financial Summary

Assets: $1,578,028
Total Giving: $7,907,846

## Grants Information

### GRANT TYPES
Awards, capital, challenge, general support, endowment, operating support, research

### TYPICAL RECIPIENTS
Arts and humanities, civic affairs, education, environment, health, international, religion, science, social services

## GRANT VALUES
NA

## PAST GRANT RECIPIENTS

*Library or School Related*
- Insurance Library Association of Boston (MA), funding for a collection of insurance-related materials to provide continuing education on insurance topics, $1,500
- Library Foundation of Los Angeles (CA), general support, $7,500
- Recording for the Blind and Dyslexic (NJ), library resources of books, reference books, and professional materials, $100
- Foundation for the Evanston Public Libraries (IL), general support, $250
- Abraham Lincoln Presidential Library Foundation (IL), general support, $25,000
- Friends of the Public Library of Charlotte and Mecklenburg County (NC), general support, $25
- Juliette Wasserman Children's Foundation (NY), funding for children's library, $975
- Colonel James N. Pritzker Library for the Citizen Soldier (IL), research library, $200

## REQUIREMENTS AND RESTRICTIONS
Applicants must have tax-exempt status.

## APPLICATION PROCEDURES
**Submission Guidelines:** The Aon Foundation is currently reviewing grant proposals by invitation only. Organizations with demonstrated successes in the foundation's areas of interest will be contacted and asked to submit a proposal.

## CONTACT
Phone: 312-381-3549

## GRANT-SPECIFIC WEBSITE
www.aon.com/usa/about-aon/community-involvement.jsp

# Argyros Foundation

## Headquarters

949 S. Coast Dr., Suite 600
Costa Mesa, CA 92626
Phone: 714-481-5000

## Description

**Founded:** NA

**Operating Locations:** California

**Foundation Information:** Private foundation

## Financial Summary

Assets: $137,790,756

Gifts Received: $8,511,125
Total Giving: $5,482,356

# Grants Information

### GRANT TYPES
Capital, project

### TYPICAL RECIPIENTS
Arts and humanities, civic affairs, education, environment, health, international, religion, science, social services

### GRANT VALUES
Total Dollar Amount of Grants:
 $5,482,356
Number of Grants: 95
Average Grant: $57,700
Highest Grant: $1,000,000
Lowest Grant: $250

### PAST GRANT RECIPIENTS

*Library or School Related*
- Harbor Day School (CA), general support, $41,000
- Pegasus School (CA), general support, $40,000
- Rice University (TX), general support, $81,797
- Servite High School (CA), general support, $10,000
- California Institute of Technology (CA), general support, $25,334
- New Hampton School (NH), general support, $25,000

*General*
- Idaho Community Foundation (ID), general support, $10,000
- Greater Houston Community Endowment (TX), general support, $100,000
- Orange County Performing Arts Center (CA), general support, $24,000
- National Park Foundation (DC), general support, $25,000
- Mount Vernon Ladies' Association of the Union (VA), general support, $100,000
- Massachusetts General Hospital (MA), research, $20,000

### REQUIREMENTS AND RESTRICTIONS
Applicants must have tax-exempt status.

### APPLICATION PROCEDURES
**Submission Guidelines:** Send a brief letter of inquiry, including

- identification and historical background of organization
- statement as to intended use of the grant
- federal ID number
- copy of IRS letter confirming tax-exempt status

**Deadlines:** June 1

### CONTACT
Daniel Russo

### GRANT-SPECIFIC WEBSITE
NA

# Arizona State Library, Archives and Public Records

## Headquarters

1700 W. Washington St., Suite 200
Phoenix, AZ 85007
Phone: 602-926-4035
www.lib.az.us

## Description

**Founded:** NA

**Operating Locations:** Arizona

The agency, a division of the Secretary of State, serves the Arizona government and Arizonans, providing public access to public information, fostering historical/cultural collaborative research and information projects, and ensuring that Arizona's history is documented and preserved.

## Grants Information

### GRANT TYPES
LSTA funds

### TYPICAL RECIPIENTS
Arizona libraries

### GRANT VALUES
Total Dollar Amount of Grants:
   $3,600,000

### NAMED GRANTS

### LSTA GRANTS
LSTA funds are intended to help libraries develop central roles as community builders. LSTA funds are used to promote improvements in services to all types of libraries; to facilitate access to, and sharing of, resources; and to achieve economical and effective delivery of service for the purpose of cultivating an educated and informed citizenry. LSTA funds are targeted for statewide library services and support a wide array of programs from family literacy to providing broad access to sophisticated databases. This program develops the role of libraries as "information brokers," helping to make resources and services, which are often prohibitively expensive, more readily available. LSTA also supports efforts to recruit and educate librarians. In Arizona, LSTA funds are available as grants to individual libraries.

**Past Grant Recipients:**

- ASU University Libraries (AZ), Expanding Access to Arizona Archives, $57,285
- City of Mesa Public Library (AZ), early childhood multimedia stations, $15,600

- Mohave County Library District (AZ), literacy collaboration, $9,820
- Snowflake-Taylor Public Library (AZ), portable computer lab, $20,779
- Phoenix Public Library (AZ), 21st Century Learning Center, $10,654
- Scottsdale Public Library (AZ), verbal and visual literacy, $11,500

**REQUIREMENTS AND RESTRICTIONS**

Funds may not be used for existing staff salaries and benefits, administrative fees, indirect costs, food or entertainment, construction, or for projects that are primarily marketing. All types of libraries recognized by the State Library are eligible for funding. Libraries are encouraged to partner with museums, archives, cultural institutions, community organizations, schools, or other organizations.

**APPLICATION PROCEDURES**

**Submission Guidelines:** A complete application consists of

- cover sheet
- project narrative
- budget form
- certification of application form (signed)
- support letters from project partners
- brief résumé from paid project consultants
- no more than two brief additional attachments

Applications can be filled out online or mailed to the address below.

**Deadlines:** March

**Decisions:** May

**CONTACT**

Grants Administrator
Library Development Division
1101 W. Washington St.
Phoenix, AZ 85007-2925
Phone: 800-255-5841 (Arizona only) or
602-542-5841

**GRANT-SPECIFIC WEBSITE**

www.lib.az.us/lsta/

# Arkansas Department of Rural Services

## Headquarters

101 E. Capitol Ave., Suite 202
Little Rock, AR 72201
Phone: 501-682-6011 or 888-787-2527
www.arkansas.gov/drs/

## Description

**Founded:** 1991

**Operating Locations:** Arkansas

The mission of the Department of Rural Services and the Arkansas Rural

Development Commission is to enhance the quality of life in rural Arkansas.

# Grants Information

## GRANT TYPES
Community enhancement

## TYPICAL RECIPIENTS
Rural Arkansas communities

## GRANT VALUES
Highest Grant: $15,000

## NAMED GRANTS

### RURAL COMMUNITY DEVELOPMENT GRANT PROGRAM
Rural communities are eligible for up to $15,000 in matching funds under this program. Match may comprise in-kind labor, in-kind materials, or cash and must be available at the time of application. Communities in the past have received funding for baseball/softball fields, community centers, walking tracks, park and playground equipment, pavilions, picnic tables, and library shelving. Eligible projects include (but are not limited to) renovations, new construction, or additions to publicly owned buildings; and new construction, new equipment, or additions to parks and other publicly owned recreational facilities.

## REQUIREMENTS AND RESTRICTIONS
Applicants must be from incorporated towns of less than 3,000 in population or unincorporated rural areas.

## APPLICATION PROCEDURES

**Submission Guidelines:** Application online. Besides the application, additional requirements include (but are not limited to)

- signed certification letter from the local governing official
- resolution passed by the city council
- backup documentation for all items listed in the project cost estimate
- proof of public ownership
- items of support (letter from your state senator and representative)

The Department of Rural Services must receive an original along with one copy. Typed applications should be mailed to the address below. Faxed applications will not be accepted.

**Deadlines:** August through March

## CONTACT
Arkansas Rural Community
    Grant Programs
101 East Capitol, Suite 202
Little Rock, AR 72201
Phone: 888-787-2527 or 501-682-6011
E-mail: Rural.Arkansas@arkansas.gov

## GRANT-SPECIFIC WEBSITE
www.state.ar.us/drs/drsgrants.html

# Arnold Fund

## Headquarters

1201 W. Peachtree St., Suite 4200
Atlanta, GA 30309
Phone: 404-881-7886

## Description

**Founded:** NA

**Operating Locations:** Georgia

**Foundation Information:** Private
foundation established by Florence
Arnold

## Financial Summary

Assets: $17,032,662
Total Giving: $847,650

## Grants Information

**GRANT TYPES**
General support

**TYPICAL RECIPIENTS**
Arts and humanities, civic affairs,
education, environment, health, religion,
social services

**GRANT VALUES**
Total Dollar Amount of Grants: $847,650
Number of Grants: 34

Average Grant: $24,900
Highest Grant: $504,000
Lowest Grant: $200

**PAST GRANT RECIPIENTS**

*Library or School Related*
- Oxford College (GA), general support,
  $50,000
- Carolina Day School (NC), general
  support, $11,000
- University of Georgia (GA), general
  support, $20,000
- Princeton University (NJ), general
  support, $3,000
- Washington and Lee University (VA),
  general support, $1,250
- Georgia Tech Foundation (GA),
  general support, $4,000

*General*
- Community Foundation of Greater
  Atlanta (GA), general support,
  $504,000
- Arts Association of Newton County
  (GA), general support, $35,000
- Highlands Community Child
  Development Center (NC), general
  support, $1,000
- Chattowah Open Land Trust (AL),
  general support, $5,000
- Leadership Georgia (GA), general
  support, $5,000

**REQUIREMENTS AND RESTRICTIONS**
NA

## APPLICATION PROCEDURES

**Submission Guidelines:** Send a brief letter of inquiry, including

- description of program or project
- purpose of funds sought
- area to be served
- budget
- any other pertinent information

## CONTACT
NA

## GRANT-SPECIFIC WEBSITE
NA

# John Arrillaga Foundation

## Headquarters

2560 Mission College Blvd., Suite 101
Santa Clara, CA 95054
Phone: 408-980-0130

## Description

**Founded:** NA

**Operating Locations:** California

**Foundation Information:** Private foundation

## Financial Summary

Assets: $37,026,054
Total Giving: $149,983

## Grants Information

### GRANT TYPES
Capital, general support, scholarship

### TYPICAL RECIPIENTS
Arts and humanities, civic affairs, education, environment, health, international, religion, science, social services

### GRANT VALUES
Total Dollar Amount of Grants: $149,983
Number of Grants: 14
Average Grant: $10,700
Highest Grant: $50,000
Lowest Grant: $1,000

### PAST GRANT RECIPIENTS
*Library or School Related*
- Stanford University (CA), athletic department, $50,000
- Stanford University (CA), housing, $25,753
- Generation Engage (DC), general support, $2,500

*General*
- Palo Alto Weekly Holiday Fund (CA), general support, $10,000
- St. Pius Church (CA), general support, $2,500

- Menlo Park Presbyterian Church (CA), contribution for VA hospital, $1,500
- St. Luke's Hospital (MO), general support, $2,500

**REQUIREMENTS AND RESTRICTIONS**
Applicants must have tax-exempt status.

**APPLICATION PROCEDURES**
**Submission Guidelines:** Send a brief letter of inquiry, including any brochures about the organization.

**CONTACT**
John Arrillaga
Phone: 408-908-0130

**GRANT-SPECIFIC WEBSITE**
NA

# Arronson Foundation

## Headquarters

2400 One Reading Center
Philadelphia, PA 19107
Phone: 215-238-1700

## Description

**Founded:** 1957

**Operating Locations:** Pennsylvania

**Foundation Information:** Private

foundation established by Gertrude Arronson

## Financial Summary

Assets: $4,088,485
Total Giving: $138,725

## Grants Information

**GRANT TYPES**
General support, endowment, research, seed money

**TYPICAL RECIPIENTS**
Arts and humanities, civic affairs, education, health, international, religion, science, social services

**GRANT VALUES**
Total Dollar Amount of Grants: $138,725
Number of Grants: 10
Average Grant: $13,800
Highest Grant: $100,000
Lowest Grant: $225

**PAST GRANT RECIPIENTS**

*Library or School Related*
- Children's Literacy Initiative (PA), general support, $10,000
- Clarkson High School North (NY), general support, $5,000
- Academy of Vocal Arts (PA), general support, $3,000
- Bryn Mawr Film Institute (PA), general support, $1,500

*General*
- Homeless Advocacy Project (PA), general support, $1,500
- Jewish Federation of Greater Philadelphia (PA), general support, $100,000
- Friends of Penn Nursing (PA), general support, $2,500
- Temple Beth Zion–Beth Israel (PA), general support, $225

**REQUIREMENTS AND RESTRICTIONS**
NA

**APPLICATION PROCEDURES**
**Submission Guidelines:** Send a brief letter, including information about the nature and work of the organization.

**CONTACT**
Joseph C. Kohn
Phone: 215-230-1700

**GRANT-SPECIFIC WEBSITE**
NA

# Art Libraries Society of North America (ARLIS/NA)

## Headquarters

7044 S. 13th St.
Oak Creek, WI 53154

Phone: 414-908-4954
www.arlisna.org

## Description

**Founded:** 1972

**Operating Locations:** Wisconsin

The Art Libraries Society of North America was founded in 1972 at the initiative of Judith Hoffberg by a group of art librarians attending the ALA Annual Conference in Chicago. This group realized that to fulfill the need among art librarians for better communication and cooperation, and to provide a forum for ideas, projects, and programs, an entirely new and separate organization was required. Inspired by the model of the Art Libraries Society, established in 1969 in the United Kingdom and Ireland, ARLIS/NA was created. The mission of ARLIS/NA is to foster excellence in art and design librarianship and image management.

## Financial Summary

Assets: $514,822
Gifts Received: $39,260

## Grants Information

**GRANT TYPES**
Conference attendance, research

## TYPICAL RECIPIENTS
Art and architecture librarians

## GRANT VALUES
Total Dollar Amount of Grants:
$8,000
Number of Grants: 6
Average Grant: $975
Highest Grant: $3,000
Lowest Grant: $750
Typical Range of Grants:
$750–$1,000

## NAMED GRANTS

### ARLIS/NA CONFERENCE ATTENDANCE AWARD
The ARLIS/NA Conference Attendance Award encourages participation in ARLIS/NA by assisting conference attendance by committee members, chapter officers, and moderators of divisions, sections, and round tables. One award of $1,000 is given to an individual member who serves as a committee member, group moderator, or chapter officer.

### ARLIS/NA STUDENT CONFERENCE ATTENDANCE AWARD
The ARLIS/NA Student Conference Attendance Award encourages participation in ARLIS/NA by assisting students considering a career in art librarianship or visual resources to attend the annual ARLIS/NA conference. The $1,000 awards will be given to student members who are active participants in ARLIS/NA and are currently enrolled in an accredited graduate program in library studies or information studies or have graduated within the past 12 months.

### AskART CONFERENCE ATTENDANCE AWARD
The AskART Conference Attendance Award encourages participation of members active in the field of American art research and bibliography who could not attend the conference without financial assistance. This $1,000 award is given to a member who is actively involved in the field of American art through reference, research, bibliographic work, or the overseeing of significant art research collections, or who is researching subjects or themes related to American art.

### HOWARD AND BEVERLY JOY KARNO AWARD
The Howard and Beverly Joy Karno Award encourages professional development of art librarians who work to advance the study of Latin American art through interaction with ARLIS/NA colleagues and conference participation. A $1,000 award is given to an art librarian residing in Latin America or an art librarian residing in North America working with significant Latin American art/architecture research collections or researching subjects or themes related to Latin American art/architecture.

## MERRILL WADSWORTH SMITH TRAVEL AWARD IN ARCHITECTURE LIBRARIANSHIP

The Merrill Wadsworth Smith Travel Award in Architecture is a $1,000 award to encourage participation of members active in the field of architecture librarianship, visual resources professionals in architecture-dominated collections, archivists, and students interested in architecture librarianship who could not attend the conference without financial assistance.

## H. W. WILSON FOUNDATION RESEARCH GRANT

The H. W. Wilson Foundation Research Grant supports research activities by ARLIS/NA individual members in the fields of librarianship, visual resources curatorship, and the arts. The award encourages the professional development of the membership in their capacities as information intermediaries and as subject specialists in the arts. Applicants may apply for award amounts of up to $3,000. If there are multiple applications deserving support but the total dollars requested in those applications exceed the committee's $3,000 annual award budget, the committee reserves the right to offer partial funding of the dollar amount requested in an application in order to provide support for more than one recipient. In that case, and based on the application materials, the committee will distribute the available funds as

it deems appropriate. Applicants may decline to accept partial funding.

**REQUIREMENTS AND RESTRICTIONS**
Vary by grant. Some awards are open to all, while others are open only to members.

**APPLICATION PROCEDURES**
**Submission Guidelines:** Vary by grant; see website for details. All grants require an application to be mailed, faxed, or preferably e-mailed.

**CONTACT**
Varies by grant. See the website for contact information.

**GRANT-SPECIFIC WEBSITE**
www.arlisna.org/about/awards/awards_index.html

# Asplundh Family Public Foundation

## Headquarters

708 Blair Mill Rd.
Willow Grove, PA 19090
Phone: 215-784-4200

## Description

**Founded:** 1955?

**Operating Locations:** Pennsylvania

**Foundation Information:** Private foundation established by Carl H. Asplundh

# Financial Summary

Assets: $48,135,425
Gifts Received: $62,000
Total Giving: $2,564,000

# Grants Information

## GRANT TYPES
General support, endowment, project, multiyear continuing support, emergency

## TYPICAL RECIPIENTS
Arts and humanities, civic affairs, education, environment, health, international, religion, science, social services

## GRANT VALUES
Total Dollar Amount of Grants: $2,564,000

## PAST GRANT RECIPIENTS

*Library or School Related*
- Princeton Public Library (NJ), general support, $1,000
- Delaware Valley Friends School (PA), endowment, $10,000
- St. Edwards School (FL), general support, $1,000

- Denison University (OH), general support, $4,000
- Marshall University (WV), general support, $1,000
- Flagler College (FL), campus recycling program, $10,000

*General*
- Colonial Williamsburg Foundation (VA), general support, $15,000
- Sanibel-Captiva Conservation Society (FL), general support, $3,000
- Chester County Community Foundation (PA), general support, $70,000
- Pennypack Ecological Restoration Trust (PA), land acquisition, $100,000
- Christiana Care Health System (DE), support for Center for Integrative Health, $100,000
- Bryn Athyn Church of the New Jerusalem (PA), emergency cash fund to classroom teachers, $12,500

## REQUIREMENTS AND RESTRICTIONS
NA

## APPLICATION PROCEDURES
**Submission Guidelines:** Send a letter of inquiry, including description of organization, amount requested, and purpose of funds sought.

## CONTACT
Asplundh Family Public Foundation
708 Blair Mill Rd.
Willow Grove, PA 19090

Phone: 215-784-4122
E-mail: contact@
asplundhpublicfoundation.org

**GRANT-SPECIFIC WEBSITE**
http://asplundhpublicfoundation.org

# Association for Library Collections and Technical Services (ALCTS)

## Headquarters

50 E. Huron St.
Chicago, IL 60611
Phone: 800-545-2433, ext. 5030
www.ala.org/ala/mgrps/divs/alcts/alcts.cfm

## Description

**Founded:** 1957

**Operating Locations:** Illinois

The Association for Library Collections and Technical Services (ALCTS), a division of the American Library Association, is the premier resource for information specialists in collection development, preservation, and technical services. ALCTS leads in the development of principles, standards, and best practices for creating, collecting, organizing, delivering, and preserving information resources in all forms.

## Financial Summary

Total Giving: $18,000

## Grants Information

**GRANT TYPES**
Professional development, conference attendance

**TYPICAL RECIPIENTS**
Technical services librarians

**GRANT VALUES**
Total Dollar Amount of Grants: $1,500
Number of Grants: 2

**NAMED GRANTS**

**ALCTS ONLINE COURSE GRANT FOR LIBRARY PROFESSIONALS FROM DEVELOPING COUNTRIES**
The ALCTS Online Course Grant for Library Professionals from Developing Countries provides one free seat per online continuing educational course session to librarians and information professionals from developing countries. The goal of this pilot project is to help library professionals from developing countries stay current with the latest trends and developments in technical services areas and enhance their professional knowledge and skills in librarianship and information science.

**Grant-Specific Website:** www.ala.org/ala/mgrps/divs/alcts/awards/grants/onlinegrant.cfm

### FIRST STEP AWARD

This Wiley Professional Development Grant awarded by the Continuing Resources Section of ALCTS is intended to provide librarians new to the continuing resources field with the opportunity to broaden their perspective and to encourage professional development in ALA Annual Conference and participation in Continuing Resources Section activities. Applicants must be ALCTS member with five or fewer years of professional experience in the continuing resources field who have not previously attended an ALA Annual Conference. The award consists of $1,500 cash and a citation. The award, donated by John Wiley and Sons, Inc., is applicable toward round-trip transportation, lodging, registration fees, etc.

**Grant-Specific Website:** www.ala.org/ala/mgrps/divs/alcts/awards/grants/firststep.cfm

### REQUIREMENTS AND RESTRICTIONS

Vary by grant; see website for details.

### APPLICATION PROCEDURES

**Submission Guidelines:** Visit the website for initial application submission information.

**Deadlines:** For most awards, the deadline for submissions is December 1 of each year.

**Decisions:** By March 1, the ALCTS executive director will distribute a press release announcing the winners of the awards. The awards are presented at the ALCTS awards ceremony during the ALA Annual Conference.

### CONTACT

Charles Wilt
Phone: 800-545-2433, ext. 5030, or 312-280-5030
E-mail: cwilt@ala.org

### GRANT-SPECIFIC WEBSITE

www.ala.org/ala/mgrps/divs/alcts/awards/

# Association for Library Service to Children (ALSC)

## Headquarters

50 E. Huron St.
Chicago, IL 60611
Phone: 800-545-2433, ext. 2163
www.ala.org/ala/mgrps/divs/alsc/

## Description

**Founded:** 1941

**Operating Locations:** Illinois

The Association for Library Service to Children (ALSC), a division of the American Library Association, was approved by ALA council in June 1941. ALSC is the world's largest organization dedicated to the support and enhancement of library service to children. Showing their commitment through creative programming and best practices, continuing education and professional connections, ALSC members are innovators in the field of children's library service. ALSC's network includes more than 4,200 children's and youth librarians, children's literature experts, publishers, education and library school faculty members, and other adults dedicated to creating a better future for children through libraries.

# Financial Summary

Total Giving: $82,000

# Grants Information

### GRANT TYPES
Project, conference attendance, continuing education, library improvement

### TYPICAL RECIPIENTS
Children's libraries and librarians

### GRANT VALUES
Total Dollar Amount of Grants: $44,400

Number of Grants: 6
Average Grant: $2,520
Highest Grant: $4,000
Lowest Grant: $600
Typical Range of Grants: $1,000–$4,000

## NAMED GRANTS

### ALSC/BWI SUMMER READING PROGRAM GRANT
The ALSC/BWI Summer Reading Program Grant, donated by Book Wholesalers, Inc. (BWI), provides financial assistance to a public library for developing outstanding summer reading programs for children. The grant is designed to encourage reading programs for children in public libraries by providing $3,000 in financial assistance, while recognizing ALSC members for innovative program development.

### MAUREEN HAYES AWARD
The Maureen Hayes Award, sponsored by Simon and Schuster Children's Publishing, is designed to provide up to $4,000 to an ALSC member library to fund a visit from an author/illustrator who will speak to children who have not had the opportunity to hear a nationally known author/illustrator. The award was established in 2005 with funding from Simon and Schuster Children's Publishing to honor its former director of library services, Maureen Hayes, for her lifelong efforts to bring together children and authors/illustrators.

## PENGUIN YOUNG READERS GROUP AWARD

The Penguin Young Readers Group Award consists of a $600 grant, sponsored by Penguin Young Readers Group, for up to four winners to attend their first ALA Annual Conference. To be considered for the award, applicants must have fewer than ten years of experience as a children's librarian and work directly with children. The award is only available to first-time conference attendees.

## LOUISE SEAMAN BECHTEL FELLOWSHIP

The Louise Seaman Bechtel Fellowship provides a $4,000 grant to a qualified children's librarian to spend a month or more reading and studying at the Baldwin Library of the George A. Smathers Libraries, University of Florida, Gainesville. The Baldwin Library contains a special collection of 85,000 volumes of children's literature published mostly before 1950. The fellowship is endowed in memory of Louise Seaman Bechtel and Ruth M. Baldwin.

## ALSC/CANDLEWICK PRESS "LIGHT THE WAY" GRANT

The ALSC/Candlewick Press "Light the Way: Outreach to the Underserved" Grant was formed in honor of Newbery Medalist and Geisel Honoree author Kate DiCamillo, and the themes represented in her books. The award consists of a $3,000 grant to assist a library in conducting exemplary outreach to underserved populations through a new program or an expansion of work already being done.

## BOOKAPALOOZA PROGRAM

Each year the ALSC office receives almost 3,000 newly published books, videos, audiobooks, and recordings from children's trade publishers. The materials are primarily for children from birth through age fourteen and are submitted to ALSC award and media evaluation selection committees for award and notables consideration. After each ALA Midwinter Meeting in January, these materials need to be removed from the ALSC office to make room for a new year of publications. The Bookapalooza Program was created to find new homes for these materials. ALSC will select three libraries to receive a Bookapalooza collection of materials to be used in a way that creatively enhances their library service to children and families. Since ALSC receives such a wide variety and assortment of materials, they are unable to guarantee the format and quality of content of all materials provided. The collections are intended to help transform each library's collection and provide an opportunity for these materials to be used in each community in creative and innovative ways. The Bookapalooza program aligns with ALSC's core purpose of creating a better future for all children through libraries. The three collections of materials are estimated to be worth $10,000 each.

**REQUIREMENTS AND RESTRICTIONS**
Almost all grants and awards require ALSC membership.

**APPLICATION PROCEDURES**

**Submission Guidelines:** Vary by grant; see the website for details.

**Deadlines:** December

**Decisions:** January

**CONTACT**
Jenny Najduch
Phone: 800-545-2433, ext. 4026, or 312-280-4026
E-mail: jnajduch@ala.org

**GRANT-SPECIFIC WEBSITE**
www.ala.org/ala/mgrps/divs/alsc/awardsgrants/profawards/

# Association of College and Research Libraries (ACRL)

## Headquarters

50 E. Huron St.
Chicago, IL 60611
Phone: 800-545-2433, ext. 2514
www.ala.org/ala/mgrps/divs/acrl/

## Description

**Founded:** 1938

**Operating Locations:** Illinois

The Association of College and Research Libraries (ACRL), a division of the American Library Association, is a professional association of academic librarians and other interested individuals. It is dedicated to enhancing the ability of academic library and information professionals to serve the information needs of the higher education community and to improve learning, teaching, and research. ACRL provides a broad range of professional services and programs for a diverse membership.

## Financial Summary

Total Giving: $40,000

## Grants Information

**GRANT TYPES**
Research

**TYPICAL RECIPIENTS**
Doctoral library students, librarians

**GRANT VALUES**
Total Dollar Amount of Grants: $5,500
Number of Grants: 3
Average Grant: $1,830
Highest Grant: $3,000
Lowest Grant: $1,000

## NAMED GRANTS

### SAMUEL LAZEROW FELLOWSHIP FOR RESEARCH IN COLLECTIONS AND TECHNICAL SERVICES IN ACADEMIC AND RESEARCH LIBRARIES

Samuel Lazerow led a distinguished career as a major contributor to the advancement of information technology at the Library of Congress, the National Library of Medicine, and the National Agriculture Library, among others. He ended his career as senior vice-president at the Institute for Scientific Information. The Samuel Lazerow Fellowship, sponsored by Thomson Reuters, fosters advances in collections or technical services by providing $1,000 fellowships to librarians for travel or writing in those fields. Research projects in the compilation of bibliographies will not be supported by this fellowship.

### DOCTORAL DISSERTATION FELLOWSHIP

The Doctoral Dissertation Fellowship, sponsored by Thomson Reuters, offers $1,500 to foster research in academic librarianship by encouraging and assisting doctoral students in the field with their dissertation research.

### WESS COUTTS NIJHOFF INTERNATIONAL WEST EUROPEAN SPECIALIST STUDY GRANT

This grant supports research pertaining to Western European studies, librarianship, or the book trade. This annual grant was established by WESS in 1985 under the sponsorship of Martinus Nijhoff International, a subscription agent and book dealer headquartered in The Hague. The grant is now sponsored by Coutts Information Services, the international academic library vendor, from its regional offices in The Netherlands (Coutts Nijhoff International). The grant consists of a maximum of $3,000 donated by Coutts Information Services to cover travel to and from Europe, transportation in Europe, and lodging and board for no more than fourteen (14) consecutive days. Funds may not be used for salaries, research-related supplies, publication costs, conference fees, or equipment purchases.

### REQUIREMENTS AND RESTRICTIONS

Eligibility for application varies according to each award or grant. Some awards and grants require the applicant to be an ALA member.

### APPLICATION PROCEDURES

**Submission Guidelines:** Applications online. Visit the website for details.

**Deadlines:** December

### CONTACT

Megan Griffin
Phone: 800-545-2433, ext. 2514, or 312-280-2514
E-mail: mgriffin@ala.org

GRANT-SPECIFIC WEBSITE
www.ala.org/ala/mgrps/divs/acrl/
awards/

# Association of Jewish Libraries (AJL)

## Headquarters

PO Box 1118
Teaneck, NJ 07666
Phone: 212-725-5359
www.jewishlibraries.org/main/

## Description

**Founded:** 1966

**Operating Locations:** New Jersey

The Association of Jewish Libraries (AJL) promotes Jewish literacy through enhancement of libraries and library resources and through leadership for the profession and practitioners of Judaica librarianship. The association fosters access to information, learning, teaching, and research relating to Jews, Judaism, the Jewish experience, and Israel.

## Financial Summary

Assets: $281,256

Gifts Received: $11,125
Total Giving: $15,992

## Grants Information

**GRANT TYPES**
Conference attendance

**TYPICAL RECIPIENTS**
AJL members

**GRANT VALUES**
Number of Grants: 2

**NAMED GRANTS**

**DORIS ORENSTEIN MEMORIAL CONVENTION TRAVEL GRANT**
The Doris Orenstein Memorial Convention Travel Grant helps defray expenses to attend the AJL convention for new members of AJL or for members who have never attended. An article describing the winner's convention experience should be submitted to the AJL Newsletter within one year of attendance. The amount of the grant varies according to costs.

**Grant-Specific Website:**
www.jewishlibraries.org/ajlweb/
scholarships/orenstein.htm

**LUCIUS LITTAUER FOUNDATION TRAVEL GRANT**
The Lucius Littauer Foundation Travel Grant helps defray expenses to attend AJL's convention. It is for current paid-

up international RAS Division members who are residing overseas and active in AJL. Applicant must be a current member of AJL at the time of application and for the convention. Full registration at the convention is required, and there is an expectation that recipients will attend the entire convention.

**Grant-Specific Website:** www.jewishlibraries.org/ajlweb/ scholarships/littauer_travel.htm

**REQUIREMENTS AND RESTRICTIONS**
Applicants must be members of AJL.

**APPLICATION PROCEDURES**
**Submission Guidelines:** Varies by grant; see the website for details. Application must be submitted to the appropriate contact person at AJL; see the website for contact information.

**Deadlines:** April 30

**CONTACT**
Phone: 212-725-5359
E-mail: ajlibs@osu.edu

**GRANT-SPECIFIC WEBSITE**
Varies by grant

# Association of Library Trustees, Advocates, Friends, and Foundations (ALTAFF)

## Headquarters

109 S. 13th St., Suite 3-N
Philadelphia, PA 19107
Phone: 800-545-2433, ext. 2161, or 312-280-2161
Fax: 215-545-3821
E-mail: altaff@ala.org
www.ala.org/ala/mgrps/divs/altaff/

## Description

**Founded:** 2009

**Operating Locations:** Illinois, Pennsylvania

In February 2009 Friends of Libraries U.S.A. (FOLUSA) and the Association for Library Trustees and Advocates (ALTA) joined forces to become an expanded division of the American Library Association: the Association of Library Trustees, Advocates, Friends and Foundations (ALTAFF). The purpose of this division is to help trustees and friends work together at the local, state, and national levels to effectively promote and advocate for libraries.

# Grants Information

## GRANT TYPES
Conference attendance, conference programming

## TYPICAL RECIPIENTS
Public library trustees, library friends groups, other nonprofit organizations

## GRANT VALUES
Total Dollar Amount of Grants: $1,250
Number of Grants: 2
Average Grant: $625
Highest Grant: $750
Lowest Grant: $500

## NAMED GRANTS

### ALTAFF/GALE OUTSTANDING TRUSTEE GRANT
The ALTAFF/Gale Outstanding Trustee Conference Grant enables a public library trustee to attend the ALA Annual Conference. A grant of $850 is awarded annually to a public library trustee who has demonstrated qualitative interests and efforts in supportive service of the local public library. Applicants must be personal members of the Trustee Section of ALTAFF, be currently serving as a member of a local public library board, and have not previously attended an ALA Annual Conference.

**Deadlines:** December 31

### ALA PRESIDENT'S AWARD FOR ADVOCACY
The ALA President's Award for Advocacy, awarded each year to a statewide advocacy campaign, was developed by and is sponsored by ALTAFF. This annual award carries with it a $1,000 grant for the development of a program or programs for Friends and Trustees at the state library association conference.

**Deadlines:** March

## REQUIREMENTS AND RESTRICTIONS
Vary by grant

## APPLICATION PROCEDURES

**Submission Guidelines:** Application online

## CONTACT
Beth Nawalinski
Phone: 800-545-2433, ext. 2161, or 312-280-2161
E-mail: bnawalinski@ala.org

## GRANT-SPECIFIC WEBSITE
www.ala.org/ala/mgrps/divs/altaff/

# Association of Research Libraries (ARL)

## Headquarters

21 Dupont Circle NW, Suite 800
Washington, DC 20036
Phone: 202-296-2296
www.arl.org

## Description

**Founded:** 1932

**Operating Locations:** District of Columbia

The Association of Research Libraries (ARL) is a nonprofit organization of 123 research libraries at comprehensive, research-extensive institutions in the United States and Canada that share similar research missions, aspirations, and achievements. The association's importance and distinction are born from its membership and the nature of the institutions represented. ARL member libraries make up a large portion of the academic and research library marketplace, spending more than $1 billion every year on library materials.

## Grants Information

### GRANT TYPES
In-kind

### TYPICAL RECIPIENTS
Research libraries

### GRANT VALUES
Total Dollar Amount of Grants: $3,200

### NAMED GRANTS

#### LibQUAL+ In-Kind Grant Program
Since 2005, LibQUAL+ has offered an in-kind grant for participation in the LibQUAL+ survey. With a goal to offer one grant for every 50 registered libraries, a total of up to five institutions are awarded grants each year. Applications will be reviewed and evaluated by an advisory committee.

### REQUIREMENTS AND RESTRICTIONS
The selection criteria are financial need, potential for contribution to the growth of LibQUAL+, and ability of the participating library to both improve overall services and contribute to the quality of service provided to students and faculty at their institution.

### APPLICATION PROCEDURES

**Submission Guidelines:** Interested applicants must submit the following materials for consideration:

- a three- to five-page narrative explaining their unique situation and how they meet the criteria above
- a brief paragraph describing their institution
- the name, phone number, e-mail address, and mailing address of the contact person for the application
- a short biography of the person applying on behalf of the institution

Applications will be accepted via e-mail, fax, or mail at the contact address below.

**Deadlines:** June and December

**CONTACT**
LibQUAL+ Grant Award
Association of Research Libraries
21 Dupont Circle NW, Suite 800
Washington DC 20036-1543
Phone: 202-296-2296
Fax: 202-872-0884
E-mail: libqual@arl.org

**GRANT-SPECIFIC WEBSITE**
www.libqual.org/about/about_lq/
   in_kind_grant

# AT&T Foundation

## Headquarters

130 E. Travis St.
San Antonio, TX 78205
Phone: 210-351-2077

## Description

**Founded:** NA

**Operating Locations:** Texas

**Foundation Information:** Corporate foundation of AT&T Corp.

## Financial Summary

Assets: $190,920,478
Gifts Received: $414,227,238
Total Giving: $57,772,461

## Grants Information

**GRANT TYPES**
Awards, conference attendance, emergency, operating support, project, multiyear continuing support, employee matching

**TYPICAL RECIPIENTS**
Arts and humanities, civic affairs, education, environment, health, international, science, social services

**GRANT VALUES**
Total Dollar Amount of Grants:
   $57,772,461

**PAST GRANT RECIPIENTS**

*Library or School Related*
- Carson City Library (NV), computer hardware, $6,548
- Cedar Park Public Library Foundation

(TX), RFID tracking system for library transactions, $5,000

- Ironwood Carnegie Library (MI), mobile computer lab upgrade, $10,173
- Elizabeth Jones Library (MS), hardware upgrade for basic adult education and literacy, $39,935
- Friends of Castroville Library (TX), laptop computer for community education, $20,000
- University of Central Oklahoma (OK), forensic training, $250,000
- University of Southern Mississippi, DuBard School for Language Disorders (MS), computer upgrade for teaching special needs students, $20,000
- University of the Incarnate Word (TX), capital campaign for science, mathematics, and engineering center, $250,000

*General*
- Youth Policy Institute (CA), computers for computer literacy course for underserved students and their families, $10,000
- The Women's Museum: An Institute for the Future (TX), sponsorship of traveling exhibits of AT&T corporate art collection, $300,000
- Washoe County Legal Aid Society (NV), technology equipment upgrade, $5,128

## REQUIREMENTS AND RESTRICTIONS

Applicants must have tax-exempt status. The foundation does not make grants to individuals or to organizations lobbying for political causes.

Technology-related grants are a priority.

## APPLICATION PROCEDURES

**Submission Guidelines:** Application online. The application form must be filled out completely and include

- signature of the organization's executive director/CEO
- indication of how the project links with the foundation's priorities
- total cost and amount requested
- statement of project goals, including issue addressed, clients served, timetable, and expected results
- details of overall fund-raising plans
- plans to sustain program after conclusion of foundation's support
- organization's mission statement
- breakdown of clients served
- copy of IRS determination letter confirming tax-exempt status
- line-item budget for the project
- list of board members with affiliations
- publicity plan to promote project and foundation's involvement
- project evaluation plan

**Decisions:** The foundation normally responds to all requests within 8 weeks after receipt.

## CONTACT

Laura P. Sanford
Phone: 210-351-5259

## GRANT-SPECIFIC WEBSITE

www.att.com/gen/corporate-
citizenship?pid = 12307
Grant application: www.att.com/
Common/files/pdf/foundation_
grant_app.doc

# Leburta Atherton Foundation

## Headquarters

c/o Bank of Hawaii
PO Box 3170, Dept. 715
Honolulu, HI 96802
Phone: 808-694-4540

## Description

**Founded:** NA

**Operating Locations:** Hawaii

**Foundation Information:** Private
foundation established by Leburta
Atherton

## Financial Summary

Assets: $14,304,023
Gifts Received: $1,392,881
Total Giving: $625,879

# Grants Information

## GRANT TYPES

General support

## TYPICAL RECIPIENTS

Arts and humanities, civic affairs,
education, environment, health, religion,
social services

## GRANT VALUES

Total Dollar Amount of Grants: $625,879
Number of Grants: 15
Average Grant: $42,000
Highest Grant: $200,000
Lowest Grant: $1,000

## PAST GRANT RECIPIENTS

*Library or School Related*
- Long Beach Public Library Foundation
  (CA), endowment for learning center,
  $25,000
- Parker School (HI), capital campaign,
  $20,000
- Hawaii Preparatory Academy (HI),
  sprinkler system, $6,678

*General*
- Hawaii Children's Discovery Center
  (HI), "Ready, Set, Grow" campaign,
  $125,000
- Long Beach Rotary Charity
  Foundation (CA), endowment for
  learning center, $25,000
- St. James Episcopal Church (HI), One
  Laptop per Child program, $3,200

- North Hawaii Community Hospital (HI), capital campaign, $50,000
- Kona Historical Society (HI), support for exhibition, $25,000
- The Contemporary Museum (HI), capital project, $200,000
- Hawaii Wildlife Center (HI), new building, $5,000

**REQUIREMENTS AND RESTRICTIONS**
NA

**APPLICATION PROCEDURES**
**Submission Guidelines:** Send a letter of inquiry.

**CONTACT**
NA

**GRANT-SPECIFIC WEBSITE**
NA

# Atran Foundation

## Headquarters

23–25 E. 21st St.
New York, NY 10010
Phone: 212-505-9677

## Description

**Founded:** NA

**Operating Locations:** New York

**Foundation Information:** Private foundation established by Frank Z. Atran

## Financial Summary

Assets: $17,563,643
Total Giving: $580,850

## Grants Information

**GRANT TYPES**
General support, endowment, fellowship, multiyear continuing support, research, operating support, seed money

**TYPICAL RECIPIENTS**
Arts and humanities, civic affairs, education, environment, health, international, religion, social services

**GRANT VALUES**
Total Dollar Amount of Grants: $580,850
Number of Grants: 30
Average Grant: $19,000
Highest Grant: $120,000
Lowest Grant: $1,000

**PAST GRANT RECIPIENTS**
*Library or School Related*
- New York Public Library (NY), general support, $4,000
- New York University (NY), Robert F. Wagner Labor Archives, $5,000
- Queens College (NY), general support, $2,500

- Columbia University (NY), general support, $55,000
- Brandeis University (MA), general support, $40,000
- Johns Hopkins University (MD), general support, $15,000
- Wurzweiler School (NY), general support, $15,000

*General*
- Folksbiene Yiddish Theatre (NY), general support, $25,000
- U.S. Holocaust Memorial Museum (NY), general support, $5,000
- Congress for Jewish Culture (NY), general support, $45,000

**REQUIREMENTS AND RESTRICTIONS**
Applicants must have tax-exempt status.

**APPLICATION PROCEDURES**
**Submission Guidelines:** Send a written proposal, including

- the nature and objectives of the project
- the estimated time period to carry out the project
- an itemized budget showing total cost of the project, contributions by the applicant and others, and amount requested for this grant
- additional financial support if project is to be continued
- dissemination of the results of the project
- a copy of the IRS ruling granting tax-exempt status to the organization

**CONTACT**
Diane Fischer
Phone: 212-505-9677

**GRANT-SPECIFIC WEBSITE**
NA

# Autry Foundation

## Headquarters

4383 Colfax Ave.
Studio City, CA 91604
Phone: 818-752-7770
Fax: 818-752-7770

## Description

**Founded:** NA

**Operating Locations:** California

**Foundation Information:** Private foundation established by Gene Autry, former actor and entertainer

## Financial Summary

Assets: $16,695,362
Total Giving: $566,307

## Grants Information

**GRANT TYPES**
General support

## TYPICAL RECIPIENTS

Arts and humanities, civic affairs, education, environment, health, international, religion, science, social services

## GRANT VALUES

Total Dollar Amount of Grants: $566,307
Number of Grants: 25
Average Grant: $22,000
Highest Grant: $300,100
Lowest Grant: $450

## PAST GRANT RECIPIENTS

*Library or School Related*

- Whittier College (CA), general support, $4,807
- UCLA Foundation (CA), scholarship support, $1,000
- Institute of American Indian Arts (NM), general support, $1,500

*General*

- Inner City Arts (CA), general support, $25,000
- American Film Institute (CA), general support, $7,500
- Alternative Living for the Aged (CA), general support, $450
- Los Angeles Philharmonic Association (CA), general support, $1,500
- Starkey Hearing Foundation (MN), general support, $10,000
- Gene Autry Courage Awards, Tempe Sports Authority (AZ), general support, $4,000

## REQUIREMENTS AND RESTRICTIONS

NA

## APPLICATION PROCEDURES

**Submission Guidelines:** Send a request on organization's letterhead.

## CONTACT

Jacqueline Autry
Phone: 878-752-7770

## GRANT-SPECIFIC WEBSITE

NA

# Milton and Ally Avery Arts Foundation

## Headquarters

c/o Radin Glass & Co.
360 Lexington Ave., 22nd fl.
New York, NY 10017
Phone: 212-557-7509, ext. 309

## Description

**Founded:** NA

**Operating Locations:** New York

**Foundation Information:** Private foundation

# Financial Summary

Assets: $4,359,492
Total Giving: $458,790

# Grants Information

## GRANT TYPES
General support

## TYPICAL RECIPIENTS
Arts and humanities, civic affairs, education, environment, international, religion, social services

## GRANT VALUES
Total Dollar Amount of Grants: $458,790
Highest Grant: $30,000
Lowest Grant: $200

## PAST GRANT RECIPIENTS

*Library or School Related*
- The Phillips Collection (DC), art links to literacy, $3,000
- Vermont Studio School (VT), school fellowship, $3,750
- University of Albany (NY), museum internship program, $1,500
- Purchase College (NY), visual arts scholarship, $15,000

*General*
- Arts in Education (NY), art education in high school, $2,000
- Jersey City Museum (NJ), art education in schools, $3,000
- Printed Matter, Inc. (NY), educational outreach, $2,000
- Brooklyn Arts Council (NY), arts in education, $5,000
- Museum of Fine Arts of Houston (TX), artist-in-residence program, $1,000
- Provincetown Fine Arts Work Center (MA), visual arts fellowships, $6,000
- Center for Book Arts (NY), general support, $1,000
- Studio Museum Harlem (NY), artist-in-residence, $3,000

## REQUIREMENTS AND RESTRICTIONS
Applicants must have tax-exempt status. Funds are restricted to art education and development of artists.

## APPLICATION PROCEDURES
**Submission Guidelines:** Send a brief letter of inquiry and a full proposal, including

- a description of organization
- amount requested
- recently audited financial statement
- proof of tax-exempt status
- purpose of funds sought

## CONTACT
NA

## GRANT-SPECIFIC WEBSITE
NA

# Aylward Family Foundation

## Headquarters

PO Box 409
Neenah, WI 54957
Phone: 920-722-0901

## Description

**Founded:** 1955?

**Operating Locations:** Wisconsin

**Foundation Information:** Private foundation established by the Aylward family of Neenah Foundry Co.

## Financial Summary

Assets: $3,958,193
Total Giving: $126,000

## Grants Information

### GRANT TYPES
Capital, general support, operating support, multiyear continuing support

### TYPICAL RECIPIENTS
Arts and humanities, civic affairs, education, health, international, religion, social services

### GRANT VALUES
Total Dollar Amount of Grants: $126,000
Number of Grants: 15
Average Grant: $8,400
Highest Grant: $15,000
Lowest Grant: $1,000

### PAST GRANT RECIPIENTS

*Library or School Related*
- Lawrence University (WI), general support, $15,000
- Ripon College (WI), general support, $15,000
- University of Wisconsin (WI), general support, $5,000
- Wayland Academy (WI), general support, $10,000

*General*
- Wisconsin Public Television (WI), general support, $6,000
- International Crane Foundation (WI), general support, $2,000
- EAA Aviation Foundation (WI), general support, $1,000
- ALS Association (CA), general support, $10,000

### REQUIREMENTS AND RESTRICTIONS
The foundation does not make grants to individuals.

### APPLICATION PROCEDURES
**Submission Guidelines:** Send a letter of request detailing need.

**Deadlines:** October 31

**CONTACT**
E. W. Aylward, President

**GRANT-SPECIFIC WEBSITE**
NA

# Azadoutioun Foundation

## Headquarters

c/o Gravestar
160 Second St.
Cambridge, MA 02142
Phone: 617-492-4118

## Description

**Founded:** 1985

**Operating Locations:** Massachusetts

**Foundation Information:** Private foundation established by Carolyn G. Mugar

## Financial Summary

Assets: $3,998,483
Gifts Received: $2,868,976
Total Giving: $674,156

## Grants Information

**GRANT TYPES**
General support, project

**TYPICAL RECIPIENTS**
Arts and humanities, civic affairs, education, environment, health, international, religion, social services

**GRANT VALUES**
Total Dollar Amount of Grants: $674,156
Number of Grants: 16
Average Grant: $42,000
Highest Grant: $302,059
Lowest Grant: $500
Typical Range of Grants: $5,000–$50,000

**PAST GRANT RECIPIENTS**

*Library or School Related*
- Armenian Library and Museum of America (MA), general support, $50,000
- St. Stephen Armenian Elementary School (MA), general support, $10,000
- Harvard Humanitarian Institute (MA), general support, $6,500
- Haigazian University (Beirut, Lebanon), general support, $25,000

*General*
- Southwestern Writers Collection (TX), general support, $10,000
- Direct Cultural Access (NY), general support, $20,000
- Public International Law and Policy Group (DC), general support, $15,000
- Bill of Rights Defense Committee (MA), general support, $10,000

- Armenia Tree Project (MA), general support, $302,059
- Reforest the Tropics (CT), general support, $10,000
- Massachusetts Council of Churches (MA), general support, $500
- Armenia Fund USA (NY), general support, $150,000

## REQUIREMENTS AND RESTRICTIONS
The foundation focuses on education and reading.

## APPLICATION PROCEDURES
**Submission Guidelines:** Send a brief letter of inquiry describing the project.

## CONTACT
Phone: 617-492-4118

## GRANT-SPECIFIC WEBSITE
NA

# George F. Baker Trust

## Headquarters

477 Madison Ave., Suite 1650
New York, NY 10022
Phone: 212-755-1890

## Description

**Founded:** NA

**Operating Locations:** New York

**Foundation Information:** Private foundation established by George F. Baker

## Financial Summary

Assets: $11,323,170
Total Giving: $1,253,980

## Grants Information

### GRANT TYPES
General support

### TYPICAL RECIPIENTS
Arts and humanities, civic affairs, education, environment, health, international, religion, science, social services

### GRANT VALUES
Total Dollar Amount of Grants:
    $1,253,980
Number of Grants: 34
Average Grant: $36,000
Highest Grant: $100,000
Lowest Grant: $400

### PAST GRANT RECIPIENTS

*Library or School Related*
- Harvard Business School (MA), upgrade of Baker Library, $100,000
- Trinity College (CT), expansion and renovation of library and its

integration with computer center, $100,000

- Purnell School (NJ), capital campaign, $10,000
- Palm Beach Day School (FL), capital campaign, $10,000
- Georgetown University (DC), scholarship and mentoring activities to business management students, $100,000

*General*

- OLPC Foundation (MA), One Laptop per Child program, $400
- New York Society for Prevention of Cruelty to Children (NY), operating support, $2,500
- Quebec-Labrador Foundation (MA), scholarships related to aircraft pilot training, $12,500
- Zoological Society of the Palm Beaches (FL), renovation support, $25,000
- Woods Hole Oceanographic Institution (MA), research on global warming, $25,000
- Laureus Sport for Good Foundation (NY), support for projects using sport as tool for social change, $10,000
- Grace Church (NY), support for outreach program for academic assistance to underperforming elementary students in Lower Manhattan, $5,000

## REQUIREMENTS AND RESTRICTIONS

Applicants must have tax-exempt status. No grants are awarded to individuals.

## APPLICATION PROCEDURES

**Submission Guidelines:** There is no formal application form; a brief letter is sufficient. The letter should state the amount requested, the reason the grant is necessary, and other funding being sought. Applications must be signed by authorized persons, and no copies are required.

**Decisions:** Notification will be made only to those who receive a grant. Decisions made take up to 6 months.

## CONTACT

NA

## GRANT-SPECIFIC WEBSITE

NA

# R. C. Baker Foundation

## Headquarters

PO Box 6150
Orange, CA 92863
Phone: 714-750-8987

## Description

**Founded:** NA

**Operating Locations:** California

**Foundation Information:** Private foundation established by R. C. Baker

# Financial Summary

Assets: $33,860,289
Total Giving: $1,333,000

# Grants Information

## GRANT TYPES
General support, operating support, research, scholarship

## TYPICAL RECIPIENTS
Arts and humanities, civic affairs, education, environment, health, international, religion, science, social services

## GRANT VALUES
Total Dollar Amount of Grants:
    $1,333,000
Number of Grants: 92
Average Grant: $123,000
Highest Grant: $280,000
Lowest Grant: $1,000

## PAST GRANT RECIPIENTS
*Library or School Related*
- Henry E. Huntington Library and Art Gallery (CA), general support, $2,500
- Family Literacy Foundation (CA), general support, $1,000
- Discovery Science Center (CA), general support, $7,500
- Muckenthaler Cultural Center (CA), general support, $1,500
- Harvey Mudd College (CA), general support, $75,000

*General*
- Baker Memorial Museum (CA), general support, $17,000
- Amigos de los Ninos (CA), general support, $12,500
- Challenged Athletes Foundation (CA), general support, $45,000

## REQUIREMENTS AND RESTRICTIONS
No grants are awarded in the eastern United States. The foundation does not award grants to individuals or to political or lobbying groups. It also does not grant funds for endowments, loans, or capital projects of tax-supported institutions. Applicants must have tax-exempt status.

## APPLICATION PROCEDURES

**Submission Guidelines:** Send a letter of inquiry, including

- description and anticipated results of the proposed project
- recently audited financial statement
- amount requested
- other sources of support funds
- proof of tax-exempt status

**Deadlines:** May 1 and October 1

## CONTACT
NA

## GRANT-SPECIFIC WEBSITE
NA

# Edward L. Bakewell, Jr., Family Foundation

## Headquarters

7800 Forsyth Blvd.
St. Louis, MO 63105
Phone: 314-862-5555

## Description

**Founded:** NA

**Operating Locations:** Missouri

**Foundation Information:** Corporate foundation of Bakewell Corp.

## Financial Summary

Assets: $4,851,162
Gifts Received: $2,200,000
Total Giving: $179,150

## Grants Information

### GRANT TYPES
General support, operating support, research, emergency

### TYPICAL RECIPIENTS
Arts and humanities, civic affairs, education, environment, health, international, religion, science, social services

### GRANT VALUES
Total Dollar Amount of Grants: $179,150
Number of Grants: 19
Average Grant: $9,400
Highest Grant: $161,000
Lowest Grant: $100

### PAST GRANT RECIPIENTS

*Library or School Related*
- Mercatus Center at George Mason University (VA), research, $2,500
- Enterprise Mentors International (UT), operating expenses, $1,000
- University of Wyoming Foundation (WY), operating expenses, $100
- Washington University School of Medicine (MO), cancer research, $100

*General*
- SLV Museum (CO), general support, $500
- Heartland Museum (IA), general support, $2,500
- BJC Hospice (MO), general support, $100
- Environic Foundation International (VA), operating expenses, $1,000
- Greater Saint Louis Community Foundation (MO), general support, $161,000
- Neighborhood Health Clinic (FL), general support, $2,500

## REQUIREMENTS AND RESTRICTIONS
NA

## APPLICATION PROCEDURES
**Submission Guidelines:** Send a written application explaining merits of request.

**Deadlines:** Applications are accepted between September 1 and November 30.

## CONTACT
Richard W. Meier
Phone: 314-862-5555

## GRANT-SPECIFIC WEBSITE
NA

# L. G. Balfour Foundation

## Headquarters

PO Box 1802
Providence, RI 02901

## Description

**Founded:** NA

**Operating Locations:** Rhode Island

**Foundation Information:** Private foundation established by Lloyd G. Balfour

## Financial Summary

Assets: $106,114,348
Total Giving: $4,136,174

## Grants Information

### GRANT TYPES
Capital, general support, scholarship

### TYPICAL RECIPIENTS
Arts and humanities, education, health, social services

### GRANT VALUES
Total Dollar Amount of Grants: $4,136,174
Typical Range of Grants: $5,000–$30,000

### PAST GRANT RECIPIENTS

*Library or School Related*
- New Orleans Foundation (LA), Afterschool Partnership, $100,000
- Indiana University School of Law (IN), general support, $100,000
- Boston Plan for Excellence (MA), public school foundation, $200,000
- Posse Foundation (NY), general support, $100,000
- North Cambridge High School (MA), corporate work-study program, $50,000

*General*
- Black Ministerial Alliance (MA), general support, $75,000

- Steppingstone Foundation (MA), general support, $100,000
- Massachusetts 2020 Foundation (MA), general support, $150,000
- Hebron Village Outreach Center (MA), Working Person's Food Pantry, $10,000
- Boston Foundation (MA), Achieve the Dream program, $179,168
- Women at Work Museum (MA), general support, $40,000

## REQUIREMENTS AND RESTRICTIONS

Priority is given to applicants from New England. No grants are given to individuals or private foundations.

## APPLICATION PROCEDURES

**Submission Guidelines:** Send a letter of intent to be reviewed before preparing formal grant proposal. Letter should include

- description of the nature and objective of project to be funded
- list of board members along with names and qualifications of officers and staff
- evidence of tax-exempt status
- detailed project budget
- most recent audited financial statement
- statement of other sources of funding
- statement of agreement to report on the results of the project and the expenditures of grant funds

Applicant will receive a packet

containing a grant application form to be completed. Applicant can also use the AGM Common Proposal Format (www.agmconnect.org) but must also complete the Grant Application Coversheet included in the packet. No videos or DVDs and no hand-delivered proposals will be accepted.

**Deadlines:** January 31 and July 31

**Decisions:** Notification ongoing

## CONTACT

Kerry Herlihy Sullivan
c/o Bank of America
100 Federal St.
Boston, MA 02110
Phone: 617-434-4846
E-mail: kerry.h.sullivan@bankofamerica.com

## GRANT-SPECIFIC WEBSITE

NA

# Baltimore Equitable Insurance Foundation

## Headquarters

100 N. Charles St., S-640
Baltimore, MD 21201
Phone: 410-727-1794

# Description

**Founded:** NA

**Operating Locations:** Maryland

**Foundation Information:** Corporate foundation of Baltimore Equity Society

# Financial Summary

Assets: $6,111,279
Total Giving: $347,280

# Grants Information

## GRANT TYPES
General support

## TYPICAL RECIPIENTS
Arts and humanities, civic affairs, education, religion, social services

## GRANT VALUES
Total Dollar Amount of Grants: $347,280
Number of Grants: 9
Average Grant: $35,000
Highest Grant: $80,000
Lowest Grant: $980

## PAST GRANT RECIPIENTS

*General*
- Pot Spring Elementary School (MD), support for environmental awareness, $1,000
- Association of Baltimore Area Grantmakers, Inc. (MD), dues and support of neighborhood alliances, $21,800
- Associated Catholic Organizations (MD), general support, $3,500
- Mercy Medical Center (MD), general support, $980
- St. Ambrose Housing Aid Center, Inc. (MD), support for strengthening neighborhoods, $70,000
- Patterson Park Community Development Corp. (MD), support for strengthening neighborhoods, $80,000

## REQUIREMENTS AND RESTRICTIONS
Applicants must be located in the state of Maryland.

## APPLICATION PROCEDURES
**Submission Guidelines:** Send a letter of inquiry.

**Deadlines:** Before January 1, April 1, July 1, and October 1

## CONTACT
Timothy J. Schwartz
Phone: 410-707-1794

## GRANT-SPECIFIC WEBSITE
NA

# Ruth Eleanor Bamberger and John Ernest Bamberger Memorial Foundation

## Headquarters

136 S. Main St., Suite 418
Salt Lake City, UT 84101
Phone: 801-364-2045
www.ruthandjohnbamberger
memorialfdn.org

## Description

**Founded:** 1947

**Operating Locations:** Utah

**Foundation Information:** Private foundation established by Ernest Bamberger and Eleanor F. Bamberger

## Financial Summary

Assets: $19,934,652
Total Giving: $1,340,915

## Grants Information

### GRANT TYPES
General support, operating support, multiyear continuing support, scholarship

### TYPICAL RECIPIENTS
Arts and humanities, civic affairs, education, environment, health, religion, science, social services

### GRANT VALUES
Total Dollar Amount of Grants:
    $1,340,915
Number of Grants: 82
Average Grant: $15,000
Highest Grant: $200,000
Lowest Grant: $1,000

### PAST GRANT RECIPIENTS

*Library or School Related*
- Westminster College (UT), general support, $100,000
- Guadalupe Schools (UT), general support, $18,000
- McGillis School (UT), general support, $10,000
- Weber State University (UT), general support, $100,000
- University of Utah College of Nursing (UT), general support, $150,000
- Utah Valley University Foundation (UT), general support, $10,000

*General*
- Center for Documentary Arts (UT), general support, $3,000
- Prevent Child Abuse Utah (UT), general support, $10,000

- Girl Scouts of Utah (UT), general support, $5,000
- Rape Recovery Center (UT), general support, $5,000
- Family Support Center (UT), general support, $16,000

## REQUIREMENTS AND RESTRICTIONS
NA

## APPLICATION PROCEDURES

**Submission Guidelines:** Send a letter of inquiry, including

- description of the program
- list of board of directors
- budget
- cost of program
- other sources of funding
- 501(c)(3) determination letter
- latest audit report, financial statements, or a copy of IRS form 990

Six legible copies should be provided.

**Deadlines:** Vary by year

## CONTACT
Eleanor Roser
Phone: 801-364-2045
E-mail: bambergermemfdn@qwestoffice. net

## GRANT-SPECIFIC WEBSITE
www.ruthandjohnbamberger memorialfdn.org

# Bandai Foundation

## Headquarters

5551 Katella Ave.
Cypress, CA 90630
Phone: 714-816-9500
www.bandai.com/about/foundation.php

## Description

**Founded:** NA

**Operating Locations:** California

**Foundation Information:** Corporate foundation of Bandai America, Inc.

## Financial Summary

Assets: $10,156,076
Total Giving: $282,500

## Grants Information

### GRANT TYPES
General support

### TYPICAL RECIPIENTS
Arts and humanities, civic affairs, education, health, international, science, social services

### GRANT VALUES
Total Dollar Amount of Grants: $282,500

Number of Grants: 4
Average Grant: $71,000
Highest Grant: $200,000
Lowest Grant: $7,500

## PAST GRANT RECIPIENTS

*General*

- Starlight Starbright (CA), computers for children in hospitals, $200,000
- Toy R Us Children's Fund (NJ), help for sick children, $7,500
- Elizabeth Glaser Pediatric AIDS Fund (DC), help for children with AIDS, $50,000
- Children's Health Fund (NY), medical care for children, $25,000

## REQUIREMENTS AND RESTRICTIONS

The foundation prefers to focus on children's issues.

## APPLICATION PROCEDURES

**Submission Guidelines:** No specific format is required.

## CONTACT

Robert L. Burkett
26 Mercy Ct.
Potomac, MD 20854

## GRANT-SPECIFIC WEBSITE

www.bandai.com/about/foundation.php

# BankAtlantic Foundation, Inc.

## Headquarters

PO Box 8608
Fort Lauderdale, FL 33310
Phone: 954-940-5058
www.bankatlantic.com/BAFoundation/default.html

## Description

**Founded:** NA

**Operating Locations:** Florida

**Foundation Information:** Corporate foundation of BankAtlantic Bancorp

## Financial Summary

Assets: $2,702,145
Gifts Received: $650,000
Total Giving: $550,373

## Grants Information

### GRANT TYPES

General support, operating support, project, emergency

### TYPICAL RECIPIENTS

Arts and humanities, civic affairs, education, international, social services

## GRANT VALUES

Total Dollar Amount of Grants: $550,373
Typical Range of Grants: $1,000–$3,000

## PAST GRANT RECIPIENTS

*Library or School Related*

- Broward Public Library Foundation, Inc. (FL), general support, $20,000
- Library Foundation of Martin County (FL), general support, $2,000
- Miami-Dade Public Library Foundation (FL), general support, $2,000
- Greater Largo Library Foundation, Inc. (FL), general support, $1,500
- After School Program, Inc. (FL), general support, $3,500
- Early Learning Coalition of Broward Country (FL), general support, $2,000
- Martin County Education Foundation, Inc. (FL), general support, $2,500
- The Education Fund, Inc. (FL), general support, $20,000
- Miami-Dade College Foundation (FL), general support, $3,000
- Hillsborough Educational Partnership (FL), general support, $1,000

*General*

- National Foundation for Teaching Entrepreneurship to Handicapped (FL), general support, $3,500
- Helping Abused Neglected Dependent Youth (HANDY) (FL), general support, $3,000

## REQUIREMENTS AND RESTRICTIONS

Applicants must be located in the state of Florida. Grants are not made to the following types of organizations or activities: capital improvement or building campaigns, courtesy or goodwill advertising, endowment campaigns, fund-raising events, travel expenses, hospitals or medical research, individual K–12 schools, national health-related organizations, organizations without 501(c)(3) status, religious organizations, veteran organizations, school athletic teams, social functions, sporting events, individuals.

## APPLICATION PROCEDURES

**Submission Guidelines:** Submit a request in writing to foundation headquarters, including

- contact information
- director's name
- brief history of organization
- project description
- anticipated benefits of the project
- total amount requested
- dates of proposed project
- operating budget
- program budget including funds already raised and potential sources of additional funding
- list of corporate and foundation funding
- project location
- copy of tax-exempt letter
- copy of Charitable Solicitation License

- list of board members and their affiliations
- list of any funding already received from BankAtlantic
- signature of executive director acknowledging application

Faxed applications will not be considered.

**Deadlines:** Applications must be received between March 1 and October 1.

**Decisions:** The foundation will notify applicants within 90 days of their decision to consider the proposal.

**CONTACT**
Shelley Levan Margolis
Phone: 954-940-5058

**GRANT-SPECIFIC WEBSITE**
www.bankatlantic.com/BAFoundation/

# Bardes Fund

## Headquarters

4730 Madison Rd.
Cincinnati, OH 45227
Phone: 513-533-6228

## Description

**Founded:** 1996

**Operating Locations:** Ohio

**Foundation Information:** Corporate foundation of Bardes Corp.

## Financial Summary

Assets: $1,843,511
Gifts Received: $50,000
Total Giving: $102,100

## Grants Information

**GRANT TYPES**
General support

**TYPICAL RECIPIENTS**
Arts and humanities, civic affairs, education, environment, health, religion, social services

**GRANT VALUES**
Total Dollar Amount of Grants: $102,100
Number of Grants: 10 +
Highest Grant: $25,000
Lowest Grant: $2,000

**PAST GRANT RECIPIENTS**

*Library or School Related*
- Lawrenceville School (NJ), capital campaign, general support, $12,000
- St. George's School (RI), general support, $2,000
- Fine Arts Fund (OH), arts programs, $3,000
- Society of the Four Arts (FL), arts programs, $12,000

*General*

- Work Resource Center (OH), community programs, $3,500
- Starfire Council (OH), capital campaign, $10,000
- Cincinnati Symphony (OH), theater programs, $2,000
- Royal Poinciana Chapel (FL), general support, $25,000

## REQUIREMENTS AND RESTRICTIONS
NA

## APPLICATION PROCEDURES
**Submission Guidelines:** Send a written request.

## CONTACT
NA

## GRANT-SPECIFIC WEBSITE
NA

# Barker Foundation

## Headquarters

PO Box 328
Nashua, NH 03061
Phone: 603-889-1763

## Description

**Founded:** 1957

**Operating Locations:** New Hampshire

**Foundation Information:** Private foundation established by Walter Barker

# Financial Summary

Assets: $6,224,651
Total Giving: $180,186

# Grants Information

## GRANT TYPES
General support, emergency

## TYPICAL RECIPIENTS
Arts and humanities, civic affairs, education, environment, health, religion, social services

## GRANT VALUES
Total Dollar Amount of Grants: $180,186
Number of Grants: 44
Average Grant: $4,000
Highest Grant: $13,000
Lowest Grant: $200

## PAST GRANT RECIPIENTS

*Library or School Related*
- Adult Learning Center (NH), general support, $10,000
- Endicott College (MA), general support, $1,500
- Masonic Learning Centers for Children, Inc. (NH), general support, $10,000

- University of New Hampshire (NH), general support, $3,500

*General*
- Special Olympics (NH), general support, $4,000
- Shriners Burns Hospital (MA), general support, $5,000
- Home Health and Hospice Care (NH), general support, $8,880
- Wildlife Rescue and Rehabilitation (TX), general support, $2,500

## REQUIREMENTS AND RESTRICTIONS
No geographic restrictions, but the majority of grants are made to organizations in New Hampshire. Grants are not made to individuals.

## APPLICATION PROCEDURES

**Submission Guidelines:** Submit a one-page concept paper, including

- a brief background statement about the applicant organization and its purposes
- an outline of the specific project to be supported
- the total project cost
- a list of directors or trustees
- evidence of tax-exempt status

## CONTACT
Douglas M. Barker
Phone: 603-889-1763

## GRANT-SPECIFIC WEBSITE
NA

# Coeta and Donald R. Barker Foundation

## Headquarters

PO Box 936
Rancho Mirage, CA 92270
Phone: 760-324-1162

## Description

**Founded:** NA

**Operating Locations:** California

**Foundation Information:** Private foundation established by Donald R. Barker

## Financial Summary

Assets: $23,240,416
Total Giving: $1,428,500

## Grants Information

### GRANT TYPES
General support, operating support

### TYPICAL RECIPIENTS
Arts and humanities, civic affairs, education, environment, health, religion, science, social services

## GRANT VALUES

Total Dollar Amount of Grants:
    $1,428,500
Number of Grants: 31
Average Grant: $46,000
Highest Grant: $400,000
Lowest Grant: $200

## PAST GRANT RECIPIENTS

*Library or School Related*
- Friends of the Rancho Mirage Public Library (CA), support for children's programs, $25,000
- Foundation for the California State University at San Bernardino (CA), construction of health sciences building, $250,000
- St. Thomas Academy (OR), operating expenses, $10,000
- University of Oregon (OR), endowment fund for art museum exhibitions, $400,000
- College of the Desert (CA), general support, $11,000
- Crafton Hills College Foundation (CA), donation toward creating pilot training program for certified respiratory therapists, $10,000

*General*
- Friends of the Cultural Center (CA), support for four programs, $36,000
- Braille Institute of America, Inc. (CA), support for Desert Center Mobile Solutions Program, $5,000
- Angel View Crippled Children's Foundation (CA), support for triannual newsletter, $10,000
- Monterey County Sheriff's Posse, Inc. (CA), scholarships for disadvantage youth, $10,000
- Desert Symphony (CA), Children's Music Discovery Series, $1,000

## REQUIREMENTS AND RESTRICTIONS

The foundation will consider only those applicants with tax-exempt and nonprofit status. Grants will not be made to influence legislation or elections, for operational deficits, for sectarian religious purposes, or to agencies that rely on tax dollars as their principal support.

## APPLICATION PROCEDURES

**Submission Guidelines:** Send an initial letter of request for a grant application on organization's letterhead, including the name, address, and telephone number of organization. The letter should be signed by the president of the organization or an authorized trustee or executive director. The initial letter request should also contain

- a brief description of the project, facility, program, or service
- why it is a community priority need
- total funding required
- amount anticipated from the foundation
- a copy of the organization's IRS tax-exemption approval

- a copy of the organization's IRS nonprofit foundation status determination letter
- a statement from an officer that the organization's status is currently in keeping with the determination letters

Upon receipt of the requested grant application, the applicant should complete the form and return it with the additional requested information.

**Deadlines:** Applications must be submitted prior to the normal May and October trustees meeting to receive spring or fall consideration by the foundation's board.

**Decisions:** Award or rejection of an application will be announced promptly to applicant after decision is made.

**CONTACT**
Nancy G. Harris
Phone: 760-324-1162

**GRANT-SPECIFIC WEBSITE**
NA

# J. M. R. Barker Foundation

## Headquarters

1350 Avenue of the Americas
New York, NY 10019
Phone: 978-282-4776

## Description

**Founded:** NA

**Operating Locations:** New York

**Foundation Information:** Private foundation

## Financial Summary

Assets: $72,152,805
Total Giving: $2,217,520

## Grants Information

**GRANT TYPES**
Capital, endowment, general support, operating support, research, project

**TYPICAL RECIPIENTS**
Arts and humanities, civic affairs, education, environment, health, religion, science, social services

**GRANT VALUES**
Total Dollar Amount of Grants:
  $2,217,520
Number of Grants: 31
Average Grant: $7,000
Highest Grant: $700,000
Lowest Grant: $1,000

**PAST GRANT RECIPIENTS**

*Library or School Related*
- Gloucester Education Foundation (MA), general support, $350,000

- Connecticut Friends School (CT), general support, $30,000
- St. Anselm College (NH), general support, $10,000
- The Grammar School (VT), general support, $5,000
- Harvard Alumni Association Early College Awareness (MA), general support, $10,000
- University of Texas Health Science Center (TX), general support, $20,000

*General*
- Poets and Writers (NY), general support, $5,000
- The Nature Museum at Grafton (VT), general support, $10,000
- Wheelchair Sports and Recreation Association (FL), general support, $30,000

**REQUIREMENTS AND RESTRICTIONS**
NA

**APPLICATION PROCEDURES**
**Submission Guidelines:** Before submitting a formal proposal, applicants should submit a formal letter of inquiry briefly describing the programs of the sponsoring organization, the amount requested, and what will be accomplished as a result of the grant. If the request is within the foundation's current interests, the foundation will require a more detailed proposal, which should include

- a budget for the project
- audited financial statements
- an IRS tax-exempt determination letter

**Deadlines:** November 1 for initial letter of inquiry

**CONTACT**
Margaret B. Clark
Phone: 978-282-4776

**GRANT-SPECIFIC WEBSITE**
NA

# Barker Welfare Foundation

## Headquarters

1007 Glen Cove Ave.
Glen Head, NY 11545
Phone: 516-759-5592
E-mail: barkersmd@aol.com
www.barkerwelfare.org

## Description

**Founded:** NA

**Operating Locations:** New York

**Foundation Information:** Private foundation established by Catherine B. Hickox

# Financial Summary

Assets: $82,920,248
Total Giving: $2,478,151

# Grants Information

## GRANT TYPES
Capital, operating support, general support, project

## TYPICAL RECIPIENTS
Arts and humanities, civic affairs, education, environment, health, religion, social services

## GRANT VALUES
Total Dollar Amount of Grants:
    $2,478,151
Highest Grant: $100,000
Lowest Grant: $500

## PAST GRANT RECIPIENTS

*Library or School Related*
- Brooklyn Public Library Foundation (NY), online homework program, $24,000
- Chicago Public Library Foundation (IL), Teacher in the Library program, $15,000
- New York Public Library (NY), revitalization of children's rooms in branch libraries, $50,000
- Queens Library Foundation (NY), funding for adult learner program, $6,000

- Literacy Partners, Inc. (NY), funding for family literacy/ESL program, $10,000
- Reading for the Blind and Dyslexic (IL), funding for educational outreach for Chicago Public Schools, $12,000
- Augusta Preparatory Day School (GA), general support, $2,005

*General*
- Center for Arts Education (NY), general support, $20,000
- Civil War Preservation Trust (MD), general support, $1,024
- First Serve (NM), funding for after-school program, $2,500

## REQUIREMENTS AND RESTRICTIONS
The foundation considers requests from organizations serving New York City; Chicago, Illinois; and Michigan City, Indiana. Applicants must have tax-exempt status. The foundation does not fund medical research, scholarships, fellowships, loans, conferences/seminars, lobbying activities, or endowment funds.

## APPLICATION PROCEDURES
**Submission Guidelines:** Send a two- to three-page letter of inquiry including a copy of the first page of IRS form 990 and a current budget for the entire organization. A follow-up phone call is recommended to determine whether the foundation is interested in the applicant's request. If a grant request is suitable, a grants process sheet, a grant

application form, and a checklist of required information will be sent.

**Deadlines:** February 1 and August 1

**CONTACT**
Sarane H. Ross
Barker Welfare Foundation
PO Box 2
Glen Head, NY 11545
Phone: 516-759-5592

**GRANT-SPECIFIC WEBSITE**
www.barkerwelfare.org

# Barnes Group

## Headquarters

123 Main St.
Bristol, CT 06010
Phone: 860-583-7070
www.barnesgroupinc.com

## Description

**Founded:** 1857

**Operating Locations:** Connecticut, California, Georgia, Illinois, Mississippi, Michigan

**Type of Product/Service:** Fabricated wire products

**In-Kind or Service Support:** Matching gifts

# BARNES GROUP FOUNDATION, INC.

123 Main St.
Bristol, CT 06010
Phone: 860-583-7070
Fax: 860-589-7466
**Foundation Information:** Corporate foundation of Barnes Group, Inc.

## Financial Summary

Assets: $2,210
Gifts Received: $1,011,830
Total Giving: $998,281

## Grants Information

**GRANT TYPES**
General support, scholarship

**TYPICAL RECIPIENTS**
Arts and humanities, civic affairs, education, environment, health, religion, science, social services

**GRANT VALUES**
Total Dollar Amount of Grants: $998,281
Number of Grants: 89
Average Grant: $11,000
Highest Grant: $125,244
Lowest Grant: $50

## PAST GRANT RECIPIENTS

*General*

- Special Olympics Connecticut (CT), general support, $2,500
- Nature Conservancy (VA), general support, $200
- Foundation Fighting Blindness (MD), general support, $2,000
- Sierra Vista Child and Family Services (CA), general support, $100
- Make a Wish Foundation of Vermont (VT), general support, $1,000
- Fidelco Guide Dog Foundation (CT), general support, $500
- Connecticut Children's Medical Center Auxiliary (CT), general support, $10,000

## REQUIREMENTS AND RESTRICTIONS

Applicants must have tax-exempt status.

## APPLICATION PROCEDURES

**Submission Guidelines:** Write or call Citizens Scholarship Foundation of America, Inc. (1505 Riverview Rd., PO Box 297, St. Peter, MN 56082, 603-627-3870) to request the application form provided by Barnes Group. Application should

- state purpose and history of organization
- describe project and its budget
- list corporate donors
- include proof of tax-exempt status

**Deadlines:** March 1

**Decisions:** Board meets four times a year.

## CONTACT

NA

## GRANT-SPECIFIC WEBSITE

NA

# Barrington Foundation

## Headquarters

7–11 S. Broadway, Suite 200
White Plains, NY 10601
Phone: 914-285-9393

## Description

**Founded:** NA

**Operating Locations:** New York

**Foundation Information:** Private foundation

## Financial Summary

Assets: $1,467,515
Total Giving: $1,313,000

## Grants Information

### GRANT TYPES

General support, project

## TYPICAL RECIPIENTS

Arts and humanities, civic affairs, education, environment, health, international, religion, social services

## GRANT VALUES

Total Dollar Amount of Grants:
   $1,313,000
Number of Grants: 123
Average Grant: $10,500
Highest Grant: $201,000
Lowest Grant: $500
Typical Range of Grants: $1,000–
   $10,000

## PAST GRANT RECIPIENTS

*Library or School Related*
- Brookline Library Foundation (MA), general support, $1,000
- Library of the Boston Athenaeum (MA), general support, $3,000
- Literacy Network of South Berkshire (MA), general support, $1,500
- Clark University (MA), general support, $6,000
- Princeton University (NJ), general support, $5,000
- Recording for the Blind (MA), general support, $15,800
- Bard College at Simon's Rock (MA), general support, $100,000

*General*
- Doctors Without Borders (NY), general support, $7,000
- Environmental Defense Fund (NY), general support, $4,000
- National Humanities Center (NC), general support, $15,000
- MMA Musical Instrument Collection (NY), general support, $1,000
- Washington Institute for Near East Policy (DC), general support, $10,000

## REQUIREMENTS AND RESTRICTIONS

There are no specific application requirements.

## APPLICATION PROCEDURES

NA

## CONTACT

David Strassler
PO Box 750
Great Barrington, MA 01230
Phone: 914-285-9393

## GRANT-SPECIFIC WEBSITE

NA

# Barstow Foundation

## Headquarters

c/o Chemical Bank and Trust
235 E. Main St.
Midland, MI 48640
Phone: 989-839-5305

## Description

**Founded:** NA

**Operating Locations:** Michigan

**Foundation Information:** Private foundation established by Florence K. Barstow

# Financial Summary

Assets: $3,388,870
Gifts Received: $186,037
Total Giving: $180,000

# Grants Information

## GRANT TYPES
General support, operating support, project

## TYPICAL RECIPIENTS
Arts and humanities, civic affairs, education, environment, health, international, religion, science, social services

## GRANT VALUES
Total Dollar Amount of Grants: $180,000
Number of Grants: 17
Average Grant: $10,600
Highest Grant: $50,000
Lowest Grant: $4,000
Typical Range of Grants: $4,000–$5,000

## PAST GRANT RECIPIENTS

*Library or School Related*
- Sedona Public Library (AZ), capital improvements, $10,000

- Western Carolina University (NC), general support, $20,000

*General*
- Catholic Charities, CYO (CA), general support, $4,000
- West Midland Family Center (MI), food pantry, $4,000
- Travis County Domestic Violence Resource Center (TX), general support, $20,000
- State YMCA of Michigan (MI), camping fund, $50,000

## REQUIREMENTS AND RESTRICTIONS
The foundation does not support individuals or research programs or make loans.

## APPLICATION PROCEDURES

**Submission Guidelines:** Send a letter of inquiry with accompanying brochures or pamphlets if available.

**Deadlines:** July 31

**Decisions:** After annual meeting at end of July

## CONTACT
John Kessler
Phone: 989-839-5305

## GRANT-SPECIFIC WEBSITE
NA

# Theodore H. Barth Foundation

## Headquarters

45 Rockefeller Plaza, Suite 2037
New York, NY 10111
Phone: 212-332-3466

## Description

**Founded:** 1953

**Operating Locations:** New York

**Foundation Information:** Private foundation established by Theodore H. Barth

## Financial Summary

Assets: $30,141,955
Total Giving: $1,366,000

## Grants Information

### GRANT TYPES
General support, scholarship

### TYPICAL RECIPIENTS
Arts and humanities, civic affairs, education, environment, health, international, religion, science, social services

### GRANT VALUES
Total Dollar Amount of Grants:
$1,366,000
Number of Grants: 85
Average Grant: $10,600
Highest Grant: $125,000
Lowest Grant: $1,000
Typical Range of Grants: $5,000–
$15,000

### PAST GRANT RECIPIENTS

*Library or School Related*
- New York Public Library (NY), general support, $15,000
- Morgan Library and Museum (NY), general support, $50,000
- National Book Foundation (NY), general support, $50,000
- Bentley College (MA), general support, $6,250
- Dartmouth College (NH), general support, $5,500
- St. Michael's College (VT), general support, $2,500

*General*
- Wolf Trap Foundation for the Performing Arts (VA), general support, $25,000
- Fidelco Guide Dog Foundation (CT), general support, $5,000
- La Clinica del Pueblo (DC), general support, $15,000
- Yorkville Common Pantry (NY), general support, $15,000

**REQUIREMENTS AND RESTRICTIONS**
NA

**APPLICATION PROCEDURES**

**Submission Guidelines:** Send a letter of inquiry.

**CONTACT**
Ellen S. Berelson
Phone: 212-332-3466

**GRANT-SPECIFIC WEBSITE**
NA

# Bay State Federal Savings Charitable Foundation

## Headquarters

55 Cambridge Pkwy.
Cambridge, MA 02142
Phone: 617-225-2822
www.baystatecharitable.com

## Description

**Founded:** 1997

**Operating Locations:** Massachusetts

**Foundation Information:** Corporate foundation of Bay State Bancorp, Inc.

## Financial Summary

Assets: $11,654,066
Total Giving: $433,383

## Grants Information

**GRANT TYPES**
General support, education

**TYPICAL RECIPIENTS**
Arts and humanities, civic affairs, education, environment, health, religion, social services

**GRANT VALUES**
Total Dollar Amount of Grants: $433,383
Number of Grants: 246
Average Grant: $1,800
Highest Grant: $54,500
Lowest Grant: $100
Typical Range of Grants: $1,000–$2,000

**PAST GRANT RECIPIENTS**

*Library or School Related*
- Brookline Library Music Association (MA), general support, $1,000
- Walpole Public Schools (MA), educational support, $1,320
- Westwood Elementary School Coalition (MA), educational support, $5,000

*General*
- Matthew C. Sellitto Foundations (NJ), educational support, $1,000

- Dedham Historical Society (MA), general support, $500
- National Braille Press (MA), educational support, $1,000
- Sandler O'Neill Foundation (NY), educational support, $3,000
- St. Matthew's House (FL), community support, $1,500

**REQUIREMENTS AND RESTRICTIONS**
Applicants must have tax-exempt status.

**APPLICATION PROCEDURES**
**Submission Guidelines:** Send a letter of inquiry with proof of tax-exempt status.

**CONTACT**
Jill Power
Phone: 617-225-6945

**GRANT-SPECIFIC WEBSITE**
www.baystatecharitable.com

# Bender Foundation

## Headquarters

1120 Connecticut Ave. NW
Washington, DC 20036
Phone: 202-828-9000

## Description

**Founded:** NA

**Operating Locations:** District of Columbia

**Foundation Information:** Private foundation established by Jack I. Bender

# Financial Summary

Assets: $23,032,932
Gifts Received: $3,697,349
Total Giving: $804,331

# Grants Information

**GRANT TYPES**
General support

**TYPICAL RECIPIENTS**
Arts and humanities, civic affairs, education, health, international, religion, science, social services

**GRANT VALUES**
Total Dollar Amount of Grants: $803,331
Number of Grants: 86
Average Grant: $9,000
Highest Grant: $100,000
Lowest Grant: $500

**PAST GRANT RECIPIENTS**

*Library or School Related*
- American Friends of the Hebrew University (DC), general support, $6,000
- Charles E. Smith Jewish Day School (MD), general support, $2,500

- Hoop Dreams Scholarship Fund (DC), general support, $5,000
- University of Wisconsin Foundation (WI), general support, $100,000

*General*
- Discovery Creek Children's Museum (DC), general support, $10,000
- Montgomery County Community Foundation (MD), general support, $1,000
- Nature Conservatory (MD), general support, $500
- National Jewish and Medical Research Center (VA), general support, $3,500
- Make a Wish Foundation (MD), general support, $500
- Keys for the Homeless Foundation (VA), general support, $5,000

**REQUIREMENTS AND RESTRICTIONS**
The foundation does not support individuals or political or lobbying groups.

**APPLICATION PROCEDURES**
**Submission Guidelines:** Send a written proposal describing charitable activity, amount requested, and purpose of funds sought, along with proof of charitable status.

**Deadlines:** November 30

**CONTACT**
NA

**GRANT-SPECIFIC WEBSITE**
NA

# Frances and Benjamin Benenson Foundation

## Headquarters

708 Third Ave., 28th fl.
New York, NY 10017
Phone: 212-716-9076
www.benensoncapital.com

## Description

**Founded:** NA

**Operating Locations:** New York

**Foundation Information:** Private foundation established by the Benenson family

## Financial Summary

Assets: $37,059,539
Gifts Received: $2,736,680
Total Giving: $2,194,732

## Grants Information

**GRANT TYPES**
General support, scholarship

**TYPICAL RECIPIENTS**
Arts and humanities, civic affairs, education, environment, health,

international, religion, science, social services

## GRANT VALUES

Total Dollar Amount of Grants:
$2,194,732

## PAST GRANT RECIPIENTS

*Library or School Related*
- Ridgefield Library (CT), general support, $1,000
- Library Foundation of Los Angeles (CA), general support, $6,200
- Reading Reform Foundation of New York (NY), general support, $11,300
- United Negro College Fund (VA), general support, $5,000
- Center for Arts Education (NY), general support, $3,500

*General*
- American Folk Art Museum (NY), general support, $10,000
- ACLU Foundation of Massachusetts (MA), general support, $5,000
- School of American Ballet (NY), general support, $6,500

## REQUIREMENTS AND RESTRICTIONS
NA

## APPLICATION PROCEDURES

**Submission Guidelines:** Send a letter stating amount requested and purpose of project.

## CONTACT
Bruce Benenson
Phone: 212-716-9076

## GRANT-SPECIFIC WEBSITE
NA

# Blood-Horse Charitable Foundation

## Headquarters

PO Box 919003
Lexington, KY 40591
Phone: 859-278-2361

## Description

**Founded:** NA

**Operating Locations:** Kentucky

**Foundation Information:** Private foundation

## Financial Summary

Assets: $44,750
Gifts Received: $23,907
Total Giving: $21,756

## Grants Information

### GRANT TYPES
General support

### TYPICAL RECIPIENTS
Arts and humanities, civic affairs, education, health, religion, social services

### GRANT VALUES
Total Dollar Amount of Grants: $21,756
Number of Grants: 37
Average Grant: $500
Highest Grant: $3,000
Lowest Grant: $10
Typical Range of Grants: $100–$1,000

### PAST GRANT RECIPIENTS

*Library or School Related*
- National Sporting Library (VA), general support, $100
- The Race for Education (KY), general support, $37

*General*
- National Museum of Racing and Hall of Fame (KY), general support, $250

### REQUIREMENTS AND RESTRICTIONS
Applicants must have tax-exempt status and conform to Kentucky law governing nonprofit corporations.

### APPLICATION PROCEDURES
**Submission Guidelines:** Request should be submitted in writing and include

- the purpose of the organization
- the amount requested
- how funds would be used
- organization/foundation status
- any other pertinent information

**Deadlines:** Requests must be received prior to the annual meeting in April.

### CONTACT
Stacy V. Bearse
Phone: 859-278-2361

### GRANT-SPECIFIC WEBSITE
NA

# Blowitz-Ridgeway Foundation

## Headquarters

1701 E. Woodfield Rd.
Schaumburg, IL 60173
Phone: 847-330-1020
Fax: 847-330-1028
www.blowitzridgeway.org

## Description

**Founded:** 1984

**Operating Locations:** Illinois

**Foundation Information:** Private foundation established using the proceeds of the sale of Chicago's Ridgeway Hospital, a nonprofit psychiatric facility focusing on low-income adolescents

## Financial Summary

Assets: $23,303,760
Total Giving: $1,384,478

## Grants Information

### GRANT TYPES
Capital, general support, operating support, project, research, scholarship

### TYPICAL RECIPIENTS
Arts and humanities, civic affairs, education, environment, health, religion, social services

### GRANT VALUES
Total Dollar Amount of Grants:
  $1,384,478
Number of Grants: 107
Average Grant: $13,000
Highest Grant: $50,000
Lowest Grant: $1,000
Typical Range of Grants: $15,000–
  $30,000

### PAST GRANT RECIPIENTS

*Library or School Related*
- Science and Arts Academy (IL), support of scholarship program for children from economically disadvantaged families, $21,000
- St. Gregory Episcopal School (IL), support of summer session and enrichment classes, $14,746
- Josephinium High School (IL), tuition-assistance program for low-income girls, $15,000

*General*
- Lumity/Information Technology Resource Center (IL), support for digital literacy services for nonprofits, $5,000
- Light Opera Works (IL), audience education and children's theater camp, $4,500
- Horses and the Handicapped of South Florida (FL), expansion of therapeutic riding program for disabled children and adults, $14,000
- Foundation Center (NY), general support, $3,500
- Grantmakers in Health (DC), general support, $2,500

### REQUIREMENTS AND RESTRICTIONS
Preference is given to applicants from Illinois; if applying for a program operating outside of Illinois, contact the foundation before submitting a grant application. Applicants must be classified as nonprofit by the Internal Revenue Service.

One of the foundation's primary funding areas is the support of nonprofit agencies which provide medical and psychological services to economically disadvantaged children and adolescents, thereby continuing the original mission of Ridgeway Hospital.

The foundation does not make grants to government agencies or to organizations that subsist mainly on third-party funding and have not tried to attract private funding. Grants will not be made for religious or political reasons or for production or writing of audiovisual materials.

Grants are reviewed and awarded in the order in which they are received. Applicants' fund-raising and administrative costs should be within reasonable limits.

## APPLICATION PROCEDURES

**Submission Guidelines:** Complete online application form, including a copy of Schedule A from IRS form 990.

## CONTACT
Serena Moy
Phone: 847-330-1020

## GRANT-SPECIFIC WEBSITE
www.blowitzridgeway.org/information/
    information.html

# Blue Bell Foundation

## Headquarters

Blue Bell Foundation
c/o Wachovia Bank and Trust Co. NA
100 N. Main St., 13th fl.
Winston Salem, NC 27150-0001

## Description

**Founded:** 1946

**Operating Locations:** North Carolina

**Foundation Information:** Private foundation

## Financial Summary

Assets: $4,520,695
Total Giving: $348,786

## Grants Information

### GRANT TYPES
General support, employee matching

### TYPICAL RECIPIENTS
Arts and humanities, civic affairs, education, environment, health, international, religion, science, social services

## GRANT VALUES

Total Dollar Amount of Grants: $348,786

Number of Grants: 100

Average Grant: $3,500

Highest Grant: $60,000

Lowest Grant: $100

Typical Range of Grants: $1,000–$4,000

## PAST GRANT RECIPIENTS

*Library or School Related*

- North Carolina Storyfest (NC), general support, $5,000
- Greensboro College (NC), general support, $2,500
- High Point University (NC), matching gift, $2,000
- Harris-Hillman School (TN), general support, $4,500
- Center for Education, Imagination and the Natural World (NC), general support, $5,000

*General*

- United Arts Council (NC), general support, $5,000
- Ronald McDonald House (NC), general support, $3,500
- Senior Resources of Guilford County (NC), general support, $1,000
- Old North State Council Boy Scouts of America (NC), general support, $5,000

## REQUIREMENTS AND RESTRICTIONS

None.

## APPLICATION PROCEDURES

**Submission Guidelines:** Send a letter of inquiry.

## CONTACT

Sam Tucker

PO Box 21488

Greensboro, NC 27420

Phone: 910-373-3412

## GRANT-SPECIFIC WEBSITE

NA

# Booth Ferris Foundation

## Headquarters

c/o JP Morgan Services

PO Box 6089

Newark, DE 19714

Phone: 212-464-2487

## Description

**Founded:** NA

**Operating Locations:** Delaware

**Foundation Information:** Private foundation established by Mrs. Chancie Ferris Booth from the estate of Willis H. Booth

# Financial Summary

Assets: $246,085,826
Total Giving: $11,315,500

# Grants Information

## GRANT TYPES
General support

## TYPICAL RECIPIENTS
Arts and humanities, civic affairs, education, environment, health, religion, science, social services

## GRANT VALUES
Total Dollar Amount of Grants:
   $11,315,500
Number of Grants: 118
Average Grant: $10,000
Highest Grant: $200,000
Lowest Grant: $50,000

## PAST GRANT RECIPIENTS

*Library or School Related*
- Bowdoin College (ME), general support, $200,000
- Literacy Partners (NY), general support, $50,000
- Gallaudet University (DC), general support, $250,000
- University of California, Santa Cruz (CA), general support, $75,000
- Building Educated Leaders (MA), general support, $75,000

*General*
- Children's Museum of Manhattan (NY), general support, $150,000
- Neighborhood Opportunities Fund (NY), general support, $150,000
- Settlement Housing Fund (NY), general support, $100,000
- Sanctuary for Families (NY), general support, $100,000

## REQUIREMENTS AND RESTRICTIONS
The foundation does not support organizations operating outside the United States or social service or cultural programs outside the New York metropolitan area. The foundation does not make grants to individuals, individual research, federated campaigns, educational scholarships and fellowships, or specific diseases and disabilities.

## APPLICATION PROCEDURES

**Submission Guidelines:** Send a written proposal, including an annual report, current budget, and latest audited financial statements.

## CONTACT
Morgan Guaranty Trust serves as
   corporate trustee.
Phone: 212-464-2487

## GRANT-SPECIFIC WEBSITE
NA

# Albert and Elaine Borchard Foundation

## Headquarters

22055 Clarendon St., Suite 210
Woodland Hills, CA 91367-6355
Phone: 818-888-2871

## Description

**Founded:** NA

**Operating Locations:** California

**Foundation Information:** Private foundation

## Financial Summary

Assets: $21,795,628
Gifts Received: $36,929
Total Giving: $1,000,518

## Grants Information

### GRANT TYPES
Project, research, emergency, fellowship

### TYPICAL RECIPIENTS
Arts and humanities, civic affairs, education, environment, health, international, religion, social services

### GRANT VALUES
Total Dollar Amount of Grants:
    $1,000,518
Number of Grants: 65
Average Grant: $15,400
Highest Grant: $40,000
Lowest Grant: $1,000
Typical Range of Grants: $5,000–
    $20,000

### PAST GRANT RECIPIENTS

*Library or School Related*
- Bookends (CA), grant for book drive in San Fernando Valley, $6,000
- University of the Pacific/McGeorge School of Law (CA), research initiatives, $40,000
- Regents of the University of California (CA), support for writing conference, $18,000

*General*
- ABA Fund for Justice and Education (DC), project support, $15,000
- Nevada Ballet Theatre, Inc. (NV), grant for Future Dance Scholars program, $10,000
- Utah Legal Services (UT), support for part-time fellowship, $12,918
- Oxfam-America (MA), grant in support of China earthquake relief, $35,000
- Smile Train (NY), grant for cleft surgery for 80 children, $20,000

## REQUIREMENTS AND RESTRICTIONS
The foundation does not make grants to individuals.

## APPLICATION PROCEDURES
**Submission Guidelines:** Send a written proposal, including tax-exempt status letter.

## CONTACT
Phone: 818-888-2871

## GRANT-SPECIFIC WEBSITE
NA

# Bretzlaff Foundation

## Headquarters

4795 Caughlin Pkwy.
Reno, NV 89619
Phone: 775-333-0300

## Description

**Founded:** 1989

**Operating Locations:** Nevada

**Foundation Information:** Private foundation established by Hazel C. Van Allen

## Financial Summary

Assets: $14,369,707
Total Giving: $473,500

## Grants Information

### GRANT TYPES
Research, scholarship

### TYPICAL RECIPIENTS
Arts and humanities, civic affairs, education, health, social services

### GRANT VALUES
Total Dollar Amount of Grants: $473,500
Number of Grants: 25
Average Grant: $6,500
Highest Grant: $50,000
Lowest Grant: $1,000

### PAST GRANT RECIPIENTS

*Library or School Related*
- Stanford University (CA), scholarship endowment, $10,000
- University of Nevada Reno Foundation (NV), capital campaign, $50,000

*General*
- Bishop Museum (HI), endowment, $5,000
- Honolulu Theatre for Youth (HI), education program, $20,000
- Foster Grandparent Program (NV), tutoring program, $10,000

- Western Folklife Center (NV), cowboy poetry/education programs, $5,000
- Arttown (NV), summer festival, $6,500
- Court Appointed Special Advocates (NV), Family Peace Center, $10,000

**REQUIREMENTS AND RESTRICTIONS**
NA

**APPLICATION PROCEDURES**

**Submission Guidelines:** Send a brief letter of inquiry, including the type of organization, its purpose, and the nature and purpose of the grant request.

**CONTACT**
Michael J. Melarkey
Phone: 775-333-0300

**GRANT-SPECIFIC WEBSITE**
NA

# Bridgestone/ Firestone Trust Fund

## Headquarters

c/o Keybank
4900 Tiedeman Rd.
Brooklyn, OH 44144
Phone: 216-689-3626
www.bridgestone-firestone.com/ trustfund.asp

## Description

**Founded:** NA

**Operating Locations:** Ohio

**Foundation Information:** Corporate foundation of Bridgestone-Firestone, Inc.

## Financial Summary

Assets: $22,730,237
Gifts Received: $5,000,000
Total Giving: $2,788,727

## Grants Information

**GRANT TYPES**
Capital, employee matching, general support, project, scholarship

**TYPICAL RECIPIENTS**
Arts and humanities, civic affairs, education, health, science, social services

**GRANT VALUES**
Total Dollar Amount of Grants:
    $2,788,727

**PAST GRANT RECIPIENTS**

*Library or School Related*
- Governor's Books from Birth Foundation (TN), general support, $5,000
- Child Development, Inc. (AR), literacy club, $500
- Alpine Public Library Association

(TX), general support, $500

- Ft. Stockton High School (TX), general support, $2,000
- W. H. & Edgar Magness Community House and Library (TN), general support, $7,500
- Indianapolis Marion County Public Library Foundation (IN), general support, $2,500

*General*
- Southeast Texas Hispanic Cultural and Education Center (TX), general support, $800
- Iowa Special Olympics (IA), general support, $12,400
- University of Akron College of Engineering (OH), leadership program, $5,000
- Aiken Technical College Foundation (SC), general support, $33,333

**REQUIREMENTS AND RESTRICTIONS**
NA

**APPLICATION PROCEDURES**

**Submission Guidelines:** Send a letter of inquiry.

**CONTACT**
Bernice Csaszar
Phone: 615-937-1415

**GRANT-SPECIFIC WEBSITE**
www.bridgestone-firestone.com/
    trustfund.asp

# Bright Family Foundation

## Headquarters

1620 N. Carpenter Rd., Bldg. B
Modesto, CA 95351
Phone: 209-526-8242

## Description

**Founded:** NA

**Operating Locations:** California

**Foundation Information:** Private foundation established by Calvin Bright

## Financial Summary

Assets: $6,429,207
Total Giving: $574,000

## Grants Information

**GRANT TYPES**
General support, operating support, scholarship

**TYPICAL RECIPIENTS**
Arts and humanities, civic affairs, education, health, science, social services

**GRANT VALUES**
Total Dollar Amount of Grants: $574,000

Number of Grants: 44
Average Grant: $14,000
Highest Grant: $45,000
Lowest Grant: $500

## PAST GRANT RECIPIENTS

*Library or School Related*
- Stanislaus County Library Foundation (CA), general support, $3,000
- Stanislaus Literacy Center (CA), general support, $2,000
- San Joaquin Valley Teen Challenge (CA), general support, $1,000
- Beggs High School (OK), scholarship, $32,000
- Dilliard University (LA), scholarship, $30,000

*General*
- Bright Media Foundation (FL), general support, $5,000
- Emanuel Medical Center (CA), general support, $20,000
- Children Crisis Center (CA), general support, $30,000

## REQUIREMENTS AND RESTRICTIONS
NA

## APPLICATION PROCEDURES
**Submission Guidelines:** Send a statement of charitable purpose on organization's letterhead, including tax ID number, or complete Bright Family Foundation's application form.

## CONTACT
Calvin Bright
Phone: 209-526-8242

## GRANT-SPECIFIC WEBSITE
NA

# Bristol-Myers Squibb Foundation, Inc.

## Headquarters

345 Park Ave.
New York, NY 10154
Phone: 212-546-4000

## Description

**Founded:** NA

**Operating Locations:** New York

**Foundation Information:** Corporate foundation of Bristol-Myers Squibb Co.

## Financial Summary

Assets: $90,450,000
Gifts Received: $75,000
Total Giving: $28,305,786

## Grants Information

### GRANT TYPES
General support, project, research, employee matching

## TYPICAL RECIPIENTS

Arts and humanities, civic affairs, education, health, sciences, social services

## GRANT VALUES

Total Dollar Amount of Grants:
$28,305,786

## PAST GRANT RECIPIENTS

*Library or School Related*
- New York Public Library (NY), $25,000
- Learning Spring Elementary School (NY), $10,000
- National Merit Scholarship (IL), $20,000
- Recording for the Blind and Dyslexic (NJ), $20,000

*General*
- Natural Science Resources Center (DC), $500,000
- Montgomery Area Mental Health (AL), $121,475
- Cancer Research Institute (NY), $45,000
- Global Health Council (DC), $50,000
- New Jersey Chamber of Commerce (NJ), $7,500

## REQUIREMENTS AND RESTRICTIONS

Applicants must have tax-exempt status under Section 501(c)(3) of the Internal Revenue code.

The foundation does not provide funding for individuals, endowments, capital campaigns, scholarships, religious or sectarian organizations, political causes, sporting events, or advertising.

## APPLICATION PROCEDURES

**Submission Guidelines:** Application must include

- federal tax ID number
- copy of organization's 501(c)(3) document
- mission statement
- certificate of incorporation or bylaws
- description of rules applicable to the distribution of the organization's income
- description of rules applicable to participation in political or similar activities
- description of applicant's other sources of financial support
- affidavit stating that the applicant is a public charity
- valid e-mail address
- verification of applicant's role within requesting organization
- list of organization's board of directors and executive officers

**Decisions:** Allow 6–8 weeks for processing.

## CONTACT

John L. Damonti
Phone: 212-546-4000

## GRANT-SPECIFIC WEBSITE

www.bms.com/foundation/Pages

# Gladys Brooks Foundation

## Headquarters

1055 Franklin Ave., Suite 208
Garden City, NY 11530
www.gladysbrooksfoundation.org

## Description

**Founded:** NA

**Operating Locations:** New York

**Foundation Information:** Private foundation created under the will of Gladys Brooks Thayer of New York to provide for the intellectual, moral, and physical welfare of the people of this country by establishing and supporting nonprofit libraries, educational institutions, hospitals, and clinics

## Grants Information

### GRANT TYPES
Endowment, capital, project

### TYPICAL RECIPIENTS
Libraries, educational institutions, hospitals, and clinics

### GRANT VALUES
Typical Range of Grants: $50,000–
$100,000

### PAST GRANT RECIPIENTS

*Library or School Related*
- Canterbury School (CT), $150,000
- Columbia University (NY), $100,000
- Rochester Institute of Technology (NY), $50,000
- Sterling College (VT), $100,000
- William D. Weeks Memorial Library (NH), $50,000

*General*
- Good Shepherd Services (NY), $50,000
- Marine Corps Heritage Foundation (VA), $100,000
- Mary Imogene Bassett Hospital (NY), $100,000
- New York Presbyterian Hospital (NY), $200,000

### REQUIREMENTS AND RESTRICTIONS
Applicants must have tax-exempt status. Grants are generally only given to applicants located in the states of Connecticut, Delaware, Florida, Illinois, Indiana, Louisiana, Maine, Maryland, Massachusetts, New Hampshire, New Jersey, New York, Ohio, Pennsylvania, Rhode Island, Tennessee, and Vermont.

Grant applications from libraries will be considered generally for resource endowments (print, film, electronic database, speakers/workshops), capital construction, and innovative equipment. Projects fostering broader public access to global information sources utilizing collaborative efforts and pioneering technologies and equipment are encouraged. Grant applications will be considered where outside funding (including governmental) is not available, where the project will be largely funded by the grant unless the grant request covers a discrete component of a larger project, and where the funds will be used for capital projects including equipment or endowments. Applications for direct salary support will not be accepted.

## APPLICATION PROCEDURES

**Submission Guidelines:** Applicants should initiate the application process by submitting a form on the website or requesting an application from the foundation at the contact address below.

**Deadlines:** The application must be completed and postmarked with all supporting documents to the foundation within 45 days from the date of the letter from the foundation furnishing the application to the applicant. Electronic submissions of the application and supporting documents are not acceptable.

## CONTACT

Jessica L. Rutledge
The Gladys Brooks Foundation
1055 Franklin Ave., Suite 208
Garden City, NY 11530

## GRANT-SPECIFIC WEBSITE

www.gladysbrooksfoundation.org/

# Charles E. and Edna T. Brundage Charitable, Scientific, and Wildlife Foundation

## Headquarters

3 Gateway Center
Newark, NY 07102
Phone: 973-622-7711

## Description

**Founded:** NA

**Operating Locations:** New York

**Foundation Information:** Private foundation established by Edna T. Brundage

## Financial Summary

Assets: $3,213,030
Total Giving: $201,500

## Grants Information

### GRANT TYPES
General support

## TYPICAL RECIPIENTS

Arts and humanities, civic affairs, education, health, science, social services

## GRANT VALUES

Total Dollar Amount of Grants: $201,500
Number of Grants: 44
Highest Grant: $20,000
Lowest Grant: $1,000

## PAST GRANT RECIPIENTS

*Library or School Related*

- Canaan Town Library (NH), general support, $6,000
- Electronic Information and Education Services of New Jersey (NJ), general support, $6,000
- Mascoma Valley Regional School District (NH), music department support, robotics project, $3,000

*General*

- Newark Museum (NJ), general support, endowment fund, capital campaign, $35,000
- Vermont Institute of Natural Sciences (VT), general support, $2,000
- Minnesota Public Radio (MN), general support, $1,500
- Community Place of Greater Rochester (NY), general support, $5,500
- Community Food Bank of New Jersey (NJ), general support, $3,000

## REQUIREMENTS AND RESTRICTIONS

NA

## APPLICATION PROCEDURES

**Submission Guidelines:** Send a letter of inquiry.

## CONTACT

Francis X. O'Brien, Esq.
Phone: 973-622-7711

## GRANT-SPECIFIC WEBSITE

NA

# Temple Hoyne Buell Foundation

## Headquarters

1666 S. University Blvd.
Denver, CO 80210
Phone: 303-744-1688
Fax: 303-744-1601
www.buellfoundation.org

## Description

**Founded:** 1962

**Operating Locations:** Colorado

**Foundation Information:** Private foundation established by Temple Hoyne Buell

# Financial Summary

Assets: $220,329,326
Total Giving: $7,695,228

# Grants Information

## GRANT TYPES
Capital, general support, operating support, project

## TYPICAL RECIPIENTS
Arts and humanities, civic affairs, education, health, social services

## GRANT VALUES
Total Dollar Amount of Grants:
$7,695,228
Highest Grant: $388,000
Lowest Grant: $437

## PAST GRANT RECIPIENTS

*Library or School Related*
- Jefferson County Library Foundation (CO), traveling children's library, $12,000
- Lake County School District R-1 (CO), STEP literacy program, $10,000
- Conejos County Library District (CO), general support, $1,500
- Denver Public Library (CO), read-aloud program, $25,000
- Salida Regional Library (CO), best practices program, $16,458
- Delta County Community Library (CO), Great Start program, $15,000

- Reach Out and Read Colorado (CO), expand program in rural Colorado, $50,000
- Adams County School District 14 (CO), English language acquisition program, $30,000

*General*
- Senior, Inc. (CO), foster grandparent program for early childhood classrooms, $20,000
- San Luis Valley Immigrant Resource Center (CO), immigrant outreach lab and x-ray services, $2,000

## REQUIREMENTS AND RESTRICTIONS
Organizations are limited to one grant request in any 12-month period.

## APPLICATION PROCEDURES

**Submission Guidelines:** The foundation accepts the Colorado Common Grant Application, which can be accessed at www.coloradocommongrantforms.org. Faxed proposals will not be accepted.

**Deadlines:** January 15 and the first business day of May and September by 5:00 p.m. If January 15 falls on a weekend or a holiday, proposals must in by 5:00 p.m. on the preceding Friday.

**Decisions:** Decisions made and money released approximately 4 months after deadlines

**CONTACT**
Grant Review Committee
Phone: 303-744-1688

**GRANT-SPECIFIC WEBSITE**
www.buellfoundation.org

# Build-A-Bear Workshop Foundation

## Headquarters

1954 Innerbelt Business Center Dr.
Saint Louis, MO 63114
Phone: 877-789-2327
www.buildabear.com

## Description

**Founded:** NA

**Operating Locations:** Missouri

**Foundation Information:** Corporate foundation of Build-A-Bear Workshop, Inc.

## Grants Information

**GRANT TYPES**
Project, research

**TYPICAL RECIPIENTS**
Children and families, health and wellness, literacy and education, animals and wildlife, environment and environmental education

**GRANT VALUES**
Average Grant: $1,500
Typical Range of Grants: $1,000–$10,000

**PAST GRANT RECIPIENTS**
NA

**REQUIREMENTS AND RESTRICTIONS**
Priority is given to organizations located near Build-A-Bear Workshop stores within the United States and Canada. U.S. requestors must be tax-exempt organizations under Section 501(c)(3) of the IRS code and "not a private foundation" within the meaning of code sections 509(a)(1) or 509(a)(2), or a state college or university within the meaning of code section 511(a)(2)(B) (a "Public Charity"). In addition, grant recipients must certify that they are not a supporting organization within the meaning of code section 509(a)(3). Canadian requestors must be registered Canadian charities. The foundation does not fund annual appeals or capital campaigns, construction or "new facility" expenses, fund-raising or event sponsorships, political activities, or religious organizations for religious purposes.

## APPLICATION PROCEDURES

**Submission Guidelines:** Applications must be filled out and submitted electronically on the Build-A-Bear Workshop Foundation's grant-giving website.

**Deadlines:** Applications are accepted between March and October.

**Decisions:** It takes approximately 4–6 months for a grant to be reviewed and processed. All grant applicants will be notified of the board's decision via e-mail.

## CONTACT

E-mail: giving@buildabear.com

## GRANT-SPECIFIC WEBSITE

www.buildabear.com/
    shopping/contents/content.
    jsp?catId = 400002&id = 700010

# Barbara Bush Foundation for Family Literacy

## Headquarters

1201 15th St. NW, Suite 420
Washington, DC 20005
Phone: 202-955-6183
Fax: 202-955-8084
www.barbarabushfoundation.com

## Description

**Founded:** NA

**Operating Locations:** District of Columbia

**Foundation Information:** Private foundation established by Barbara Bush

## Financial Summary

Total Giving: $634,070

## Grants Information

### GRANT TYPES
Project

### TYPICAL RECIPIENTS
Education, social services

### GRANT VALUES
Total Dollar Amount of Grants: $650,000
Number of Grants: 10
Average Grant: $65,000
Highest Grant: $65,000
Lowest Grant: $50,000

### PAST GRANT RECIPIENTS

*Library or School Related*
- Cambodian Association of America (CA), support for ongoing Cambodian family literacy program, $64,984
- The Family Place (DC), funding to expand Comprehensive Family Literacy Project for low-income Latino families, $65,000

- Mary's Center for Maternal and Child Care, Inc. (DC), support for Even Start Multicultural Literacy Project, early childhood education in conjunction with adult education for low-income immigrant families, $50,000
- Union Mission, Inc. (GA), support for New Chapter for Homeless Families focusing on comprehensive literacy and educational assistance, $65,000
- Howard Area Community Center (IL), support for Family Literacy Project focusing on low-income, low-literacy adults and their children, $64,086
- Whiteside County Regional Office of Education (IL), support for Family Literacy Program, $65,000

**REQUIREMENTS AND RESTRICTIONS**
The foundation funds projects that support the development of literacy skills for adult primary caregivers and their children.

**APPLICATION PROCEDURES**
**Submission Guidelines:** Application online, including

- letters of support from collaborating organizations
- key staff résumés or job descriptions
- budget for proposed project
- state of fiscal accountability
- a site authorization if other than the applicant

Do not include narrative-related information such as objectives,

evaluation design, and schedules. See the guidelines on the website.

**CONTACT**
Phone: 202-955-6183

**GRANT-SPECIFIC WEBSITE**
www.barbarabushfoundation.com

# Laura Bush Foundation for America's Libraries

## Headquarters

1201 15th St. NW
Washington, DC 20005
Phone: 202-955-5890
Fax: 202-955-4541
www.laurabushfoundation.org

## Description

**Founded:** NA

**Operating Locations:** District of Columbia

**Foundation Information:** Private foundation established by Laura Bush. The Laura Bush Foundation is a component fund of the Community Foundation for the National Capital Region (CFNCR).

# Financial Summary

Total Giving: $1,071,000

# Grants Information

### GRANT TYPES
Library improvement

### TYPICAL RECIPIENTS
School libraries

### GRANT VALUES
Total Dollar Amount of Grants:
   $1,071,000
Number of Grants: 158
Average Grant: $6,000

### PAST GRANT RECIPIENTS
NA

### REQUIREMENTS AND RESTRICTIONS
All grants are made to individual schools, rather than to school districts, county systems, private organizations, or other entities. Neither public and rural libraries nor homeschools are eligible for the grant. The Laura Bush Foundation gives preference to schools in which 90 percent or more of the students receive free or reduced lunches and are likely to have the fewest books at home. Funds must be spent within the school year following the award of the grant. The grant cannot be spent for DVD versions of books, for processing expenses, or for shelving and/or equipment.

### APPLICATION PROCEDURES
**Submission Guidelines:** Application online. Faxed, mailed, or e-mailed applications are not accepted. Applicants must submit two budget figures: Dollars spent on books in previous year from all sources, and how many dollars applicant expects to spend in current year from all sources.

### CONTACT
Alicia Reid
Phone: 202-263-4774
Fax: 202-955-4541
E-mail: areid@cfncr.org

### GRANT-SPECIFIC WEBSITE
www.laurabushfoundation.org

# California Community Foundation

## Headquarters

445 S. Figueroa St., Suite 3400
Los Angeles, CA 90071
Phone: 213-413-4130
www.calfund.org

## Description

**Founded:** 1915

**Operating Locations:** California

**Foundation Information:** Community foundation. The California Community Foundation is a nonprofit organization committed to improving the lives of all Los Angeles County residents. We do this by helping individuals, families, and organizations meet their own philanthropic goals and by supporting Los Angeles nonprofits through our grant making, program-related investments, and endowment-building services.

# Financial Summary

Assets: $1,117,071,883
Gifts Received: $183,392,219
Total Giving: $202,071,241

# Grants Information

### GRANT TYPES
Competitive, donor-advised, program-related investments, and special initiative grants to support community needs

### TYPICAL RECIPIENTS
Arts and humanities, civic affairs, education, health

### GRANT VALUES
Total Dollar Amount of Grants:
$202,071,241

## PAST GRANT RECIPIENTS

*Library or School Related*
- Friends of Westwood Library (CA), general support, $10,000
- Julliard School (NY), development, $29,947
- Library Foundation of Los Angeles (CA), general support, $25,000
- Literacy First Charter School (CA), general support, $500
- Rx for Reading (CA), general support, $20,000
- Springboard for Improving Schools (CA), general support, $200,000

*General*
- Art Institute of Chicago (IL), general support, $5,000
- Bilingual Foundation of the Arts (CA), general support, $25,000
- The Pew Charitable Trust (PA), general support, $5,000
- Volunteers of America (CA), general support, $10,016

## REQUIREMENTS AND RESTRICTIONS
Applicants must be
- nonprofit agencies with evidence of tax-exempt status under Section 501(c)(3) of the Internal Revenue Code and not classified as a private foundation
- located within and primarily serving residents of Los Angeles County, except for regional, statewide, or national public policy efforts that may

benefit a substantial portion of the local population

- operated and organized so that they do not discriminate in the hiring of staff or in providing services on the basis of race, religion, gender, sexual orientation, age, national origin, or disability

## APPLICATION PROCEDURES
**Submission Guidelines:** Submit a letter of intent online, including acknowledgement of submission by organization's president or executive director and most recent IRS form 990. Staff will review letters of intent within 6–8 weeks of corresponding deadline. Applicants will then receive an invitation to submit a full application or a notice that the request has been declined.

**Deadlines:** March, June, and October

**Decisions:** Grant decisions can be expected within 4–5 months of application submission.

## CONTACT
Phone: 213-239-2330

## GRANT-SPECIFIC WEBSITE
www.calfund.org/how_to_apply.php

# California State Library

## Headquarters

PO Box 942837
Sacramento, CA 94237-0001
Phone: 916-654-0266
www.library.ca.gov

## Description

**Founded:** 1850

**Operating Locations:** California

The California State Library provides its customers with accurate, up-to-date information. Whether you are an elected official, a state employee, a representative of one of California's libraries, a person with special reading needs, or a member of the general public, the California State Library is here for you. It collects, preserves, generates, and disseminates information. It advises, consults with, and provides technical assistance to California's public libraries, and it directs state and federal funds to support local public libraries and statewide library programs.

## Financial Summary

Assets: $5,218,855
Gifts Received: $244,093

# Grants Information

## GRANT TYPES
LSTA funds, education, library improvement, cultural preservation

## TYPICAL RECIPIENTS
California libraries, California residents

## GRANT VALUES
NA

## NAMED GRANTS

### LSTA COMPETITIVE GRANT
LSTA funding is used each year to support three key areas: (1) statewide initiatives that provide libraries with the opportunity to support their local communities with programs and information services; (2) a competitive grant process to provide local libraries with funding to develop programs and innovative initiatives; (3) services and access to resources available through the California State Library.

### Past Grant Recipients:

- Alameda County Library, Ashland READS, $46,705
- Banning Library District, Catching Up with the 21st Century, $7,000
- Corona Public Library, Teens on Main—Technology Center, $100,000
- Folsom Public Library, "There's an App for All That," $20,000
- Rancho Cucamonga Public Library, Local History 2.0—Rancho Cucamonga Portal to the Past, $75,000

**Requirements and Restrictions:** A completed application and participation in mandatory webinar.

**Contact:** Library Development Services; Phone: 916-653-5217

**Grant-Specific Website:** www.library.ca.gov/grants/lsta/

### PUBLIC LIBRARY FUND
The intent of the program is to embody the state's interest in the dissemination of information and knowledge through free public libraries; encourage lifelong learning; supplement the system of free public education; help libraries serve as sources of information and inspiration to persons of all ages, cultural backgrounds, and economic status; and furnish a resource for continuing education. The funds ensure the availability to every resident of the state an adequate level of public library service regardless of the taxable wealth of the local jurisdiction providing the service. Funds are appropriated annually in the state budget to support the program.

**Requirements and Restrictions:** Applicants must be located in the state of California. To qualify, the local governing body (county, city, district) must appropriate funds to the library that are at least equal to its appropriation for the immediately preceding year. Funds must be used for library procedures. Funds must supplement, not supplant, local revenue.

**Contact:** Ira Bray, PLF Program Coordinator; Phone: 916-653-0171; E-mail: ibray@library.ca.gov

**Grant-Specific Website:** www.library. ca.gov/services/libraries/plf.html

## CALIFORNIA CIVIL LIBERTIES PUBLIC EDUCATION PROGRAM

The California Civil Liberties Public Education Program (CCLPEP) is a state-funded grant project administered by the California State Library. The program provides competitive grants for public educational activities and for the development of educational materials to ensure that the events surrounding the exclusion, forced removal, and incarceration of civilians and permanent resident aliens of Japanese ancestry during World War II will be remembered and so that causes and circumstances of this and similar events may be illuminated and understood. The program is open to individuals, 501(c)(3) organizations, and other nonprofit organizations. Applicants in the past have included artists, writers, journalists, scholars, educators, community organizations, colleges and universities, cultural institutions, and arts organizations.

**Past Grant Recipients:**
- The California Museum, Uprooted! Oral History Project: Japanese Americans Remember World War II Internment, $25,000
- Center for Multicultural Cooperation, Nisei Voices, $10,000
- San Leandro Public Library, Legacy of the Nisei Veterans, $23,000
- Watsonville Public Library, Japanese American Digital Storytelling (California Central Coast), $14,000

**Requirements and Restrictions:** Handwritten applications will not be accepted.

**Contact:** Linda Springer, CCLPEP Project Manager; Phone: 916-651-6509; E-mail: CivilLiberties@library.ca.gov

**Grant-Specific Website:** www.library. ca.gov/grants/cclpep/

## CALIFORNIA CULTURAL AND HISTORICAL ENDOWMENT

The California Cultural and Historical Endowment was established in 2003 to raise the profile and scope of California's historic and cultural preservation program in an era of dwindling historic structures and cultural homogeneity. The endowment is devoted to telling California's history as experienced by the many diverse peoples of California and is intended to help strengthen and deepen Californians' understanding of the state's history, its present society, and themselves.

**Grant-Specific Website:** www.library. ca.gov/grants/cche/

**REQUIREMENTS AND RESTRICTIONS**
The California State Library administers and hosts grant programs that help make California an information rich, culturally responsive state. Most of the grant programs are competitive, unless announced otherwise. Each grant program housed at the California State Library has its own application processes, criteria, deadlines, and governances.

**APPLICATION PROCEDURES**
Vary by grant

**CONTACT**
Varies by grant

**GRANT-SPECIFIC WEBSITE**
Varies by grant

# Campbell Soup Co.

## Headquarters

One Campbell Pl.
Camden, NJ 08103
www.campbellsoup.com

## Description

**Founded:** 1922

**Operating Locations:** California, Connecticut, Florida, Illinois, Michigan, North Carolina, New Jersey, Ohio, Pennsylvania, South Carolina, Texas, Utah, Washington, Wisconsin

**Type of Product/Service:** Foods

**In-Kind or Service Support:** In-kind services, donated products; supports employee volunteers

**Corporate Sponsorship:** Arts and cultural events

# CAMPBELL SOUP FOUNDATION

One Campbell Pl.
Camden, NJ 08103
Phone: 856-342-4800
www.campbellsoupcompany.com/
    Foundation.aspx
**Foundation Information:** Corporate foundation of Campbell Soup Co.

## Financial Summary

Assets: $17,337,629
Total Giving: $1,524,916

## Grants Information

### GRANT TYPES
General support, project, employee matching

## TYPICAL RECIPIENTS

Arts and humanities, civic affairs, education, health, science, social services

## GRANT VALUES

Total Dollar Amount of Grants:
$1,524,916

## PAST GRANT RECIPIENTS

*Library or School Related*
- Literacy Today (NJ), general support, $1,000
- Scotland County Literacy Council (NC), literacy and job-readiness training, $15,000
- Children's Literacy Initiative (NJ), general support, $3,708

*General*
- Camden County Technical Schools (NJ), general support, $10,000
- Philadelphia's Children's Alliance (PA), general support, $2,000
- Perkins Center for the Arts (NJ), summer program, $28,000
- Please Touch Museum (PA), general support, $20,000

## REQUIREMENTS AND RESTRICTIONS

The foundation limits grants to nonprofit organizations that are tax exempt under Section 501(c)(3) of the Internal Revenue Code. Grants are made to institutions that serve Camden, New Jersey, and locations where the Campbell Soup Company has plant facilities in the United States. The foundation focuses its giving on childhood obesity and hunger relief programming. It also supports organizations that make a positive impact on the lives of youth living in Campbell's operating communities. Applicants must take an eligibility survey online.

## APPLICATION PROCEDURES

**Submission Guidelines:** The foundation has a two-part grant proposal process that includes a letter of intent and a request for proposal. Letters of intent must be submitted by e-mail to the address below. Submission by regular mail will not be reviewed. Letter must include documentation verifying the organization's eligibility under the Section 501(c)(3) of the IRS code.

**Deadlines:** January and August

**Decisions:** March and October

## CONTACT

Jerry S. Buckley
Phone: 856-342-4800
E-mail: community_relations@
    campbellsoup.com

## GRANT-SPECIFIC WEBSITE

www.campbellsoupcompany.com/
    Foundation.aspx

# Carlson Family Foundation

## Headquarters

550 Tonkawa Rd.
Long Lake, MN 55356
Phone: 952-404-5605
www.clcfamilyfoundation.com

## Description

**Founded:** 1950

**Operating Locations:** Minnesota

**Foundation Information:** Private foundation established by Curtis L Carlson

## Financial Summary

Assets: $73,141,534
Total Giving: $4,329,106

## Grants Information

### GRANT TYPES
General support, matching

### TYPICAL RECIPIENTS
Arts and humanities, civic affairs, education, health, social services

### GRANT VALUES
Total Dollar Amount of Grants:
$4,329,106

### PAST GRANT RECIPIENTS

*Library or School Related*
- New York Public Library (NY), general support, $50,000
- Friends of the Minneapolis Public Library (MN), general support, $4,000
- Mentoring Partnership of Minnesota (MN), general support, $40,000
- Serve Minnesota (MN), MN Reading Corps, $35,000

*General*
- San Francisco Museum of Art (CA), general support, $12,500
- AARP Foundation (DC), Women's Scholarship Program, $20,000
- Boys and Girls Club (MN), Gang Prevention Program, $30,000
- Guthrie Theater (MN), Kushner Celebration, $100,000
- Mayo Clinic (MN), general support, $200,000

### REQUIREMENTS AND RESTRICTIONS
NA

### APPLICATION PROCEDURES
**Submission Guidelines:** Application online. The following documents must accompany the application (either online or by mail before deadline):

- copy of IRS determination letter certifying organization's current 501(c)(3) tax-exempt status
- organization's annual operating budget for current fiscal year
- organization's project or program budget
- organization's most recent audit or financial statement
- list of board of directors and affiliations
- most recent annual report

**Deadlines:** January 1, April 1, or July 1

**Decisions:** All applicants will receive notification of the trustees' decisions following a board meeting.

**CONTACT**
Phone: 952-404-5605

**GRANT-SPECIFIC WEBSITE**
www.clcfamilyfoundation.com/apply.asp

# Carnahan-Jackson Foundation

## Headquarters

9–11 E. Fourth St.
Jamestown, NY 14701
Phone: 716-483-1015 or 716-661-3389
E-mail: grants@ChautauquaGrants.org
www.chautauquagrants.org/Funders/
CarnahanJacksonFoundation/tabid/287/Default.aspx

## Description

**Founded:** NA

**Operating Locations:** New York

**Foundation Information:** Private foundation established by Katherine J. Carnahan

## Financial Summary

Assets: $11,848,136
Total Giving: $587,155

## Grants Information

**GRANT TYPES**
General support, capital, project

**TYPICAL RECIPIENTS**
Arts and humanities, civic affairs, education, health, social services

**GRANT VALUES**
Total Dollar Amount of Grants: $587,155
Number of Grants: 24
Highest Grant: $150,000
Lowest Grant: $1,100

**PAST GRANT RECIPIENTS**

*Library or School Related*
- Lakewood Memorial Library (NY), general support, $25,000

- Denison University (OH), general support, $20,000
- Jamestown Community College (NY), general support, $50,000
- Fredonia College Foundation (NY), general support, $150,000
- United Negro College Fund (VA), general support, $5,250
- James Audubon Society (NY), general support, $15,000

**REQUIREMENTS AND RESTRICTIONS**
NA

**APPLICATION PROCEDURES**
**Submission Guidelines:** Send a letter of inquiry. The foundation does not accept online applications. The letter should describe the organization and contain

- a descriptive title for the project
- dollar amount requested
- why funds are needed
- current funders and amount of their support
- project budget
- what will be accomplished if funding is received

If the letter is accepted, applicant will receive confirmation that a full proposal may be submitted.

**Deadlines:** April 30 and September 30

**CONTACT**
Phone: 716-483-1015
Fax: 716-483-6556
E-mail: stephen@sellstromlaw.com

**GRANT-SPECIFIC WEBSITE**
www.chautauquagrants.org/Funders/
CarnahanJacksonFoundation/
tabid/287/Default.aspx

# Carnegie Corporation of New York

## Headquarters

437 Madison Ave.
New York, NY 10022
Phone: 212-371-3200
Fax: 212-754-4073
http://carnegie.org

## Description

**Founded:** 1911

**Operating Locations:** New York

**Foundation Information:** Private foundation established by Andrew Carnegie

## Financial Summary

Assets: $2,662,702,247
Gifts Received: $30,000,000
Total Giving: $2,400,000,000

# Grants Information

## GRANT TYPES
General support to increase knowledge, foster education, and promote international peace

## TYPICAL RECIPIENTS
Arts and humanities, civic affairs, education, social services

## GRANT VALUES
Number of Grants: 300
Highest Grant: $2,163,000
Lowest Grant: $20,000

## PAST GRANT RECIPIENTS
*Library or School Related*
- New York Public Library (NY), Islam studies, $150,000
- Library of America (IA), special opportunities, $45,000
- University of Chicago (IL), urban and higher education, $2,053,300
- University of Southern California (CA), urban and higher education, $660,000
- Teach for America, Inc. (NY), urban and higher education, $1,000,000
- Paley Center for Media (NY), journalism education, $100,000
- University of Ghana (Accra, Ghana), Libraries in Africa, $50,000

*General*
- National Academy of Sciences (DC), urban and higher education, $1,484,400
- Council on Foreign Relations (NY), international peace and security, $300,000
- Center for the Advancement of Women (NY), special opportunities, $50,000
- Achieve, Inc. (DC), education, $2,163,300

## REQUIREMENTS AND RESTRICTIONS
The foundation awards the majority of its grants to support public agencies, universities, and public charities that are tax exempt under section 501(c)(3) of the U.S. Internal Revenue Code. The foundation does not fund for-profit institutions; endowments, buildings, or fund-raising drives; political campaigns; religious organizations; or capital costs, including construction, renovation, or equipment.

## APPLICATION PROCEDURES

**Submission Guidelines:** Submit a letter of inquiry online. If letter passes staff review, grant seeker will be invited to submit a formal grant proposal.

**Decisions:** Organizations invited to submit formal grant proposal will be contacted 4–6 weeks following their online submission of letter of inquiry.

## CONTACT
No phone calls

GRANT-SPECIFIC WEBSITE
http://carnegie.org/grants/grantseekers/
submitting-a-letter-of-inquiry/

# Thomas and Agnes Carvel Foundation

## Headquarters

35 E. Grassy Sprain Rd.
Yonkers, NY 10710
Phone: 914-793-7300

## Description

**Founded:** 1977

**Operating Locations:** New York

**Foundation Information:** Private foundation established by Agnes Carvel and Thomas Carvel

## Financial Summary

Assets: $33,609,447
Gifts Received: $1,718,914
Total Giving: $1,640,400

## Grants Information

### GRANT TYPES
General support, capital

### TYPICAL RECIPIENTS
Arts and humanities, civic affairs, education, health, religion, social services

### GRANT VALUES
Total Dollar Amount of Grants:
   $1,640,400
Number of Grants: 87
Highest Grant: $250,000
Lowest Grant: $1,000

### PAST GRANT RECIPIENTS

*Library or School Related*
- Pines Plains Library (NY), general support, $50,000
- Fordham University (NY), general support, $35,000
- Cristo Rey High School (NY), general support, $20,000
- Drew University (NJ), general support, $10,000
- Enrico Fermi Educational Fund (NY), general support, $10,000
- Recording for the Blind and Dyslexic (NJ), general support, $5,000

*General*
- New Jersey Historical Society (NJ), general support, $1,000
- League for Hard of Hearing (NY), general support, $50,000
- Leukemia Society (NY), general support, $40,000

**REQUIREMENTS AND RESTRICTIONS**
NA

**APPLICATION PROCEDURES**
**Submission Guidelines:** Send a letter accompanied by budget for expenditure of requested grant.

**Deadlines:** October 1

**CONTACT**
William Griffin
Phone: 914-793-7300

**GRANT-SPECIFIC WEBSITE**
NA

# Roy J. Carver Charitable Trust

## Headquarters

202 Iowa Ave.
Muscatine, IA 52761
Phone: 563-263-4010
www.carvertrust.org

## Description

**Founded:** 1982

**Operating Locations:** Iowa

**Foundation Information:** Private foundation established by Roy J. Carver

## Financial Summary

Assets: $206,615,523
Total Giving: $12,147,930

## Grants Information

### GRANT TYPES
General support, project, research, scholarship

### TYPICAL RECIPIENTS
Arts and humanities, civic affairs, education, health, religion, science, social services

### GRANT VALUES
Total Dollar Amount of Grants:
    $12,147,930
Highest Grant: $3,200,000
Lowest Grant: $1,940

### PAST GRANT RECIPIENTS

*Library or School Related*
- Crew Public Library (IA), general support, $60,000
- Davenport Public Library (IA), general support, $60,000
- Dunkerton Public Library (IA), general support, $60,000
- Fontanelle Public Library (IA), general support, $45,000
- Red Oak Public Library (IA), general support, $60,000
- Wellsburg Public Library IA), general support, $60,000

- West Liberty School District (IA), middle school library materials, $183,511
- City of Thornton Public Library (IA), general support, $1,940

## REQUIREMENTS AND RESTRICTIONS

Applicant must be a tax-exempt charitable, educational, or scientific organization under Section 501(c)(3) of the IRS code.

## APPLICATION PROCEDURES

**Submission Guidelines:** Send a written or online letter of inquiry, including

- brief background of the organization
- the history of its existence
- the size of staff and board
- the type of service provided
- a succinct description of the project
- what it is designed to achieve and how this will be accomplished
- a proposed budget for the total cost of the project
- the amount requested from the trust
- how participation of the Carver Trust is vital to the success of the proposed project

Should it be determined from the letter of inquiry that a clear fit with the trust's interests exists, an applicant may be asked to submit a complete proposal.

## CONTACT

Troy K. Ross, Ph.D.
Executive Administrator

Roy J. Carver Charitable Trust
202 Iowa Ave.
Muscatine, IA 52761-3733
E-mail: info@carvertrust.org

**GRANT-SPECIFIC WEBSITE**
www.carvertrust.org

# Louis N. Cassett Foundation

## Headquarters

One Penn Center
Philadelphia, PA 19103
Phone: 215-563-8886

## Description

**Founded:** 1948

**Operating Locations:** Pennsylvania

**Foundation Information:** Private foundation established by Louis N. Cassett

## Financial Summary

Assets: $8,063,059
Total Giving: $408,000

## Grants Information

**GRANT TYPES**
General support, capital

## TYPICAL RECIPIENTS

Arts and humanities, civic affairs, education, health, religion, social services

## GRANT VALUES

Total Dollar Amount of Grants: $408,000

## PAST GRANT RECIPIENTS

*Library or School Related*

- Abington Township Public Library (PA), general support, $10,000
- Adopt a Classroom (FL), general support, $7,500
- JHM Center for Literacy (PA), general support, $1,500
- Pennsylvania School for the Deaf (PA), general support, $1,500
- Reading Buddies (PA), general support, $3,000
- United Negro College Fund (FL), general support, $2,500
- Royer Greaves School for the Blind (PA), general support, $2,000

*General*

- National Liberty Museum (PA), general support, $2,500
- Curtis Institute of Music (PA), general support, $5,000

## REQUIREMENTS AND RESTRICTIONS

NA

## APPLICATION PROCEDURES

**Submission Guidelines:** Send a letter including background information on purpose and funding.

## CONTACT

Malcolm B. Jacobson
Phone: 215-563-8886

## GRANT-SPECIFIC WEBSITE

NA

# Catholic Library Association (CLA)

## Headquarters

100 North St., Suite 224
Pittsfield, MA 01201-5109
Phone: 413-443-2252
Fax: 413-442-2252
www.cathla.org/index.php

## Description

**Founded:** 1921

**Operating Locations:** Massachusetts, Illinois

Established in 1921, the Catholic Library Association (CLA) is an international membership organization, providing its members professional development through educational and networking experiences, publications, scholarships, and other services. The CLA coordinates the exchange of ideas, provides a source of inspirational support and guidance in ethical issues related to librarianship, and offers fellowship for those who seek, serve, preserve, and share the word in all its forms.

## Financial Summary

Assets: $640,184
Gifts Received: $6,500
Total Giving: $5,482

## Grants Information

**GRANT TYPES**
Continuing education, conference attendance

**TYPICAL RECIPIENTS**
CLA chapters and CLA individual members

**GRANT VALUES**
Total Dollar Amount of Grants: $1,500
Number of Grants: 2

**NAMED GRANTS**

**JOHN T. CORRIGAN, CFX MEMORIAL CONTINUING EDUCATION GRANT**
The John T. Corrigan, CFX Memorial Continuing Education Grant was reestablished in 2008 to assist chapters of the CLA in their mission of providing quality continuing education opportunities to their members. Applications must be submitted in writing to the Scholarships and Awards Committee of the association. Chapters receiving Corrigan Grant funds must also submit a written evaluation of their approved program to the committee within 90 days after the program is held.

**Submission Guidelines:** Application online

**Deadlines:** July 15

**Decisions:** August 15

**Contact:** John T. Corrigan Grant, Catholic Library Association, 100 North Street, Suite 224, Pittsfield, MA 01201-5178

**Grant-Specific Website:** www.cathla.org/scholarships-a-grants/john-t-corrigan-cfx-memorial-continuing-education-grant

**SISTER SALLY DALY MEMORIAL GRANT**
The CLA together with the Junior Library Guild established a grant in 2007 in memory of Sister Sally Daly, an ardent supporter of recruiting new members to CLA and its Children's Library Services Section. The purpose of the $1,500 grant is to enable a new member of CLA's Children's Library Services Section to attend the annual convention. The recipient will be selected by the CLA Scholarship Committee and will be notified in time to make travel arrangements.

**Submission Guidelines:** Application online

**Deadlines:** December 1

**Contact:** Sister Sally Daly Memorial Grant, Catholic Library Association, 205 West Monroe Street, Suite 314, Chicago, IL 60606-5061

**Grant-Specific Website:** www.cathla. org/scholarships-a-grants/the-sister-sally-daly-memorial-grant

## REQUIREMENTS AND RESTRICTIONS
Vary by grant

## APPLICATION PROCEDURES
**Submission Guidelines:** Application online

## CONTACT
Varies by grant

## GRANT-SPECIFIC WEBSITE
www.cathla.org/scholarships-a-grants/

# Chinese American Librarians Association (CALA)

## Headquarters

PO Box 6341
Alhambra, CA 91802-6341
www.cala-web.org

## Description

**Founded:** 1973

**Operating Locations:** California

The Chinese American Librarians Association (CALA) started in 1973 as Mid-West Chinese American Librarians Association, a regional organization in Illinois. A year later, Chinese Librarians Association was formed in California. In 1976, Mid-West Chinese American Librarians Association was expanded to a national organization as Chinese American Librarians Association. By 1979, CALA had five chapters in Northeast, Mid-West, Atlantic, Southwest, and California. Chinese American Librarians Association and Chinese Librarians Association were merged in 1983. The merged organization retains CALA's English name and Chinese Librarians Association's Chinese name 華人圖書館員協會.

## Financial Summary

Assets: $178,561
Gifts Received: $57,825
Total Giving: $9,550

## Grants Information

### GRANT TYPES
Professional development, conference attendance

## TYPICAL RECIPIENTS

Chinese American (of Chinese descent) librarians who are CALA members

## GRANT VALUES

Total Dollar Amount of Grants: $1,500
Number of Grants: 2
Highest Grant: $1,000
Lowest Grant: $500

## NAMED GRANTS

### SALLY C. TSENG'S PROFESSIONAL DEVELOPMENT GRANT

Sally C. Tseng's Professional Development Grant of $1,000 supports programs and research by CALA members. Proposals must focus on programs and research in library and information science for which the applicant is highly qualified and which would result in the advancement of the individual's professional status and contributions to the community.

**Deadlines:** March 15

### C. C. SEETOO CONFERENCE TRAVEL SCHOLARSHIP

The C. C. Seetoo Conference Travel Scholarship awards an amount of $500 each year to a library school student for his or her attendance of the CALA program at an ALA Annual Conference. Designed to provide an opportunity for networking and being mentored at the ALA conference, the award is available to all students of Chinese heritage who are currently enrolled in ALA-accredited master's or doctoral programs of library and information science in a higher education institution in North America.

**Deadlines:** April 15

## REQUIREMENTS AND RESTRICTIONS

Must be of Chinese nationality or descent.

## APPLICATION PROCEDURES

**Submission Guidelines:** Application online

**Decisions:** Prior to ALA Annual Conference

## CONTACT

Varies by grant

## GRANT-SPECIFIC WEBSITE

www.cala-web.org/node/203/

# Colorado State Library (CSL)

## Headquarters

201 E. Colfax Ave., Rm. 309
Denver, CO 80203
Phone: 303-866-6900
www.cde.state.co.us/cdelib/

# Description

**Founded:** NA

**Operating Locations:** Colorado

A division of the Colorado Department of Education, the Colorado State Library provides leadership and expertise in developing library-related policies, activities, and assistance for school, public, academic, and special libraries. The goal of the Colorado State Library is to improve the ability of libraries to provide quality services to all Coloradans.

# Grants Information

### GRANT TYPES
LSTA funds, summer reading programs

### TYPICAL RECIPIENTS
Colorado libraries

### GRANT VALUES
Total Dollar Amount of Grants: $412,250
Number of Grants: 80

### NAMED GRANTS

### LSTA GRANTS
LSTA Grants are provided by the Colorado State Library to assist libraries and library-related agencies in developing or enhancing programs and projects that enable Coloradans to receive improved library services.

**Typical Recipients:** Officially recognized Colorado libraries and library-related agencies or organizations, including school (public, charter, nonprofit private), public, academic, and special libraries; BOCES; library consortia; and library professional organizations

**Grant Values:** Total Dollar Amount of Grants, $300,000

**Past Grant Recipients:**

- McClave School (CO), improving technology integration and student writing skills through digital scrapbooking, $3,923
- Colorado Libraries for Early Literacy (CLEL) (CO), Creating an Online Road to Reading, $23,500
- Southern Peaks Public Library (CO), San Luis Valley Libraries technology learning project, $72,559
- Pikes Peak Library District (CO), Play and Learn Colorado, $15,000
- Salida Regional Library (CO), mobile computer education lab, $12,000
- High Plains Library District (CO), Southeast Greeley literacy center, $20,000
- Auraria Library (CO), Latinos in Colorado: Research Sources and Research Strategies, $20,000
- Adams State College, Nielsen Library (CO), San Luis Valley historic digitization project, $12,739

- Automated Systems Colorado Consortium (ASCC) (CO), The Power of Synergy in Action (Migration Project), $200,000

**Requirements and Restrictions:** Applicants must meet the purpose of the grant offering and address stated goals from Colorado's LSTA Five-Year Plan.

**Deadlines:** August 1

**Contact:** Colorado Department of Education, Colorado State Library, Attn: LSTA Project Proposals, 201 E. Colfax Ave., Rm. 309, Denver, CO 80203-1799; Phone: 303-866-6731; E-mail: heilig_j@cde.state.co.us

**Grant-Specific Website:** www.cde.state.co.us/cdelib/LSTA/

### MINIGRANT FOR STATEWIDE SUMMER READING PROGRAM

The Colorado State Library awards minigrants of $200 each to public libraries to support and promote the Collaborative Summer Library Program (CSLP) statewide Summer Reading Program in their local communities.

**Typical Recipients:** Public libraries, in particular those below 10,000 Legal Service Area and in nonmetro locations

**Grant Values:** Number of Grants, 70; Average Grant, $200

**Requirements and Restrictions:** Applicants may request funds from the children's or the teen program, but not both for the same library.

1. Library must submit report information from their previous year's summer reading program.
2. Library must register for and use the statewide Summer Reading Program theme.
3. Library must submit their previous year's LSTA Minigrant Report (for minigrant recipients only).
4. Library identifies planning for the summer reading program which incorporates the Outcomes Based Evaluation Statement.
5. Library plans to offer each of the following:
   - library outreach to daycare/recreational/community programs
   - school visits in April/May to promote program and follow-up in August/September
   - partnerships established in community
   - some examples of community visibility
6. Library must meet the definition of a public library in Colorado AND will commit to a local funding match of at least $50.

**Deadlines:** January 30

**Contact:** Michelle Gebhart; Phone: 303-866-6900; Fax: 303-866-6940; E-mail: Gebhart_m@cde.state.co.us

**Grant-Specific Website:** www.cde.state.co.us/cdelib/SummerReading/minigrants.htm#Application_Information

## REQUIREMENTS AND RESTRICTIONS
Vary by grant

## APPLICATION PROCEDURES
**Submission Guidelines:** Application online

## CONTACT
Varies by grant

## GRANT-SPECIFIC WEBSITE
Varies by grant

# Connecticut Library Association (CLA)

## Headquarters

PO Box 75
Middletown, CT 06457
Phone: 860-346-2444
www.ctlibraryassociation.org

## Description

**Founded:** 1891

**Operating Locations:** Connecticut

The Connecticut Library Association (CLA) aims to improve library service to Connecticut; to advance the interests of librarians, library staff, and librarianship; and to increase public awareness of libraries and library services.

## Financial Summary

Assets: $88,527
Gifts Received: $1,410

## Grants Information

### GRANT TYPES
Professional development

### TYPICAL RECIPIENTS
CLA members

### GRANT VALUES
Total Dollar Amount of Grants: $2,500 per year; $625 per quarter
Highest Grant: $400

### NAMED GRANTS

### PROGRAM FOR EDUCATIONAL GRANTS (PEG)
PEG provides funding to help members of CLA improve their knowledge and skills. PEG funds some expenses for continuing education programs, workshops, seminars, courses, institutes, and other activities. PEG is especially designed for CLA members who want to learn something new, or build upon an existing knowledge base, to improve library service. PEG is not available

for coursework leading to or part of a professional library degree and is not designed for attendance at events that are general in nature or for the building of expertise in areas that are not related to library service. PEG is a reimbursement program. The application must be made in advance of the program/event, and payment will be made when the applicant has submitted receipts and a written report about the program/event.

**REQUIREMENTS AND RESTRICTIONS**
Applicants must be members of CLA.

**APPLICATION PROCEDURES**

**Submission Guidelines:** Print a grant application from the website and mail or fax the completed form to the address below.

**Deadlines:** September 1, November 1, January 2, and July 1

**CONTACT**
Peter Ciparelli, PEG Chair
Killingly Public Library
25 Westcott Rd.
Danielson, CT 06239
Phone: 860-779-5383
Fax: 860-779-1823
E-mail: pciparelli@biblio.org

**GRANT-SPECIFIC WEBSITE**
www.ctlibraryassociation.org/
    content.php?page = Program_for_
    Educational_Grants_PEG_

# Connecticut State Library (CSL)

## Headquarters

231 Capitol Ave.
Hartford, CT 06106
Phone: 866-886-4478
www.cslib.org

## Description

**Founded:** NA

**Operating Locations:** Connecticut

The mission of the Connecticut State Library is to preserve and make accessible Connecticut's history and heritage and to advance the development of library services statewide.

## Grants Information

**GRANT TYPES**
Library support, library construction

**TYPICAL RECIPIENTS**
Connecticut public libraries

**GRANT VALUES**
Total Dollar Amount of Grants:
    $9,000,000
Highest Grant: $1,000,000
Lowest Grant: $1,200

## NAMED GRANTS

### STATE AID GRANT

Principal public libraries in the state that meet the eligibility requirements may apply for and receive an annual state aid grant. A principal public library is one which has been so designated by the local municipal governing board. A municipality may have more than one public library, but may designate only one library as its principal public library. The application form is combined with the Public Library Annual Statistical Report.

**Typical Recipients:** Connecticut principal public libraries

**Grant Values:** Total Dollar Amount of Grants, $207,692; Average Grant, $1,200, plus additional amounts for equalization based on town AENGLC rankings and each town's per capita library expenditures

**Past Grant Recipients:**

- Andover Public, $1,336
- Ansonia Library, $2,149
- Avon Free Public, $1,897
- Babcock Library, $1,427
- Beacon Falls Public, $1,436
- Berlin-Peck Memorial Library, $2,222

**Requirements and Restrictions:** Applicants must be located in the state of Connecticut. Funds may only be used for general library purposes (including the purchase of land or the construction, alteration, or remodeling of buildings). State aid funds must be expended within two years of receipt, unless a library has applied to the State Library Board and received authority to carry over funds beyond the two-year limit.

**Submission Guidelines:** Applicant must electronically submit a locked Public Library Annual Statistical Report and Application for State Aid with the State Library, participate in Connecticard, provide equal access to library materials without charging individuals residing in the town for borrower cards or for use of the library's basic collections and services, not discriminate, and certify that the library's annual tax levy or appropriation has not been reduced to an amount less than the average amount levied or appropriated for the library in the preceding three years.

**Deadlines:** November 15

**Decision Notification:** June 1

**Contact:** Tom Newman; Phone: 860-757-6573; Fax: 860-757-6503; E-mail: Tom.Newman@ct.gov

**Grant-Specific Website:** http://ct.webjunction.org/510/articles/content/1090780

### STATE PUBLIC LIBRARY CONSTRUCTION GRANT

The State Public Library Construction Grant program provides grants for public library construction projects to improve their facilities to meet their communities' needs. The grant is one-third of the total cost of the project. Public libraries can apply under two grant categories:

- 80 percent of total monies fund projects that create additional usable space (i.e., new buildings, additions, and renovations).
- 20 percent of total monies fund projects that improve existing space (i.e., handicapped accessibility, correcting building and fire code violations, remodeling to accommodate new technologies, and energy conservation).

**Typical Recipients:** Connecticut public libraries

**Grant Values:** Total Dollar Amount of Grants, $5,200,000 for distressed municipalities; Highest Grant, $1,000,000; Lowest Grant, $6,666

**Past Grant Recipients:**

- Avon Free Public Library, $1,000,000
- James Blackstone Memorial Library, Branford, $1,000,000
- Canterbury Public Library, $793,666
- Belden Public Library, Cromwell, $1,000,000
- Raymond Library, East Hartford, $1,000,000
- Hagaman Memorial Library, East Haven, $184,000

**Requirements and Restrictions:** Applicants must be located in the state of Connecticut. Total project cost must be more than $20,000; grants shall not exceed $1,000,000.

**Submission Guidelines:** Application online

**Deadlines:** Letter of intent, early June; completed application, September 1

**Contact:** Mary Louise Jensen; Phone: 800-253-7944 or 860-456-1717, ext. 306; Fax: 860-423-5874; E-mail: MaryLouise.Jensen@ct.gov

**Grant-Specific Website:** http://ct.webjunction.org/510/articles/content/1090915

## REQUIREMENTS AND RESTRICTIONS
Vary by grant

## APPLICATION PROCEDURES
Vary by grant

## CONTACT
Varies by grant

## GRANT-SPECIFIC WEBSITE
Varies by grant

# Cummins Foundation

## Headquarters

PO Box 3005, M/C 60113
Columbus, IN 47202
Phone: 812-377-1439
www.cummins.com/cmi/navigation
Action.do?nodeId=6&siteId=1&node
Name=Cummins+Foundation&menu
Id=1003

## Description

**Founded:** NA

**Operating Locations:** Indiana

**Foundation Information:** Corporate
foundation of Cummins, Inc.

## Financial Summary

Assets: $16,063,403
Gifts Received: $5,531,800
Total Giving: $5,716,992

## Grants Information

### GRANT TYPES
General support, continuing support

### TYPICAL RECIPIENTS
Arts and humanities, civic affairs,
education, health, social services

### GRANT VALUES
Total Dollar Amount of Grants:
$5,716,992

### PAST GRANT RECIPIENTS

*Library or School Related*
- The Library Project (AZ),
  support for elementary and middle
  school libraries in China, $50,000
- Mineral Point Public Library (WI),
  library expansion/improvement in
  computer equipment and software,
  $10,000
- Bartholomew Consolidated School
  Corporation (IN), Book Buddies
  Program expansion, $5,000
- New Haven Elementary School (KY),
  literacy program, $25,000
- Franklin College (IN), support lecture
  series, $25,000

*General*
- The Mind Trust (IN), educational
  entrepreneurship, $100,000
- Kidscommons Children's Museum
  (IN), general support, $20,000

### REQUIREMENTS AND RESTRICTIONS
The foundation funds only IRS-
designated 501(c)(3) nonprofit
organizations or equivalent charitable
international organizations. The
foundation does not support political
causes or candidates or sectarian
religious activities. No grants are made
to individuals.

## APPLICATION PROCEDURES

**Submission Guidelines:** Submit a written inquiry, including

- brief description of the problem being addressed
- what the program hopes to achieve
- operating plan and cost
- description of key leadership
- proposed measurement of the program's success

## CONTACT

Tracy Souza, President/Secretary
Phone: 812-377-3746

## GRANT-SPECIFIC WEBSITE

NA

# Dime Bank

## Headquarters

290 Salem Turnpike
Norwich, CT 06360
www.dime-bank.com

## Description

**Founded:** 1869

**Operating Locations:** Connecticut

**Type of Product/Service:** Bank

# DIME BANK FOUNDATION, INC.

290 Salem Turnpike
Norwich, CT 06360
Phone: 860-859-4300
www.dime-bank.com/foundation/
**Foundation Information:** Corporate foundation of Dime Bank

## Financial Summary

Assets: $3,097,674
Total Giving: $142,528

## Grants Information

### GRANT TYPES
General support

### TYPICAL RECIPIENTS
Arts and humanities, civic affairs, education, health, science, social services

### GRANT VALUES
Total Dollar Amount of Grants: $142,528
Number of Grants: 40
Average Grant: $3,500
Highest Grant: $12,000
Lowest Grant: $1,200

### PAST GRANT RECIPIENTS

*Library or School Related*
- Bill Library (CT), general support, $3,000

- Sprague Public Library (CT), general support, $3,000
- Ledyard High School Agri-Science Department (CT), general support, $2,500
- R.I.S.E.N. at Sacred Heart School (CT), subsidy for special education program, $1,500

*General*
- High Hopes Therapeutic Riding, Inc. (CT), therapeutic services to eligible students, $5,000
- VNS Home Health Services (CT), senior wellness and disease prevention, $2,500
- Furniture Bank of Southeastern Connecticut (CT), furniture for needy families, $5,000

**REQUIREMENTS AND RESTRICTIONS**
Applicants must have tax-exempt status.

**APPLICATION PROCEDURES**

**Submission Guidelines:** Application online. Application must include

- a written proposal for needs and use of the grant, including objectives, purposes, and goals of the project; description of plans designed to achieve objectives and goals; location and estimated duration of the program; and number of people expected to benefit from the program
- budget summary identifying expenses and income for the program
- a list of members of the governing board or description of organizational structure
- two copies of the most recent financial statement and program brochure
- a copy of the IRS tax classification letter under 501(c)(3) dated after 1969
- any additional materials that will further define the program

**CONTACT**
Cheryl Calderado
Phone: 860-859-4300
E-mail: ccalderado@dime-bank.com

**GRANT-SPECIFIC WEBSITE**
www.dime-bank.com/foundation/grant_
   application.pdf

# Cleveland H. Dodge Foundation

## Headquarters

420 Lexington Ave., Suite 2331
New York, NY 10170
Phone: 212-972-2800
Fax: 212-972-1049
E-mail: info@chdodgefoundation.org
www.chdodgefoundation.org

# Description

**Founded:** 1917

**Operating Locations:** New York

**Foundation Information:** Private foundation established by Cleveland Hoadley Dodge

# Financial Summary

Assets: $33,876,779
Total Giving: $1,698,364

# Grants Information

**GRANT TYPES**
Capital, general support, matching, operating support, project

**TYPICAL RECIPIENTS**
Arts and humanities, civic affairs, education, science, social services

**GRANT VALUES**
Total Dollar Amount of Grants:
  $1,698,364

**PAST GRANT RECIPIENTS**

*Library or School Related*
- New York Public Library (NY), general support, $5,000
- Kingsbridge Heights Community Center (NY), youth literacy programs, $35,000
- Literacy Partners, Inc. (NY), family literacy, English as a second language programs, $15,000
- Recording for the Blind and Dyslexic (NJ), AudioPlus program, $25,000
- East Harlem Tutorial Program (NY), capital campaign, $50,000

*General*
- New York Restoration Project (NY), Million Trees Apprentice Program, $10,000
- Episcopal Social Services (NY), after-school program, $25,000
- American Farm School (Thessaloniki, Greece), education dairy and milk processing center, $10,000

**REQUIREMENTS AND RESTRICTIONS**
Grants are made only to organizations on the exempt list of the Internal Revenue Service, excluding private foundations as defined in the Tax Reform Act of 1969 in Section 509 of the Internal Revenue Code. The foundation does not make grants to individuals, and does not fund medical research or health care, or most schools, colleges, and universities.

**APPLICATION PROCEDURES**
**Submission Guidelines:** Send a letter describing project and budget, along with annual report and proof of tax-exempt status.

**Deadlines:** January 15, April 15, and September 15

**CONTACT**
Phyllis Criscuoli
Phone: 718-543-1220

**GRANT-SPECIFIC WEBSITE**
www.chdodgefoundation.org/grants.shtml

# Dodge Jones Foundation

## Headquarters

PO Box 176
Abilene, TX 79604
Phone: 325-673-6429

## Description

**Founded:** 1956

**Operating Locations:** Texas

**Foundation Information:** Private foundation established by Ruth Leggett Jones

## Financial Summary

Assets: $55,023,724
Total Giving: $155,484,680

## Grants Information

### GRANT TYPES
General support, capital, operating support, challenge

### TYPICAL RECIPIENTS
Arts and humanities, civic affairs, education, environment, health, international, religion, social services

### GRANT VALUES
Total Dollar Amount of Grants:
$155,484,680

### PAST GRANT RECIPIENTS

*Library or School Related*
- Abilene Library Consortium (TX), support for digital archives project, $500,105
- Friends of the Abilene Public Library Fund (TX), sponsorship of West Texas Book and Author Festival, $5,000
- Recording Library of West Texas (TX), general support, $5,000
- Paint Creek Independent School District (TX), purchase of library books, $5,000

*General*
- American Spectator Educational Foundation (VA), general support, $2,500
- Center for Educational Reform (DC), general support, $5,000
- Foundation for Teaching Economics (CA), funding for professional development, $5,000

### REQUIREMENTS AND RESTRICTIONS
The foundation does not make grants to individuals.

## APPLICATION PROCEDURES

**Submission Guidelines:** Send a letter describing request and purpose of grant.

## CONTACT

Larry Gill
Phone: 325-673-6429

## GRANT-SPECIFIC WEBSITE

NA

# Dollar General Literacy Foundation

## Headquarters

100 Mission Ridge
Goodlettsville, TN 37072
Phone: 615-855-5208
www.dgliteracy.com

## Description

**Founded:** NA

**Operating Locations:** Tennessee

**Foundation Information:** Corporate foundation of Dollar General Corporation

## Financial Summary

Assets: $25,911,062
Gifts Received: $44,579,066
Total Giving: $7,889,989

# Grants Information

## GRANT TYPES

Literacy programs

## TYPICAL RECIPIENTS

Arts and humanities, civic affairs, education, social services

## GRANT VALUES

Total Dollar Amount of Grants:
$7,889,989
Number of Grants: 350
Highest Grant: $520,000
Lowest Grant: $3,000
Typical Range of Grants: $10,000–
$20,000

## NAMED GRANTS

### YOUTH LITERACY GRANTS

Dollar General Literacy Foundation Youth Literacy Grants provide funding to schools, public libraries, and nonprofit organizations to help students who are below grade level or experiencing difficulty reading.

### ADULT LITERACY GRANTS

Dollar General Literacy Foundation Adult Literacy Grants award funding to nonprofit organizations that provide direct service to adults in need of literacy assistance. Organizations must provide help in one of the following instructional areas: adult basic education, general education diploma preparation, or English as a second language.

## BACK TO SCHOOL LITERACY GRANTS

Dollar General Literacy Foundation Back to School Grants provide funding to assist school libraries or media centers in meeting some of the financial challenges they face in the following areas: implementing new or expanding existing literacy programs, purchasing new technology or equipment to support literacy initiatives, and purchasing books, materials, or software for literacy programs.

## FAMILY LITERACY GRANTS

Dollar General Literacy Foundation Family Literacy Grants provide funding to family literacy service providers. The foundation uses the federal government's definition of family literacy when reviewing grant applications. Organizations applying for funding must have the following four components: adult education instruction, children's education, parent and child together time (PACT), and parenting classes.

## SUMMER READING GRANTS

Dollar General Literacy Foundation Summer Reading Grants provide funding to local nonprofit organizations and libraries to help with the implementation or expansion of summer reading programs. Programs must target pre-K through 12th-grade students who are new readers, below-grade-level readers, or readers with learning disabilities.

## PAST GRANT RECIPIENTS

*Library or School Related*
- Pioneer Library System (OK), $14,762
- Mansfield/Richmond Country Public Library (OH), $5,000
- Nashville Public Library System (TN), $20,000
- Friends of Westfield Washington Public Library (IN), $9,210
- Carl Sandburg College Literacy Coalition (IL), $12,500
- Clayton Public Library (OH), $5,000

*General*
- Aiken County Public Schools Family Literacy Parenting Program (SC), $20,000
- Association for Advancement of Mexican-Americans (TX), $10,000
- Jobs for the Future (MA), $370,000
- ProLiteracy America (NY), $110,000
- Read Write Adult Literacy (NM), $10,000
- Reading Is Fundamental (DC), $222,500

## REQUIREMENTS AND RESTRICTIONS
Vary by grant

## APPLICATION PROCEDURES

**Submission Guidelines:** Application online

## CONTACT
NA

GRANT-SPECIFIC WEBSITE
www.dollargeneral.com/dgliteracy/
Pages/grant_programs.aspx

# Dow Jones Foundation

## Headquarters

Dow Jones Foundation
PO Box 1802
Providence, RI 02901-1802

## Description

**Founded:** NA

**Operating Locations:** Rhode Island

**Foundation Information:** Corporate foundation of Dow Jones and Co., Inc.

## Financial Summary

Assets: $916,256
Gifts Received: $1,100,000
Total Giving: $737,032

## Grants Information

### GRANT TYPES
General support

### TYPICAL RECIPIENTS
Arts and humanities, civic affairs, education, health, social services

### GRANT VALUES
Total Dollar Amount of Grants: $737,032
Number of Grants: 19
Highest Grant: $350,000
Lowest Grant: $5,000
Typical Range of Grants: $5,000–
$10,000

### PAST GRANT RECIPIENTS

*Library or School Related*
- Chicopee Public Library (MA), general support, $5,000
- South Brunswick Public Library (NJ), general support, $5,000
- Literacy Partners (NY), general support, $5,000
- New York Public Library (NY), general support, $5,000
- Princeton Public Library (NJ), general support, $5,000
- Trustees of Columbia University (NY), general support, $10,000

*General*
- National Merit Scholarship (IL), general support, $256,792

### REQUIREMENTS AND RESTRICTIONS
Applicants must have tax-exempt status.

### APPLICATION PROCEDURES

**Submission Guidelines:** Send a letter stating purpose of proposal.

### CONTACT
Thomas McGuirl

c/o Dow Jones Foundation
PO Box 300
Princeton, NJ 08540

## GRANT-SPECIFIC WEBSITE
NA

# The Dreyer's Foundation

## Headquarters

5929 College Ave.
Oakland, CA 94618
Phone: 510-450-4586

## Description

**Founded:** 1987

**Operating Locations:** California

**Foundation Information:** Corporate foundation of Dreyer's, Inc.

## Grants Information

### GRANT TYPES
Capital, project, general support, operating support, start-up costs, in-kind donations, employee matching

### TYPICAL RECIPIENTS
Education

### GRANT VALUES
Highest Grant: $3,000

### NAMED GRANTS

#### LARGE GRANTS
Dreyer's Large Grants (over $3,000) focus on young people from preschool to grade 12, primarily in Oakland and the East Bay. A limited number of requests will be considered from markets across the country where Dreyer's or Edy's employees are involved. Grants will be given to K–12 public education and programs that help students to succeed in core academic subjects and graduate to postsecondary education or vocational training. Priority will be given to programs, either in school or after school, that are provided in sequential, consistent basis to students throughout the year.

Organizations may request support for capital items, program expenses, operating expenses, start-up costs, materials, or supplies. Priority will be given to those programs/projects that support low- and middle-income youth and minority youth. The foundation supports ongoing programs with long-term results. One-day or short-term events will not be considered. The foundation does not fund basic health, clothing, or shelter needs.

**Submission Guidelines:** To apply for a Dreyer's Large Grant, please submit a proposal no longer than three pages on your organization's stationery. Please include the following information:

- history/description of organization
- nature of request and specific use of funding
- how proposal addresses grant criteria
- copy of current tax-exemption letter
- copy of current operating budget and budget for the specific project for which funds will be used
- copy of most recent audited financial statement
- list of previous Dreyer's contributions and list of pending proposals or anticipated support from other organizations
- name, address, e-mail and daytime telephone number of contact person
- current membership list of board of directors

**Deadlines:** Large grant proposals are reviewed on an annual basis and must be submitted prior to January 15 of each year.

## SMALL GRANTS AND PRODUCT DONATIONS

The foundation makes small grants ($3,000 or less) and donates ice cream products, gift certificates, and auction items to bona fide nonprofit organizations for events. These proposals are reviewed on a monthly basis.

**Submission Guidelines:** To request a small grant, products, gift certificates, or auction item donations, please send a one-page letter on organization stationery with the following information:

- current tax-exemption number
- date of event
- brief description of organization and purpose of event
- specific item or product request
- for product donation, please state number of people to be served and specific product request (e.g., ice cream, yogurt, sherbet)
- name, e-mail address and daytime telephone number of a contact person

Due to the number of requests the foundation receives, we are no longer able to accept e-mails or faxes. We only accept hard copies in the mail.

**Deadlines:** We ask that all requests be submitted in writing at least 8 weeks prior to your event. Requests are reviewed monthly.

**REQUIREMENTS AND RESTRICTIONS**
Vary by grant

**APPLICATION PROCEDURES**
Vary by grant

**CONTACT**
Phone: 510-450-4586
Fax: 510-601-4400

**GRANT-SPECIFIC WEBSITE**
http://scoopnet.icecream.com/scoopnet/
    company/foundation.asp

# Dyson Foundation

## Headquarters

25 Halcyon Rd.
Millbrook, NY 12545
Phone: 845-677-0644
www.dysonfoundation.org

## Description

**Founded:** 1957

**Operating Locations:** New York

**Foundation Information:** Private foundation established by Charles and Margaret Dyson

## Financial Summary

Assets: $231,468,267
Total Giving: $16,148,797

## Grants Information

### GRANT TYPES
General support, project, research, matching

### TYPICAL RECIPIENTS
Arts and humanities, civic affairs, education, health, religion, science, social services

### GRANT VALUES
Total Dollar Amount of Grants:
    $16,148,797

### PAST GRANT RECIPIENTS

*Library or School Related*
- Pierpont Morgan Library (NY), renovation and expansion, $100,000
- Stone Ridge Library Foundation (NY), resource development planning, $4,400
- New York Public Library (NY), support for research libraries, $10,000
- Millbrook Free Library (NY), general support, $1,000
- Hudson Area Association Library (NY), ESL literacy program and management support, $65,000

*General*
- Ulster Literacy Association (NY), support for ESL programming, $25,000
- Literacy Connections (NY), literacy programs, $2,500
- Literacy, Inc. (NY), early literacy programs, $25,000
- Literacy Volunteers of Eastern Orange County (NY), merger between Literacy Volunteers chapters, $32,000

### REQUIREMENTS AND RESTRICTIONS
Applicants must have tax-exempt status. The foundation does not make grants to individuals; for fund-raising events, dinners, or tickets; in response to direct mail campaigns; to service

clubs; or for debt or deficit reduction. Each proposal will be reviewed on its fit with the foundation's priorities, significance of need addressed, potential to achieve significant results, capacity of applicant to accomplish the goals, and appropriateness of budget.

### APPLICATION PROCEDURES
**Submission Guidelines:** Application online

**Decisions:** The time it takes to evaluate a proposal varies but may take as long as 6 months.

### CONTACT
Phone: 845-677-0644
E-mail: submissions@dyson.org

### GRANT-SPECIFIC WEBSITE
www.dysonfoundation.org/
    grantmaking/how-to-apply

# Educational Foundation of America

## Headquarters

35 Church La.
Westport, CT 06880
Phone: 203-226-6498
www.efaw.org

## Description

**Founded:** 1959

**Operating Locations:** Connecticut

**Foundation Information:** Private foundation established by Richard Prentice Ettinger and his wife, Elsie P. Ettinger

## Financial Summary

Assets: $143,087,852
Total Giving: $11,220,241

## Grants Information

### GRANT TYPES
Project, general support

### TYPICAL RECIPIENTS
Arts and education, environment, sustainable population

### GRANT VALUES
Total Dollar Amount of Grants:
    $11,220,241
Number of Grants: 73
Highest Grant: $100,000
Lowest Grant: $20,000

### PAST GRANT RECIPIENTS

*Library or School Related*
- Queens Library Foundation, Inc. (NY), Bes-Out-of-School Time, $70,000
- Teach for America (LA), expansion of

program, $100,000
- Teach for America (NY), early childhood education, $100,000
- Center for Summer Learning (MD), improvement of summer program, $40,000

*General*
- LibForAll Foundation (NC), educational programs, $30,000
- Connecticut Fund for the Environment (CT), clean air campaign, $80,000
- Human Rights Campaign Foundation (DC), children and family support, $80,000
- Big Brothers/Big Sisters of Greater Miami Mentoring Center (FL), mentoring project, $60,000

**REQUIREMENTS AND RESTRICTIONS**
NA

**APPLICATION PROCEDURES**
**Submission Guidelines:** Visit the website for application information.

**CONTACT**
E-mail: loi@efaw.org

**GRANT-SPECIFIC WEBSITE**
www.efaw.org/apply.htm

# Margaret Alexander Edwards Trust

## Headquarters

600 Wyndhurst Ave, Suite 246
Baltimore, MD 21210
Phone: 410-464-0100

## Description

**Founded:** NA

**Operating Locations:** Maryland

**Foundation Information:** Private foundation established by Margaret Alexander Edwards

## Financial Summary

Assets: $972,994
Total Giving: $29,450

## Grants Information

**GRANT TYPES**
General support, project

**TYPICAL RECIPIENTS**
Young adult librarians, programs to promote young adults' reading

**GRANT VALUES**
Total Dollar Amount of Grants: $29,450
Number of Grants: 6

Average Grant: $4,900
Highest Grant: $10,000
Lowest Grant: $2,000

## PAST GRANT RECIPIENTS

*Library or School Related*
- Young Adult Library Services Association (IL), $10,000
- EPFL Teen Summer Reading (MD), $10,000
- Institute of Notre Dame (MD), $2,500
- University of Delaware (DE), $2,500
- Roberto Clemente Middle School (MD), $2,450
- Cristo Rey Jesuit High School (MD), $2,000

## REQUIREMENTS AND RESTRICTIONS
The foundation issues grants only to promote reading among young adults.

## APPLICATION PROCEDURES

**Submission Guidelines:** Call to request an application, or download application from website.

## CONTACT
Julian L. Lapides, Esquire
Margaret Alexander Edwards Trust
Baltimore, MD 21210
Phone: 410-464-0100
E-mail: jllethics@msn.com

## GRANT-SPECIFIC WEBSITE
www.carr.org/mae/trust.html

# Essick Foundation

## Headquarters

1379 La Solana Dr.
Altadena, CA 91001
Phone: 626-794-7992

## Description

**Founded:** 1949

**Operating Locations:** California

**Foundation Information:** Private foundation established by Jeannette Marie Essick and Bryant Essick

## Financial Summary

Assets: $2,391,996
Total Giving: $129,100

## Grants Information

### GRANT TYPES
General support

### TYPICAL RECIPIENTS
Arts and humanities, civic affairs, education, health, social services

### GRANT VALUES
Total Dollar Amount of Grants: $129,100
Number of Grants: 7

Average Grant: $1,845
Highest Grant: $63,100
Lowest Grant: $1,000

## PAST GRANT RECIPIENTS

*Library or School Related*
- Henry E. Huntington Library and Art Gallery (CA), general support, $63,100
- University of North Carolina (NC), general support, $46,500
- University of Rochester (NY), general support, $8,500
- California Institute of Technology (CA), general support, $2,500

*General*
- The Da Camera Society (CA), general support, $2,500
- Boy Scouts of America (WA), general support, $1,000

## REQUIREMENTS AND RESTRICTIONS
NA

## APPLICATION PROCEDURES
NA

## CONTACT
Robert N. Essick
Phone: 626-794-7992

## GRANT-SPECIFIC WEBSITE
NA

# Harvey Firestone, Jr., Foundation

## Headquarters

2000 Brush St.
Detroit, MI 48226
Phone: 313-961-0500

## Description

**Founded:** 1983

**Operating Locations:** Michigan

**Foundation Information:** Private foundation

## Financial Summary

Assets: $16,810,971
Total Giving: $1,103,000

## Grants Information

### GRANT TYPES
General support

### TYPICAL RECIPIENTS
Arts and humanities, civic affairs, education, health, religion, science, social services

### GRANT VALUES
Total Dollar Amount of Grants:
    $1,103,000

Number of Grants: 130
Highest Grant: $179,000
Lowest Grant: $500
Typical Range of Grants: $1,000–
$10,000

**PAST GRANT RECIPIENTS**

*Library or School Related*
- Danen Library (CT), general support, $500
- Greenwich Library (CT), general support, $2,500
- Buckingham, Browne, and Nichols School (MA), general support, $3,000
- Vassar College (NY), general support, $15,000
- Miss Porter's School (CT), general support, $52,000

*General*
- Martin Luther King Community Center (RI), general support, $500
- Abilities United (CA), general support, $10,000

**REQUIREMENTS AND RESTRICTIONS**
NA

**APPLICATION PROCEDURES**
NA

**CONTACT**
Christine Jaggi
Phone: 313-961-0500

**GRANT-SPECIFIC WEBSITE**
NA

# State Library and Archives of Florida

## Headquarters

R. A. Gray Bldg.
500 S. Bronough St.
Tallahassee, FL 32399-0250
Phone: 850-245-6600
http://dlis.dos.state.fl.us/library/

## Description

**Founded:** NA

**Operating Locations:** Florida

The State Library and Archives of Florida serves as the designated information resource provider for the Florida Legislature and all state agencies. It coordinates and helps fund activities of public libraries, provides a framework for statewide library initiatives, provides archival and records management services, and preserves, collects, and makes available the published and unpublished documentary history of the state.

## Grants Information

**GRANT TYPES**
LSTA funds, library construction, library cooperation, library support

## TYPICAL RECIPIENTS

Florida libraries and nonprofit organizations primarily related to the provision or support of library services, eligible Florida governmental entities, multitype library cooperatives

## GRANT VALUES

Total Dollar Amount of Grants:
$40,000,000

## NAMED GRANTS

### PUBLIC LIBRARY CONSTRUCTION GRANT PROGRAM

The Public Library Construction grant program provides state funding to governments for the construction of public libraries. This includes the construction of new buildings and the acquisition, expansion, or remodeling of existing buildings to be used for public library service. Funds are reimbursed to local government entities based on stages of project completion.

**Typical Recipients:** Any eligible Florida governmental entity may apply, including county governments, incorporated municipalities, special districts, and special tax districts that establish or maintain a public library and provide free public library service.

**Grant Values:** Total Dollar Amount of Grants, $5,000,000; Number of Grants, 10; Highest Grant, $500,000; Lowest Grant, $10,000

**Requirements and Restrictions:** The minimum allowable project size is 3,000 square feet. A dollar-for dollar match is required for all construction grants. Matching funds must be available and unencumbered at the time of the grant award. (A library in a county or community with rural status may request a waiver of the match requirement at the time of the grant application in compliance with Section 288.06561, Florida Statutes.) Grant funds must be used for the following: architectural services; acquisition of land; new construction; expansion; remodeling; site preparation, including the provision of parking spaces; engineering costs and legal fees directly related to the construction of the library; and initial or fixed equipment, including shelving, tables, chairs, information and building technologies, video and telecommunications equipment, machinery, utilities, built-in equipment and enclosures or structures necessary to house them, opening day collections, and all other items necessary to furnish and operate a new or improved facility for the provision of library services.

**Deadlines:** April 1

**Decisions:** July (15 months after date of application)

**Grant-Specific Website:** http://dlis.dos.state.fl.us/bld/grants/Construction/Construction.html

## LSTA Grants

LSTA Grant funds are designated principally for direct support of services and programs to targeted audiences.

**Typical Recipients:** Florida libraries and nonprofit organizations primarily related to the provision or support of library services, including public libraries; public elementary, secondary, or charter school libraries; academic libraries; library consortia; and special libraries.

**Grant Values:** Total Dollar Amount of Grants, $8,425,488

**Past Grant Recipients:**

- Broward County Division of Libraries (FL), Literacy Help Center, $152,572
- Bureau of Braille and Talking Book Services (FL), digital program, $80,000
- Jacksonville Public Library (FL), Expanding Horizons Adult Literacy Project, $78,512
- Polk County Library Cooperative (FL), Bringing Library Services to Northridge, $176,415
- St. Johns County Public Library (FL), Library Express Outreach (LEO) project, $63,850

**Requirements and Restrictions:** Local matching funds must equal a minimum of one-third of the amount of federal funds requested or awarded, and may be in-kind or cash contributions. (A library in a county or community with rural status may request a waiver of the match requirement at the time of the grant application in compliance with Section 288.06561, Florida Statutes.) Eligible entities must apply for funds under two categories: Access for Persons Having Difficulty Using Libraries or Library Technology Connectivity and Services.

**Deadlines:** March 15

**Grant-Specific Website:** http://dlis.dos. state.fl.us/bld/grants/Lsta/LSTA.html

## State Aid to Libraries Grant Program

*This program comprises three interrelated grants: Equalization, Multicounty, and Operating grants. All three grant types are matching grants.*

**Typical Recipients:** Equalization grants are available to counties that qualify for Operating grants and serve counties with limited local tax resources. Multicounty grants are available to the administrative unit of the multicounty library that qualifies for Operating grants. Operating grants are available to any county or municipality that qualifies for the State Aid to Libraries grant program.

**Grant Values:** Total Dollar Amount of Grants, $26,719,200

**Past Grant Recipients:**

- Alachua County (FL), operating grant, $499,635

- Altamonte Springs (FL), operating grant, $16,211
- Baker County (FL), operating grant and equalization grant, $5,198 and $62,645, respectively
- Bay County (FL), operating grant, $77,481
- Boynton Beach (FL), operating grant, $72,894
- Bradford County (FL), operating grant and equalization grant, $17,670 and $425,180, respectively

**Requirements and Restrictions:** State Aid to Libraries grant funds must be expended for the operation and maintenance of the library and not for the purchase or construction of a library building or library quarters.

**Deadlines:** October 1

**Grant-Specific Website:** http://dlis.dos. state.fl.us/bld/grants/StateAid/StateAid. html

## LIBRARY COOPERATIVE GRANT

The priority for use of Library Cooperative grant and local matching funds is for the continual maintenance of the statewide database of library materials. Maintenance of this database involves bibliographic enhancement and related training for all Florida Library Information Network (FLIN) member libraries within each multitype library cooperative's geographic service area.

**Typical Recipients:** Multitype library cooperatives are eligible to apply. These will be not-for-profit corporations qualified or registered pursuant to Chapter 617, Florida Statutes, and in good standing, consisting of two or more libraries under separate governance and of more than one type, including any combination of academic, school, special, state institution, and public libraries as required by Section 257.41(1), Florida Statutes.

**Grant Values:** Highest Grant, $400,000

**Requirements and Restrictions:** A 10 percent cash match is required for Library Cooperative grants. Library cooperatives are generally required to spend at least 50 percent of the grant and local matching funds on bibliographic enhancement activities and related training within each grant period. The remaining 50 percent of the grant and matching funds may either be used to provide services to all FLIN member libraries for additional bibliographic enhancement activities or for other resource sharing activities as identified in the cooperative's long-range plan and annual plan of service.

**Deadlines:** April 15

**Grant-Specific Website:** http://dlis.dos.state.fl.us/bld/grants/ Cooperative/Cooperative.html

## REQUIREMENTS AND RESTRICTIONS

Applicants must be located in the state of Florida. Other requirements vary by grant.

## APPLICATION PROCEDURES

**Submission Guidelines:** Application online

## CONTACT

Phone: 850-245-6620
Fax: 850-245-6643
E-mail: grantsoffice@dos.state.fl.us

## GRANT-SPECIFIC WEBSITE

http://dlis.dos.state.fl.us/bld/grants/

# Ford Motor Co. Fund

## Headquarters

One American Rd.
Dearborn, MI 48126
Phone: 313-845-8711
www.community.ford.com

## Description

**Founded:** 1949

**Operating Locations:** Michigan

**Foundation Information:** Corporate foundation of Ford Motor Co.

## Financial Summary

Assets: $51,275,883
Gifts Received: $10,000,000
Total Giving: $34,261,532

## Grants Information

### GRANT TYPES

Capital, general support, employee matching

### TYPICAL RECIPIENTS

Education, auto-related safety education, community development

### GRANT VALUES

Total Dollar Amount of Grants:
$34,261,532

### PAST GRANT RECIPIENTS

*Library or School Related*
- San Antonio Public Library Foundation (CA), support for public arts program, $25,000

*General*
- National Engineers Week (DC), Future City national finals, $30,000
- Smithsonian Institute (DC), Smithsonian Scholars in the Schools program, $50,000
- Field Museum of Natural History (IL), Calumet Environmental Education Project, $55,000
- Henry Ford Learning Institute (MI), operations, $1,000,000

- Oakwood Healthcare System Foundation (MI), Women's Health Resource Center, $200,000
- Latin Americans for Social and Economic Development (MI), Senior Center funding grant, $100,000
- National Park Foundation (PA), Gettysburg National Battlefield Museum Foundation's capital campaign, $600,000

**REQUIREMENTS AND RESTRICTIONS**
Applicants must have tax-exempt status.

**APPLICATION PROCEDURES**
**Submission Guidelines:** Complete application online, including organization information, budget information, and grant details.

**CONTACT**
Phone: 888-320-7129
E-mail: FordMotor@Easymatch.com

**GRANT-SPECIFIC WEBSITE**
https://secure4.easymatch.com/
 FordGrants/CustomerContent/
 Grants/FundingAndGrants.asp

# Freas Foundation

## Headquarters

483 Main St.
Harleysville, PA 19438

Phone: 484-232-6234

## Description

**Founded:** 1953

**Operating Locations:** Pennsylvania

**Foundation Information:** Private foundation

## Financial Summary

Assets: $2,752,117
Total Giving: $209,096

## Grants Information

**GRANT TYPES**
General support

**TYPICAL RECIPIENTS**
Arts and humanities, civic affairs, education, health, religion, social services

**GRANT VALUES**
Total Dollar Amount of Grants: $209,096
Number of Grants: 42
Highest Grant: $15,000
Lowest Grant: $500

**PAST GRANT RECIPIENTS**

*Library or School Related*
- Kaltreider-Benfer Library (PA), general support, $3,000
- Martin Library Association (PA),

general support, $4,500
- Schlow Centre County Library (PA), general support, $1,600
- Capon Bridge Elementary School (WV), general support, $3,000

*General*
- York County Literacy Council (PA), general support, $3,000
- Dreamwrights Youth and Family Theatre (PA), general support, $6,000
- Thomas Jefferson Area United Way (VA), Smart Beginnings for Parents Program, $500
- Mt Carmel Continuing Care Retirement Community (IA), general support, $1,010

**REQUIREMENTS AND RESTRICTIONS**
NA

**APPLICATION PROCEDURES**
**Submission Guidelines:** Call for application information.

**CONTACT**
Phone: 484-232-6234

**GRANT-SPECIFIC WEBSITE**
NA

# Freedom to Read Foundation (FTRF)

## Headquarters

50 E. Huron St.
Chicago, IL 60611
Phone: 800-545-2433, ext. 4226
Fax: 312-280-4227
E-mail: ftrf@ala.org
www.ftrf.org

## Description

**Founded:** 1969

**Operating Locations:** Illinois

The First Amendment to the U.S. Constitution guarantees all individuals the right to express their ideas without governmental interference, and to read and listen to the ideas of others. The Freedom to Read Foundation was established to promote and defend this right, to foster libraries and institutions wherein every individual's First Amendment freedoms are fulfilled, and to support the right of libraries to include in their collections and make available any work which they may legally acquire.

## Financial Summary

Assets: $792,548

Gifts Received: $160,049

Total Giving: $42,500

# Grants Information

## GRANT TYPES

Conference attendance, general support of organizations to defend intellectual freedom rights

## TYPICAL RECIPIENTS

Librarians, libraries, and professional organizations that defend First Amendment rights

## GRANT VALUES

Total Dollar Amount of Grants: $20,500

Number of Grants: 6

Average Grant: $3,416

Highest Grant: $22,000

Lowest Grant: $1,500

Typical Range of Grants: $1,500–$2,000

## NAMED GRANTS

### GORDON M. CONABLE CONFERENCE SCHOLARSHIP

The Freedom to Read Foundation (FTRF) offers an annual scholarship for library school students and new professionals to attend ALA Annual Conference. The goal of the Gordon M. Conable Conference Scholarship is to advance two principles that Conable held dear: intellectual freedom and mentoring. The Conable Scholarship provides for conference registration, transportation, housing for six nights, and per diem

expenses. In return, the recipient will be expected to attend various FTRF and other intellectual freedom meetings and programs at conference, consult with a mentor/board member, and present a report about their experiences and thoughts.

Only students currently enrolled in a library and information studies degree program, and new professionals (those who received their library school degree no more than three years ago) are eligible to receive the Conable Scholarship. Those interested must submit an application including two references and an essay detailing their interest in intellectual freedom issues and how conference attendance will help further that interest. Applicants also are asked to attach a résumé, particularly those who are working professionals.

**Grant-Specific Website:** www.ala.org/ ala/aboutala/offices/oif/oifprograms/ ifawards/conablescholarship/conable.cfm

### JUDITH KRUG FUND'S BANNED BOOKS WEEK EVENT GRANTS

The Judith Krug Fund is dedicated to continuing and promoting the remarkable legacy of Judith Krug, founding executive director of the Freedom to Read Foundation and founding director of the ALA Office for Intellectual Freedom. For more than 40 years, Krug made it her life's work to protect the First Amendment to the U.S. Constitution and the principles of intellectual freedom, in libraries and beyond. The first project of the Judith Krug Fund is to disburse grants to organizations to assist them in staging "Read-Outs" or other events during Banned Books Week. (A Banned Books Week Read-Out is an event at which people gather to read from books that have been banned or challenged over the years, in order to celebrate the freedom to read.) Applicants must provide planning and budget outlines for their projects; agree to record the event, if selected; and provide a written narrative afterward, for use by the Freedom to Read Foundation and American Library Association.

**Grant-Specific Website:** www.ala.org/ala/mgrps/affiliates/relatedgroups/freedomtoreadfoundation/ftrfinaction/krugfund/index.cfm

**REQUIREMENTS AND RESTRICTIONS**
Vary by grant

**APPLICATION PROCEDURES**
**Submission Guidelines:** Application online

**CONTACT**
Jonathan Kelley
Phone: 800-545-2433, ext. 4226, or 312-280-4226
Fax: 312-280-4227
E-mail: jkelley@ala.org

**GRANT-SPECIFIC WEBSITE**
Varies by grant

# Bill and Melinda Gates Foundation

## Headquarters

PO Box 23350
Seattle, WA 98102
Phone: 206-709-3100
www.gatesfoundation.org

## Description

**Founded:** 1994

**Operating Locations:** Washington

**Foundation Information:** Private foundation established by William H. Gates III and his wife, Melinda French Gates

## Financial Summary

Assets: $29,673,548,843
Gifts Received: $1,856,600,807
Total Giving: $1,851,998,519

## Grants Information

**GRANT TYPES**
Education, library improvement, technology support

**TYPICAL RECIPIENTS**
Arts, libraries, education, health, civic affairs, social services

## GRANT VALUES

Total Dollar Amount of Grants:
    $1,851,998,519

## PAST GRANT RECIPIENTS

*Library or School Related*

- Libraries for the Future (PA), EqualAccess Libraries, transforming libraries into information and education centers, $1,050,000
- New York State Library (NY), computers, Internet access, and technical training for public libraries, $7,700,000
- Chelsea District Library (MI), support for rural library services, $19,670
- The Library of Virginia (VA), improving technology access in libraries serving low-income patrons, $652,155
- Southeastern Library Network, Inc. (GA), support for Mississippi and Louisiana libraries damaged or destroyed by Hurricanes Katrina and Rita, $2,547,929
- International City County Management Association (DC), facilitating partnerships between libraries and local governments and position libraries as relevant community institutions through a set of demonstration projects throughout the United States, $476,323
- University of Texas (TX), support for secondary literacy and mathematics instruction, $73,123

- University of Chicago (IL), providing training to school researchers and administrators, $150,223
- Denver School of Science and Technology (CO), support for secondary school model expansion and development of critical systems to support future replication, $73,441
- KnowledgeWorks Foundations (OH), expanding development of an Ohio-based network of early college high schools, $520,000
- Greater Kansas City Community Foundation (MO), improving urban high schools in Kansas City, $1,120,729
- Fund for Educational Excellence (MD), support for district reform initiatives to increase college-ready graduation rates in Baltimore, $853,530

## REQUIREMENTS AND RESTRICTIONS

The foundation looks for library programs that evaluate local technology needs, purchase equipment, train library staff, help libraries build public support for long-term funding, provide up-to-date Internet connections, and support free access to computers and the Internet. The foundation does not accept unsolicited letters of inquiry (LOIs) and does not fund individuals. However, the foundation does accept LOIs from 501(c)(3) organizations. The foundation also does not fund building or capital campaigns, projects that exclusively serve religious purposes, political campaigns, or projects addressing health problems in developed countries.

### APPLICATION PROCEDURES

**Submission Guidelines:** Grants for U.S. libraries are by invitation only. The foundation encourages grant seekers to watch for RFPs on the foundation website.

### CONTACT

Phone: 206-709-3140
E-mail: info@gatesfoundation.org

### GRANT-SPECIFIC WEBSITE

www.gatesfoundation.org/grantseeker/

# General Mills Foundation

## Headquarters

PO Box 1113
Minneapolis, MN 55440
www.generalmills.com/Responsibility/
Community_Engagement/general_mills_
foundation_2010.aspx

## Description

**Founded:** NA

**Operating Locations:** Minnesota

**Foundation Information:** Corporate foundation of General Mills, Inc.

## Financial Summary

Assets: $37,432,110
Total Giving: $21,099,998

## Grants Information

### GRANT TYPES

General support, capital, employee matching, scholarship

### TYPICAL RECIPIENTS

Arts and humanities, civic affairs, health, science, social services

### GRANT VALUES

Total Dollar Amount of Grants:
    $21,099,998
Average Grant: $10,000
Highest Grant: $3,649,334
Lowest Grant: $1,000
Typical Range of Grants: $5,000–
    $30,000

### PAST GRANT RECIPIENTS

*Library or School Related*
- Carlisle Public Library (IA), summer reading program, $2,700
- Friends of the Vineland Free Public Library (NJ), purchase of computers, $1,000
- Minnesota Literacy Council., Inc. (MN), early literacy and families program, $10,000

- Minnesota Early Learning Foundation (MN), operating support, $300,000
- Luzerne County Head Start, Inc. (PA), Reading Is Fundamental program, $4,300

*General*
- Hempstead Boys and Girls Club (NY), operating support, $5,000
- Kentucky Special Olympics (KY), track and field, $5,000
- Lyric Opera of Chicago (IL), student matinees, $10,000

**REQUIREMENTS AND RESTRICTIONS**
Applicants must have tax-exempt status.

**APPLICATION PROCEDURES**
**Submission Guidelines:** Application online. Application should include

- proof of tax-exempt status
- objective of proposal
- list of officers and board members
- recently audited financial statement
- list of major donors for previous year

**Deadlines:** Grant requests are accepted on an ongoing basis.

**CONTACT**
Christina L. Shea, President
PO Box 1113
Minneapolis, MN 55440
Phone: 763-764-2211
Fax: 763-764-4114
E-mail: Community.ActionQA@genmills. com

**GRANT-SPECIFIC WEBSITE**
www.generalmills.com/en/
    Responsibility/Community_
    Engagement/Grants.aspx

# Georgia-Pacific Foundation

## Headquarters

133 Peachtree St. NE
Atlanta, GA 30303
Phone: 404-652-4000
www.gp.com/gpfoundation/

## Description

**Founded:** NA

**Operating Locations:** Georgia

**Foundation Information:** Corporate foundation of Georgia-Pacific Corp.

## Financial Summary

Assets: $460,421
Total Giving: $3,397,636

## Grants Information

**GRANT TYPES**
General support, capital, employee matching, scholarship

**TYPICAL RECIPIENTS**

Arts and humanities, civic affairs, education, environment, health, religion, science, social services

**GRANT VALUES**

Total Dollar Amount of Grants:
    $3,397,636

**PAST GRANT RECIPIENTS**

*Library or School Related*

- Thompson Sawyer Public Library (TX), general support, $2,500
- Jasper County Library (GA), general support, $5,000
- Pine Mountain Regional Library (GA), general support, $500
- Bedford Public Library System (VA), general support, $1,000
- Taylorsville Friends of the Library (NC), general support, $100
- Winston County Library (MS), general support, $500
- Seminole County Public Library (FL), general support, $500
- Plattsburgh Public Library (NY), general support, $100
- Literacy Action (GA), general support, $10,000
- Early County Literacy Task Force (GA), general support, $5,000

**REQUIREMENTS AND RESTRICTIONS**

Applicants must have tax-exempt status. The foundation does not make grants to individuals.

**APPLICATION PROCEDURES**

**Submission Guidelines:** Complete application online, including eligibility test.

**CONTACT**

Curley Dossman, Jr.
Phone: 404-652-4000

**GRANT-SPECIFIC WEBSITE**

www.gp.com/gpfoundation/
    grantprocess.html

# Georgia Public Library Service

## Headquarters

1800 Century Pl., Suite 150
Atlanta, GA 30345-4304
Phone: 404-235-7200
www.georgialibraries.org

## Description

**Founded:** NA

**Operating Locations:** Georgia

The Georgia Public Library Service provides and encourages visionary leadership, ensures equal access to information and technology, promotes the value and joy of lifelong reading and learning, and facilitates collaboration and innovation in the broader library community.

## Grants Information

**GRANT TYPES**
Library construction

**TYPICAL RECIPIENTS**
Georgia libraries

**GRANT VALUES**
Highest Grant: $150,000
Lowest Grant: $2,500

**NAMED GRANTS**

### MAJOR REPAIR AND RENOVATION GRANT PROGRAM
Grant will pay up to 90 percent, up to $150,000, of approved costs associated with major repairs and renovations of existing library facilities that are closed due to catastrophic events. Grant will pay up to 50 percent, up to $100,000, of approved costs associated with all other major repairs and renovations of existing library facilities.

**REQUIREMENTS AND RESTRICTIONS**
Funds will not be provided to pay for the cost of repairs that are covered by existing insurance or warranties given at the time of initial installation of construction. A library system may apply for as many projects as needed, but only two awards will be granted per county in any given fiscal year. Assurance of local funds availability for matching costs will be required. Evidence of state or local governmental support for this grant application is strongly recommended. A library system may submit more than one project per facility.

**APPLICATION PROCEDURES**
**Deadlines:** January

**CONTACT**
Nathan Rall
Phone: 404-235-7153
Fax: 404-235-7201
E-mail: nrall@georgialibraries.org

**GRANT-SPECIFIC WEBSITE**
www.georgialibraries.org/lib/
   construction/

# Getty Foundation

## Headquarters

1200 Getty Center Dr., Suite 800
Los Angeles, CA 90049-1685
www.getty.edu/foundation/

## Description

**Founded:** NA

**Operating Locations:** California

**Foundation Information:** Private foundation of the J. Paul Getty Trust

# Financial Summary

Assets: $10,837,340,620
Total Giving: $18,759,273

# Grants Information

## GRANT TYPES
General support, project, research, matching, fellowship

## TYPICAL RECIPIENTS
Arts and humanities, civic affairs, education, environment, health, international, religion, science

## GRANT VALUES
Total Dollar Amount of Grants:
$18,759,273

## PAST GRANT RECIPIENTS

*Library or School Related*
- Henry E. Huntington Library and Art Gallery (CA), multicultural internships, $12,000
- Library Foundation of Los Angeles (CA), multicultural internships, $8,000
- Southern California Library for Social Studies (CA), multicultural internships, $4,000
- University of Chicago (IL), reference works, $200,000

- New York Public Library (NY), general support, $20,000
- Recording for the Blind and Dyslexic (NJ), general support, $8,000

*General*
- Somerset House of Art History Foundation (NY), general support, $8,000
- Mayo Foundation (MN), general support, $15,000

## REQUIREMENTS AND RESTRICTIONS
The Getty Foundation supports individuals and institutions committed to advancing the understanding and preservation of the visual arts locally and throughout the world. The majority of funding is through initiatives that target a particular issue or region, and that are carried out in collaboration with the other Getty programs—the J. Paul Getty Museum, the Getty Research Institute, and the Getty Conservation Institute. The foundation focuses on the following four broad areas: access to museum and archival collections, art history as a global discipline, advancing conservation practice, leadership and professional development.

## APPLICATION PROCEDURES
**Submission Guidelines:** Submit a brief preliminary letter describing the project and its financial requirements to the Getty Foundation before developing a formal grant proposal.

**Deadlines:** Submission deadlines vary depending on grant category. See the website for details.

**CONTACT**
Phone: 310-440-7320
Fax: 310-440-7703
E-mail: GettyFoundation@getty.edu

**GRANT-SPECIFIC WEBSITE**
www.getty.edu/foundation/

# Florence Gould Foundation

## Headquarters

c/o Cahill Cordon & Reindel
80 Pine St.
New York, NY 10005
Phone: 212-701-3400

## Description

**Founded:** 1957

**Operating Locations:** New York

**Foundation Information:** Private foundation established by Florence J. Gould

## Financial Summary

Assets: $66,131,003
Total Giving: $7,570,652

# Grants Information

**GRANT TYPES**
General support, project, endowment, exhibition

**TYPICAL RECIPIENTS**
Arts and humanities, civic affairs, education, health, international, science, social services

**GRANT VALUES**
Total Dollar Amount of Grants:
    $7,570,652

**PAST GRANT RECIPIENTS**

*Library or School Related*
- New York Public Library (NY), exhibition, $250,000
- Newberry Library (IL), acquisition support, $10,000
- The Library of America (NY), cost of shipping volumes to American libraries in France, $1,194
- Yale University (CT), acquisition of Benjamin Franklin papers, $75,000

*General*
- The Grolier Club (NY), acquisition of materials relating to Napoleon's libraries, $50,000
- Massachusetts Historical Society (MA), acquisition of the Adams papers, $20,000
- Metropolitan Museum of Art (NY), exhibition, $500,000

- Philadelphia Museum of Art (PA), exhibition, $100,000
- Animal Medical Center (NY), support of pet care for the elderly, $25,000
- Lincoln Center for the Performing Arts (DC), French programming, $100,000

## REQUIREMENTS AND RESTRICTIONS

The foundation's aim is to promote French-American exchange and goodwill.

## APPLICATION PROCEDURES

**Submission Guidelines:** Send a letter of inquiry.

## CONTACT

John R. Young
Phone: 212-701-3400

## GRANT-SPECIFIC WEBSITE

NA

# Grable Foundation

## Headquarters

650 Smithfield St.
Pittsburgh, PA 15222
Phone: 412-471-4550
www.grablefdn.org

## Description

**Founded:** 1976

**Operating Locations:** Pennsylvania

**Foundation Information:** Private foundation established by Minnie K. Grable

## Financial Summary

Assets: $208,427,438
Total Giving: $11,510,882

## Grants Information

### GRANT TYPES

General support, operating support, project

### TYPICAL RECIPIENTS

Arts and humanities, civic affairs, education, environment, health, religion, science, social services

### GRANT VALUES

Total Dollar Amount of Grants:
$11,510,882
Number of Grants: 244
Average Grant: $48,000
Highest Grant: $750,000
Lowest Grant: $2,500

### PAST GRANT RECIPIENTS

*Library or School Related*

- Community Center and Library Association (PA), general support for branch library, $15,000
- Andrew Carnegie Free Library and Music Hall (PA), children's services, $28,500

- C. C. Mellor Memorial Library (PA), programs, $8,743
- German Masontown Public Library (PA), after-school program, $20,000
- Allegheny County Library Association (PA), programs, $125,000
- Greater Pittsburgh Literacy Council (PA), Families for Learning program, $40,000

*General*
- Reading Is Fundamental (PA), literacy programs, $40,000
- Beginning with Books, Inc. (PA), neighborhood-based early literacy outreach, $150,000
- Leadership Foundation (DC), International Women's Forum Conference, $2,500
- North Carolina Arts in Action (NC), Building Community One Step at a Time program, $15,000

## REQUIREMENTS AND RESTRICTIONS

The foundation does not make grants to individuals or to conduit organizations that pass on funds to other organizations.

## APPLICATION PROCEDURES

**Submission Guidelines:** Letter of inquiry online. Letter should include

- a one- or two-page summary of the proposal
- information about the applicant organization
- statement of need for the proposed project
- description of the project and rationale for its approach
- qualifications of organization and staff
- project budget
- organization's current operating budget
- description of how the project will be sustained after grant ends
- list of board members or advisors
- letters of support from applicant's board
- a copy of the IRS tax-exempt certification

Upon request of the foundation applicant may submit a full proposal.

**Deadlines:** January 1, May 1, and September 1

## CONTACT

Gregg Behr
Phone: 412-471-4550
E-mail: grable@grable.org

## GRANT-SPECIFIC WEBSITE

www.grablefdn.org/inquiries.html

# The Hearst Foundations

## Headquarters

300 W. 57th St.
New York, NY 10019

Phone: 212-586-5404
E-mail: hearst@fdn.org
www.hearstfdn.org

# Description

**Founded:** 1945

**Operating Locations:** New York,
California

**Foundation Information:** Private
foundation established by publisher/
philanthropist William Randolph Hearst

# Financial Summary

Assets: $200,128,336
Total Giving: $11,229,000

# Grants Information

### GRANT TYPES
General support, project, endowment,
research, scholarship

### TYPICAL RECIPIENTS
Arts and humanities, civic affairs,
education, science, social services

### GRANT VALUES
Total Dollar Amount of Grants:
    $11,229,000

### PAST GRANT RECIPIENTS
*Library or School Related*
- Henry E. Huntington Library and
  Art Gallery (CA), general support,
  $100,000
- Winterthur Museum, Garden, and
  Library (DE), general support,
  $75,000
- Brooklyn Public Library Foundation
  (NY), general support, $125,000
- Queens Borough Public Library (NY),
  general support, $250,000
- DePauw University (IN), general
  support, $100,000

*General*
- Bushnell Center for the Performing
  Arts (CT), general support, $50,000
- Kansas City Symphony (MO), general
  support, $75,000
- Children and Family Services Center
  (NC), general support, $75,000
- Greater Pittsburgh Community Food
  Bank (PA), general support, $100,000

### REQUIREMENTS AND RESTRICTIONS
The foundation does not make annual
or multiyear grants, and favors private-
sector organizations over those funded
by taxation. The Hearst Foundation and
the William Randolph Hearst Foundation
are independent private philanthropies
operating independently from the Hearst
Corporation. However, charitable goals
of the two foundations are the same, and
they are administered as one. Therefore,
only one proposal need be submitted. A
site visit is required before board review.

### APPLICATION PROCEDURES
**Submission Guidelines:** Submit a one-
page executive summary accompanied

by a full proposal. The summary should describe the applicant's organization's mission and the dollar amount of the request. The proposal should include

- project budget
- current fiscal year operating budget
- most recent audited financial report
- primary affiliations of officers and board members
- proof of tax-exempt status

**Deadlines:** Board meetings on grant decisions are held in March, June, September, and December.

## CONTACT

Organizations located EAST of the
    Mississippi River should send
    requests to
The Hearst Foundations
300 W. 57th St., 26th fl.
New York, NY 10019-3741
Phone: 212-586-5404
Fax: 212-586-1917
Organizations located WEST of the
    Mississippi River should send
    requests to
The Hearst Foundations
90 New Montgomery St., Suite 1212
San Francisco, CA 94105
Phone: 415-908-4500
Fax: 415-348-0887

## GRANT-SPECIFIC WEBSITE

www.hearstfdn.org

# A. D. Henderson Foundation

## Headquarters

PO Box 14096
Fort Lauderdale, FL 33302-4096
Phone: 954-764-2819
www.hendersonfdn.org/index.htm

## Description

**Founded:** 1959

**Operating Locations:** Florida, Vermont

**Foundation Information:** Private foundation established by A. D. and Lucy E. Henderson

## Grants Information

### GRANT TYPES
Project, program

### TYPICAL RECIPIENTS
Education, literacy

### GRANT VALUES
Total Dollar Amount of Grants:
    $1,500,000

### PAST GRANT RECIPIENTS
*Library or School Related*
- Broward College Foundation, Inc. (FL), Stars Summer Academy, $20,000

- Broward Public Library Foundation, Inc. (FL), continuation of Para los Niños program, $35,000
- Children's Literacy Foundation (VT), CLIF child-care program, $12,250
- Reach Out and Read Inc. (MA), Reach Out and Read Vermont, $25,000

*General*
- Big Brothers Big Sisters of Broward, Inc. (FL), innovations in data analysis project, $30,000
- Bonnyvale Environmental Education Center (VT), Nature Detectives: A Science Inquiry Program, $15,056
- Family Central, Inc. (FL), early childhood educators conference, $35,050
- N.E. Focal Point Casa, Inc. (FL), Early Language and Literacy for Life project, $12,841
- VSA Arts Vermont, Inc. (VT), Start with the Arts library outreach, $20,000

**REQUIREMENTS AND RESTRICTIONS**
The foundation limits its grant making to Broward County in Florida and the State of Vermont. The foundation makes grants to public entities and IRS 501(c)(3) tax-exempt organizations that are not classified as private foundations. It also looks for organizations that do not discriminate in the hiring of staff or providing of services on the basis of race, age, sex, national origin, religion, disabilities, ancestry, marital status, or sexual orientation.

The foundation seeks to fund programs that enhance and promote the literacy and learning skills of children and families; improve the quality of child care and the expertise of child-care providers; promote mentoring and positive relationships between children and adults; provide in-school and out-of-school activities for children with a focus on child care, literacy, art, science, and culture; utilize computer technology to improve the learning capabilities of children; strengthen the organizational capacity of nonprofits with a focus on board and staff development, fundraising, utilization of technology, and program delivery; address the educational aspects of family planning; and improve the lives of children through interaction with animals.

**APPLICATION PROCEDURES**
**Submission Guidelines:** Applicants must contact a foundation program director to discuss their project idea prior to submitting a formal application. If the project is a potential match with the foundation's funding priorities, the applicant will be asked to submit an application, including a proposal, project budget, an IRS tax-exempt status letter, and additional documentation.

**CONTACT**
Phone: 954-764-2819 (Florida office); 802-888-1188 (Vermont office)
E-mail: staff@hendersonfdn.org

GRANT-SPECIFIC WEBSITE
www.hendersonfdn.org/page3.htm

# William and Flora Hewlett Foundation

## Headquarters

2121 Sand Hill Rd.
Menlo Park, CA 94025
Phone: 650-234-4500
E-mail: info@hewlett.org
www.hewlett.org

## Description

**Founded:** 1967

**Operating Locations:** California

**Foundation Information:** Private foundation established by William Hewlett (of Hewlett-Packard Co.) and his wife Flora Lamson Hewlett

## Financial Summary

Assets: $6,208,980,453
Gifts Received: $30,000
Total Giving: $379,599,742

## Grants Information

**GRANT TYPES**
General support, project, matching

**TYPICAL RECIPIENTS**
Arts and humanities, civic affairs, education, environment, health, international, science, social services

**GRANT VALUES**
Total Dollar Amount of Grants:
   $379,599,742
Number of Grants: 596
Average Grant: $397,000

**PAST GRANT RECIPIENTS**

*Library or School Related*
- National Academy of Sciences (DC), study of reading comprehension from grade 4 onward, $100,000
- President and Fellows of Harvard College (MA), support of literacy research, $119,000
- San Mateo Public Library (CA), general support, $6,000

*General*
- Pratham USA (TX), program to improve students' literacy and numeracy skills, $3,038,000
- Boys and Girls Club of the Peninsula (CA), after-school literacy club, $100,000
- Center for the Future of Teaching and Learning (CA), general support, $400,000
- Room to Read (CA), primary reading enhancement program in India, $238,685

## REQUIREMENTS AND RESTRICTIONS

Almost all grants are awarded to organizations identified by the foundation. The foundation does accept unsolicited letters of inquiry from organizations looking for funding in limited areas, but only on very rare occasions are grants awarded in response to these unsolicited funding inquiries. There are no deadlines for their submission.

## APPLICATION PROCEDURES

**Submission Guidelines:** Submit a letter of inquiry online.

## CONTACT

Paul Brest
Phone: 650-234-4500

## GRANT-SPECIFIC WEBSITE

www.hewlett.org/grants/grantseekers/

# Home Depot Foundation

## Headquarters

2455 Paces Ferry Rd.
Atlanta, GA 30339
E-mail: hd_foundation@homedepot.com
www.homedepotfoundation.org/

## Description

**Founded:** 2002

**Operating Locations:** Georgia

**Foundation Information:** Corporate foundation of The Home Depot

## Financial Summary

Total Giving: $10,000,000

## Grants Information

### GRANT TYPES

Construction, general support

### TYPICAL RECIPIENTS

Arts and humanities, civic affairs, environment, education, social services

### GRANT VALUES

Total Dollar Amount of Grants:
$10,000,000
Highest Grant: $5,000

### PAST GRANT RECIPIENTS

*Library or School Related*
- Melba Cottage Library (ID)
- Omak Public Library (WA)
- Judith Morton Johnston Elementary School (IN)
- Le Comte Middle School (CA)
- Kempre County High School (MS)
- United Negro College Fund (GA)

*General*
- Green Infrastructure Foundation (VA)
- Trees Forever (IA)
- Spokane County Parks (WA)
- Center for Women in Transition (IL)

- St. Joseph's School for the Blind (NJ)
- Atlanta Opera (GA)

## REQUIREMENTS AND RESTRICTIONS

Grants are available to registered 501(c)(3) nonprofit organizations, public schools, or tax-exempt public service agencies in the United States that are using the power of volunteers to improve the physical health of their community. Grants are given in the form of The Home Depot gift cards for the purchase of tools, materials, or services. More competitive grant proposals will specifically identify projects for veterans, seniors, or the disabled and will include housing repairs, modifications, and weatherization work.

## APPLICATION PROCEDURES

**Submission Guidelines:** Only proposals submitted through the online application process will be considered for funding. Donation requests submitted by mail, phone, or e-mail will not receive funding and will be directed to the online application process.

**Decisions:** Once grant applications are reviewed, all applicants will receive a written response within 6 weeks of receipt of a request.

## CONTACT

E-mail: team_depot@homedepot.com

## GRANT-SPECIFIC WEBSITE

www.homedepotfoundation.org/grants.html

# Humana Foundation

## Headquarters

500 W. Main St., Suite 208
Louisville, KY 40202
Phone: 502-580-4140
Fax: 502-580-1256
www.humanafoundation.org

## Description

**Founded:** 1981

**Operating Locations:** Kentucky

**Foundation Information:** Corporate foundation of Humana, Inc.

## Financial Summary

Assets: $66,013,934
Total Giving: $4,807,682

## Grants Information

### GRANT TYPES
Capital, general support, project, research, scholarship

### TYPICAL RECIPIENTS
Arts and humanities, civic affairs, education, health, social services

### GRANT VALUES
Total Dollar Amount of Grants:
    $4,807,682

Highest Grant: $310,000
Lowest Grant: $1,000

## PAST GRANT RECIPIENTS

*Library or School Related*

- Middlebury College (VT), capital campaign for new library, $150,000

*General*

- Junior Achievement for Kentuckiana (KY), capital campaign for new enterprise center, $25,000
- Kentucky Author Forum (KY), author interview series, $50,000
- Business Higher Education Forum (DC), program support, $75,000
- San Antonio River Foundation (TX), capital campaign, $50,000
- International Women's Media Foundation (DC), Courage in Journalism Awards Program, $25,000
- Business Committee for the Arts (NY), program support, $10,000
- Family/Children's Place (KY), general support, $75,000
- Juvenile Diabetes Research Foundation (GA), program support, $10,500

## REQUIREMENTS AND RESTRICTIONS

Applicants must have tax-exempt status. Grants are made to organizations where Humana has a meaningful presence; see the website for a list of eligible locations.

## APPLICATION PROCEDURES

**Submission Guidelines:** Application online

**Deadlines:** Vary by location

## CONTACT

Phone: 502-580-4140
E-mail: HumanaFoundation@humana.com

## GRANT-SPECIFIC WEBSITE

www.humanafoundation.org/
philanthropy/grant_application.asp

# Idaho Commission for Libraries (ICFL)

## Headquarters

325 W. State St.
Boise, ID 83702
Phone: 800-458-3271 (in Idaho), or 208-334-2150
Fax: 208-334-4016
http://libraries.idaho.gov

## Description

**Founded:** 1901

**Operating Locations:** Idaho

The mission of the Idaho Commission for Libraries (ICFL) is to assist libraries to build the capacity to better serve their clientele.

# Grants Information

## GRANT TYPES
LSTA funds

## TYPICAL RECIPIENTS
Idaho public, school, and academic libraries; special libraries; library consortia; nonlibrary entities

## GRANT VALUES
NA

## NAMED GRANTS

### LSTA Grants
The Board of Library Commissioners invites applications for projects that, if successful, will make a significant long-term contribution to local, regional, or statewide library development. Successful proposals clearly describe a well-planned project that supports at least one of the Board of Library Commissioners' strategic issues for Idaho's libraries, is consistent with LSTA's priorities, and supports the 2020 Vision for Idaho's Library Future 2007–2020. LSTA priorities include

- library technology, connectivity, and services
- services for lifelong learning
- services to people having difficulty using libraries

**Past Grant Recipients:**

- Stanley Public Library, advocacy grant for teen gaming
- Ada Community, advocacy grant for a digital native summit
- Boise Basin Library District, advocacy grant for e-audiobooks
- Lewiston City Library, Access for All grant for seniors outreach–homebound program
- Kootenai Shoshone Library, Access for All grant for seniors outreach program

## REQUIREMENTS AND RESTRICTIONS
Applicants must contact the Commission for Libraries' consultant in their area to discuss the project. They must arrange project-related training in advance.

## APPLICATION PROCEDURES

**Submission Guidelines:** Application online. Applicants must submit a complete eligibility checklist with their grant application.

**Deadlines:** Draft application, October; final application, January. Digital applications are due two days earlier than paper applications.

**Decisions:** March

## CONTACT
Sonja Hudson
Phone: 208-639-4136
E-mail: sonja.hudson@libraries.idaho.gov

## GRANT-SPECIFIC WEBSITE
http://libraries.idaho.gov/page/lsta-library-services-technology

# Illinois State Library

## Headquarters

300 S. Second St.
Springfield, IL 62701
Phone: 217-785-5600
www.cyberdriveillinois.com/
departments/library/home.html

## Description

**Founded:** 1839

**Operating Locations:** Illinois

The Illinois State Library promotes excellence in information access and innovative services for government, libraries, and people.

## Grants Information

**GRANT TYPES**
Library improvement, library construction, literacy

**TYPICAL RECIPIENTS**
Illinois libraries

**GRANT VALUES**
NA

**NAMED GRANTS**

**PUBLIC LIBRARY PER CAPITA AND EQUALIZATION GRANTS**
Equalization grants were established

to help public libraries that have a low library tax base. In providing up to $4.25 per person served, these grants help ensure a minimum level of funding for library services. Per capita grants are authorized to help public libraries improve and increase library services to their service areas. A grant amount of up to $1.25 per person served is made available to local public libraries.

**Typical Recipients:** Public libraries that are members of the regional library system

**Grant Values:** Total Dollar Amount of Grants, $14,200,000; Number of Grants, 634 per capita grants and 10 equalization grants

**Past Grant Recipients:**
- Aurora Public Library (IL), per capita grant, $199,221
- Broadview Public Library District (IL), per capita grant, $10,005
- Cairo Public Library (IL), per capita grant and equalization grant, $4,397 and $336
- Mount Prospect Public Library (IL), per capita grant, $68,120
- Washington Park Public Library (IL), per capita grant and equalization grant, $7,194 and $11,201
- Yorkville Public Library (IL), per capita grant, $13,565

**Submission Guidelines:** Applicants may complete the application form online. Once the required fields have been filled, the form must be printed, signed, and returned to the Illinois State Library. Applicants must also include an updated County Clerk Page. Faxed applications will not be accepted.

**Deadlines:** October

**Decisions:** July

**Contact:** Phone: 217-524-8836; E-mail: mdowning@ilsos.net OR jurbanek@ilsos.net

**Grant-Specific Website:** www.cyberdriveillinois.com/departments/library/what_we_do/equalizationgrant.html

## ADULT LITERACY GRANT PROGRAM

The Adult Literacy Grant Program consists of three different categories. The Adult Volunteer Literacy Tutoring program utilizes volunteer tutors to provide one-on-one instruction for adults who want to improve their reading, math, writing, and language skills. The Family Literacy program equips parents and their children, together and separately, to improve their basic reading, math, writing, or language skills. The Workplace Skills Enhancement program provides on-site basic skills learning opportunities for working adults at their workplace.

**Typical Recipients:** Nonprofit agencies that provide direct adult literacy instruction using upaid, trained volunteer tutors to at least 50 students while recruiting and training at least 25 volunteers.

**Grant Values:** Number of Grants, 1 Adult Volunteer Literacy Tutoring grant per application, 5 Family Literacy grants per application, 12 Workplace Skills Enhancement grants per application; Highest Grant, $75,000 Adult Volunteer Literacy Tutoring grant (first year awards do not exceed $25,000), $35,000 Family Literacy grant, $15,000 Workplace Skills Enhancement grant. A combined grant award to any one grantee will not exceed $180,000.

**Submission Guidelines:** The online grant application is divided into four sections. All applications must include section 1. Section 2 should be completed if you are applying for an Adult Volunteer Literacy Tutoring grant; section 3 if you are applying for a Family Literacy grant; and section 4 if you are applying for a Workplace Skills Enhancement grant. Applications should be sent to the address below.

**Deadlines:** April

**Contact:** Illinois State Library Literacy Office, Rm. 422, Gwendolyn Brooks Bldg., 300 S. Second St., Springfield, IL 62701; Phone: 217-785-6921 or 800-665-5576, ext. 3

**Grant-Specific Website:**
www.cyberdriveillinois.com/
departments/library/who_we_are/
literacy/adultlit-grantapps.html

## LIVE AND LEARN CONSTRUCTION GRANT PROGRAM

This program has three categories:
(1) Remodeling for Accessibility, used
to remodel for compliance with the
Americans with Disabilities Act; (2)
Minigrants, used to remodel or refurbish
existing library facilities in libraries with
an income of less than $15 per capita;
and (3) New Construction/Remodeling,
used for new construction, remodeling,
or conversion of existing buildings.

**Typical Recipients:** Public libraries that
are full members of a regional library
system and permit intersystem reciprocal
borrowing. For minigrants, applicants
must also meet the eligibility criteria to
qualify for an Illinois Public Library Per
Capita and Equalization Aid Grant.

**Grant Values:** Total Dollar Amount of
Grants, $810,800; Number of Grants, 17;
Typical Range of Grants, Remodeling for
Accessibility, $2,500–$50,000, Minigrants,
$2,500–$25,000, New Construction/
Remodeling, $25,000–$125,000

**Past Grant Recipients:**
• Benton Public Library District (IL),
  $16,600
• Prairie Trails Public Library District
  (IL), $26,000
• Carmi Public Library (IL), $17,400

• Chester Public Library (IL), $25,000
• Coulterville Public Library (IL),
  $25,000
• Freeburg Area Library District (IL),
  $125,000

**Requirements and Restrictions:**
Remodeling for Accessibility and New
Construction/Remodeling grants require
local matching funds.

**Submission Guidelines:** Send a
statement of interest, including the
applying agency's name, the category of
construction grant for which the agency
is applying, and the estimated amount
of the grant request, via e-mail to Becky
Hunter at bhunter1@ilsos.net.

Completed grant applications must
be legibly postmarked or hand delivered
to the Illinois State Library, Gwendolyn
Brooks Bldg., 300 S. Second St., Rm.
410, Springfield, IL 62701 no later than
the application due date. Application
should include
• application form with verification of
  local matching funds attached
• preliminary drawings, including floor
  plan, site plan, and elevations as
  applicable
• a map of Illinois indicating the
  location of the library in the state
• a detailed map indicating the
  street location of the library and its
  relation to the surrounding area and
  community
• outline specifications of the work to
  be done

- library building program completed within the last two years (not required for Minigrants)
- subsurface soil analysis by a soil engineer (for new construction, additions, or projects involving the evacuation of soil)
- deed of ownership or proof of long-term (20 years) occupancy (not required for Minigrants)
- sign-off letter from the Illinois Historic Preservation Agency
- Special Flood Hazard Area documentation (for new construction, additions, or projects involving the evacuation of soil)
- environmental site assessment by licensed environmental/hazardous materials consultant (for new construction, additions, or projects involving the evacuation of soil)
- letter of acknowledgement from the regional library system director
- ADA self-evaluation (not required for new building construction)
- sign-off letter from Library Building Consultant (for projects over $150,000)

**Deadlines:** Statement of interest, December; completed grant application, February

**Decisions:** April

**Contact:** H. Neil Kelley; Phone: 217-782-1891; E-mail: nkelley@ilsos.net; OR Mark Shaffer; Phone: 217-524-4901; E-mail: mshaffer@ilsos.net

**Grant-Specific Website:** www.cyberdriveillinois.com/departments/library/what_we_do/constructgrant.html

**REQUIREMENTS AND RESTRICTIONS**
Applicants must be located in the state of Illinois.

**APPLICATION PROCEDURES**
Vary by grant

**CONTACT**
Varies by grant

**GRANT-SPECIFIC WEBSITE**
www.cyberdriveillinois.com/departments/library/what_we_do/

# Indiana State Library

## Headquarters

140 N. Senate Ave.
Indianapolis, IN 46204
Phone: 317-232-3675
www.in.gov/library/

## Description

**Founded:** 1825

**Operating Locations:** Indiana

The Indiana State Library is responsible for providing library services to the state government; providing for the individual citizens of the state those specialized library services not generally available in other libraries of the state; encouraging and supporting the development of the library profession; and strengthening services of all types of publicly and privately supported special, school, academic, and public libraries.

# Grants Information

## GRANT TYPES
LSTA funds

## TYPICAL RECIPIENTS
Indiana academic, public, and school libraries; cultural institutions and special libraries partnering with libraries; institutional libraries

## GRANT VALUES
NA

## NAMED GRANTS

### LSTA DIGITIZATION GRANT
The Indiana State Library offers LSTA subgrants to libraries in Indiana for the purpose of digitizing Indiana's historical records. Libraries should use these funds to digitize artifacts important to Indiana history and relevant to researchers today. Projects awarded grant funding must evidence the ability to produce at least one of the following outcomes: expanded access to unique cultural heritage artifacts of Indiana; increased knowledge about Indiana history among state residents, researchers, and students; increased awareness of Indiana memory among educators, researchers, and students. Projects given preference will have at least one of the following outcomes: digitization of a unique and important collection housed outside a library; digitization of collections which meet specifically identified needs of researchers or students; development of a partnership between libraries and outside cultural institutions.

**Typical Recipients:** Academic, public, and school libraries. In addition, cultural institutions and special libraries may partner with any of the libraries listed above to digitize unique historical documents that they house.

**Grant Values:** Total Dollar Amount of Grants, $150,000; Number of Grants, 8; Highest Grant, $20,000

**Past Grant Recipients:**

- Ball State University (IN), digital collection of aerial plat maps for Delaware County, Indiana, $24,000
- IUPUI (IN), digitization of Conner Prairie's traditional craft collection, $11,245
- Eckhart Public Library (IN), IHSBCA Newsletter and Manufacturer's Catalog Digital Preservation Project, $17,371

- Saint Mary's College (IN), digitization of William W. Dunkle's weekly newspaper collection, $4,000
- Butler University Libraries (IN), digitization project of Indiana ferns and orchids, $8,015
- Indiana University Purdue University Fort Wayne (IN), digitization of Native American collections in northeastern Indiana, $23,799

**Requirements and Restrictions:** Applicants must be located in the state of Indiana. All libraries must meet federal and state regulations to be eligible. Public libraries must meet library standards and both public and school libraries must meet CIPA requirements to be eligible for grant funds. Applicants may not purchase digital collection management software. A local cash match of 10 percent of the total requested amount is required. Individual equipment pieces costing $5,000 or more are subject to preapproval from the IMLS.

**Submission Guidelines:** Libraries are strongly encouraged to submit a project proposal form (available on the website) before completing a digitization grant application. The grant application consists of an application form and budget worksheet (available on the website). These documents must be submitted by BOTH hard copy and e-mail to be reviewed. Incomplete applications will not be reviewed. Mail

or hand deliver one signed original of your completed application materials to the address below. E-mail your completed application materials to the e-mail address below.

**Deadlines:** February

**Decisions:** March

**Contact:** LSTA Digitization Grant Application, Library Development Office, Rm. 413, Indiana State Library, 315 W. Ohio St., Indianapolis, IN 46202; Phone: 317-234-6550; Fax: 317-232-0002; E-mail: jclifton@library.in.gov

**Grant-Specific Website:** www.in.gov/library/3729.htm

## LSTA TECHNOLOGY GRANT

The Indiana State Library offers LSTA subgrants to help Indiana libraries provide their users with the new and improved technology necessary to meet their residents' ever-changing needs for library services and access to information. Projects awarded grant funding must evidence the ability to produce at least one of the following outcomes: increased effectiveness of telecommunications, technology, and resources used in the library; increased availability of up-to-date and reliable information; delivery of new and improved programs that meet Indiana residents' constantly changing needs for library services. Projects given preference will have at least one of the following outcomes: increased access to information for underserved urban and rural persons; increased computer and information literacy skills among digital immigrants; increased participation in statewide resource sharing; enhanced online presence of Indiana libraries.

**Typical Recipients:** Academic, public (including branches), school media, and special libraries. Preference is given to those that are active lenders to other libraries and those that have not received a technology grant in the past two years.

**Grant Values:** Total Dollar Amount of Grants, $225,000; Highest Grant, $10,000

**Past Grant Recipients:**

- Yorktown–Mt. Pleasant Township Public Library (IN), mobile computer lab upgrade, $6,455
- Greenwood Public Library (IN), wireless upgrade, $5,280
- Marion Public Library (IN), mini-laptop project, $6,311
- Morgan County Public Library (IN), improving patron access to resources, $6,512
- Waterloo Grant Township Public Library (IN), public assistance, $4,379
- Washington Carnegie Public Library (IN), technology additions, $2,006

**Requirements and Restrictions:** Applicants must be located in the state of Indiana. Libraries must comply with federal and state statutes and regulations and with the Children's Internet and Safety Protection Act (CIPA). Public libraries must meet Indiana Public Library Standards. Applicants must show they will provide a cash match equal to at least 10 percent of the awarded amount of LSTA funds.

**Submission Guidelines:** The grant application consists of an application form and budget worksheet (available on the website). These documents must be submitted by BOTH hard copy and e-mail to be reviewed. Incomplete applications will not be reviewed. Mail or hand deliver one signed original of your completed application materials to the address below. E-mail your completed application materials to the e-mail address below.

**Deadlines:** February

**Decisions:** March

**Contact:** LSTA Technology Grant Application, Library Development Office, Rm. 413, Indiana State Library, 315 W. Ohio St., Indianapolis, IN 46202; Phone: 317-234-6550; Fax: 317-232-0002; E-mail: jclifton@library.in.gov

**Grant-Specific Website:** www.in.gov/library/3729.htm

## LSTA INSTITUTIONAL LITERACY GRANT

The Indiana State Library offers grants to institutional libraries in Indiana for the primary purpose of facilitating improved literacy among the individuals they serve. Institutions should meet literacy goals at multiple educational levels (e.g., for new readers, for those preparing to enter the labor market, for those who speak a language other than English, etc.), and should request funds for library materials that meet the specific literacy needs of the populations they serve.

**Typical Recipients:** All 32 institutional libraries in Indiana. Applications will not be accepted from any academic, public, school, or other special library.

**Grant Values:** Highest Grant, $5,000

**Requirements and Restrictions:** A principal officer or superintendent must submit a letter along with the application materials detailing his or her involvement in ensuring the overall success of the project and cooperation of the fiscal office in completing all financial documents and reports and in a timely manner.

**Submission Guidelines:** Applications are available on the website. Mail or hand-deliver one original and seven copies of your completed application with duplexed pages to the address below.

**Deadlines:** March

**Decisions:** June

**Contact:** Special Services Consultant, Library Development Office, Rm. 413, Indiana State Library, 315 W. Ohio St., Indianapolis, IN 46202; Phone: 317-232-3719; E-mail: mwoodard@library.in.gov

**Grant-Specific Website:** www.in.gov/library/3373.htm

## LSTA INNOVATIVE LIBRARY TECHNOLOGY GRANT

The Indiana State Library offers federal funds for the purpose of developing innovative library technology projects with the potential for statewide impact. Projects awarded grant funding must evidence the ability to produce at least one of the following outcomes: increased effectiveness of telecommunications, technology, and resources used in the library; increased availability of up-to-date and reliable information; delivery of new and improved programs that anticipate and meet Indiana residents' constantly changing needs for library services. Projects evidencing the ability to produce at least one of the following desired outcomes are given preference: increased access to information for underserved urban and rural persons; increased computer and information literacy skills among digital immigrants; increased participation in statewide resource sharing; enhanced online presence of Indiana libraries.

**Typical Recipients:** Public, school, academic, and special libraries in Indiana

**Grant Values:** Highest Grant, $500,000

**Requirements and Restrictions:** A library may submit only one application for an innovative library technology subgrant. A local cash match equal to at least 10 percent of the requested amount of LSTA funds is required.

**Submission Guidelines:** The grant application consists of an application form and budget worksheet (available on the website). A copy of these documents must be submitted by BOTH hard copy and e-mail to be reviewed. Incomplete applications will not be reviewed. Mail or hand deliver one signed original of your completed application to the address below. E-mail your completed application materials to the e-mail address below.

**Deadlines:** The Innovative Library Technology Grant application deadline is open-ended. Applications will be reviewed upon submission based on the quality of the project, its relevance to desired outcomes, and its potential for statewide impact.

**Contact:** LSTA Innovative Library Technology Grant Application, Library Development Office, Rm. 413, Indiana State Library, 315 West Ohio Street, Indianapolis, IN 46202; Phone: 317-234-6550; E-mail: jclifton@library.in.gov

**Grant-Specific Website:** www.in.gov/library/3731.htm

## LSTA Information Access for the Unserved Grant

The Indiana State Library uses these grants to provide support for Indiana libraries making a concerted effort to extend their current service area or services such that unserved or underserved populations gain increased access to library services and electronic resources. Methods public libraries have used in the past to provide services for unserved populations include consolidation with annexation, annexing unserved areas, and creating outreach programs such as bookmobiles. Funds will be available for creating shared public access catalogs, purchasing technological equipment, or increasing networking capabilities.

**Typical Recipients:** Public libraries

**Grant Values:** The specific amount of assistance provided will be determined by the individual needs of libraries interested in this project.

**Submission Guidelines:** Contact the State Library.

**Deadlines:** Open-ended

**Contact:** Phone: 317-234-6550 or 317-232-3715; E-mail: jclifton@library.in.gov or jfields@library.in.gov

**Grant-Specific Website:** www.in.gov/library/3731.htm

**REQUIREMENTS AND RESTRICTIONS**
Vary by grant

**APPLICATION PROCEDURES**
Vary by grant

**CONTACT**
Varies by grant

**GRANT-SPECIFIC WEBSITE**
Varies by grant

# Institute of Museum and Library Services (IMLS)

## Headquarters

1800 M St. NW, 9th fl.
Washington, DC 20036
Phone: 202-653-4657
www.imls.gov/index.shtm

## Description

**Founded:** 1996

**Operating Locations:** District of Columbia

The Institute of Museum and Library Services is the primary source of federal support for the nation's 122,000 libraries and 17,500 museums. The institute's mission is to create strong libraries and museums that connect people to information and ideas. The institute works at the national level and in coordination with state and local organizations to sustain heritage, culture, and knowledge; enhance learning and innovation; and support professional development.

## Financial Summary

Total Giving: $231,235,000

## Grants Information

**GRANT TYPES**
Conservation, collection management, community engagement, digital collections/tools, informal learning, partnerships, professional development/ continuing education, public programs, research, awards, formal education, population-based grants to state library administrative agencies

**TYPICAL RECIPIENTS**
Each U.S. state, public or private nonprofit institutions of higher education, universities, individual libraries, individual museums and organizations, professional associations, state library administrative agencies, historical societies, federally recognized Native American tribes, organizations supporting Native American tribes by strengthening museum services

## GRANT VALUES

Total Dollar Amount of Grants:
$231,235,000

Number of Grants: 613

Average Grant: $377,218

Highest Grant: $10,000,000

Lowest Grant: $5,000

## NAMED GRANTS

### NATIVE AMERICAN LIBRARY SERVICES ENHANCEMENT GRANTS

Native American Library Services Enhancement Grants are competitive grants to support activities to advance the applicant library's operations to new levels of service for activities specifically identified in the Library Services and Technology Act. These competitive grants are intended to encourage the implementation of both mainstream and innovative library practices.

**Typical Recipients:** Indian tribes, Alaska Native villages, regional corporations, village corporations

**Grant Values:** Highest Grant, $150,000

**Requirements and Restrictions:** Tribes and Alaska Native villages are eligible to apply for the Enhancement Grant only if they have applied for a Native American Library Services Basic Grant in the same fiscal year. Grant funds may not be used for construction, contributions to endowment funds, social activities, ceremonies, entertainment, or pre-grant costs. All listed expenses, including all cost sharing, must be incurred during the grant period. IMLS and government-wide administrative, cost, and audit rules and requirements apply, including appropriate OMB Circulars and regulations.

**Submission Guidelines:** Applications must be submitted through the online system at www.grants.gov/applicants/apply_for_grants.jsp. Mailed applications will not be accepted. Applications must be submitted by an authorized organizational representative of an eligible Indian tribe.

**Deadlines:** May

**Contact:** *For questions regarding the grant program*: Phone: 202-653-4665; *for assistance submitting your application*: Phone: 800-518-4726; E-mail: support@grants.gov

**Grant-Specific Website:** www.imls.gov/applicants/grants/nativeEnhance.shtm

### NATIVE AMERICAN LIBRARY SERVICES BASIC GRANT

Native American Library Services Basic Grants are noncompetitive grants available to support existing library operations and to maintain core library services. The Education/Assessment Option is supplemental to the Basic Grant and provides funding for library staff to attend continuing education courses and training workshops on- or off-site, to attend or give presentations at conferences related to library services, and to hire a consultant for an on-site professional library assessment.

**Typical Recipients:** Indian tribes, Alaska Native villages, regional corporations, village corporations

**Grant Values:** Average Grant, $6,000 for the Basic Grant and $1,000 for the Education/Assessment Option

**Requirements and Restrictions:** Grant funds may not be used for construction, contributions to endowment funds, social activities, ceremonies, entertainment, pre-grant costs, or indirect costs. IMLS and government-wide administrative, cost, and audit rules and requirements apply, including appropriate OMB Circulars. An Indian tribe may receive only one Basic Grant in a fiscal year.

**Submission Guidelines:** Applications must be submitted through the online system at www.grants.gov/applicants/ apply_for_grants.jsp. Mailed applications will not be accepted. Applications must be submitted by an authorized organizational representative of an eligible Indian tribe. Required components of the application include

- Application for Federal Domestic Assistance/Short Organizational Form
- Program Information Sheet
- Project Budget for Basic Grant
- Project Budget for Education/ Assessment Option
- long-range plan

**Deadlines:** March

**Contact:** *For questions regarding the grant program*: Phone: 202-653-4665; *for assistance submitting your application*: Phone: 800-518-4726; E-mail: support@ grants.gov

**Grant-Specific Website:** www.imls.gov/ applicants/grants/nativeAmerican.shtm

## SWIM: REGIONAL COLLABORATIVE LIBRARY EDUCATIONAL PROJECT

The IMLS SWIM: Regional Collaborative Library Educational Project gives scholarships to 50 students from South Dakota, Wyoming, Idaho, and Montana to earn a master's degree in library and information science from the University of North Texas's distance education program or to earn a school library media endorsement from distance programs at Black Hills State University, Montana State University, or the University of Montana.

**Requirements and Restrictions:** Applicant must be a resident of Idaho, Montana, South Dakota, or Wyoming; have a BA/BS degree (a teaching degree is required for the endorsement program); not be currently enrolled or have been previously enrolled in an MLIS or endorsement program; apply and be accepted to one of the stipulated MLIS distance programs; complete the program in accordance with the agreement; agree to work in an Idaho,

Montana, South Dakota, or Wyoming academic, public, school, special, or tribal library in a professional librarian position for 24 months after obtaining degree or endorsement.

**Submission Guidelines:** Required components of the application include

- application form
- essay on rural library services
- résumé
- three letters of support
- community involvement statement
- signed agreement
- essay on purpose and goals

**Deadlines:** March

**Contact:** Sue Jackson, Library Development Consultant; Phone: 406-444-5350; E-mail: sujackson@mt.gov

**Grant-Specific Website:** www.imls.gov/news/2009/061709b_list.shtm#MT

**PAST GRANT RECIPIENTS**
*Library or School Related*
- Alabama Public Library Service (AL), grants to state library agencies, $2,545,491
- University of Illinois at Urbana-Champaign (IL), Laura Bush 21st Century Librarian Program, $499,895
- University of Colorado, Denver (CO), Laura Bush 21st Century Librarian Program, $99,981
- Minnesota Historical Society (MN), national leadership grants for libraries, $243,363

- Cheyenne-Arapaho Tribes of Oklahoma (OK), Native American library services, $6,000
- ALU LIKE, Inc. (HI), Native American library services, $510,500

*General*
- New England Aquarium (MA), 21st Century Museum Professionals, $228,825
- Balboa Park Cultural Partnership (CA), 21st Century Museum Professionals, $500,000
- Indiana Historical Society (IN), Connecting to Collections Statewide Planning Grants, $39,983
- Chester County Historical Society (PA), conservation project support—survey of collections, $25,025
- River Road African American Museum (LA), Museum Grants for African American History and Culture, $114,920
- Children's Discovery Museum (IL), Museums for America—Engaging Communities, $147,267

**REQUIREMENTS AND RESTRICTIONS**
Applicant must be located in one of the 50 states of the United States, the District of Columbia, the Commonwealth of Puerto Rico, Guam, American Samoa, the Virgin Islands, the Commonwealth of the Northern Mariana Islands, the Republic of the Marshall Islands, the Federated States of Micronesia, or the Republic of Palau.

Each grant program has specific eligibility requirements; there is a general eligibility criteria for museums, libraries, and tribal organizations, but please note that additional organizations may be eligible for grants under certain programs. Additionally, ineligible organizations may still be able to participate in grant programs through partnerships with eligible organizations.

**APPLICATION PROCEDURES**
Vary by grant

**CONTACT**
E-mail: imlsinfo@imls.gov

**GRANT-SPECIFIC WEBSITE**
www.imls.gov/applicants/
http://grants.gov

# International Federation of Library Associations and Institutions (IFLA)

## Headquarters

Prins Willem-Alexanderhof 5
2595 BE
The Hague, Netherlands
Phone: 31-70-3140884
E-mail: ifla@ifla.org

## Description

**Founded:** 1927

**Operating Locations:** The Netherlands, South Africa, Singapore, Brazil

The International Federation of Library Associations and Institutions (IFLA) and libraries and information services share the common vision of an Information Society for all. That vision promotes an inclusive society in which everyone will be able to find, create, access, use, and share information and knowledge. To enable access to information by all peoples, ILFA is committed to the fundamental human rights to know, learn, and communicate without restriction. It opposes censorship and supports balance and fairness in intellectual property regulation. IFLA is also vitally concerned with promoting multilingual content, cultural diversity, and the special needs of indigenous peoples, minorities, and those with disabilities. IFLA, working with its members, the profession, and other partners, will advance the position of libraries and information services and their capacity to contribute to the development of individuals and communities through access to information and culture.

## Grants Information

**GRANT TYPES**
Conference attendance

## TYPICAL RECIPIENTS

Librarians from Arab countries

## GRANT VALUES

Total Dollar Amount of Grants: $1,900
Number of Grants: 1

## NAMED GRANTS

### DR. SHAWKY SALEM CONFERENCE GRANT (SSCG)

The Dr. Shawky Salem Conference Grant (SSCG) is an annual grant established by Dr. Shawky Salem and IFLA. The aim of the grant is to enable one expert in library and information sciences from the Arab countries (AC) to attend the IFLA Annual Conference. The winner of the grant will write a report on the conference and distribute copies to IFLA, the grantee's organization, and Dr. Salem. The grant meets, up to a maximum of US$1,900, the cost of travel (economy class air transportation) to and from the host country of the conference, registration, hotel costs, and a per diem allowance.

## REQUIREMENTS AND RESTRICTIONS

Candidates should be attending an IFLA conference for the first time, be an Arab national, not exceed 45 years of age, have experience of at least five years in an LIS profession or teaching, and have the approval of his or her organization. Winning persons/organizations may not apply a second time.

## APPLICATION PROCEDURES

**Deadlines:** February 1

**Decisions:** April 1

## CONTACT

Jennefer Nicholson, Secretary General
Phone: +31-70-3834827
E-mail: ifla@ifla.org

## GRANT-SPECIFIC WEBSITE

www.ifla.org/en/funds-grants-awards/
    SSCG

# State Library of Iowa

## Headquarters

1112 E. Grand Ave.
Des Moines, IA 50319
Phone: 515-281-4105
www.statelibraryofiowa.org

## Description

**Founded:** NA

**Operating Locations:** Iowa

The main roles of the State Library are improving library services in Iowa and delivering specialized information services to state government and to Iowans. Their mission is to advocate for Iowa libraries and to promote excellence and innovation in library services, in order to provide statewide access to information for all Iowans.

# Grants Information

## GRANT TYPES
LSTA funds

## TYPICAL RECIPIENTS
Iowa libraries

## GRANT VALUES
Highest Grant: $3,000

## NAMED GRANTS

### LSTA SPACE PLANNING GRANT
LSTA Space Planning Grants allow librarians to get professional advice from impartial consultants who provide guidance and recommendations to library staff about use of existing space or preparing for a building project. Grants may be requested for the following services:
- space needs assessment of current facility
- library building process overview, including staff and board training on the process of planning for a new library facility
- evaluation of library sites
- building program review and building program statement
- hiring an architect
- ADA compliance—evaluation and planning
- architectural drawing review
- funding consultation

## PAST GRANT RECIPIENTS
- Algona Library (IA), space needs assessment, $3,000
- Asbury Library (IA), needs assessment, $3,000
- Bellevue Library (IA), space utilization study, $3,000
- Cedar Rapids Library (IA), space utilization study, $1,296
- Donnellson Library (IA), space needs assessment, $3,000
- Dubuque (IA), needs assessment, $3,000

## REQUIREMENTS AND RESTRICTIONS
Applicants must be located in the state of Iowa. LSTA funds for library building consultation may not be used for the following: architect or engineer services; equipment, installation, or implementation; fund-raising; a summary of project activities or outcomes; or to evaluate the impact of the project on customer service. Applicant should contact a library building consultant and must negotiate fees with the consultant prior to submitting the grant application. Only qualified building consultants with prior library building experience are eligible.

## APPLICATION PROCEDURES
**Submission Guidelines:** Complete the application online and submit it to the address below.

**CONTACT**
East Central Library Services
222 Third St. SE, Suite 402
Cedar Rapids, IA 52401
Phone: 319-365-0521
E-mail: llau@ecls.lib.ia.us

**GRANT-SPECIFIC WEBSITE**
www.statelibraryofiowa.org/ld/a-b/lib-
build/space

# Kansas Library Association

## Headquarters

1020 SW Washburn Ave.
Topeka, KS 66604
Phone: 785-580-4518
http://kslibassoc.org/home/

## Description

**Founded:** 1900

**Operating Locations:** Kansas

The Kansas Library Association is
the common bond, public voice, and
collective power for the Kansas library
community.

## Grants Information

**GRANT TYPES**
Professional development/continuing
education

**TYPICAL RECIPIENTS**
Kansas librarians

**GRANT VALUES**
Typical Range of Grants: $200–$500

**NAMED GRANTS**

**PROFESSIONAL DEVELOPMENT/
CONTINUING EDUCATION GRANT**
The Continuing Education Committee
of the Kansas Library Association offers
grant support for librarians to pursue
continuing education opportunities.
Applicants who have been KLA members
less than 12 months qualify for a
maximum grant of $200; for those who
have been members longer than 12
months, the maximum grant is $500.

**REQUIREMENTS AND RESTRICTIONS**
Applicants must be current members
of the Kansas Library Association.
The funded activity should support
the performance of the applicant's
work-related duties. Eligible expenses
include costs for items such as tuition
for classes not leading to a degree or
certification, registration, lodging, food,
transportation, substitute help, and child
care. Car mileage should be calculated at
the current IRS-defined rate per mile.

**APPLICATION PROCEDURES**
**Submission Guidelines:** Application
online. Required attachments include

- a brief description of the program
  (if possible, include printed material

---

or URL describing the program or activity)
- a description of how this activity will support your work-related duties
- a budget of your anticipated expenses, describing your financial need for the funds and listing other sources from which you have asked for or received funds

Mail complete application to the address below.

**CONTACT**
Kansas Library Association
1020 SW Washburn Ave.
Topeka, KS 66604
Attn: CE Committee
Phone: 785-580-4518
E-mail: kansaslibraryassociation@yahoo.com

**GRANT-SPECIFIC WEBSITE**
http://kslibassoc.org/conedcommittee.htm

# Ezra Jack Keats Foundation

## Headquarters

450 14th St.
Brooklyn, NY 11215
E-mail: foundation@ezra-jack-keats.org
www.ezra-jack-keats.org/programs/minigrantapp.pdf

## Description

**Founded:** 1964

**Operating Locations:** New York

**Foundation Information:** Private foundation established by Ezra Jack Keats. The Ezra Jack Keats Foundation is known for its pioneering support of bookmaking programs, portrait projects, book festivals, libraries, and mural projects throughout the United States.

## Grants Information

**GRANT TYPES**
Programs, events

**TYPICAL RECIPIENTS**
Public schools and public libraries

**GRANT VALUES**
Average Grant: $500

**PAST GRANT RECIPIENTS**
NA

**REQUIREMENTS AND RESTRICTIONS**
Funds will not be granted for general operating costs; administrative costs; transportation of the audience; or purchase of books, tapes, software, or equipment unrelated to a specific program. Applications cannot be accepted if they are for programs in any type of private or parochial school

or library; if they are for duplicated programs; if they are e-mailed; if they are sent registered mail; or if they require a signature on delivery.

**APPLICATION PROCEDURES**
**Submission Guidelines:** Application online

**Deadlines:** March 15

**Decisions:** Decisions will be made by mid-May of each year, and all applicants will be notified of decisions.

**CONTACT**
Ezra Jack Keats Minigrant Program
E-mail: foundation@ezra-jack-keats.org

**GRANT-SPECIFIC WEBSITE**
www.ezra-jack-keats.org/index.
    php?option=com_content&view=ar
    ticle&id=103&Itemid=65

# Kentucky Department for Libraries and Archives (KDLA)

## Headquarters

PO Box 537
300 Coffee Tree Rd.
Frankfort, KY 40602-0537
Phone: 502-564-8300
http://kdla.ky.gov

## Description

**Founded:** NA

**Operating Locations:** Kentucky

The mission of the Kentucky Department for Libraries and Archives (KDLA) is to support and promote access to library services and to ensure that documentation of government activities is created, preserved, and made available for public use.

## Grants Information

**GRANT TYPES**
LSTA funds, scholarship

**TYPICAL RECIPIENTS**
Kentucky libraries, librarians, and full-time employees of Kentucky libraries

**GRANT VALUES**
NA

**NAMED GRANTS**

**GRADUATE LIBRARY SCHOOL TUITION REIMBURSEMENT**
KDLA encourages the pursuit of graduate library science degrees by full-time public library staff by offering tuition reimbursement for the successful completion of classes from ALA-accredited graduate programs.

**Grant Values:** Average Grant, 100 percent reimbursement for in-state tuition (This amount may be prorated to a lesser percentage, and libraries may be limited in the number of applicants approved in relation to available funds and the number of applications received.)

**Requirements and Restrictions:** Applicant must be a full-time employee at a Kentucky public library and working a minimum of 100 hours a month. Applicant must successfully complete coursework from an in-state or out-of-state university with an accredited library science program and earn at least an A or a B final grade. At the conclusion of the coursework, the applicant must submit a final report, a request for payment form, an official proof of tuition payment form, and a final grade report. Applicant must be properly certified by the Kentucky State Board for the Certification of Librarians.

**Submission Guidelines:** Applicant completes the application and has the library director or board president/designee sign as well (a library director cannot sign as both student and supervisor). Application must include a letter of recommendation from the student's supervisor, the library director, or board president/designee. For subsequent semester applications during the same federal fiscal year (fall-spring school year), a second letter of recommendation will be required only if the student has a new supervisor.

Completed application with original signatures must be postmarked by indicated deadline dates and mailed to the address below. Faxed copies will not be accepted.

**Deadlines:** Application and letter of recommendation are due no later than 30 days after the first day of the class. The final report and payment request for tuition reimbursement are due no later than 60 days after the last day of a fall or spring semester class.

**Contact:** Kentucky Department for Libraries and Archives, PO Box 537, 300 Coffee Tree Rd., Frankfort, KY 40602-0537; Phone: 502-564-8300, ext. 219; E-mail: beth.milburn@ky.gov

**Grant-Specific Website:** http://kdla. ky.gov/librarians/funding/Pages/LibrarySchoolGrants.aspx

### LSTA LIBRARY ASSISTIVE TECHNOLOGY GRANT

The LSTA Library Assistive Technology Grant provides funding to public libraries for technologies that assist patrons with special needs. A library assistive technology project uses technology solutions to address a service problem encountered by library patrons with special needs, introduce or expand library services to currently unserved or underserved populations, or improve access to information and library services for physically challenged library patrons.

**Grant Values:** Typical Range of Grants, $500–$5,000

**Requirements and Restrictions:** Applicants must be located in the state of Kentucky.

**Deadlines:** June

**Contact:** Nicole Bryan; Phone: 502-564-8300, ext. 304; E-mail: nicole.bryan@ky.gov

**Grant-Specific Website:** http://kdla.ky.gov/librarians/funding/Pages/LSTAGrantApplications.aspx

## LSTA PUBLIC LIBRARY AUTOMATION GRANT

The LSTA Public Library Automation Grant provides funding to assist libraries in automating their systems. These grants are divided into two categories: academic and public. A library automation project addresses the need for modern library services, provides patrons with improved access to library collections, expands patron access to multiple information resources, and improves the efficiency of library staff.

**Grant Values:** Typical Range of Grants, $500–$25,000

**Requirements and Restrictions:** Applicants must be located in the state of Kentucky. All Kentucky full-service academic libraries associated with recognized institutions of higher education are eligible to apply. High

school, middle school, and elementary school libraries are not eligible.

**Deadlines:** June

**Contact:** Nicole Bryan; Phone: 502-564-8300, ext. 304; E-mail: nicole.bryan@ky.gov

**Grant-Specific Website:** http://kdla.ky.gov/librarians/funding/Pages/LSTAGrantApplications.aspx

## LSTA LIBRARY EQUIPMENT GRANT

The LSTA Library Equipment Grant provides funding to public libraries for the purchase of equipment that will provide patrons with improved access to library and information resources. A library equipment project addresses the need to replace outdated library equipment, provides patrons with improved access to library or Internet resources, expands patron access to multiple information resources, and improves the efficiency of library staff.

**Grant Values:** Typical Range of Grants, $1,000–$10,000

**Requirements and Restrictions:** Applicants must be located in the state of Kentucky. Private, institutional, academic libraries and high school, middle school, and elementary school libraries are not eligible to apply.

**Deadlines:** June

**Contact:** Nicole Bryan; Phone: 502-564-8300, ext. 304; E-mail: nicole.bryan@ky.gov

**Grant-Specific Website:** http://kdla. ky.gov/librarians/funding/Pages/ LSTAGrantApplications.aspx

## LSTA LIBRARY INNOVATION GRANT

The LSTA Library Innovation Grant provides funding to public libraries for innovative and creative technological solutions to service problems in libraries. A library innovation project uses technology solutions to address patron service problems in new and creative ways, provide new or enhanced library services, reach existing customers in nontraditional ways, or improve services to currently underserved or unserved populations.

**Grant Values:** Typical Range of Grants, $500–$20,000

**Requirements and Restrictions:** Applicants must be located in the state of Kentucky.

**Deadlines:** June

**Contact:** Nicole Bryan; Phone: 502-564-8300, ext. 304; E-mail: nicole.bryan@ ky.gov

**Grant-Specific Website:** http://kdla. ky.gov/librarians/funding/Pages/ LSTAGrantApplications.aspx

## LSTA PUBLIC LIBRARY PROGRAMMING GRANT

The LSTA Public Library Programming Grant provides funding to public libraries to enhance, expand, or provide programming that will meet the specific needs of their community. A well planned and executed library program matches the appropriateness of a subject to the target audience; addresses a need of the target audience; promotes appreciation of books and reading; introduces a range of library services; enhances the use of the library's collection; improves access to information for specific audiences; encourages positive community cooperation and support; and results in changes in attitudes, behaviors, knowledge, or skill levels of program participants.

**Grant Values:** Typical Range of Grants, $2,000–$15,000

**Requirements and Restrictions:** Applicants must be located in the state of Kentucky. Applicant must be a legally established public library, have a library director who is properly certified by the Kentucky Board for Certification of Librarians, and provide free countywide library services.

**Submission Guidelines:** Applicant libraries may submit up to two grant proposals.

**Deadlines:** June

**Contact:** Nicole Bryan; Phone: 502-564-8300, ext. 304; E-mail: nicole.bryan@ky.gov

**Grant-Specific Website:** http://kdla. ky.gov/librarians/funding/Pages/ LSTAGrantApplications.aspx

## LOCAL RECORDS GRANT PROGRAM

The Local Records Grant Program provides funds to local government agencies to improve their recordkeeping practices and to preserve the information as a strategic resource.

**Grant Values:** Total Dollar Amount of Grants, $406,604; Number of Grants, 16

**Contact:** Sunnye Smith; Phone: 502-564-8300, ext. 257; E-mail: sunnye.smith@ky.gov

**Grant-Specific Website:** http://kdla.ky.gov/records/recmgmtservices/Pages/LocalGovernmentRecordsServices.aspx

### REQUIREMENTS AND RESTRICTIONS

Vary by grant

### APPLICATION PROCEDURES

**Submission Guidelines:** For LSTA grants, a proposal for grant projects must be made on the application form provided by KDLA. Altered forms will not be accepted. The original application with original signatures should be mailed to KDLA. Faxed copies are not acceptable. Applicant libraries may submit one grant proposal in each category unless otherwise noted above.

### CONTACT

Varies by grant

### GRANT-SPECIFIC WEBSITE

Varies by grant

# Knapp Foundation

## Headquarters

1103 S. Talbot St.
St. Michaels, MD 21663
Phone: 410-745-5660

## Description

**Founded:** 1932

**Operating Locations:** Maryland

**Foundation Information:** Private foundation established by Cleon T. Knapp

## Financial Summary

Assets: $17,216,477
Total Giving: $274,100

## Grants Information

### GRANT TYPES

General support

### TYPICAL RECIPIENTS

Arts and humanities, civic affairs, education, environment, health, science, social services

### GRANT VALUES

Total Dollar Amount of Grants: $274,100
Number of Grants: 19

Average Grant: $5,000
Highest Grant: $45,000
Lowest Grant: $4,100
Typical Range of Grants: $5,000–$10,000

## PAST GRANT RECIPIENTS

*Library or School Related*
- American Foundation for the Blind (NY), annual contributions to library collections, $10,000
- Recording for the Blind and Dyslexic (NJ), library education materials, $10,000
- Randolph-Macon College (VA), equipment acquisitions, $24,000
- Anderson University (SC), computer acquisitions, $11,000
- Clemson University (SC), equipment acquisitions, $45,000

*General*
- Boys Club of New York (NY), acquisition of Project Read materials, $5,000
- National Wildlife Federation (VT), equipment acquisitions, $5,000
- Humane Society of Dorchester County (MD), equipment acquisitions, $5,000
- North Carolina Aquarium Society (NC), equipment acquisitions, $5,000

## REQUIREMENTS AND RESTRICTIONS
NA

## APPLICATION PROCEDURES
**Submission Guidelines:** Send a detailed letter.

**CONTACT**
Antoinette P. Vojvoda
Phone: 410-745-5660

**GRANT-SPECIFIC WEBSITE**
NA

# John S. and James L. Knight Foundation

## Headquarters

200 S. Biscayne Blvd., Suite 3300
Miami, FL 33131
Phone: 305-908-2600
www.knightfoundation.org

## Description

**Founded:** 1950

**Operating Locations:** Florida

**Foundation Information:** Private foundation established by John S. and James L. Knight

## Financial Summary

Assets: $1,806,388,618
Gifts Received: $80,000
Total Giving: $116,206,415

# Grants Information

## GRANT TYPES
Capital, general support, multiyear continuing support, endowment, operating support

## TYPICAL RECIPIENTS
Arts and humanities, civic affairs, education, environment, health, international, science, social services

## GRANT VALUES
Total Dollar Amount of Grants:
$116,206,415

## PAST GRANT RECIPIENTS

*Library or School Related*
- San Jose Public Library Foundation (CA), community programs, $246,420
- The Free Public Library of Philadelphia (PA), growth of the Philadelphia Book Festival, $100,000
- Duluth Public Library (MN), community programs, $160,000
- Allen County Public Library (IN), community programs, $135,000
- Harrison County Library System (MS), community programs, $160,000
- University of Maryland (MD), multimedia, digital learning center, $375,000
- Colby College (ME), program to improve news literacy of liberal arts students, $246,612

*General*
- Fort Wayne Museum of Art (IN), funding to strengthen the museum's collections and library, $500,000
- Opportunity Project Learning Center (KS), funding for early learning centers in Wichita and to provide potential model for statewide pre-kindergarten program, $485,000
- Pro-Literacy Detroit (MI), funding to connect segment of Detroit workforce to job opportunities through support of pilot project using Internet-based literacy programs, $200,000
- Salvation Army (KY), literacy program for children ages 3–8 to become proficient in reading by grade 3, $100,000
- Tides Center (CA), news literacy project, $187,500

## REQUIREMENTS AND RESTRICTIONS
Applicants must be tax exempt under section 501(c)(3) of the Internal Revenue code.

## APPLICATION PROCEDURES

**Submission Guidelines:** Letter of inquiry online. Application should include

- the impact of the project
- how it was identified
- why the time is right for the project
- other partners or funders involved in the project

- how success will be measured
- how applicant is qualified to implement project
- organizational and financial capacity to implement project, including any business plan
- how project will be sustained beyond Knight Foundation funding

**CONTACT**

Phone: 305-908-2600

E-mail: web@knightfoundation.org

**GRANT-SPECIFIC WEBSITE**

www.knightfoundation.org/apply/

# Library Leadership and Management Association (LLAMA)

## Headquarters

50 E. Huron St.
Chicago, IL 60611
Phone: 800-545-2433, ext. 5032
www.ala.org/llama/

## Description

**Founded:** 1957

**Operating Locations:** Illinois

The mission of the Library Leadership and Management Association (LLAMA), a division of the American Library Association, is to encourage and nurture current and future library leaders, and to develop and promote outstanding leadership and management practices. Since its establishment in 1957, LLAMA has been a powerful catalyst in the development of leadership in the library and information science field. Attuned to ever-changing technological, economic, political, and cultural conditions, LLAMA equips library professionals with dynamic tools for building vibrant library services and successful careers. Highlighting all aspects of library management, LLAMA's sections (special interest groups) offer not only opportunities to connect with people of similar interests, but also to exchange ideas, collaborate on projects, publish research, mentor future leaders, and hone leadership and managerial skills.

## Grants Information

**GRANT TYPES**

Library marketing, conference attendance

**TYPICAL RECIPIENTS**

Individual libraries

**GRANT VALUES**

Total Dollar Amount of Grants: $6,000
Number of Grants: 2
Average Grant: $3,000
Highest Grant: $5,000
Lowest Grant: $1,000

## NAMED GRANTS

### JOHN COTTON DANA AWARD

The John Cotton Dana Award, sponsored by H. W. Wilson, honors outstanding library public relations, whether a summer reading program, a yearlong centennial celebration, fund-raising for a new college library, an awareness campaign, or an innovative partnership in the community. In recognition of their achievement, John Cotton Dana Award winners receive a cash development grant of $5,000 from the H. W. Wilson Foundation.

**Requirements and Restrictions:** Strategic library communication campaigns may be submitted by any library, Friends group, consulting agency, or service provider, excluding libraries represented by the JCD Committee members. All sizes and types of libraries-and all budget levels-are encouraged to enter. International entries are welcome.

**Submission Guidelines:** Application online

**Deadlines:** December

**Contact:** John Cotton Dana Library PR Awards, ALA/LLAMA, 50 E. Huron St., Chicago, IL 60611; Phone: 800-545-2433, ext. 5036; E-mail: freuland@ala.org

**Grant-Specific Website:** www.hwwilson.com/jcdawards/nw_jcd.htm

### LLAMA/YBP STUDENT WRITING AND DEVELOPMENT AWARD

The LLAMA/YBP Student Writing and Development Award is given to honor the best article on a topic in the area of library leadership and management written by a student enrolled in a library and information studies graduate program. The purpose of this award is to enhance the professional development of students of library and information studies through publication of the winning article in Library Leadership and Management, the LLAMA magazine, and enabling the award recipient to attend the ALA Annual Conference. The award winner will receive a travel grant of up to $1,000, funded by YBP, Inc., to be used to attend the ALA Annual Conference, where he or she will be recognized at the LLAMA President's Program, the first meeting of the LLAMA Board of Directors, and have the opportunity to attend other conference programs.

**Requirements and Restrictions:** At the time the paper is submitted, the applicant must be currently enrolled in an ALA-accredited program of library and information studies at the master's or Ph.D. level, be a current student member of ALA and LLAMA, and submit an original manuscript according to the guidelines and criteria outlined on the website.

**Submission Guidelines:** Application online

**REQUIREMENTS AND RESTRICTIONS**
Vary by grant

**APPLICATION PROCEDURES**
Vary by grant

**CONTACT**
Fred Reuland
Phone: 800-545-2433, ext. 5032,
     or 312-280-5032
Fax: 312-280-5033
E-mail: freuland@ala.org

**GRANT-SPECIFIC WEBSITE**
www.ala.org/ala/mgrps/divs/llama/
     awards/index.cfm

# The Libri Foundation

## Headquarters

PO Box 10246
Eugene, OR 97440-2246
Phone: 541-747-9655
www.librifoundation.org

## Description

**Founded:** 1989

**Operating Locations:** Oregon

**Foundation Information:** The Libri
Foundation was established in 1989
for the sole purpose of helping rural
libraries acquire new, high-quality,
hardcover children's books they could
not otherwise afford to buy.

## Financial Summary

Assets: $408,139
Gifts Received: $352,361
Total Giving: $283,018

## Grants Information

**GRANT TYPES**
Books for children, disaster relief

**TYPICAL RECIPIENTS**
U.S. libraries serving small, rural
populations

**GRANT VALUES**
NA

**NAMED GRANTS**

**BOOKS FOR CHILDREN PROGRAM**
Since October 1990, the Libri
Foundation has donated more than
$3,500,000 worth of new children's
books to more than 2,600 libraries
in 49 states, including Alaska and
Hawaii. The foundation works with
the library's Friends of the Library or
other local organizations in order to
encourage and reward local support of
libraries. Friends or other local sponsors
contribute between $50 and $350, which
the foundation matches two to one.

Thus, a library can receive up to $1,050 worth of new, high-quality, hardcover children's books.

**Requirements and Restrictions:** Only libraries within the United States are eligible to apply. County libraries should serve a population under 16,000 and town libraries should serve a population under 10,000 (usually under 5,000). Libraries should be in a rural area, have a limited operating budget, and have an active children's department. Rural is usually considered to be at least 30 miles from a city with a population over 40,000. The average total operating budget of a Books for Children grant recipient is less than $40,000.

**Submission Guidelines:** Application online

**Grant-Specific Website:** www.librifoundation.org/apps.html

### DISASTER RELIEF GRANT

The Libri Foundation offers a limited number of special nonmatching Books for Children grants to libraries serving rural communities affected by hurricanes, floods, or other natural disasters. Libraries receiving these grants will be able to select $700 worth of new, high-quality, hardcover children's books from the foundation's 700-plus-title booklist. No local matching funds are required. Only libraries within the United States are eligible to apply.

**Requirements and Restrictions:** Only libraries within the United States are eligible to apply. County libraries should serve a population under 16,000 and town libraries should serve a population under 10,000 (usually under 5,000). Libraries should be in a rural area, have a limited operating budget, and have an active children's department. Rural is usually considered to be at least 30 miles from a city with a population over 40,000.

**Submission Guidelines:** Application packets for these special grants may be requested by mail, telephone, fax, or e-mail at the contact address below.

**Grant-Specific Website:** www.librifoundation.org/relief.html

### REQUIREMENTS AND RESTRICTIONS
Vary by grant

### APPLICATION PROCEDURES
**Deadlines:** January and May

### CONTACT
Barbara J. McKillip, President
The Libri Foundation
PO Box 10246
Eugene, OR 97440-2246
Phone: 541-747-9655
Fax: 541-747-4348
E-mail: libri@librifoundation.org

### GRANT-SPECIFIC WEBSITE
Varies by grant

# State Library of Louisiana

## Headquarters

701 N. Fourth St.
Baton Rouge, LA 70802
Phone: 225-342-4923
www.state.lib.la.us

## Description

**Founded:** 1920

**Operating Locations:** Louisiana

The mission of the State Library of Louisiana is to build an informed, literate, and democratic society by ensuring access to informational, cultural, and recreational resources, especially those resources unique to Louisiana.

## Grants Information

**GRANT TYPES**
Library support

**TYPICAL RECIPIENTS**
Louisiana public libraries

**GRANT VALUES**
Lowest Grant: $18,000

**NAMED GRANTS**

**STATE AID TO PUBLIC LIBRARIES**
The State Aid to Public Libraries Program distributes state funds directly to eligible public libraries for two purposes: technology and books. Each parish receives a base grant of $18,000 from the State Library budget. The remainder of the available funds in the State Library budget are distributed by population, with each eligible entity—parish or municipal library—receiving the appropriate per capita amount.

**REQUIREMENTS AND RESTRICTIONS**
(1) The library must be legally established according to Louisiana Revised Statue 25:211 et seq., (2) the library must agree to serve all patrons with free basic library service with no denial of service, (3) the library must show evidence of working toward the Louisiana Library Association's Standards for Public Libraries, (4) the library must endorse the interlibrary loan code adopted by the Louisiana Library Association to ensure interlibrary availability of materials purchased with state aid funds, and (5) state aid funds are to be expended only for library collection materials and technology enhancement, not for personnel or other operating expenditures.

**APPLICATION PROCEDURES**
**Submission Guidelines:** Complete and

submit the state aid application form found on the website.

### CONTACT
Phone: 225-342-4923
Fax: 225-219-4804

### GRANT-SPECIFIC WEBSITE
www.state.lib.la.us/statewide-services/
state-aid
www.state.lib.la.us/public-libraries/
grant-opportunities

# Lowe's Charitable and Educational Foundation

## Headquarters

PO Box 1111
North Wilkesboro, NC 28656
Phone: 704-758-2009
www.lowes.com

## Description

**Founded:** 1957

**Operating Locations:** North Carolina

**Foundation Information:** Corporate foundation of Lowe's

## Financial Summary

Assets: $20,161,306

Gifts Received: $19,057,529
Total Giving: $15,318,980

## Grants Information

### GRANT TYPES
General support, project

### TYPICAL RECIPIENTS
Arts and humanities, civic affairs, education

### GRANT VALUES
Total Dollar Amount of Grants:
$15,318,980

### PAST GRANT RECIPIENTS

*Library or School Related*
- Roberto Clemente Charter School (PA), update of library media resources, $19,854
- Pendleton Elementary School (SC), general support, $3,500
- North Learning Community (NC), technology upgrade, $250,000
- Mooresville Graded School District (NC), technology upgrade, $250,000
- Mount Vernon Elementary School (GA), general support, $10,000
- Golden Valley Charter School (CA), general support, $5,000

*General*
- National Trust for Historic Preservation (DC), general support, $1,000,000
- Neighborhood Improvement Development (WI), neighborhood

improvement, $20,000
- Home Safety Council (DC), promote and support safety awareness, $1,500,000
- Greater Pittston YMCA (PA), playground construction, $20,000

**REQUIREMENTS AND RESTRICTIONS**
Only tax-exempt organizations, registered charities, or government entities will be considered for grants. Community/school projects preferred.

**APPLICATION PROCEDURES**
**Submission Guidelines:** Application online

**CONTACT**
NA

**GRANT-SPECIFIC WEBSITE**
www.lowes.com/cd_The + Lowes + Chari
    table + and + Educational + Foundati
    on_474741445_

# John D. and Catherine T. MacArthur Foundation

## Headquarters

140 S. Dearborn St., no. 1200
Chicago, IL 60603

Phone: 312-726-8000
E-mail: 4answers@macfound.org
www.macfound.org

## Description

**Founded:** 1970

**Operating Locations:** Illinois

**Foundation Information:** Private foundation established by John D. MacArthur and his wife, Catherine T. MacArthur

## Financial Summary

Assets: $5,014,059,259
Total Giving: $228,248,284

## Grants Information

### GRANT TYPES
General support, project, research, fellowship, matching, multiyear continuing support

### TYPICAL RECIPIENTS
Arts and humanities, civic affairs, education, environment, health, international, science, social services

### GRANT VALUES
Total Dollar Amount of Grants:
    $228,248,284

## PAST GRANT RECIPIENTS

*Library or School Related*

- American Library Association (DC), funding for work on implications of digital copyright for libraries, $210,000
- Friends of the Evanston Public Library (IL), general support, $900
- Public Library of Science (CA), support for open access publishing initiatives, $250,000
- Newberry Library (IL), general support, $75,000
- Chicago Public Library Foundation (IL), science lecture series, $50,000
- Online Computer Library Center (OH), development of search engine based on citations of librarians, $100,000

*General*

- After School Matters (IL), youth development programs in neighborhoods, $200,000
- American Academy of Arts and Sciences (MA), general support, $3,000
- SeaWeb (MD), ocean conservation in Fiji, $65,000
- Sargent Shriver National Center on Poverty Law (IL), general support, $125,000
- Comprehensive AIDS Program (FL), general support, $300
- Civil War Preservation Trust (MD), general support, $150

## REQUIREMENTS AND RESTRICTIONS

The foundation does not support political activities or attempts to influence action on specific legislation. The foundation does not provide scholarships or tuition assistance for undergraduate, graduate, or postgraduate studies, nor does it support annual fund-raising drives, institutional benefits, honorary functions, or similar projects.

## APPLICATION PROCEDURES

**Submission Guidelines:** Submit a cover sheet and a letter of inquiry about the proposed work. The cover sheet should include

- information regarding who will carry out the work
- name of organization (and acronym if commonly used)
- name of parent organization, if any
- name of chief executive officer or person holding similar position
- organization's address (and courier address if different)
- organization's phone number, fax number, and e-mail address, if any
- name and title of the principal contact person, if different from the above
- address (and courier address if different), phone number, fax number, and e-mail address of principal contact
- web address, if any

The letter of inquiry should include

- name or topic of the proposed project or work to be done
- a brief statement (two or three sentences) of the purpose and nature of the proposed work
- the significance of the issue addressed by the project and how it relates to a stated MacArthur program strategy
- how the work will address the issue
- how the issue relates to your organization, and why your organization is qualified to undertake the project
- geographic area or country where the work will take place
- time period for which funding is requested
- information about those who will be helped by and interested in the work and how you will communicate with them
- amount of funding requested from MacArthur and total cost (estimates are acceptable)

**Decisions:** Applicant will receive immediate e-mail acknowledgement of receipt of application. Final decision may take up to 8 weeks.

### CONTACT
MacArthur Foundation, Office of Grants Management (at above address)
Phone: 312-726-8000
E-mail: 4answers@macfound.org

### GRANT-SPECIFIC WEBSITE
www.macfound.org/site/c.
   lkLXJ8MQKrH/b.913959/k.E1BE/
   Applying_for_Grants.htm

# Maine State Library (MSL)

## Headquarters

64 State House Station
Augusta, ME 04333-0064
Phone: 888-577-6690
www.maine.gov/msl/

## Description

**Founded:** 1836

**Operating Locations:** Maine

The purpose of the Maine State Library is to lead in efforts that will provide, broaden, and improve access to information and library services regardless of location of residency.

## Grants Information

### GRANT TYPES
Library construction

### TYPICAL RECIPIENTS
Maine libraries

## GRANT VALUES
Total Dollar Amount of Grants: $400,000
Highest Grant: $50,000

## NAMED GRANTS

### NEW CENTURY CONSTRUCTION/ RENOVATION GRANT
New Century Construction/Renovation Grant funding can be used toward new construction, facilities renovation, projects to meet ADA requirements, and internal wiring. Library must be able to match the grant amount it is applying for.

**Past Grant Recipients:**

- Calais Free Library (ME), air-conditioning in the children's section, $4,430
- Carrabassett Valley Public Library (ME), Building for the Future, $45,000
- Cary Library (ME), new energy efficient furnace, $16,016
- Charlotte Hobbs Memorial Library (ME), expansion and renovation of 100-year-old building, $45,000
- Edythe L. Dyer Community Library (ME), central air-conditioning, $24,631
- Shaw Public Library (ME), renovating building to improve accessibility and compliance with ADA, $29,000

## REQUIREMENTS AND RESTRICTIONS
All organizations applying for a New Century Community Grant must be nonprofit organizations, legally incorporated in the state of Maine, or a unit of local, county, or state government. Items that are not a permanent part of the library building itself, such as furniture (including bookshelves), carpets, interior painting, restoration of art work, and computers, are not eligible.

## APPLICATION PROCEDURES

**Submission Guidelines:** Applicants must use the application form as presented by the Library Commission. Applications may be e-mailed or faxed, but six print copies with signatures must be mailed. Font must be 12-point and cannot be bold.

## CONTACT
Linda Lord
Phone: 207-287-5620
Fax: 207-287-5624
E-mail: Linda.Lord@maine.gov

## GRANT-SPECIFIC WEBSITE
www.maine.gov/msl/libs/grants/

# Massachusetts Board of Library Commissioners (MBLC)

## Headquarters

98 N. Washington St., Suite 401
Boston, MA 02114
Phone: 617-725-1860
http://mblc.state.ma.us/

## Description

**Founded:** 1890

**Operating Locations:** Massachusetts

The Massachusetts Board of Library Commissioners is the agency of state government with the statutory authority and responsibility to organize, develop, coordinate, and improve library services throughout the Commonwealth.

## Grants Information

### GRANT TYPES
LSTA funds, library improvement, library construction, programs

### TYPICAL RECIPIENTS
Massachusetts libraries

### GRANT VALUES
NA

### NAMED GRANTS

#### CONSTRUCTION GRANT PROGRAM
There are two grants available through the Construction Grant Program. The Project for Planning and Design grant assists libraries in the preliminary planning stages of a construction project. Funds from this grant may be used for development of the library building program, architectural studies including feasibility and schematic design, cost estimates, soil studies, and site investigation. The Project for New Construction, Addition/Renovation, or Renovation grant assists libraries in the design development and construction stages of their project. Both grants are offered on a cyclical basis. The grant cycle depends on authorizing legislature, administrative approval, and availability of funds.

**Typical Recipients:** Public libraries

**Grant Values:** Average Grant, 50 percent of eligible costs; Highest Grant, 75 percent of eligible costs

**Requirements and Restrictions:** Landscaping, parking lots, and furnishings are not eligible for funding.

**Contact:** *For towns with populations over 10,000*: Phone: 617-725-1860, ext. 245; *for towns with populations under 10,000*: Phone: 617-725-1860, ext. 246

**Grant-Specific Website:** http://mblc
.state.ma.us/grants/construction/

## LSTA GRANTS

Massachusetts receives several million
dollars in federal LSTA funds from
the Institute of Museum and Library
Services. A portion of these funds is then
awarded as competitive direct grants to
libraries of all types. A competitive grant
round is announced yearly in November.
Awards are made in July for projects to
begin the following October.

**Contact:** Phone: 800-952-7403, ext. 232
or 234

**Grant-Specific Website:**
http://mblc.state.ma.us/grants/lsta/
opportunities/

## ACADEMIC LIBRARY INCENTIVE MINIGRANT

Academic Library Incentive Minigrants
are intended to help academic libraries
carry out the goals in their long-range
plans. Projects must include a significant
program component to ensure that
the specific target population will be
directly served by the grant. Projects
may address the unique challenges
that academic libraries face, such as
communication and collaboration
within library departments, as well as
across campus and with the outside
community, instruction, collections, and
access, among others.

**Typical Recipients:** Academic libraries

**Grant Values:** Highest Grant, $5,000

**Submission Guidelines:** The original
plus seven copies of the application must
be mailed to the MBLC at the address
below. The application should also be
e-mailed to the MBLC grants manager.
Faxed applications will not be accepted.

**Deadlines:** March

**Contact:** 98 N. Washington St., Suite
401, Boston, MA 02114; Phone: 800-
952-7403, ext. 232 or 234

**Grant-Specific Website:** http://mblc.
state.ma.us/grants/lsta/forms/index.php

## CONVERSATION CIRCLES MINIGRANT

Through the Conversation Circles
Minigrant program, libraries receive
funding to develop a volunteer-led
program of conversation circles.
Conversation circles provide a structured
setting for second-language learners in
need of opportunities to practice basic
conversational English. These programs
may be supervised by library staff
and conducted by trained volunteers.
Funds would be used to pay for a
part-time volunteer coordinator and
support materials on English-language
instruction and citizenship.

**Typical Recipients:** Public libraries

**Grant Values:** Highest Grant, $12,500

**Submission Guidelines:** The original plus seven copies of the application must be mailed to the MBLC at the address below. The application should also be e-mailed to the MBLC grants manager. Faxed applications will not be accepted.

**Deadlines:** March

**Contact:** 98 N. Washington St., Suite 401, Boston, MA 02114; Phone: 800-952-7403, ext. 232 or 234

**Grant-Specific Website:** http://mblc .state.ma.us/grants/lsta/forms/

### DIGITIZING HISTORICAL RESOURCES MINIGRANT

Through the Digitizing Historical Resources Minigrant, libraries will receive funding support for creating digital images of historically valuable library resources and making them available on the Internet. Creating digital images and making them accessible online makes the images available for use by researchers anywhere in the world. Original documents can then be preserved and stored in secure, climate-controlled storage for those who need them in person. This program is not to be considered a preservation program.

**Typical Recipients:** Libraries that have completed a formal preservation survey within five years and developed a preservation action plan

**Grant Values:** Typical Range of Grants, $5,000–$30,000

**Submission Guidelines:** The original plus seven copies of the application must be mailed to the MBLC at the address below. The application should also be e-mailed to the MBLC grants manager. Faxed applications will not be accepted.

**Deadlines:** March

**Contact:** 98 N. Washington St., Suite 401, Boston, MA 02114; Phone: 800-952-7403, ext. 232 or 234

**Grant-Specific Website:** http://mblc. state.ma.us/grants/lsta/forms/

### HOW GREEN IS MY LIBRARY GRANT

The multifaceted How Green Is My Library Grant gives funds to libraries that may be used to provide resources, programming, and improved access to materials. Funds should be used to raise awareness and use of the statewide licensed database programs to engage and educate their constituencies about environmental literacy while improving communication technology literacy skills. Funds may be spent on web support, collections, speakers, supplies, stipends for students or faculty as needed, promotions, and equipment other than computers.

**Typical Recipients:** Academic, school, and public libraries

**Grant Values:** Highest Grant, $7,500; Lowest Grant, $5,000

**Submission Guidelines:** The original plus seven copies of the application must be mailed to the MBLC at the address below. The application should also be e-mailed to the MBLC grants manager. Faxed applications will not be accepted.

**Deadlines:** March

**Contact:** 98 N. Washington St., Suite 401, Boston, MA 02114; Phone: 800-952-7403, ext. 232 or 234

**Grant-Specific Website:** http://mblc .state.ma.us/grants/lsta/forms/

## LIBRARIES FOR JOB SEEKERS GRANT

The Libraries for Job Seekers Grant provides funds for libraries to carry out a program aimed at serving the needs of job and career seekers in their communities. Collaboration with governmental and local civic and community partners must be demonstrated.

**Typical Recipients:** Public libraries

**Grant Values:** Highest Grant, $7,500

**Submission Guidelines:** The original plus seven copies of the application must be mailed to the MBLC at the address below. The application should also be e-mailed to the MBLC grants manager. Faxed applications will not be accepted.

**Deadlines:** March

**Contact:** 98 N. Washington St., Suite 401, Boston, MA 02114; Phone: 800-952-7403, ext. 232 or 234

**Grant-Specific Website:** http://mblc .state.ma.us/grants/lsta/forms/

## MOTHER GOOSE ON THE LOOSE GRANT

Mother Goose on the Loose is an early-childhood literacy program for babies and young children and their caregivers pioneered at the Enoch Pratt Free Library in Baltimore. Grant funds may be used to plan and implement a project using the material developed for MGOL. Components of the project include agreement to use the MGOL program model and to participate in the training sessions; agreement to offer programs to a minimum of 15 families; agreement to publicize the program as appropriate; commitment to collaborate with local schools, museums, and other agencies; and agreement to participate in a statewide evaluation of MGOL to determine the effectiveness of the program.

**Typical Recipients:** Public libraries

**Grant Values:** Highest Grant, $7,500

**Submission Guidelines:** The original plus seven copies of the application must be mailed to the MBLC at the address below. The application should also be e-mailed to the MBLC grants manager. Faxed applications will not be accepted.

**Deadlines:** March

**Contact:** 98 N. Washington St., Suite 401, Boston, MA 02114; Phone: 800-952-7403, ext. 232 or 234

**Grant-Specific Website:** http://mblc .state.ma.us/grants/lsta/forms/

## ON THE SAME PAGE GRANT (COMMUNITY READING CAMPAIGN PROGRAM)

This program is aimed at building a community of readers through providing a "one book" experience that will initiate thoughtful discussion of the same book among local residents. Grant funds can be used to purchase books (print and audio), to develop public relations strategies and readers' advisory support tools, and to support a part-time staff person to help the library coordinate the campaign.

**Typical Recipients:** All libraries

**Grant Values:** Highest Grant, $7,500

**Submission Guidelines:** The original plus seven copies of the application must be mailed to the MBLC at the address below. The application should also be e-mailed to the MBLC grants manager. Faxed applications will not be accepted.

**Deadlines:** March

**Contact:** 98 N. Washington St., Suite 401, Boston, MA 02114; Phone: 800-952-7403, ext. 232 or 234

**Grant-Specific Website:** http://mblc .state.ma.us/grants/lsta/forms/

## OPEN PROJECTS GRANTS

The Open Projects grant program allows librarians to satisfy needs that are not being met by current programs. Applicants are allowed to apply new methods to solve problems, build programs, and best carry out their library's mission and plan. This program allows applicants as much flexibility in the development of their projects as possible. Applicants should speak with a consultant about their project ideas for feedback prior to submitting an application.

**Typical Recipients:** All libraries

**Grant Values:** Typical Range of Grants, $5,000–$30,000 (regions and cooperatives may exceed)

**Submission Guidelines:** The original plus seven copies of the application must be mailed to the MBLC at the address below. The application should also be e-mailed to the MBLC grants manager. Faxed applications will not be accepted.

**Deadlines:** March

**Contact:** 98 N. Washington St., Suite 401, Boston, MA 02114; Phone: 800-952-7403, ext. 232 or 234

**Grant-Specific Website:** http://mblc .state.ma.us/grants/lsta/forms/

## PRESERVATION SURVEY GRANT

Funds from the Preservation Survey Grant allow libraries to perform a preservation survey to determine individual item conservation requirements and needs for proper storage, care, and handling. Once the survey has been completed, it will be up to the library to pursue the recommendations of the consultant. A five-year preservation long-range plan based on the recommendations of the consultant is a required outcome of this grant. Library must pay a minimum of $500.

**Typical Recipients:** All libraries

**Grant Values:** Highest Grant, $2,500

**Submission Guidelines:** The original plus seven copies of the application must be mailed to the MBLC at the address below. The application should also be e-mailed to the MBLC grants manager. Faxed applications will not be accepted.

**Deadlines:** March

**Contact:** 98 N. Washington St., Suite 401, Boston, MA 02114; Phone: 800-952-7403, ext. 232 or 234

**Grant-Specific Website:** http://mblc .state.ma.us/grants/lsta/forms/

### READERS' ADVISORY: PUTTING THE "RA" BACK IN LIBRARY GRANT

The Readers' Advisory grant project will provide funds for training staff in the use of electronic and print readers' advisory tools, as well as enable libraries to purchase popular reading collections in multiple formats. Libraries receiving funding will be requested to study a selected genre during the course of the project. Funds may be used to support a limited number of staff hours as well as program materials and outreach to communities.

**Typical Recipients:** Public and institutional libraries

**Grant Values:** Highest Grant, $7,500–$10,000

**Submission Guidelines:** The original plus seven copies of the application must be mailed to the MBLC at the address below. The application should also be e-mailed to the MBLC grants manager. Faxed applications will not be accepted.

**Deadlines:** March

**Contact:** 98 N. Washington St., Suite 401, Boston, MA 02114; Phone: 800-952-7403, ext. 232 or 234

**Grant-Specific Website:** http://mblc .state.ma.us/grants/lsta/forms/

### SCHOOL LIBRARY INCENTIVE GRANT

The School Library Incentive Grant provides funding for K–12 library teachers to update collections to meet current curriculum frameworks or to create a project to help their students develop information literacy skills. Recipients should develop programs that meet the needs of their users based on their approved long-range plans.

**Typical Recipients:** School libraries

**Grant Values:** Highest Grant, $5,000

**Submission Guidelines:** The original plus seven copies of the application must be mailed to the MBLC at the address below. The application should also be e-mailed to the MBLC grants manager. Faxed applications will not be accepted.

**Deadlines:** March

**Contact:** 98 N. Washington St., Suite 401, Boston, MA 02114; Phone: 800-952-7403, ext. 232 or 234

**Grant-Specific Website:** http://mblc state.ma.us/grants/lsta/forms/

## SERVING 'TWEENS AND TEENS GRANT

The purpose of the Serving 'Tweens and Teens grant program is to allow libraries to develop programs and services that meet the needs of the young adult population in their community. In particular, grant funds can be used to carry out a targeted program aimed at middle- and high-school-age 'tweens and teens. Libraries must conduct a preliminary needs assessment including focus groups with teens and interviews with community leaders, parents, and teachers.

**Typical Recipients:** Public libraries

**Grant Values:** Highest Grant, $20,000

**Submission Guidelines:** The original plus seven copies of the application must be mailed to the MBLC at the address below. The application should also be e-mailed to the MBLC grants manager. Faxed applications will not be accepted.

**Deadlines:** March

**Contact:** 98 N. Washington St., Suite 401, Boston, MA 02114; Phone: 800-952-7403, ext. 232 or 234

**Grant-Specific Website:** http://mblc .state.ma.us/grants/lsta/forms/

## VITAL AGING FOR OLDER ACTIVE ADULTS GRANT

Funds from the Vital Aging for Older Active Adults Grant will allow libraries to carry out a program aimed at serving the older active adults in their communities. Libraries must conduct a preliminary needs assessment including focus groups or surveys with this population.

**Typical Recipients:** Public libraries

**Grant Values:** Highest Grant, $7,500

**Submission Guidelines:** The original plus seven copies of the application must be mailed to the MBLC at the address below. The application should also be e-mailed to the MBLC grants manager. Faxed applications will not be accepted.

**Deadlines:** March

**Contact:** 98 N. Washington St., Suite

401, Boston, MA 02114; Phone: 800-952-7403, ext. 232 or 234

**Grant-Specific Website:** http://mblc.state.ma.us/grants/lsta/forms/

**REQUIREMENTS AND RESTRICTIONS**
Vary by grant

**APPLICATION PROCEDURES**
Vary by grant

**CONTACT**
Varies by grant

**GRANT-SPECIFIC WEBSITE**
Varies by grant

# Robert R. McCormick Foundation

## Headquarters

205 N. Michigan Ave.
Chicago, IL 60601
Phone: 312-445-5000
Fax: 312-445-5001
E-mail: info@mccormickfoundation.org
www.mccormickfoundation.org

## Description

**Founded:** 1955

**Operating Locations:** Illinois

**Foundation Information:** Private foundation established by Robert R. McCormick, longtime editor and publisher of the Chicago Tribune

## Financial Summary

Assets: $967,483,707
Total Giving: $22,052,225

## Grants Information

**GRANT TYPES**
General support, awards, matching

**TYPICAL RECIPIENTS**
Arts and humanities, civic affairs, education, health, international, science, social services

**GRANT VALUES**
Total Dollar Amount of Grants:
    $22,052,225

**PAST GRANT RECIPIENTS**
*Library or School Related*
- Arapahoe Library Foundation (CO), Begin with Books program, $10,000
- Chicago Public Library Foundation (IL), Chicago Reads Together early literacy program, $35,000
- Denver Public Library Friends Foundation (CO), children and youth programs, $20,000
- Indianapolis–Marion County Public Library Foundation (IN), summer reading program, $10,000

- Los Angeles County Public Library Foundation (CA), oral history program for East Los Angeles, $10,000
- Pritzker Military Library (IL), general support, $50,000

*General*
- Adult Literacy League (FL), family literacy services, $10,000
- De La Salle Institute (IL), adult and family literacy programs, $65,000
- El Centrito Family Learning Centers (CA), family literacy and school reading programs, $20,000
- Greater Reading or Writing Skills Literacy Council (FL), GROWS family literacy program, $24,000
- Reading Is Fundamental of Southern California (CA), WIC family literacy program, $20,000
- Westside Children's Center (CA), funding to promote Early Literacy in Disadvantaged Children program, $10,000

## REQUIREMENTS AND RESTRICTIONS

The foundation only funds not-for-profit 501(c)(3) organizations. The foundation does not fund personal research projects, endowments, capital campaigns, or individual scholarships.

## APPLICATION PROCEDURES

**Submission Guidelines:** Review grant programs on the website before calling or e-mailing the foundation.

## CONTACT

Phone: 312-445-5000
E-mail: info@mccormickfoundation.org

## GRANT-SPECIFIC WEBSITE

www.mccormickfoundation.org/grants
.aspx

# MDU Resources Foundation

## Headquarters

PO Box 5650
Bismarck, ND 58506
Phone: 701-530-1040
www.mdu.com/corporateresponsibility/
foundation/

## Description

**Founded:** NA

**Operating Locations:** North Dakota

**Foundation Information:** Corporate foundation of MDU Resources Group, Inc.

## Financial Summary

Assets: $3,551,523
Gifts Received: $2,746,045
Total Giving: $1,997,830

# Grants Information

## GRANT TYPES
General support, operating support, construction, awards

## TYPICAL RECIPIENTS
Arts and humanities, civic affairs, education, environment, health, science, social services

## GRANT VALUES
Total Dollar Amount of Grants:
$1,997,830

## PAST GRANT RECIPIENTS

*Library or School Related*
- Sheridan County Library Foundation (WY), general support, $10,000
- Parmly Billings Library Foundation (MT), general support, $12,000
- Library Foundation, Inc. (ND), construction, $15,000
- Mandan Public Library (ND), general support, $3,500
- Marshall Lyon County Public Library (MN), construction and civic grants, $20,000
- Dickinson Area Public Library (ND), construction, $10,000
- Dickinson Public Library Foundation (ND), civic/community grants, $5,000

*General*
- Citizens for Bay Area Youth (OR), general support, $10,000
- Children's Alliance of Hawaii (HI), general support, $7,000
- Food Bank of Alaska (AK), general support, $6,000
- Good Shepherd's Clothes Closet (NV), general support, $3,000

## REQUIREMENTS AND RESTRICTIONS
Applicants must have tax-exempt status and be located within the service territory of MDU Resources and its subsidiaries (i.e., central and northwest United States).

## APPLICATION PROCEDURES
**Submission Guidelines:** Application online. Application should include

- the name and address of the organization or charity as shown on the IRS determination letter
- the name, address, and telephone number of contact person
- a copy of an Internal Revenue Service determination letter indicating tax-exempt status under section 501(c)(3) of the Internal Revenue Code, OR evidence of eligibility under Section 170(c)(1) of the code
- purpose or use of the requested grant
- other information deemed appropriate, including program or project brochures that will be helpful in understanding the request

**Deadlines:** October 1 of the year prior to the year for which funding is sought

**CONTACT**
Rita O'Neill
Phone: 701-530-1087
E-mail: rita.oneill@mduresources.com

**GRANT-SPECIFIC WEBSITE**
www.mdu.com/CorporateResponsibility/
Foundation/Pages/Qualified.aspx

# Medical Library Association (MLA)

## Headquarters

65 E. Wacker Pl.
Chicago, IL 60601-7298
Phone: 312-419-9094
www.mlanet.org

## Description

**Founded:** 1898

**Operating Locations:** Illinois

The Medical Library Association (MLA) is a nonprofit, educational organization of more than 1,100 institutions and 3,600 individual members in the health sciences information field, committed to educating health information professionals, supporting health information research, promoting access to the world's health sciences information, and working to ensure that the best health information is available to all.

## Financial Summary

Assets: $3,144,854
Total Giving: $213,756

## Grants Information

**GRANT TYPES**
Research, conference attendance, continuing education, career development, scholarship

**TYPICAL RECIPIENTS**
Health sciences information professionals in the United States or Canada

**GRANT VALUES**
Total Dollar Amount of Grants: $75,117
Number of Grants: 9
Highest Grant: $9,945
Lowest Grant: $100

**NAMED GRANTS**

**CONTINUING EDUCATION AWARD**
MLA members may submit applications for these awards of $100–$500 to develop their knowledge of the theoretical, administrative, or technical aspects of librarianship. More than one continuing education award may be offered in a year and may be used either for MLA courses or for other continuing education activities.

## MLA RESEARCH, DEVELOPMENT, AND DEMONSTRATION PROJECT GRANT

The purpose of this grant is to provide support for research, development, or demonstration projects that will help to promote excellence in the field of health sciences librarianship and information sciences. Grants range from $100 to $1,000. Grants will not be given to support an activity that is operational in nature or has only local usefulness. More than one award may be granted in a year.

## HOSPITAL LIBRARIES SECTION/ MLA PROFESSIONAL DEVELOPMENT GRANT

This award, sponsored by the Hospital Libraries Section, provides librarians working in hospital and similar clinical settings with the support needed for educational or research activities. Up to two awards of up to $800 may be granted each year.

## DONALD A. B. LINDBERG RESEARCH FELLOWSHIP

The Lindberg Research Fellowship Endowment, established in 2003, will provide a $9,945 grant, awarded annually by MLA through a competitive grant process. The purpose of this fellowship is to fund research aimed at expanding the research knowledge base, linking the information services provided by librarians to improved health care and advances in biomedical research.

The application deadline is November 15.

## MEDICAL INFORMATICS SECTION/ MLA CAREER DEVELOPMENT GRANT

This award provides up to two individuals $1,500 to support a career development activity that will contribute to advancement in the field of medical informatics.

## EBSCO/MLA ANNUAL MEETING GRANT

This scholarship is sponsored by EBSCO Information Services and enables MLA members to attend the association's annual meeting. Each year awards of up to $1,000 for travel and conference-related expenses will be given to four librarians who would otherwise be unable to attend the meeting. Applicants must be currently employed as health sciences librarians and have between two and five years of experience in a health sciences library.

## REQUIREMENTS AND RESTRICTIONS

Vary by grant. Some grants require MLA membership or a specific number of years in the health-care librarianship field.

## APPLICATION PROCEDURES

**Submission Guidelines:** Application online

**Deadlines:** December 1 unless otherwise noted

**CONTACT**
Carla Funk
Phone: 312-419-9094, ext. 14
E-mail: mlapd2@mlahq.org

**GRANT-SPECIFIC WEBSITE**
www.mlanet.org/awards/grants/

# Andrew W. Mellon Foundation

## Headquarters

140 E. 62nd St.
New York, NY 10065
Phone: 212-838-8400
www.mellon.org

## Description

**Founded:** 1969

**Operating Locations:** New York

**Foundation Information:** Private foundation established by the children of Pittsburgh financier Andrew W. Mellon

## Financial Summary

Assets: $4,363,563,181
Total Giving: $267,479,576

## Grants Information

### GRANT TYPES
General support, awards, research, matching

### TYPICAL RECIPIENTS
Higher education and scholarship, scholarly communications and information technology, museums and art conservation, performing arts, conservation and the environment

### GRANT VALUES
Total Dollar Amount of Grants:
$267,479,576

### PAST GRANT RECIPIENTS

*Library or School Related*
- Appalachian College Association (NC), expansion of central library online shared catalog, $500,000
- Duke University (NC), support for Open Library Initiative, shared technology services environment for research and academic libraries, $475,700
- Oberlin College (OH), collaborative program to strengthen academic libraries, $500,000
- Southeastern Library Network, Inc. (GA), strengthening of libraries of historically black colleges and universities, $600,000
- Henry E. Huntington Library and Art Gallery (CA), cataloguing of

unprocessed manuscript collections in the library, $700,000

- University of Virginia (VA), establishment of library preservation system, $750,000
- Council on Library and Information Resources (DC), fellowship program for humanities students to conduct research in original sources, $1,378,000

*General*

- Children's Defense Fund (DC), inventory and assessment of papers of civil rights leader Marian Wright Edelman, $5,000
- Council on the Environment (NY), general support, $30,000
- Louisiana Philharmonic Orchestra (LA), purchase of acoustical shell and floor for Mahalia Jackson Theatre and performances at reopening of theatre, $400,000
- Eviction Intervention Services Homeless Prevention, Inc. (NY), general support, $40,000

**REQUIREMENTS AND RESTRICTIONS**
Applicants must prove tax-exempt status.

**APPLICATION PROCEDURES**
**Submission Guidelines:** Applicants should review the foundation's general requirements for grant proposals in the Grant Inquiries section of the website before sending a brief e-mail describing their funding needs to one of the contacts below. Letters of inquiry regarding ideas that fall within the program description are reviewed throughout the year.

**CONTACT**
Donald J. Waters
E-mail: djw@mellon.org
OR
Helen Cullyer
E-mail: hc@mellon.org

**GRANT-SPECIFIC WEBSITE**
www.mellon.org/grant_programs/
    programs/
www.mellon.org/contact_information/
    grantinquiries/

# Michigan Center for the Book (MCFB)

## Headquarters

702 W. Kalamazoo St.
PO Box 30007
Lansing, MI 48909
Phone: 517-241-0021
www.michigan.gov/mcfb/

## Description

**Founded:** 1986

**Operating Locations:** Michigan

The Michigan Center for the Book draws from the Library of Michigan and its affiliate institutions to encourage and produce local and statewide programs and resources that promote books, reading, authors, and libraries.

# Grants Information

## GRANT TYPES
Project

## TYPICAL RECIPIENTS
Michigan-based nonprofit organizations, libraries, and schools

## GRANT VALUES
Highest Grant: $500

## PAST GRANT RECIPIENTS

*Library or School Related*
- Bayliss Public Library (MI), Curious Creatures with Unkle Ake Larson
- Chesterfield Township Library (MI), Giggle Poetry Concert with Bruce Lansky
- Genesee District Library (MI), Meet the Author with Juan Williams
- Grand Rapids Public Library (MI), Celebration of the Book
- Hillsdale Community Library (MI), Hillsdale County Reads Jeannette Wall's The Glass Castle
- Kalkaska County Library (MI), An Evening with Joe Heywood

## REQUIREMENTS AND RESTRICTIONS
Applicant must be a Michigan-based nonprofit organization, library, or school. The request for funds must be no more than 50 percent of the total budget of the project/event or no more than $500, whichever is less. Michigan Center for the Book affiliates may receive priority. The event sponsored must be free and open to the public. Within 30 days of event completion, an activity report must be turned in to the Michigan Center for the Book. Review criteria for requests may include Center for the Book affiliate status, impact of the program, uniqueness of the program, geographic area of the institution, community size, and previous Center for the Book funding. Programs that provide new opportunities to participants are preferred.

## APPLICATION PROCEDURES
**Submission Guidelines:** Application online

**Deadlines:** January

## CONTACT
Karren Reish
Phone: 517-241-0021
Fax: 517-373-5700
E-mail: reishk@michigan.gov

## GRANT-SPECIFIC WEBSITE
www.michigan.gov/mde/0,1607,7-140
-54574_36788_36790-118794--,00
.html

# Michigan Humanities Council

## Headquarters

119 Pere Marquette, Suite 3B
Lansing, MI 48912
Phone: 517-372-7770
www.michiganhumanities.org

## Description

**Founded:** 1974

**Operating Locations:** Michigan

The Michigan Humanities Council connects people and communities by fostering and creating high-quality cultural programs.

## Grants Information

**GRANT TYPES**
Project

**TYPICAL RECIPIENTS**
Michigan cultural, educational, and community-based organizations and institutions

**GRANT VALUES**
NA

### NAMED GRANTS

### MAJOR GRANTS

Major grants emphasize collaboration among cultural, educational, and community-based organizations and institutions to serve Michigan's people with public humanities programming. Up to $15,000 is awarded per major grant.

**Submission Guidelines:** The grant application form is available on the website. It has four sections: the cover sheet, the narrative section, the budget, and the appendixes. Submit one original and nine copies to the address below. A draft may be submitted for Council staff to review and provide feedback up to 2 weeks before the deadline.

**Deadlines:** March and September

**Decisions:** May and November

**Contact:** Michigan Humanities Council, 119 Pere Marquette Dr., Suite 3B, Lansing, MI 48912-1270; Phone: 517-372-7770

**Grant-Specific Website:** www.michiganhumanities.org/grants/index.php#major_grants

### QUICK GRANTS AND PLANNING GRANTS

Support for programs that fall outside the design and deadline schedules of the major grants is made through Quick Grants and Planning Grants.

Quick Grants provide up to $500 and Planning Grants provide up to $1,000 to Michigan-based, nonprofit organizations for public humanities programs or services. Organizations may only receive one quick or planning grant per year and the project activities must be free or very low cost and open to the public. Eligible expenses include program expenses supporting the Great Michigan Read; guest speakers; reading/discussion programs; honoraria and travel expenses for humanities professionals serving as consultants in developing a public humanities project or program that will result in a nonprofit organization applying for a major grant through the Michigan Humanities Council.

**Typical Recipients:** Michigan-based, nonprofit organizations for public humanities programs or services

**Requirements and Restrictions:** Programs and presenters already supported through the Arts and Humanities Touring Program are not eligible for additional Quick Grant support. Additional ineligible expenses include advocacy or action programs, social services, travel for study or to attend conferences, scholarships for academic credit, construction or renovation, property or equipment purchases, general operating expenses, microfilming newspapers, food, and individuals.

**Submission Guidelines:** Applications may be filled out online or downloaded and mailed to the address below. Applicants must also mail a signed copy of the certification proving nonprofit status, and a copy of the curriculum vitae or résumé of the humanities professional involved in the project. Faxed applications will not be accepted.

**Deadlines:** The Council must receive applications for Quick Grants or Planning Grants at least 4 weeks prior to the program or planning date.

**Contact:** Michigan Humanities Council, 119 Pere Marquette, Suite 3B, Lansing, MI 48912-0027; Phone: 517-372-7770

**Grant-Specific Website:** www.michiganhumanities.org/grants/quickgrants.php

### PRIME TIME FAMILY READING TIME LIBRARY GRANTS

PRIME TIME is a 6-week program of reading, discussion, and storytelling that targets low-income, low-literacy families. Grant funds in the amount of $9,000 will cover the majority of expenses so that select libraries may host the program.

**Typical Recipients:** Any public library system in the state of Michigan

**Submission Guidelines:** All interested libraries must first submit a one-page letter of interest to the Michigan Humanities Council for consideration as a PRIME TIME site. A library system must commit to hosting a minimum of three PRIME TIME series over a two-year period.

**Contact:** Cynthia Dimitrijevic, Grants Director; Phone: 517-372-0029, ext. 29; E-mail: cdimitrijevic@ mihumanities.org

**Grant-Specific Website:** www.michiganhumanities.org/ programs/primetime/

### PRIME TIME MINIGRANTS FOR REPEAT PROGRAMS

Minigrants of up to $2,000 are currently available to library systems that have previously implemented a Council-sponsored PRIME TIME program and are in need of additional funds to support repeat programs.

**Submission Guidelines:** Letter of intent on library letterhead including the following:

- proposed dates and location of repeat PRIME TIME program
- names of all PRIME TIME team members, including library coordinator, scholar, and storyteller
- target audience and plans for recruiting families
- partner agencies that will assist with program implementation and family recruitment
- total program budget and detail of how grant funds will be expended

**Contact:** Cynthia M. Dimitrijevic, Grants Director, Michigan Humanities Council, 119 Pere Marquette, Suite 3B, Lansing, MI 48912; Phone: 517-372-7770; Fax: 517-372-0027; E-mail: cdimitrijevic@ mihumanities.org

**Grant-Specific Website:** www.michiganhumanities.org/grants/ primetime/

### ARTS AND HUMANITIES TOURING PROGRAM GRANT

Touring Program grant funds help cover the costs of bringing humanities performers, presenters, artists, and exhibitors to Michigan nonprofit organizations. Organizations may request up to 40 percent of presenters'/ exhibitors' fees and travel expenses. Request for a grant may not exceed $3,000 per application, and an organization may not submit more than four grant applications or request more than $4,000 in a fiscal year. Applications are awarded on a first come, first served basis.

**Typical Recipients:** Libraries, schools, museums, civic and service groups, festival organizers, and other Michigan nonprofits

**Submission Guidelines:** Applications must be typed or computer generated. The application can be printed and typed or downloaded and completed in MS Word format from the website. Required attachments include proof of nonprofit status and a copy of the contract signed by the sponsoring organization's project director or authorizing official and performer/presenter/exhibitor. The original application (with original signatures) and a copy of the grant application, along with two copies of the required attachments, must be sent to the address below.

**Deadlines:** Applications must be postmarked at least 4 weeks prior to the contracted program or exhibition date.

**Contact:** Michigan Humanities Council, 119 Pere Marquette Dr., Suite 3B, Lansing, MI 48912-1270; Phone: 517-372-7770

**Grant-Specific Website:** www.michiganhumanities.org/grants/touring/index.php

### REQUIREMENTS AND RESTRICTIONS
Vary by grant

### APPLICATION PROCEDURES
Vary by grant

### CONTACT
Varies by grant

### GRANT-SPECIFIC WEBSITE
www.michiganhumanities.org/grants/

# Minnesota Department of Education, State Library Services Division

## Headquarters

1500 Hwy. 36 W.
Roseville, MN 55113
Phone: 651-582-8791
http://education.state.mn.us/MDE/Learning_Support/Library_Services/index.html

## Description

**Founded:** NA

**Operating Locations:** Minnesota

The Minnesota State Library Agency is a division of the Minnesota Department of Education. The state library provides leadership and support to the Minnesota library community in planning, developing, and implementing high-quality library and information services statewide.

## Grants Information

### GRANT TYPES
LSTA funds

## TYPICAL RECIPIENTS

Academic, public, and special libraries and public school media centers

## GRANT VALUES

Total Dollar Amount of Grants: $400,000

## NAMED GRANTS
## LSTA COMPETITIVE GRANT PROGRAM

An estimated allocation of $400,000 is available to fund eligible library and school media center projects from funds made available through the Library Services and Technology Act. Grants will be made for projects in two categories: (1) targeted areas of underserved populations and barrier-free access to library services and programs, and (2) upgrades, improvements, and enhancements to library automation and technology issues.

## REQUIREMENTS AND RESTRICTIONS

See the website for details.

## APPLICATION PROCEDURES

**Submission Guidelines:** There is a two-part application process. Interested eligible libraries must submit a letter of intent which will be reviewed and accepted before applicant can move forward to the full competitive grant application. Application packets are available on the website.

**Deadlines:** January

## CONTACT

James V. Wroblewski
LSTA Coordinator/
    Grant Administrator
Phone: 651-582-8805
E-mail: jym.wroblewski@state.mn.us

## GRANT-SPECIFIC WEBSITE

http://education.state.mn.us/MDE/
    Learning_Support/Library_Services/
    Grants_and_Aid/Library_Services_
    and_Technology_Act/

# Mississippi Library Commission

## Headquarters

3881 Eastwood Dr.
Jackson, MS 39211-6439
Phone: 800-647-7542
www.mlc.lib.ms.us

## Description

**Founded:** 1926

**Operating Locations:** Mississippi

The Mississippi Library Commission is committed—through leadership, advocacy, and service—to strengthening and enhancing libraries and library services for all Mississippians.

# Grants Information

## GRANT TYPES
LSTA funds

## TYPICAL RECIPIENTS
Public libraries, public library systems, consortia led by a public library or library system

## GRANT VALUES
NA

## NAMED GRANTS

### LSTA LIBRARY 2.0 SERVICES COMPETITIVE GRANT
Priority is given to projects that focus on user assessment and identified needs by adding new services or expanding/improving current services and evaluating new or expanded services frequently. Project must reflect priority with activities/methods described and address state goals defined by agency's current LSTA Five-Year Plan.

**Typical Recipients:** Public libraries, public library systems, consortia led by a public library or library system

**Grant Values:** Total Dollar Amount of Grants, $75,000; Highest Grant, $15,000; Lowest Grant, $2,500

### LSTA PUBLIC LIBRARY PROGRAMMING COMPETITIVE GRANT
Priority is given to programs aimed at an identified target audience, using input from local community leaders and the target audience.

**Typical Recipients:** Public libraries, public library systems, consortia led by a public library or library system

**Grant Values:** Total Dollar Amount of Grants, $50,000; Highest Grant, $15,000; Lowest Grant, $2,500

### LSTA TECHNOLOGY COMPETITIVE GRANT
Priority is given to projects that complete one of the following: upgrade/replacement of integrated library system (ILS) for full participation in Virtual Union Catalog/Interlibrary Loan System including patron-initiated interlibrary loan functions; installation of systems to manage public-access Internet, workstations, printers; assistive devices to enable persons with disabilities to use library services; improved network security; dedicated computers and related software for targeted populations.

**Typical Recipients:** Public libraries, public library systems, consortia led by a public library or library system

**Grant Values:** Total Dollar Amount of Grants, $200,000; Highest Grant, $20,000; Lowest Grant, $2,500

### LSTA FOCUSED DEVELOPMENT NONCOMPETITIVE GRANT
Priority is given to projects that enhance

identified areas of existing nonfiction/ specialized fiction collections, introduce a new collection format, or improve a picture book collection.

**Typical Recipients:** Public libraries, public library systems

**Grant Values:** Total Dollar Amount of Grants, $293,000 (for all noncompetitive categories); Average Grant, $3,000

## LSTA FOCUSED TECHNOLOGY NONCOMPETITIVE GRANT

Priority is given to projects that enhance technologies used by library staff to deliver services or carry out operations, or that enhance technologies used by library patrons to access or use services.

**Typical Recipients:** Public libraries, public library systems

**Grant Values:** Total Dollar Amount of Grants, $293,000 (for all noncompetitive categories); Average Grant, $3,000

## LSTA PROFESSIONAL ASSISTANCE CONSULTING NONCOMPETITIVE GRANT

Priority is given to projects that enhance the ability of libraries to address specific local needs for library services and the effect on end users through the services of a consultant or other appropriate professional.

**Typical Recipients:** Public libraries, public library systems

**Grant Values:** Total Dollar Amount of Grants, $293,000 (for all noncompetitive categories); Highest Grant, $7,500; Lowest Grant, $2,000

**Requirements and Restrictions:** There is no limit on the number of applications a library/library system can submit.

## LSTA SKILLS DEVELOPMENT NONCOMPETITIVE GRANT

This grant funds opportunities to aid in developing skills and knowledge of library staff to improve library resources, services, systems, and tools so that all Mississippians have access to quality library service.

**Typical Recipients:** Public libraries, public library systems

**Grant Values:** Total Dollar Amount of Grants, $293,000 (for all noncompetitive categories); Highest Grant, $3,500; Lowest Grant, $1,500

**Requirements and Restrictions:** Applicants must complete and submit a Training Plan with the application. Applicants are allowed to submit only one application.

## REQUIREMENTS AND RESTRICTIONS

Applicant must be located in the state of Mississippi. Funds cannot be used for capital improvements, repair, or renovation as defined by IMLS; library materials for general collection updates;

staff costs; administrative overhead fees; general office supplies unrelated to project; costs related to events and services primarily for entertainment; or other costs not eligible or allowable under federal or state regulations. There is a 10 percent cash match of project total required for competitive grants. Unless otherwise noted, applicants are allowed to submit up to two applications in each grant category.

## APPLICATION PROCEDURES

**Submission Guidelines:** Applications must be on the prescribed application forms supplied by the Library Commission on the website below, and they must be filled out on the computer. No cover sheets or transmittal letters are allowed. Applications must be submitted by e-mail to the address below; any required attachments to the application must be submitted in the same e-mail. Only one application per e-mail. Subject of e-mail must be title of project. Internet Certification (CIPA) and Assurances must be printed out, signed, and a hard copy mailed to the Library Commission at the following address: Mississippi Library Commission, LSTA Subgrant Program, 3881 Eastwood Dr., Jackson, MS 39211.

**Deadlines:** April

**CONTACT**
Grant Programs Management
Phone: 800-647-7542
E-mail: grantsprog@mlc.lib.ms.us

**GRANT-SPECIFIC WEBSITE**
www.mlc.lib.ms.us/ServicesToLibraries/
    Grants.html

# Missouri State Library

## Headquarters

600 W. Main St.
PO Box 387
Jefferson City, MO 65102-0387
www.sos.mo.gov/library/

## Description

**Founded:** NA

**Operating Locations:** Missouri

The major functions of the state library are to provide direct library and information service in support of the Missouri state government, to provide library service to blind and physically handicapped residents of Missouri, and to promote the development and improvement of library services throughout the state.

# Grants Information

## GRANT TYPES
Project, programs

## TYPICAL RECIPIENTS
Missouri public, academic, special, institutional, and public school libraries and library consortia

## GRANT VALUES
NA

## NAMED GRANTS

### EXCELLENCE IN LIBRARY SERVICE GRANT
The Excellence in Library Service Grant is intended to help libraries plan and train staff for improved library services. Libraries receive funds to contract with a trainer, qualified consultant, professional librarian, technology expert, child development specialist, or other expert with a skill or knowledge that would help the library to better serve its community.

**Typical Recipients:** Libraries that do not have local funding available for such an expense

**Grant Values:** Highest Grant, $15,000; Lowest Grant, $500

**Past Grant Recipients:**

- Kirkwood Public Library (MO), $1,125
- George A. Spiva Library, Missouri Southern State University (MO), $1,966
- Saint Charles City-County Library District (MO), $3,669
- Spring-Greene County Library District (MO), $3,381

**Requirements and Restrictions:**
Unallowable costs include hiring a member of the applicant's library or regional contractual members; food expenses (for events not open to outside registrants); equipment purchases; furniture; collection development acquisitions; planning for a tax levy campaign; any costs related to building, planning and design, remodeling, or new construction; and on-call maintenance contracts. Grant winners are required to submit narrative, statistical, financial, and evaluative reports regarding the project. Copies of surveys, promotional materials, brochures, evaluation results, and other documents produced as part of the grant project must accompany the final narrative report.

**Deadlines:** January

**Grant-Specific Website:** www.sos .mo.gov/library/development/grants.asp

### PROGRAMS FOR TARGETED POPULATIONS
The Programs for Targeted Populations grant is designed to assist libraries in providing events for youth, adults,

families, and intergenerational audiences. Programs will stimulate interest in books, technology, and other library services among the targeted population and provide opportunities for collaboration between libraries and community agencies. The grant is $2,500 per library outlet per program for up to three different programs in a series ($7,500). Libraries with multiple branches or service centers may replicate the program(s) at one additional site for maximum funding of $15,000.

**Typical Recipients:** Public, academic, special, institutional, and public school libraries in Missouri

**Grant Values:** Highest Grant, $15,000; Lowest Grant, $500

**Past Grant Recipients:**

- Cape Girardeau Public Library (MO), $6,041
- Mid-Continent Public Library (MO), $1,086
- Morgan County R-1 School Library (MO), $4,744
- Saint Louis County Library (MO), $3,582

**Requirements and Restrictions:** Unallowable costs include events primarily for entertainment with little educational focus, existing staff costs, transportation, incentives, prizes, gifts, refreshments, movie and database licensing/subscription fees, collection development purchases, equipment, gaming software, furniture, and vehicles. Grant winners are required to submit narrative, statistical, financial, and evaluative reports regarding the project. Copies of surveys, promotional materials, brochures, evaluation results, and other documents produced as part of the grant project must accompany the final narrative report.

**Deadlines:** January

**Grant-Specific Website:** www.sos .mo.gov/library/development/grants.asp

### SHOW ME STEPS TO CAREER DEVELOPMENT GRANT

Show Me Steps to Career Development grants provide financial assistance for library staff to participate in continuing education and training opportunities when local funds cannot finance the entire cost. Eligible activities include regional, state, and national workshops; preconferences, conferences, seminars or other development programs offered by professional associations or other appropriate public or nonprofit entities; web-based instructional courses; and technical or special training sessions offered by nonprofit providers. There is no maximum amount of funds that may be requested. However, a maximum dollar amount available per request, per educational activity, may be set by the State Library in order to maintain funding throughout the current calendar year.

**Typical Recipients:** Missouri librarians

**Grant Values:** Lowest Grant, $100

**Requirements and Restrictions:** The State Library determines the amount of local matching funds required. The minimum is 25 percent, but a larger match may be required. Unallowable costs include, but are not limited to, late registration fees; hotel room service fees; charges for academic course credit; personal entertainment; transportation charges for sightseeing, shopping, etc.; and Internet connectivity or computer upgrades to hardware or software for the purpose of participating in web-based instruction. Additional activities ineligible for funding include library management activities such as leadership development, staff management, fund-raising, advocacy, general marketing, and library design and construction.

**Deadlines:** Applications may be submitted at any time throughout the year, but must be received at least 6 weeks before the activity begins.

**Grant-Specific Website:** www.sos .mo.gov/library/development/grants .asp#lsta

## SPANISH THAT WORKS GRANT PROGRAM
Spanish That Works grant funds are intended to help libraries train staff for improved library service to Spanish speakers. Funds may be used by libraries to hire an instructor to teach the prepackaged "Spanish That Works" curriculum, provided by the state library, to its staff. Grant provides $3,000 per course for three courses (for a total of $9,000).

**Typical Recipients:** Missouri libraries

**Grant Values:** Highest Grant, $9,000; Lowest Grant, $500

**Past Grant Recipients:**

- Kansas City Public Library (MO), $2,714
- Saint Louis Public Library (MO), $5,000

**Requirements and Restrictions:** Unallowable costs include hiring a member of the applicant's own library or applicant's regional library, refreshments, equipment purchases, furniture, and collection development acquisitions. Grant winners are required to submit final financial and narrative reports.

**Deadlines:** January

**Grant-Specific Website:** www.sos .mo.gov/library/development/grants/ ShortTerm.asp

## TECHNOLOGY MINIGRANT
Technology Minigrants provide funding for technology- and automation-related equipment—hardware and software—to improve network infrastructure. These grant funds can be used to replace older

or purchase new equipment in order to provide improved library services.

**Typical Recipients:** Public libraries certified to receive state aid

**Grant Values:** Highest Grant, $19,000; Lowest Grant, $500

**Past Grant Recipients:**

- Bollinger County Library (MO), $3,161
- Jefferson County Library (MO), $9,053
- Kansas City Public Library (MO), $12,342
- Rolling Hills Consolidated Library (MO), $14,775

**Requirements and Restrictions:** Academic, school, and special libraries are not eligible. A 25 percent minimum match is required for all grants. A 50 percent match is required for individual pieces of equipment in excess of $15,000.

**Deadlines:** January

**Contact:** Phone: 573-751-1822 or 800-325-0131, ext. 9

**Grant-Specific Website:** www.sos .mo.gov/library/development/grants/ ShortTerm.asp

## COOPERATION PROJECTS GRANT PROGRAM

The Cooperation Projects Grant will allow libraries of all types to try out new and different ideas, in cooperation with library and community partners. These include partnerships between public libraries and senior centers; projects designed for underserved groups; partnerships between libraries and medical programs in an educational role; or other great ideas that involve all types of libraries partnering together or with other community/state agencies with an end result of improved or expanded services for the citizens of Missouri.

**Typical Recipients:** All public libraries certified to receive state aid, school libraries, academic libraries, special libraries, and library consortia

**Grant Values:** Highest Grant, $50,000; Lowest Grant, $2,500

**Requirements and Restrictions:** Unallowable costs include, but are not limited to, costs for basic library service operations, equipment needed for basic library operations, existing staff costs, collection development acquisitions, vehicles or bookmobiles, speakers or other activities used for entertainment, transportation for field trips, and materials delivery services.

**Deadlines:** March

**Grant-Specific Website:** www.sos .mo.gov/library/development/grants.asp

## RETROSPECTIVE CONVERSION GRANT

The Retrospective Conversion Grant

provides funding for libraries to convert card catalogs, other print inventories, or non-MARC electronic records for library materials to the MARC21 format. This lays the basis for libraries to display their local holdings in the Missouri Group Catalog or other union catalogs. Prepares libraries for implementation of local online automation systems and facilitates greater resource sharing among institutions. There is no limit to the maximum amount of funds that can be requested.

**Typical Recipients:** Academic, public, and special libraries

**Grant Values:** Lowest Grant, $5,000

**Past Grant Recipients:**

- Jackson County Missouri Historical Society (MO), $5,000
- State Historical Society of Missouri (MO), $70,952

**Requirements and Restrictions:** Unallowable costs include, but are not limited to, subscriptions to bibliographic databases; installation charges, equipment training fees, extended warranties and service contracts, furnishings, signage, coin-operated devices on equipment, RFID tags, vehicles; ongoing operating costs; equipment for new facilities that are less than 75 percent complete at the time of application; administrative overhead; "in-house" original cataloging or copy-cataloging projects; and existing staff costs.

**Deadlines:** March

**Contact:** Phone: 573-751-1822 or 800-325-0131, ext. 9

**Grant-Specific Website:** www.sos.mo.gov/library/development/grants.asp

**SPOTLIGHT ON LITERACY GRANT**

The Spotlight on Literacy grant program offers Missouri libraries the opportunity to serve patrons of all ages through programs that support an educated and informed citizenry. Programs may encourage reading, language skills development, academic improvement, and GED instruction. Collaborative efforts to better serve low-literacy populations are strongly encouraged.

**Typical Recipients:** Public, academic, and secondary or postsecondary school libraries

**Grant Values:** Highest Grant, $10,000; Lowest Grant, $2,000

**Past Grant Recipients:**

- Bollinger County Library (MO), $9,288
- Maryville Public Library (MO), $5,090
- Morgan County R-1 School Library (MO), $10,000
- Southern Reynolds County R-2 School Library (MO), $9,981

- Pickler Memorial Library, Truman State University (MO), $10,000

**Requirements and Restrictions:** Unallowable costs include, but are not limited to, paying existing staff costs, costs to provide classes that are part of a school or institution's usual curriculum, transportation, incentives/prizes, refreshments, movie and database licensing or subscription fees, collection development purchases, equipment, furniture, or vehicles. Libraries may apply for up to three grants per grant period, choosing among the following categories: at-risk youth; families; persons who may be low literate; and persons who lack a high school diploma. Each grant proposal must be submitted on a separate application. Grant funds may be used to cover the costs for planning and implementing the project.

**Deadlines:** March

**Grant-Specific Website:** www.sos.mo.gov/library/development/grants/LongTerm.asp

## TECHNOLOGY LADDER GRANT PROGRAM

The Technology Ladder grant provides funds for technology- and automation-related equipment and software. Specifically, this application is designed to help libraries move up the technology ladder to a higher level of service. These grant funds can be used to replace older equipment and software or to purchase new equipment or software. There is no limit on the maximum amount that can be requested.

**Typical Recipients:** Public libraries

**Grant Values:** Lowest Grant, $5,000

**Requirements and Restrictions:** Libraries that are eligible for the Gates Opportunity Online Hardware Grants will be a low priority for patron-use computer equipment requested through this application. See the website for list of unallowable costs. A 25 percent minimum match is required. A 50 percent match is required for individual pieces of equipment in excess of $15,000.

**Deadlines:** March

**Contact:** Phone: 573-751-1822 or 800-325-0131, ext. 9

**Grant-Specific Website:** www.sos.mo.gov/library/development/grants/LongTerm.asp

## REQUIREMENTS AND RESTRICTIONS

Applicants must be located in the state of Missouri.

## APPLICATION PROCEDURES

**Submission Guidelines:** Applications may be downloaded from the website. Original completed application forms and two additional copies must be mailed to the address below.

**CONTACT**
Debbie Musselman
LSTA Grants Officer
Missouri State Library
600 W. Main St.
PO Box 387
Jefferson City, MO 65102-0387
Phone: 573-526-6734 or 800-325-0131,
      ext. 14
E-mail: debbie.musselman@sos.mo.gov

**GRANT-SPECIFIC WEBSITE**
www.sos.mo.gov/library/development/
      grants.asp

# Montana Library Association (MLA)

## Headquarters

PO Box 1352
Three Forks, MT 59752
Phone: 406-285-3090
Fax: 406-285-3091
www.mtlib.org/index.php

## Description

**Founded:** 1906

**Operating Locations:** Montana

The purpose of the Montana Library Association is to promote library interest and library development and to raise standards of library service in the state of Montana.

## Financial Summary

Assets: $92,148
Gifts Received: $2,731

## Grants Information

**GRANT TYPES**
Conference attendance, professional development

**TYPICAL RECIPIENTS**
Montana librarians

**GRANT VALUES**
NA

**NAMED GRANTS**

**ALA EMERGING LEADERS GRANTS**
The selected MLA participant will join other ALA members and attend Emerging Leaders meetings at the ALA Midwinter Meeting and Annual Conference. MLA will provide one member with a $500 stipend for travel to each conference for a total grant amount of $1,000.

**Requirements and Restrictions:**
Applicant must meet Emerging Leaders application requirements and have been accepted to the program. Applicant must be able to attend the two ALA conferences for the year of participation

and be willing to serve MLA for two years in a leadership position within the association. Recipients will be required to present a program at an MLA-sponsored retreat or conference and/or to serve as a mentor in the MLA mentor program. Grant recipients unable to serve as Emerging Leaders through ALA and/or unable to serve MLA for two years following the program will be required to reimburse MLA for the grant amount.

## MLA CONFERENCE GRANTS

MLA Conference Grants are available for members who want to attend the association's annual conference. Fifteen $150 grants are available; of these, up to five are available to those members new to MLA and the library profession.

**Requirements and Restrictions:**
Recipients must live further than 50 miles from the conference site. Applicants must not have received an MLA Conference Grant in the last two calendar years. Applicants applying for one of the grants designated for new members must have no more than two years as an MLA member. Grant recipients unable to attend the annual conference will not receive the award.

**Deadlines:** March

## LEADERSHIP INSTITUTE GRANTS

Leadership Institute grants of $1,000 per institute are available to those association members who want to further their professional development by attending the Leadership Institutes hosted by MPLA or PNLA.

**Requirements and Restrictions:**
Applicant must be a current MLA member and must have been a member for at least two previous years. Leadership Institute grants are designated for leadership institutes specified by the MLA board. Applicants must not have received a Leadership Institute grant previously. Leadership Institute grants will not exceed the actual amount associated with the program/event for which the grant is requested. Recipients will be required to present a program at an MLA-sponsored retreat or conference and/or to serve as a mentor in the MLA mentor program.

## PROFESSIONAL DEVELOPMENT GRANTS

Professional Development grants of $800 are available to those association members who want to further their professional development by attending a national or regional conference or professional development event.

**Requirements and Restrictions:**
Professional Development grants cannot be applied to the MLA annual conference. Applicant must not have received a Professional Development grant in the last five calendar years and must have been an MLA member for at least three consecutive

years. Applications must be submitted prior to professional development event for which funds are being sought. Professional Development grants will not exceed the actual amount associated with the program/event for which the grant is requested. Award will be based upon the budget submitted by the applicant.

**Deadlines:** April and October

## REQUIREMENTS AND RESTRICTIONS

Applicants must be located in the state of Montana and be current MLA members.

## APPLICATION PROCEDURES

**Submission Guidelines:** Application may be downloaded from the website. E-mail one copy (preferred) or mail three copies of the completed application to the address below.

## CONTACT

Mary Drew Powers
Parmly Billings Library
510 North Broadway
Billings, MT 59101
Phone: 406-657-8258
Fax: 406-657-8293
E-mail: powersmd@ci.billings.mt.us

## GRANT-SPECIFIC WEBSITE

www.mtlib.org/Handbook/grant_
guidelines.html

# Motorola Mobility Foundation

## Headquarters

600 N. US Highway 45
Libertyville, IL 60048
Phone: 847-523-3597
E-mail: giving@motorola.com
http://responsibility.motorola.com/
index.php/society/comminvest/
motofoundation/

## Description

**Founded:** 1928/2011

**Operating Locations:** Illinois

**Foundation Information:** Corporate foundation of Motorola Mobility, Inc.

## Financial Summary

Assets: $159,131,143
Gifts Received: $88,639,315
Total Giving: $15,117,528

## Grants Information

### GRANT TYPES

Capital, employee matching, general support, multiyear continuing support, project, scholarship

## TYPICAL RECIPIENTS

Arts and humanities, civic affairs, education, environment, health, religion, science, social services

## GRANT VALUES

Total Dollar Amount of Grants:
$15,117,528
Highest Grant: $5,000,000
Lowest Grant: $25

## NAMED GRANTS

### EMPOWERMENT GRANTS

Empowerment Grants support programs that leverage technology to build stronger communities and will provide nonprofit organizations with funding to close the digital divide. Successful programs may include providing technology, and the skills needed to use it, for teachers, mentors, and community leaders.

## REQUIREMENTS AND RESTRICTIONS

Eligible organizations must be U.S. registered or incorporated 501(c) (3) nonprofit organizations or NCES schools or school districts; must have an operating budget under $5 million; must serve communities in California, Illinois, Massachusetts, or Pennsylvania; must be aligned with funding priorities in education, health, and wellness or community. Successful applications must demonstrate the ways that digital technology can be used to further a nonprofit organization's mission.

## APPLICATION PROCEDURES

**Submission Guidelines:** As part of the application process, applicants are required to submit a 3–5 minute video describing the program and how digital technology could be used to further enhance that program. All videos must be uploaded to YouTube prior to submission of the written application.

**Deadlines:** July

**Decisions:** September

## CONTACT

E-mail: giving@motorola.com

## GRANT-SPECIFIC WEBSITE

http://responsibility.motorola.com/
index.php/society/comminvest/
empowermentgrants/

# Motorola Solutions Foundation

## Headquarters

1303 E. Algonquin Rd.
Schaumburg, IL 60196
Phone: 847-576-6200
Fax: 847-576-9440
E-mail: foundation@motorolasolutions
.com
http://responsibility.motorolasolutions.
com/index.php/communityinvestment/
motosolutionsfoundation/

# Description

**Founded:** 1928/2011

**Operating Locations:** Illinois

**Foundation Information:** Corporate foundation of Motorola Solutions, Inc.

# Financial Summary

Assets: $159,131,143
Gifts Received: $88,639,315
Total Giving: $15,117,528

# Grants Information

## GRANT TYPES
Employee matching, general support, multiyear continuing support, project, scholarship

## TYPICAL RECIPIENTS
Arts and humanities, civic affairs, education, environment, health, religion, science, social services

## GRANT VALUES
Total Dollar Amount of Grants:
    $15,117,528
Highest Grant: $5,000,000
Lowest Grant: $25

## PAST GRANT RECIPIENTS

*Library or School Related*
- Forsyth County Public Library Fund (GA), general support, $50
- Library Foundation of Needham, Inc. (MA), general support, $150
- Sonoma County Public Library Fund (CA), general support, $25
- St. Theresa School (IL), general support, $11,765
- Morehouse College (GA), general support, $5,000

*General*
- National Merit Scholarship (IL), general support, $150,000
- YMCA of Metropolitan Chicago (IL), general support, $25,000

## REQUIREMENTS AND RESTRICTIONS
The foundation gives priority to programs in communities where Motorola Solutions has a significant presence. The foundation does not lease or donate Motorola Solutions products or equipment. Additionally, the foundation does not contribute to individuals; political or lobbying organizations, candidates, or campaigns; endowment funds; sport sponsorships; capital fund drives; or private foundations described under the U.S. IRS Code Section 509(a).

## APPLICATION PROCEDURES
**Submission Guidelines:** Complete eligibility quiz online.

## CONTACT
E-mail: foundation@motorolasolutions.
    com

**GRANT-SPECIFIC WEBSITE**
http://responsibility.
    motorolasolutions.com/index.
    php/communityinvestment/
    motosolutionsfoundation/
    applyforgrant/

# Music Library Association (MLA)

## Headquarters

8551 Research Way, Suite 180
Middleton, WI 53562
Phone: 608-836-5825
www.musiclibraryassoc.org

## Description

**Founded:** 1931

**Operating Locations:** Wisconsin

The Music Library Association (MLA) is the professional association for music libraries and librarianship in the United States. Founded in 1931, it has an international membership of librarians, musicians, scholars, educators, and members of the book and music trades. Complementing the association's national and international activities are eleven regional chapters that carry out its programs on the local level. MLA provides a professional forum for librarians, archivists, and others who support and preserve the world's musical heritage.

## Financial Summary

Assets: $991,138
Total Giving: $6,950

## Grants Information

### GRANT TYPES
Research, conference attendance

### TYPICAL RECIPIENTS
Music librarians or students of music librarianship

### GRANT VALUES
Total Dollar Amount of Grants: $4,850
Number of Grants: 4
Average Grant: $1,212
Highest Grant: $2,100
Lowest Grant: $750

### NAMED GRANTS

### DENA EPSTEIN AWARD FOR ARCHIVAL AND LIBRARY RESEARCH IN AMERICAN MUSIC
The Dena Epstein Award for Archival and Library Research in American Music was created through a generous endowment from Morton and Dena Epstein to the MLA in 1995. These $2,100 grants are awarded to support research in archives or libraries internationally on any aspect of American music. There are no

restrictions as to an applicant's age, nationality, profession, or institutional affiliation. All proposals are reviewed entirely on the basis of merit. Calls for applications are issued in the spring, and awards are announced at the MLA annual meeting.

### KEVIN FREEMAN TRAVEL GRANT

The Kevin Freeman Travel Grant is intended to support travel and hotel expenses to attend the MLA annual meeting. Grants include the conference registration fee and a cash award of up to $750, subject to approval of the current year's budget by the MLA board. Applicant must be a member of MLA and be in the first three years of his or her professional career, a graduate library school student aspiring to become a music librarian, or a recent graduate (within one year of degree) of a graduate program in librarianship who is seeking a professional position as a music librarian. Calls for applications are issued in the spring, and awards are announced at the MLA annual meeting.

### WALTER GERBOTH AWARD

The Walter Gerboth Award was established by MLA in memory of its past president and honorary member Walter Gerboth. The award of $1,000 is made to members of MLA who are in the first five years of their professional library careers, to assist research in progress in music or music librarianship. Calls for applications are issued in the

spring, and awards are announced at the MLA annual meeting.

### CAROL JUNE BRADLEY AWARD FOR HISTORICAL RESEARCH IN MUSIC LIBRARIANSHIP

In 2003, MLA established this annual award in honor of Carol June Bradley, librarian emeritus at the State University of New York at Buffalo, who has been the foremost historian of music librarianship. The award, in the amount of $1,000, is granted to support studies that involve the history of music libraries or special collections, biographies of music librarians, studies of specific aspects of music librarianship, and studies of music library patrons' activities. The grant will be awarded to support costs associated with the research process, which may include travel, lodging, meals, supplies, and digital, photocopy, or microfilm reproduction of source material. There are no restrictions as to applicant's age, nationality, profession, or institutional affiliation. All proposals will be reviewed entirely on the basis of merit.

### REQUIREMENTS AND RESTRICTIONS

Some grants require MLA membership and a specific number of years in the music librarianship profession.

### APPLICATION PROCEDURES

**Deadlines:** Vary according to grant but are usually in June or July.

**Decisions:** Vary according to grant but are all announced at the MLA annual conference.

## CONTACT

Michael J. Rogan, Treasurer
Phone: 608-836-5825
Fax: 608-831-8200
E-mail: michael.rogan@tufts.edu

## GRANT-SPECIFIC WEBSITE

www.musiclibraryassoc.org/awards.
    aspx?id = 42

# National Center for Family Literacy (NCFL)

## Headquarters

325 W. Main St., Suite 300
Louisville, KY 40202
Phone: 502-584-1133
www.famlit.org

## Description

**Founded:** 1989

**Operating Locations:** Kentucky

It is the mission of the National Center for Family Literacy (NCFL) to provide every family not only with the opportunity to learn, but with the ability to learn and grow together. Family literacy ensures the cycle of learning and progress passes from generation to generation.

## Grants Information

### GRANT TYPES

Family literacy

### TYPICAL RECIPIENTS

Friends of the Library groups, public/ academic libraries, urban libraries

### GRANT VALUES

Number of Grants: 3
Average Grant: $10,000

### NAMED GRANTS

#### BETTER WORLD BOOKS/NCFL LIBRARIES AND FAMILIES

Through the Better World Books/NCFL Libraries and Families Award, NCFL and Better World Books will reward and enhance existing family programming and expand literacy-building practices of families in library settings. The grants will connect more families to their local libraries and expand their literacy efforts in new and innovative ways. One winner will be chosen from each of the following three categories: local Friends of the Library programs, public/ academic libraries, and urban libraries. Winners will also receive scholarships to NCFL's National Conference on Family Literacy.

**REQUIREMENTS AND RESTRICTIONS**
NA

**APPLICATION PROCEDURES**
**Submission Guidelines:** Application online

**Deadlines:** March

**CONTACT**
Phone: 502-584-1133

**GRANT-SPECIFIC WEBSITE**
www.famlit.org/award-grant
   -opportunities/ncfl-awards/

# National Endowment for the Humanities (NEH)

## Headquarters

1100 Pennsylvania Ave. NW
Washington, DC 20506
Phone: 202-606-8400
www.neh.gov

## Description

**Founded:** 1965

**Operating Locations:** District of Columbia

The National Endowment for the Humanities (NEH) is an independent grant-making agency of the U.S. government dedicated to supporting research, education, preservation, and public programs in the humanities.

## Grants Information

**GRANT TYPES**
Capital, project, training

**TYPICAL RECIPIENTS**
Colleges and universities, museums, public libraries, research institutions, historical societies and historic sites, scholarly associations, state humanities councils, nonprofit organizations, state and local governmental agencies, tribal governments

**GRANT VALUES**
NA

**NAMED GRANTS**

**CHALLENGE GRANTS**
Challenge Grants are capacity-building grants, intended to help institutions and organizations secure long-term improvements in and support for their humanities programs and resources. Grants may be used to establish or enhance endowments or spend-down funds that generate expendable earnings to support ongoing program activities. Funds may also be used for one-time capital expenditures (such as construction and renovation, purchase of equipment, and acquisitions) that bring

long-term benefits to the institution and to the humanities more broadly. Applicants wishing to apply for a grant of more than $500,000 should consult with NEH staff about the size of their requests. The federal portions of NEH challenge grants have ranged in recent years from $30,000 to $1,000,000.

**Typical Recipients:** Colleges and universities, museums, public libraries, research institutions, historical societies and historic sites, scholarly associations, state humanities councils, and other nonprofit entities

**Grant Values:** Typical Range of Grants, $30,000–$1,000,000

**Requirements and Restrictions:** Institutions may apply for only one NEH challenge grant in a calendar year. An institution is eligible to apply for a subsequent challenge grant beginning in the third year after the closing date of its most recent NEH challenge grant.

**Deadlines:** May

**Decisions:** December

**Contact:** Office of Challenge Grants, National Endowment for the Humanities, Rm. 420, 1100 Pennsylvania Ave. NW, Washington, DC 20506; *for assistance using Grants.gov*: Phone: 800-518-4726; E-mail: support@grants.gov; *for questions about the grant program*: Phone: 202-606-8309; E-mail: challenge@neh.gov

**Grant-Specific Website:** www.neh.gov/grants/guidelines/challenge.html

## PICTURING AMERICA SCHOOL COLLABORATION PROJECT GRANTS

The NEH invites proposals for local and regional projects that foster collaboration between K–12 educators and humanities scholars to encourage engagement with the rich resources of American art to tell America's story. The Picturing America School Collaboration Project grant opportunity is designed to help teachers and librarians whose schools display the Picturing America images form connections with courses in the core curriculum. Funded projects should support one or more conferences of one or two days each; accommodate at each conference 24–100 (or more) participants, all of whom would have access to the Picturing America portfolio; and provide opportunities for participants to engage with scholars, museum and library professionals, and other experts.

**Typical Recipients:** Any U.S. nonprofit organization is eligible, as are state and local governmental agencies and tribal governments. Individuals are not eligible to apply.

**Grant Values:** Highest Grant, $75,000

**Deadlines:** October

**Decisions:** April

**Contact:** Picturing America School Collaboration Projects, Division of Education Programs, Rm. 302, National Endowment for the Humanities, 1100 Pennsylvania Ave. NW, Washington, DC 20506; *for questions about the grant program*: Phone: 202-606-8500; E-mail: education@neh.gov; *for assistance using Grants.gov*: Phone: 800-518-4726; E-mail: support@grants.gov

**Grant-Specific Website:** www.neh.gov/grants/guidelines/PASCP.html

## PRESERVATION AND ACCESS EDUCATION AND TRAINING GRANT

Preservation and Access Education and Training grants help the staff of cultural institutions, large and small, obtain the knowledge and skills needed to serve as effective stewards of humanities collections. Grants also support educational programs that prepare the next generation of conservators and preservation professionals, as well as projects that introduce the staff of cultural institutions to new information and advances in preservation and access practices. Grants to regional preservation field service organizations typically range from $50,000 to a maximum of $250,000 per year. For all other applicants, the maximum award is $125,000 per year.

**Typical Recipients:** Any U.S. nonprofit organization is eligible, as are state and local governmental agencies and tribal governments. Individuals are not eligible to apply.

**Grant Values:** Typical Range of Grants, $50,000–$250,000

**Deadlines:** June

**Decisions:** January

**Contact:** Preservation and Access Education and Training, Division of Preservation and Access, Rm. 411, National Endowment for the Humanities, 1100 Pennsylvania Ave. NW, Washington, DC 20506; *for questions about the grant program*: Phone: 202-606-8570; E-mail: preservation@neh.gov; *for assistance using Grants.gov*: Phone: 800-518-4726; E-mail: support@grants.gov

**Grant-Specific Website:** www.neh.gov/grants/guidelines/pet.html

## SUSTAINING CULTURAL HERITAGE COLLECTIONS GRANT

The Sustaining Cultural Heritage Collections program helps cultural institutions meet the complex challenge of preserving large and diverse holdings of humanities materials for future generations by supporting preventive conservation measures that mitigate deterioration and prolong the useful life of collections. NEH invites proposals that explore and implement energy-efficient and cost-effective preventive conservation measures designed to mitigate the greatest risks to collections. Two kinds of grants are available: (1) Planning and Evaluation Grants may encompass such activities as site visits, planning sessions, monitoring, testing, project-specific research, and preliminary designs for implementation projects. Planning and evaluation grants may be especially helpful to institutions interested in exploring sustainable preventive conservation strategies. (2) Implementation Grants funds projects based on planning that is specific to the needs of the institution and its collections within the context of its local environment.

**Typical Recipients:** Any U.S. nonprofit organization is eligible, as are state and local governmental agencies and tribal governments. Individuals are not eligible to apply.

**Grant Values:** Highest Grant, $40,000 (Planning and Evaluation Grant), $400,000 (Implementation Grant)

**Deadlines:** December

**Decisions:** August

**Contact:** Sustaining Cultural Heritage Collections, Division of Preservation and Access, Rm. 411, National Endowment for the Humanities, 1100 Pennsylvania Ave. NW, Washington, DC 20506; *for questions about the grant program*: Phone: 202-606-8570; E-mail: preservation@neh.gov; *for assistance using Grants.gov*: Phone: 800-518-4726; E-mail: support@grants.gov

**Grant-Specific Website:**
www.neh.gov/grants/guidelines/SCHC.html

## REQUIREMENTS AND RESTRICTIONS
Vary by grant

## APPLICATION PROCEDURES

**Submission Guidelines:** Prior to submitting a proposal, applicants are encouraged (though not required) to contact program officers who can offer advice about preparing the proposal and read draft proposals. Draft proposals should be submitted at least 6 weeks before the deadline. The final application must be prepared and submitted via Grants.gov. Applicants must create an account and are strongly encouraged to do so at least 2 weeks before the application deadline. If you are sending supplementary materials (that cannot be scanned and converted to an electronic form and submitted via Grants.gov), please send eight copies of each item and include a list of these supplementary materials in the application's table of contents with an indication that they have been mailed separately.

## CONTACT
Varies by grant

## GRANT-SPECIFIC WEBSITE
www.neh.gov/grants/

# Neal-Schuman Publishers

## Headquarters

100 William St., Rm. 2004
New York, NY 10038-4512
Phone: 212-925-8650
www.neal-schuman.com

## Description

**Founded:** 1976

**Operating Locations:** New York, London

**Type of Product/Service:** Independent, privately owned publisher of professional books for librarians, archivists, and knowledge managers

# NEAL-SCHUMAN FOUNDATION

100 William St., Rm. 2004
New York, NY 10038-5017
**Foundation Information:** Corporate foundation of Neal-Schuman Publishers

## Financial Summary

Assets: $69,821

## Grants Information

**GRANT TYPES**
Project

**TYPICAL RECIPIENTS**
Library associations, foundations, or nonprofit organizations

**GRANT VALUES**
Typical Range of Grants: $250–$1,000

**NAMED GRANTS**

**CONFERENCE PROGRAMMING GRANTS**
Conference Programming Grants are given to state and regional library associations in support of programming for local, regional, and national library conferences.

**REQUIREMENTS AND RESTRICTIONS**
NA

**APPLICATION PROCEDURES**

**Submission Guidelines:** Application online

**CONTACT**
Charles Harmon
Phone: 212-925-8650, ext. 310
Fax: 212-219-8916
E-mail: info@neal-schumanfoundation.org

GRANT-SPECIFIC WEBSITE
www.neal-schuman.com/the-neal
-schuman-foundation

# Nebraska Library Commission

## Headquarters

1200 North St., Suite 120
Lincoln, NE 68508-2023
Phone: 402-471-2045
www.nlc.state.ne.us

## Description

**Founded:** 1901

**Operating Locations:** Nebraska

The mission of the Nebraska Library Commission is statewide promotion, development, and coordination of library and information services. As the state library agency, the commission advocates for the library and information service needs of all Nebraskans.

## Grants Information

### GRANT TYPES
Continuing education, library improvement, youth programs

### TYPICAL RECIPIENTS
Accredited public libraries, accredited public libraries in conjunction with recognized community organizations or agencies, groups of public libraries, regional library systems, consortia of public libraries, state-run institutions, institutional libraries, individual children's librarians

### GRANT VALUES
NA

### NAMED GRANTS

#### CONTINUING EDUCATION AND TRAINING GRANTS
The purpose of Continuing Education and Training grants is to assist Nebraska libraries to provide improved library services to their communities through continuing education and training for their library personnel and supporters.

**Typical Recipients:** Accredited public libraries, accredited public libraries in conjunction with recognized community organizations or agencies, groups of public libraries, regional library systems, consortia of public libraries, and state-run institutions

**Grant Values:** Highest Grant, $5,000; Lowest Grant, $250

**Requirements and Restrictions:** Applicants must be located in the state of Nebraska. This grant may not be applied toward the cost of attending statewide professional conferences. This grant may not be applied toward the cost of academic education for an individual or individuals. Each grant requires a match of 25 percent of the total cost of the project. Applications from libraries cooperating with other libraries or entities will be given first consideration. Applications from libraries which have never received a Continuing Education and Training Grant will also be given preference.

**Submission Guidelines:** Applications are available online. Applications will be accepted by mail or e-mail. Faxes and in-person delivery are not accepted.

**Deadlines:** December

**Decisions:** January

**Contact:** Laura Johnson, Continuing Education Coordinator, Nebraska Library Commission, The Atrium, 1200 N St., Suite 120, Lincoln, NE 68508-2023; Phone: 800-307-2665 or 402-471-2694; E-mail: laura.johnson@nebraska.gov

**Grant-Specific Website:** www.nlc.state.ne.us/grants/ce/

### LIBRARY IMPROVEMENT GRANT

The Library Improvement Grant program is designed to facilitate growth and development of library programs and services in Nebraska public and institutional libraries, by supplementing local funding with federal funds designated for these purposes. Projects seeking funding must meet one or more of the six "LSTA Purposes" on the Nebraska Library Commission's Long Range Plan.

**Typical Recipients:** Nebraska public libraries, identified institutional libraries, Nebraska regional library systems

**Grant Values:** Lowest Grant, $500

**Past Grant Recipients:**

- Alliance Public Library (NE), replacement of 30-year-old microfilm reader machine, $8,550
- Bennington Public Library (NE), electronic materials format collection development, $2,475
- Blair Public Library (NE), portable computer lab, $5,195
- Clay Center Public Library (NE), youth space project, $300
- Kearney Public Library (NE), historic newspaper project, $12,140
- Panhandle Library System (NE), rotating DVD collection, $5,160

**Requirements and Restrictions:** Applicant is required to make a 25 percent local match, of which at least 10 percent is a cash match.

**Submission Guidelines:** Applications are available online. Applications should be submitted electronically, postmarked, or hand-delivered no later than the due date. Faxes are not accepted.

**Deadlines:** January

**Decisions:** February

**Contact:** Richard Miller, Library Improvement Grant Applications, Nebraska Library Commission, The Atrium, 1200 N St., Suite 120, Lincoln, NE 68508-2023; Phone: 800-307-2665 or 402-471-3175; Fax: 402-471-2083; E-mail: richard.miller@nebraska.gov

**Grant-Specific Website:** www.nlc.state.ne.us/grants/LSTA/

## YOUTH GRANTS FOR EXCELLENCE

The Youth Grants for Excellence program is designed to encourage creative, new approaches to address problems and needs of children and young adults in the community. It is expected that funding will provide a foundation for ongoing, rather than one-time, services that can be continued with community support.

**Typical Recipients:** Any children's librarian, young adult librarian, or adult librarian (in an accredited public library or a state-run institutional library) in charge of children's or young adult services may apply. Schools, service agencies, or organizations may be involved through collaborative planning and programming.

**Grant Values:** Lowest Grant, $250

**Past Grant Recipients:**

- Collaboration: Eastern Library System, Southeast Library System (NE), youth services retreat, $700
- Lied Randolph Public Library (NE), Explore the Arts program, $1,495
- South Sioux City Public Library (NE), infant and toddler storytime, $600
- Stromsburg Public Library (NE), youth gaming program, $809
- Tekamah Public Library (NE), video game nights for teens, $831
- Scottsbluff Public Library (NE), teen technology grant, $782

**Requirements and Restrictions:** The purchase of furniture, computer equipment, or food with grant funds is not allowed. Grant funds may not be used for payment of salary or wages for permanent library staff. Each project must have at least one program for community youth to attend. Applicant is required to make a 25 percent local match, of which at least 10 percent is a cash match.

**Submission Guidelines:** Applications are available online. For projects requesting $250–$1,000 in grant funds, applicants should use the short application form. For projects requesting more than $1,000, applicants should use the longer form. Applications must be postmarked or submitted electronically no later than the due date. Faxes will not be accepted. Application must include a brief statement of the need for the project, details about how the project will be implemented, a description of the program to be held, and information about how the success of the project will be determined.

**Deadlines:** October

**Decisions:** November

**Contact:** Sally Snyder, Nebraska Library Commission, The Atrium, 1200 N St., Suite 120, Lincoln, NE 68508-2023; Phone: 800-307-2665 or 402-471-4003; E-mail: sally.snyder@nebraska.gov

**Grant-Specific Website:** www.nlc.state.ne.us/grants/youth/

**REQUIREMENTS AND RESTRICTIONS**
Applicants must be located in the state of Nebraska. Other requirements vary by grant.

**APPLICATION PROCEDURES**
Vary by grant

**CONTACT**
Varies by grant

**GRANT-SPECIFIC WEBSITE**
Varies by grant

# Nevada State Library and Archives

## Headquarters

100 N. Stewart St.
Carson City, NV 89701-4285
Phone: 800-922-2880 (in Nevada) or 775-684-3360
http://nsla.nevadaculture.org

## Description

**Founded:** NA

**Operating Locations:** Nevada

The Nevada State Library and Archives provides full access to a range of information services that enhance the quality of life for all and center on creating an educated and enlightened citizenry while supporting the best interests of the state of Nevada.

## Grants Information

**GRANT TYPES**
LSTA funds

**TYPICAL RECIPIENTS**
Academic, public, and school libraries; governmental agency libraries and eligible information centers; special libraries with public access

## GRANT VALUES
NA

## NAMED GRANTS

### LSTA COMPETITIVE GRANTS AND MINIGRANTS

The purpose of LSTA grants is to provide assistance to eligible libraries in the areas of technology innovation, resource sharing, and targeted services to people who are underserved, disadvantaged, geographically isolated, illiterate, and so forth.

## REQUIREMENTS AND RESTRICTIONS

Applicants must be located in the state of Nevada. LSTA funds will not cover any food, entertainment, indirect, or administrative costs. An applicant may submit more than one application in a grant cycle, but must rank applications by priority before final submission.

The following factors are considered in evaluating each application: (1) evidence of need, (2) degree of preplanning, (3) client or community involvement in project development, (4) clarity, (5) quality of the plan, including its likelihood of success and continuation at the local level, (6) adequacy and realism of the budget, (7) potential benefit of the project and its contribution toward meeting local and statewide goals, objectives, and needs and meeting LSTA purposes.

## APPLICATION PROCEDURES

**Submission Guidelines:** The application form is available online. The format of this application form must be maintained and all information sections must be included on the same page as, and with the dimensions shown on, the original application form. Applicants are required to submit one electronic copy of the application (via e-mail or on disk) and one hard copy (with original signatures). Mailed applications should be sent to the address below. All applications received by the due date stand in competition for the available federal funds. Applications received late will not be considered.

**Deadlines:** December

## CONTACT
Nevada State Library and Archives
Attn: LSTA Applications
100 N. Stewart St.
Carson City, NV 89701
Phone: 775-684-3407 or 775-684-3324

## GRANT-SPECIFIC WEBSITE
http://nsla.nevadaculture.org/index.
php?option = com_content&task = vie
w&id = 537&Itemid = 421

# New Hampshire Library Association (NHLA)

## Headquarters

PO Box 617
Concord, NH 03302-0617
www.nhlibrarians.org

## Description

**Founded:** NA

**Operating Locations:** New Hampshire

The purpose of the New Hampshire Library Association (NHLA) is to advance the interests of its members through advocacy on library issues and increasing public awareness of library service, to support the professional development of its members, to foster communication and encourage the exchange of ideas among its members, and to promote participation in the association and its sections.

## Grants Information

### GRANT TYPES
Continuing education, literacy, LSTA funds

### TYPICAL RECIPIENTS
Agencies or individuals in New Hampshire; school library media centers, academic libraries, qualified private/research libraries, special libraries, library consortia, libraries in residential and correctional institutions, and public libraries

### GRANT VALUES
NA

### NAMED GRANTS

#### ADAM AND JANE MACDONALD MINI-MONEY GRANT
The Adam and Jane Macdonald Mini-money Grant may be used for credit or noncredit courses, workshops and seminars, State Library Education modules, NELINET classes, online education classes, and classes offered by local educational institutions.

**Typical Recipients:** New Hampshire librarians

**Grant Values:** Highest Grant, $200

**Requirements and Restrictions:** Grant funds may not be used for conference attendance.

**Submission Guidelines:** Completed applications should be mailed to the address below.

**Contact:** Continuing Education Committee, Hanover Town Library, PO Box 207, Etna, NH 03750

**Grant-Specific Website:** www.nhlibrarians.org/scholarshipsgrants.html

## GRANITE STATE READS GRANT

The annual Granite State Reads grant program, supported by a partnership between the Verizon Foundation and the Park Street Foundation, provides financial support to New Hampshire organizations providing literacy assistance to New Hampshire residents. Any project that improves the literacy skills of New Hampshire children or adults is eligible for a Granite State Reads grant.

**Typical Recipients:** Any agency or individual in New Hampshire who can comply with the requirements of this grant may apply.

**Grant Values:** Total Dollar Amount of Grants, $21,859 was distributed in the 2009 grant cycle; Lowest Grant, $500

**Past Grant Recipients:**

- Boscawen Public Library (NH), babies and books program
- Children's Literacy Foundation (CLiF) (NH), new books and support to refugee children in Hanover
- Grantham Village School Books and Beyond (NH), high-interest books for older readers
- Hills Garrison School (NH), Book WALK (We Are Literate Kids)
- The Parent Information Center (NH), Let's Read Together Early-Literacy Volunteer Program in Concord
- Rockingham Community Action (NH), Reading Is Fundamental local match in Exeter

**Requirements and Restrictions:** Applicants must be located in the state of New Hampshire. Grant recipients are required to complete a report, using the form provided on the website, by November of the grant year.

**Submission Guidelines:** Application form is available on the website. Applicants should download the form, either as a PDF or as a Word document; fill it out on the computer; save it; and send a printed copy to the address below, or create a PDF of the completed form and e-mail it as an attachment.

**Deadlines:** December

**Decisions:** February

**Contact:** Center for the Book at the NHSL, Attn: Granite State Reads, 20 Park St., Concord, NH 03301; Phone: 603-271-2866; E-mail: gsr@dcr.nh.gov

**Grant-Specific Website:** www.nh.gov/nhsl/bookcenter/programs/gs_reads.html

## LSTA GRANTS

LSTA funds are available to all New Hampshire libraries to carry out the goals and objectives of the New Hampshire LSTA Five-Year Plan. Priority goals include increased access to information through improved technology, and training and education of librarians, library staff, public officials, and the public in the importance of the library in an information environment.

**Typical Recipients:** School library media centers, academic libraries, qualified private/research libraries, special libraries, library consortia, libraries in residential and correctional institutions, and public libraries

**Grant Values:** Total Dollar Amount of Grants, $880,000 per year

**Requirements and Restrictions:** Applicants must be located in the state of New Hampshire.

**Contact:** Phone: 603-271-2393

**Grant-Specific Website:** www.nh.gov/nhsl/nhlac/lsta_2000.html

## REQUIREMENTS AND RESTRICTIONS
Vary by grant

## APPLICATION PROCEDURES
Vary by grant

## CONTACT
Varies by grant

## GRANT-SPECIFIC WEBSITE
Varies by grant

# New Jersey Council for the Humanities (NJCH)

## Headquarters

28 W. State St., 6th fl.
Trenton, NJ 08608
Phone: 609-695-4838
www.njch.org

## Description

**Founded:** 1972

**Operating Locations:** New Jersey

The New Jersey Council for the Humanities (NJCH) is a nonprofit organization whose mission is to serve the people of New Jersey by developing, supporting, and promoting projects that explore and interpret the human experience, foster cross-cultural understanding, and engage people in dialogue about matters of individual choice and public responsibility.

## Grants Information

### GRANT TYPES
Project

### TYPICAL RECIPIENTS
New Jersey nonprofit organizations and cultural institutions

## GRANT VALUES
Highest Grant: $20,000
Lowest Grant: $500

## NAMED GRANTS

### MAJOR AND MINIGRANTS
Major and Minigrants are awarded in support of public humanities projects. Major grants of up to $20,000 are awarded twice a year; minigrants of up to $3,000 are awarded four times a year. NJCH has a special interest in funding projects that address the council's theme of justice.

**Typical Recipients:** Registered New Jersey nonprofit organizations and government agencies operating within New Jersey

**Past Grant Recipients:**

• Rutgers Institute for Women and Art (NJ), series of five public programs exploring the themes of gender, transnationalism, and postcolonialism in contemporary Middle Eastern culture to be held in association with three exhibitions of work by women artists from the Middle East, Major Grant
• Camden County College Foundation (NJ), seven-part lecture series on Ancient Egyptian history, culture, and study to be held in association with the Franklin Institute's Cleopatra exhibit, "The Search for the Last Queen of Egypt," Major Grant
• Crossroads of the American Revolution, Inc. (NJ), creation of an online digital library containing photographs of National Heritage Area sites accompanied by interpretive text, Major Grant
• African American Heritage Museum of Southern New Jersey (NJ), development of a plan for the preservation, cataloging, digitalization, public accessibility, and interpretation of the museum's permanent collection, Minigrant
• Rutgers University Libraries, Special Collections and University Archives (NJ), exhibition and related programming on the life and works of John Milton, Minigrant
• Parsippany Troy Hills Public Library System (NJ), series of four film screenings focused on adaptations of Edith Wharton's written works, Minigrant

**Requirements and Restrictions:** To be considered for support, projects are required to have the humanities at their core; actively involve a humanities scholar; involve public discussion or distribution of humanistic work; present objective points of view; primarily serve an adult or intergenerational New Jersey audience; feature free and open access for any public events (nominal donations may be requested but cannot be required for admission; regular museum entrance fees may be collected, but no additional fee may be charged for a funded exhibit or event). Applicant must provide a 100 percent match of funds granted by NJCH.

**Submission Guidelines:** All drafts and applications must be submitted online. A draft narrative and budget must be submitted at least 1 month prior to the application deadline for review.

**Deadlines:** For Major Grants, May and October; for Minigrants, February, May, August, and November

**Decisions:** For Major Grants, June and November; for Mini Grants, March, June, September, and December

**Contact:** Grants Officer, New Jersey Council for the Humanities, 28 W. State St., 6th fl., Trenton, NJ 08608; Phone: 888-394-6524

**Grant-Specific Website:** www.njch.org/ grants_major-mini.html

## HUMANITIES FESTIVAL GRANTS

NJCH provides awards of up to $500 annually in celebration of National Arts and Humanities Month. Humanities Festival Grant programs must use at least one of the humanities disciplines, but the council is open to a variety of formats: lecture and discussion, oral histories, walking tours, reading or film discussion programs, and storytelling.

**Typical Recipients:** Libraries, museums, historical societies, religious and community groups, and other nonprofit organizations

**Past Grant Recipients:**

- Nutley Public Library (NJ), panel discussion exploring the history and philosophy of the environmental justice movement in the United States
- Woodbury Public Library (NJ), four-part lecture series on the topics of gay and lesbian rights, cyber-liberties, student and youth rights, and free speech and expression
- Ocean County Library, Toms River Branch (NJ), two programs exploring the relationship between social justice and Ben Shahn's artistic works

**Requirements and Restrictions:** Applicants must be registered New Jersey nonprofit organizations or government agencies operating within the state. The humanities must be central to the project. Programs must be introduced by a person possessing at least a master's degree in a humanities discipline, who will provide a context for the program. Applicants must present a plan for attracting a diverse audience. All programs must be open to the public, free of charge, and scheduled during the month of October. Grant funds cannot be used to cover salaries, indirect costs, capital purchases, refreshments, or entertainment expenses.

**Submission Guidelines:** Applications must be completed online. Applicants should consult with the NJCH Grants Officer well in advance of the deadline.

**Deadlines:** June

**Decisions:** July

**Contact:** Grants Officer, New Jersey Council for the Humanities, 28 W. State St., 6th fl., Trenton, NJ 08608; Phone: 888-394-6524

**Grant-Specific Website:** www.njch.org/grants_HFG.html

**REQUIREMENTS AND RESTRICTIONS**
Vary by grant

**APPLICATION PROCEDURES**
Vary by grant

**CONTACT**
Varies by grant

**GRANT-SPECIFIC WEBSITE**
www.njch.org/grants.html

# New Mexico Library Association (NMLA)

## Headquarters

PO Box 26074
Albuquerque, NM 87125
Phone: 505-400-7309
Fax: 505-891-5171

E-mail: admin@nmla.org
http://nmla.org

## Description

**Founded:** NA

**Operating Locations:** New Mexico

The New Mexico Library Association (NMLA) is a nonprofit organization dedicated to the support and promotion of libraries and the development of library personnel through education and the exchange of ideas to enrich the lives of all New Mexicans.

## Grants Information

**GRANT TYPES**
Continuing education

**TYPICAL RECIPIENTS**
New Mexico librarians

**GRANT VALUES**
Highest Grant: $200

**NAMED GRANTS**
CONTINUING EDUCATION GRANT
To promote professional development, NMLA, through the Continuing Education Fund, supports requests to attend workshops, conferences, and related activities. Awards are made on the basis of financial need.

**REQUIREMENTS AND RESTRICTIONS**
NA

## APPLICATION PROCEDURES

**Submission Guidelines:** Application online. A copy of the workshop brochure, conference agenda, or registration form should accompany the completed application form. Completed applications should be sent to the address below. Applicants must apply in advance of the event. No reimbursements will be made.

## CONTACT

Kevin Comerford, Education Committee Chair
Digital Initiatives Librarian
Zimmerman Library, MSC05 3020
University of New Mexico
Albuquerque NM 87131-0001

## GRANT-SPECIFIC WEBSITE

http://nmla.org/scholarships-grants/

# New Mexico Library Foundation (NMLF)

## Headquarters

PO Box 30572
Albuquerque, NM 87190-0572
www.nm-lf.org

## Description

**Founded:** NA

**Operating Locations:** New Mexico

The NMLF supports libraries in New Mexico by allocating funds to libraries of all types and to nonprofit organizations that directly benefit libraries.

# Grants Information

## GRANT TYPES

Library improvement, programs, technology

## TYPICAL RECIPIENTS

New Mexico public, academic, school, special, and private libraries; nonprofit groups that directly benefit New Mexico libraries

## GRANT VALUES

Highest Grant: $1,000

## PAST GRANT RECIPIENTS

NA

## REQUIREMENTS AND RESTRICTIONS

Funding will not be considered for normal operating expenses, salaries for regular staff, employee benefits, construction, or endowment funds.

## APPLICATION PROCEDURES

**Submission Guidelines:** Application online

**Deadlines:** May

**CONTACT**
Valerie Nye
Grants Liaison
Phone: 505-473-6575
E-mail: valnye@gmail.com

**GRANT-SPECIFIC WEBSITE**
www.nm-lf.org/index.php?option = com_co
ntent&view = article&id = 6&Itemid = 5

# New Mexico State Library

## Headquarters

1209 Camino Carlos Rey
Santa Fe, NM 87507
Phone: 505-476-9700
www.nmstatelibrary.org/index.php

## Description

**Founded:** 1929

**Operating Locations:** New Mexico

The New Mexico State Library is committed to providing leadership that promotes effective library services and access to information to all citizens of New Mexico.

## Grants Information

**GRANT TYPES**
LSTA funds, tribal libraries

**TYPICAL RECIPIENTS**
New Mexico libraries and librarians

**GRANT VALUES**
NA

**NAMED GRANTS**

**LSTA DIGITAL PROJECT GRANTS**
LSTA Digital Project Grants provide public library staff access to the skills needed to complete digital projects in their libraries.

**Typical Recipients:** Public library staff involved in digital preservation projects in their libraries

**Grant Values:** Highest Grant, $400

**Requirements and Restrictions:** Applicants and grantees must meet eligibility and grant management requirements for LSTA funds; see website for details.

**Submission Guidelines:** Application online. Completed application should be e-mailed to the e-mail address below, and mailed or hand-delivered (hard copy with original signatures) to the address below.

**Deadlines:** March

**Contact:** Geraldine Hutchins, Federal Programs Coordinator, New Mexico State Library, 1209 Camino Carlos Rey, Santa Fe, NM 87509; Phone: 505-476-9727; E-mail: geraldine.hutchins@state.nm.us

**Grant-Specific Website:** www .nmstatelibrary.org/component/content/ article/36-programs-service/1637-digital-project-grants-lsta-2010

## LSTA Technology Support Grants

Many New Mexico public libraries lack local technology support for computers and networks; for example, 30 percent of New Mexico public libraries report that computers are down for more than two days. Technology Support grants will help provide affordable tech support and encourage local tech consultants to become familiar with libraries' unique tech needs.

**Typical Recipients:** New Mexico public libraries

**Grant Values:** Highest Grant, $15,000

**Requirements and Restrictions:** Grant recipients must contribute 10 percent of the total cost of the project using local cash funds (no in-kind matching funds may be used). Grant funds may be used for outside technology contractors or software (for example, security-related, antivirus, or remote support software). Licensing and maintenance costs may be included as part of the software purchase.

**Submission Guidelines:** Application online. Completed application should be mailed to the address below.

**Deadlines:** November

**Contact:** Patricia Moore, Technology Support Grant Applications, New Mexico State Library, 1209 Camino Carlos Rey, Santa Fe, NM 87507; Phone: 800-340-3890 or 505-476-9724; E-mail: patricia. moore@state.nm.us

**Grant-Specific Website:** www .nmstatelibrary.org/component/content/ article/38-funding-for-libraries/1462-technology-support-grants-lsta-2011

## LSTA E-audio/E-book Grants

The purpose of the E-audio/E-book Grants is to expand the availability of e-audiobooks and e-books to New Mexico residents.

**Typical Recipients:** Consortia of New Mexico public libraries (grants will not be awarded to individual libraries)

**Grant Values:** Highest Grant, $80,000

**Requirements and Restrictions:** Grant recipients must contribute 10 percent of the total cost of the project using local cash funds (no in-kind matching funds may be used). Grant funds may be used for subscriptions for e-audiobook/e-book collections for the consortium of libraries. Indirect costs for the administrative charges of the fiscal agent are limited to 4 percent of the total LSTA funds requested.

**Submission Guidelines:** Application online. Completed application should be e-mailed to the e-mail address below, and mailed or hand-delivered (hard copy with original signatures) to the address below. Faxed copies will not be accepted.

**Decisions:** November

**Contact:** Geraldine Hutchins, Federal Programs Coordinator, New Mexico State Library, 1209 Camino Carlos Rey, Santa Fe, NM 87509; Phone: 505-476-9727; E-mail: geraldine.hutchins@state.nm.us

**Grant-Specific Website:** www.nmstatelibrary.org/component/content/article/38-funding-for-libraries/1464-e-audioebook-grants-lsta-20102011

## STATE GRANTS-IN-AID
The purpose of the State Grants-in-Aid program is to provide financial assistance that encourages and supports public library service by public libraries and developing public libraries. The program is intended to supplement and encourage local effort in providing local library service. The program consists of developing library grants and public library grants that may be used for library collections, library staff salaries, library staff training, library equipment, or other operational expenditures associated with delivery of library services. Eligible developing libraries shall receive a minimum grant of $1,500. The remaining funds shall be divided equally among all eligible public libraries, branches, and bookmobiles.

**Grant Values:** Lowest Grant, $1,500

**Contact:** Geraldine Hutchins; Phone: 505-476-9727; E-mail: geraldine.hutchins@state.nm.us

**Grant-Specific Website:** www.nmstatelibrary.org/services-libraries/funding-libraries/state-aid

## TRIBAL LIBRARIES PROGRAM GRANT
The purpose of the Tribal Libraries Program grant is to provide financial assistance that encourages and supports tribal library services. The grant is intended to supplement and encourage local effort in providing local library service. Grant funds may be used for library collections, library programming, library staff salaries, library staff professional development, library equipment, or other operational expenditures associated with delivery of library services.

**Typical Recipients:** All tribal libraries that currently meet the criteria for developing library, public library, or branch library as defined in section 4.5.2 of the state code and receive a State Grants-in-Aid for Public Libraries grant

**Grant Values:** The amount of funding varies from year to year depending on the allocation of the state legislature.

**Requirements and Restrictions:**
Funds are limited to New Mexico Tribal libraries only. TLP grant funds cannot be used to replace local funds from tribal budgets. Additionally, funds cannot be used for pre-grant costs or indirect (administrative) costs.

**Submission Guidelines:** Completed applications should be sent to the address below.

**Contact:** Tribal Libraries Program, New Mexico State Library, Attn: Grant Application, 1209 Camino Carlos Rey, Santa Fe, NM 87507; Phone: 800-340-3890 or 505-786-7391, ext. 7205

**Grant-Specific Website:** www.nmstatelibrary.org/services-libraries/programs-services/tribal-libraries/tribal-libraries-grants

**REQUIREMENTS AND RESTRICTIONS**
Vary by grant

**APPLICATION PROCEDURES**
Vary by grant

**CONTACT**
Varies by grant

**GRANT-SPECIFIC WEBSITE**
Varies by grant

# New York State Library (NYSL)

## Headquarters

310 Madison Ave.
Empire State Plaza
Albany, NY 12230
Phone: 518-474-5355
www.nysl.nysed.gov

## Description

**Founded:** 1818

**Operating Locations:** New York

The New York State Library's collections include over 20 million items that support state government work and the research needs of the general public.

## Grants Information

**GRANT TYPES**
LSTA funds, literacy, conservation

**TYPICAL RECIPIENTS**
Public and association libraries that are members of a public library system, public library systems; libraries, archives, historical societies, and similar agencies

## GRANT VALUES

NA

## NAMED GRANTS

### ADULT LITERACY SERVICES GRANT PROGRAM

NYSL's Adult Literacy Library Services grants help libraries offer services that will improve adult literacy on the job and in the home. The grants encourage libraries to become community literacy leaders and to strengthen partnerships among local literacy providers. These grants operate on a two-year cycle. Education law provides $200,000 for each year. The actual amount available for grants will depend on the appropriation by the New York State Legislature. The maximum amount that may be requested is $20,000 per year; the minimum amount that may be requested is $10,000 per year.

**Typical Recipients:** Public and association libraries that are members of a public library system, public library systems

**Grant Values:** Total Dollar Amount of Grants, $200,000; Highest Grant, $20,000; Lowest Grant, $10,000

**Past Grant Recipients:**

- Andover Free Library (NY), adult literacy computer cafe, $37,749
- Brooklyn Public Library (NY), technology literacy for English language learners, $37,749
- Hempstead Public Library (NY), The New Road to Citizenship, $37,749
- James Prendergast Library Association (NY), Log On for Literacy, $36,812
- Mahopac Public Library (NY), Opening Doors: Workforce Empowerment through Literacy Education, $29,659
- The New York Public Library (NY), integrated technology-assisted ESOL instruction at Aguilar Branch Library, $37,749

**Requirements and Restrictions:** Funds may not be used to replace funds for existing programs or staff, building modification, construction, or overhead and administrative costs. Funds can be used for the following: partnership expansions and projects that establish a new collaboration; collection development that supports enhanced adult literacy services; projects that encourage adult literacy students and their families to become lifelong library users; library literacy–related materials; project equipment; project personnel; supplies; contracts for services; evaluation and publication of a report for project replication; other purposes directly related to project's success.

**Submission Guidelines:** Applications must be submitted through the online system—no other form of submission will be accepted. Items to submit in paper format: cover page (two with original signatures); board certification (two with original signatures); and three copies of Form FS-10 with original signatures in blue ink. These items may be printed from the online application. Send by U.S. mail or another carrier to the address below.

**Deadlines:** December

**Contact:** New York State Library, Division of Library Development, Albany, NY 12230; Phone: 518-474-1479 or 518-486-4863

**Grant-Specific Website:** www.nysl.nysed.gov/libdev/literacy/

## FAMILY LITERACY SERVICES GRANT PROGRAM

Through the Family Literacy Services Grant Program, public libraries have access to resources to help children learn to use the library as an integral part of their education. The projects involve parents in their student's education from an early age and their parents or caregivers often make successful programs. These grants operate on a two-year cycle and the program theme changes for every cycle. Priority is given to projects that include partnerships between libraries or library systems and community organizations. Education law provides $300,000 for each year. The actual amount available for grants will depend on the appropriation by the New York State Legislature. The maximum amount that may be requested is

$45,000 per year; the minimum amount that may be requested is $10,000 per year.

**Typical Recipients:** Public and association libraries that are members of a public library system, public library systems

**Grant Values:** Total Dollar Amount of Grants, $300,000; Highest Grant, $45,000; Lowest Grant, $10,000

**Past Grant Recipients:**
- Brooklyn Public Library (NY), Para los Niños workshop, $92,076
- Buffalo and Erie County Public Library (NY), Get Graphic: Building Literacy and Community with Graphic Novels, $92,420
- Town of Indian Lake Public Library (NY), Bright Beginnings, $36,715
- Irondequoit Public Library (NY), Let's Get Ready to Read, $44,102
- Oneida Public Library (NY), Standing Tall, $88,326
- Richmond Memorial Library (NY), Giving Reading Opportunities, $31,139

**Requirements and Restrictions:** Funds may not be used to replace funds for existing programs or staff, building modification, construction, or overhead and administrative costs.

**Submission Guidelines:** Applications must be submitted through the online system—no other form of submission will be accepted. Items to submit in paper format: cover page (two with original signatures); board certification (two with original signatures); and three copies of Form FS-10 with original signatures in blue ink. These items may be printed from the online application. Send by U.S. mail or another carrier to the address below.

**Deadlines:** December

**Contact:** New York State Library, Division of Library Development, Albany, NY 12230; Phone: 518-474-1479 or 518-486-4863

**Grant-Specific Website:** www.nysl.nysed.gov/libdev/familylit/

## LSTA SERVICE IMPROVEMENT GRANT PROGRAM

NYSL has allocated a total of $1.6 million in federal LSTA funds for a two-year invitational grant program focused on assisting library systems to help their member libraries improve library services for their customers and to implement New York State's 2008–2012 LSTA Five-Year Plan.

**Typical Recipients:** Public library systems

**Grant Values:** Total Dollar Amount of Grants, $800,000 per year

**Requirements and Restrictions:** Each library system is eligible to submit only one application. Applicants are required

to use an outcome-based evaluation approach for measuring the results of projects whose activities involve proposed changes in participants' knowledge, skills, attitude, or behavior. Project ideas should be discussed with the State Library's LSTA Coordinator early on in the project development process to ensure that the project is approvable. Matching funds of 35 percent are required for all equipment and software of $5,000 or more.

**Submission Guidelines:** Application online. Two hard copies of the completed application (one with original signatures), budget (FS-20), and all related forms must be mailed to the address below. Additionally, an electronic copy of the narrative and the FS-20 must be sent to the LSTA coordinator.

**Deadlines:** March

**Contact:** New York State Library, Division of Library Development, Rm. 10B41, CEC, Albany, NY 12230; Phone: 518-474-1565

**Grant-Specific Website:** www.nysl.nysed.gov/libdev/lsta/

## LSTA SUMMER READING MINIGRANT PROGRAM

NYSL has allocated LSTA funds for an invitational grant program focused on assisting library systems to help their member libraries support and carry out activities related to the Statewide Summer Reading Program. Grant projects must be linked to one or more of the four goals in New York's LSTA Five-Year Plan and to one or more of the six federal LSTA purposes and to the library system's Five-Year Plan of Service.

**Typical Recipients:** Public library systems

**Grant Values:** Total Dollar Amount of Grants, $222,000

**Past Grant Recipients:**

- Brooklyn Public Library (NY), $12,000
- Buffalo and Erie County Public Library System (NY), $12,000
- Chautauqua-Cattaraugus Library System (NY), $6,000
- Clinton Essex Franklin Library System (NY), $6,000
- Finger Lakes Library System (NY), $6,000
- Four County Library System (NY), $6,000

**Requirements and Restrictions:** Applicants must limit the use of funds for supplies and materials to items that are directly related to the purpose of the SRMG (e.g., bookmarks, reading records, and certificates). If LSTA funds are used to purchase supplies which might be considered of a promotional nature, the application must justify such purchases on the grounds of educational or informational benefit.

**Submission Guidelines:** Application online. Two hard copies of the completed application (one with original signatures), budget (FS-20), and all related forms must be mailed to the address below. Additionally, one electronic copy should be sent to the LSTA Coordinator.

**Deadlines:** March

**Contact:** LSTA Coordinator, New York State Library, Library Development, Rm. 10B41, CEC, Albany, NY 12230; Phone: 518-486-4858 or 518-474-1565

**Grant-Specific Website:** www.nysl.nysed.gov/libdev/lsta/

## CONSERVATION AND PRESERVATION GRANT PROGRAM

Conservation and Preservation grants support projects for the protection, care, and treatment of library materials valuable to New York State, preventing loss of their informational or intellectual content or the objects themselves through such activities as evaluating the condition of the collection and making a preservation plan; environmental control; disaster prevention, preparedness, and recovery; preparation of library materials for storage; cleaning, repairing, and maintaining collection materials; screening items for preservation; reformatting to microform, tape, or photocopy; cleaning, deacidification; and staff training and patron awareness programs.

**Typical Recipients:** Libraries, archives, historical societies, and similar agencies

**Grant Values:** Highest Grant, $40,000

**Past Grant Recipients:**

- Barnard College Archives–Wollman Library (NY), restoration and conservation of one thousand seminal documents in the history of Barnard College, 1883–1910, $29,022
- Brewster Public Library (NY), preservation and microfilming of Brewster Standard newspapers, $11,574
- Northern New York Library Network (NY), preservation and microfilming of the Plattsburgh Republican and the Plattsburgh Press-Republican, $9,163
- Rudolf Steiner Library of the Anthroposophical Society in America (NY), conservation and preservation survey, $2,436

**Requirements and Restrictions:**
The following institutions are not eligible to apply: the eleven designated comprehensive research libraries: Columbia University Libraries; Cornell University Libraries; New York State Library; New York University Libraries; University of Rochester Libraries; Syracuse University Libraries; the Research Libraries of The New York

Public Library; and the libraries of the State University of New York centers at Albany, Binghamton, Buffalo, and Stony Brook. Institutions wholly or in part under the control of any religious denominations in which any denominational tenet or doctrine is taught are constitutionally ineligible to receive state financial assistance.

**Submission Guidelines:** Applications must be submitted through the online system—no other form of submission will be accepted.

**Deadlines:** May

**Contact:** Phone: 518-474-7890 or 518-486-4864

**Grant-Specific Website:** www.nysl. nysed.gov/libdev/cp/

## REQUIREMENTS AND RESTRICTIONS
Vary by grant

## APPLICATION PROCEDURES
Vary by grant

## CONTACT
Varies by grant

## GRANT-SPECIFIC WEBSITE
Varies by grant

# State Library of North Carolina

## Headquarters

109 E. Jones St.
Raleigh, NC 27601-1023
Phone: 919-807-7430
http://statelibrary.ncdcr.gov/index.html

## Description

**Founded:** 1812

**Operating Locations:** North Carolina

The State Library of North Carolina is the principal library of state government. It builds the capacity of all libraries in North Carolina and develops and supports access to specialized collections for the people of North Carolina, including genealogy, North Caroliniana, and resources for the blind and physically handicapped.

## Grants Information

### GRANT TYPES
LSTA funds

### TYPICAL RECIPIENTS
Public and academic libraries, including public, private, and community college libraries; qualified state agency libraries; qualified special libraries; public school libraries and public school district media services administrative units

### GRANT VALUES
NA

### NAMED GRANTS

**LSTA ECHO DIGITIZATION GRANT**
The ECHO Digitization Grant program supports libraries in the creation of online resources that focus on topics important to the cultural heritage of North Carolina and that improve access to the state's special collections. Digitization Grant project activities will focus on digital imaging of primary materials (manuscripts, artifacts, artwork, photographs, rare books, broadsides, pamphlets, etc.) and presentation of the images and contextual information over the Internet, or the conversion of existing finding aids for archival or manuscript collections and presentation of encoded finding aids online. Conversion must include encoding using EAD (Encoded Archival Description) or other metadata schema as appropriate.

**Typical Recipients:** Public and academic libraries, including public, private, and community college libraries; qualified state agency libraries; qualified special libraries

**Grant Values:** Highest Grant, $75,000 for a single applicant or $150,000 for a collaborative project; Lowest Grant, $2,500

**Requirements and Restrictions:** At least 10 percent in matching funds is required. Eligible expenses include equipment, computer furniture, contractual service, software or software-based services, supplies, travel and subsistence, cost of project personnel training, personnel, outsourcing. Grant funds may not be used for the following: collection development activities, including the identification or acquisition of new materials; preservation activities or materials; costs of conventional arrangement, description, or cataloging of original material; retrospective conversion of catalog records; ongoing operating costs; wages and benefit supplements/reimbursements for existing full-time employees; entertainment or social events; costs of promotional items; administrative overhead or indirect costs.

**Submission Guidelines:** Libraries must first submit a letter of intent and receive authorization before submitting a full application.

## LSTA LIBRARY OUTREACH SERVICES GRANT

The Library Outreach Services grant program is intended to enable libraries to implement services for specific communities of users who are currently unserved or underserved. Services must be based on an analysis and assessment of local needs.

**Typical Recipients:** Public and academic libraries, including public, private, and community college libraries; public school libraries and public school district media services administrative units

**Grant Values:** Highest Grant, $50,000 for a single applicant or $100,000 for a collaborative project; Lowest Grant, $5,000

**Requirements and Restrictions:** The local contribution to the project must equal a minimum of 10 percent of the amount of federal funds requested for a one-year project or the first year of a multiyear project. For multiyear projects, the local contribution is 25 percent in the second year and 50 percent in the third year. Eligible expenses include wages and benefits for temporary staff to be employed for the project, contractual services, equipment, furniture that the applicant demonstrates is crucial to the success of the project, library materials that support the programs and services that are the project's main focus, travel and training expenses, supplies, postage and printing costs. Ineligible expenses include ongoing expenditures for normal operations (such as utilities, Internet access, etc.); entertainment or social events; wages and benefit supplements/reimbursements for existing full-time employees; costs of most promotional items and memorabilia, including models, gifts, and souvenirs; administrative overhead or indirect costs.

**Submission Guidelines:** Libraries must first submit a letter of intent and receive authorization before submitting a full application.

## LSTA TECHNOLOGY GRANT

Technology Grants are intended to provide applicant libraries with the opportunity to carry out technology-intensive projects to improve library services or access to resources.

**Typical Recipients:** Public and academic libraries, including public, private, and community college libraries; qualified state agency libraries; qualified special libraries

**Grant Values:** Highest Grant, $100,000 for a single applicant or $150,000 for a collaborative project

**Requirements and Restrictions:** LSTA Technology Grant proposals will consist largely of technology expenditures, including such items as hardware, software, network infrastructure, and installation costs. Other allowable expenditures may include nontechnology items such as training and furniture. A proposal that includes nontechnology expenditures totaling 25 percent or more of total project costs may not be suitable

for this grant category, and strong justification will be required for such a proposal to be competitive. The local contribution to the project must equal a minimum of 25 percent of the amount of federal funds requested.

**Submission Guidelines:** Libraries must first submit a letter of intent and receive authorization before submitting a full application.

**Contact:** Grant Pair, Assistant State Librarian for Statewide Development Programs; Phone: 919-807-7408; E-mail: grant.pair@ncdcr.gov

## LSTA STRENGTHENING PUBLIC AND ACADEMIC LIBRARY COLLECTIONS GRANT

The Strengthening Public and Academic Library Collections Grant program is designed to help North Carolina public and academic libraries develop or strengthen subject areas in their print book collection to meet users' needs. Libraries serving low-wealth communities and institutions are given priority for this grant program, assuming their application is eligible and meets the criteria.

**Typical Recipients:** Public and academic libraries, including public, private, and community college libraries that have not received this grant in the last three years

**Grant Values:** Highest Grant, $20,000; Lowest Grant, $1,000

**Requirements and Restrictions:**
The local contribution must equal a minimum of 25 percent of the amount of federal funds requested.

**Submission Guidelines:** A complete application will include application signature page signed by appropriate persons; complete proposal that responds to every required section of the application; complete budget table, with figures that add up correctly; and budget narrative and explanation of source and availability of matching funds. Send the original application with certifying signatures in blue ink, plus 15 copies (16 total), and the original of the required CIPA certification form (public libraries only).

## LSTA BASIC EQUIPMENT GRANT

The Basic Equipment Grant program is intended to help eligible libraries have sufficient up-to-date computers to ensure that their users have access to the Internet and online content. These grants are to fund basic hardware and equipment needs (e.g., computers for public access, equipment and software for persons with disabilities using public access computers, computer training lab equipment, scanners).

**Typical Recipients:** Public and academic libraries, including public, private, and community college libraries; qualified state agency libraries; qualified special libraries

**Grant Values:** Highest Grant, $25,000; Lowest Grant, $2,500

**Requirements and Restrictions:**
The local contribution must equal a minimum of 25 percent of the amount of federal funds requested.

**Submission Guidelines:** A complete application will include application signature page signed by appropriate persons; complete proposal that responds to every required section of the application; complete budget table, with figures that add up correctly; and budget narrative and explanation of source and availability of matching funds. Send the original application with certifying signatures in blue ink, plus 15 copies (16 total), and the original of the required CIPA certification form (public libraries only).

## LSTA PLANNING GRANT

The Planning Grant program supports libraries seeking to engage in effective planning. The planning activities and outcomes must be consistent with the library's mission and strategic goals. Planning should have its primary focus on the needs of library users rather than on the library itself. Federal law prohibits the use of LSTA funds to support construction or renovation projects.

**Typical Recipients:** Public and academic libraries, including public, private, and community college libraries;

public school libraries and public school district media services administrative units; qualified state agency libraries; qualified special libraries

**Grant Values:** Highest Grant, $20,000 for a single applicant or $35,000 for a collaborative project

**Requirements and Restriction:** No local matching funds are required for an LSTA Planning Grant.

**Submission Guidelines:** A complete application will include application signature page signed by appropriate persons; complete proposal that responds to every required section of the application; complete budget table, with figures that add up correctly; and budget narrative and explanation of source and availability of matching funds. Send the original application with certifying signatures in blue ink, plus 15 copies (16 total), and the original of the required CIPA certification form (public libraries only).

## LSTA School Library Collection and Development Grant

The School Library Collection and Development Grant program is designed to help school library media centers provide a current, accurate, and attractive collection of books that supports student achievement and the importance of reading. The availability of grant funds and the requirement

for matching funds are designed to leverage additional money to help build print collections and bring heightened attention to the need for improvement of the school library's current collection.

**Typical Recipients:** Public school libraries that have not received this grant in the last three years

**Grant Values:** Highest Grant, $10,000; Lowest Grant, $1,000

**Requirements and Restrictions:** The local contribution must equal a minimum of 25 percent of the amount of federal funds requested. Applicants must complete the online survey by the deadline to be considered for funds (printed surveys received in the mail will not be accepted).

**Submission Guidelines:** A complete application will include the following: application signature page, signed by appropriate persons; answers to questions 1 and 3–7 (narrative sections and budget); appendix A: Collection Development Plan; appendix B: Match Certification; appendix C: Media and Technology Advisory Committee commitment statement. Send the original application with certifying signatures in blue ink, plus nine copies (ten total), and the original of the required CIPA certification form.

## REQUIREMENTS AND RESTRICTIONS
Vary by grant

## APPLICATION PROCEDURES
**Submission Guidelines:** All applications are available online.

**Deadlines:** February

## CONTACT
For delivery by Fedex, UPS, or in person (recommended):
LSTA Grant Applications
Library Development Section, Rm. 310A
State Library of North Carolina
Archives and State Library Bldg.
109 E. Jones St., Raleigh, NC 27601
For delivery by U.S. Postal Service:
LSTA Grant Applications
Library Development Section
State Library of North Carolina
4640 Mail Service Center
Raleigh, NC 27699-4640
Unless otherwise noted above, questions about grants should be directed to
Penny Hornsby
Federal Programs Consultant
Phone: 919-807-7420
E-mail: penny.hornsby@ncdcr.gov

## GRANT-SPECIFIC WEBSITE
http://statelibrary.ncdcr.gov/lsta/2010-2011Grants.htm

# North Dakota Library Association (NDLA)

## Headquarters

PO Box 1595
Bismarck, ND 58502-1595
www.ndla.info

## Description

**Founded:** NA

**Operating Locations:** North Dakota

The purpose of the North Dakota Library Association (NDLA)is to exercise professional leadership and to promote library services and librarianship.

## Grants Information

### GRANT TYPES
Conference attendance, continuing education

### TYPICAL RECIPIENTS
North Dakota librarians

### GRANT VALUES
NA

### NAMED GRANTS

### NEW MEMBERS ROUND TABLE GRASSROOTS GRANT
The Grassroots Grant gives new librarians and future librarians a chance

to go to the NDLA annual conference. One award will be given to a student currently enrolled in an ALA-accredited MLS program. The second award will be given to a librarian with less than six years of experience who is attending an NDLA conference for the first time. The full registration cost (including meals) for each recipient will be waived. The grant does not cover the cost of travel, lodging, or any other expenses.

**Requirements and Restrictions:** Applicants must be current members of NDLA. Recipients of the Grassroots Grant must agree to confirm in writing with the NMRT Grassroots Grant Committee that they will accept the grant and will attend the NDLA annual conference, provide confirmation in writing from their employing institutions that they have approval to accept this grant and to meet the requirements of conference attendance, attend all three days of the conference, attend the executive board meeting (as a guest) on the third day, and submit an article for publication in the NDLA newsletter about their experiences at the conference.

**Submission Guidelines:** Application online

**Deadlines:** August

**Contact:** Laura Trude, Chair, New Members Round Table, Health Workforce Information Center, University of North Dakota, 501 N.

Columbia Rd., Stop 9037, Grand Forks, ND 58202-9037; Phone: 701-777-8003; E-mail: laura.trude@med.und.edu

**Grant-Specific Website:** www.ndla.info/awards.htm

## NDLA PROFESSIONAL DEVELOPMENT GRANT

NDLA believes that furthering an individual's skills is beneficial to the North Dakota library environment. Each year NDLA sets aside general fund dollars for this purpose. The Professional Development grant may be used for college or university classroom work, independent study, workshops, conferences, or participation in any activity that will benefit the library community in North Dakota.

**Requirements and Restrictions:** Applicants must be North Dakota residents or employed in North Dakota, be current members of NDLA and must have been members for the past two years, submit a detailed budget of expected expenses, submit a narrative describing personal growth and career development expectations from the proposed program, and submit printed materials that describe the program. Applicants need not be currently employed in a library. Applicants must submit an evaluative report to NDLA upon program completion for publication in the NDLA newsletter. A copy of CEU certificate or letter of recognition should accompany the report, if applicable. Grant money will be awarded after the evaluative report has been received by the NDLA president. No applicant may receive more than one grant per 18 months.

## RON RUDSER MEMORIAL CONTINUING EDUCATION GRANT

Ron Rudser was a librarian and library science instructor at Minot State University at the time of his death in 1986. This memorial grant fund was initiated by his wife, Kay. The Ron Rudser Memorial Continuing Education Grant may be used for credit courses, workshops, seminars, or preconference programs that enhance the education of a practicing librarian in any type of library. Regular conference programs or conventions do not qualify.

### Requirements and Restrictions:

Applicants must be North Dakota residents or employed in North Dakota, be current members of NDLA and must have been members for the past two years, submit a detailed budget of expected expenses, submit a narrative describing personal growth and career development expectations from the proposed program, and submit printed materials that describe the program. Applicants need not be currently employed in a library. Applicants must submit an evaluative report to NDLA upon program completion for publication in the NDLA newsletter.

A copy of CEU certificate or letter of recognition should accompany the report, if applicable. Grant money will be awarded after the evaluative report has been received by the NDLA president. No applicant may receive more than one grant per 18 months.

## M. VIVIAN HUBBARD MEMORIAL GRANT

M. Vivian Hubbard was state president of the Federated Women's Clubs in the early 1950s. The rural bookmobile program originated in North Dakota with much influence from the Federated Women's Clubs. Hubbard believed in this program and requested that upon her death memorial funds be donated to NDLA to further interest in bookmobiles. The grant may be used for formal college or university classroom work, independent study, workshops, conferences, or participation in any other activity that will further the work of the bookmobile, including the purchase of books or other materials.

### Requirements and Restrictions:

Applicants must be current members of NDLA and agree to submit an evaluative report of how the grant was used to be published in the NDLA newsletter.

## MIKE JAUGSTETTER LEADERSHIP MEMORIAL GRANT

The Mike Jaugstetter Leadership Memorial Grant honors the superb leadership skills in librarianship that Mike Jaugstetter demonstrated while he was employed as the State Librarian of North Dakota. The grant money may be used for library leadership institutes or programs.

**Requirements and Restrictions:**
Applicants must be current individual members of NDLA and must have been members for the past two years, must be currently employed in a North Dakota library, and must submit a detailed budget of expected expenses, a narrative statement describing personal growth and career development expectations from the program they plan to attend, and printed materials that describe the program. Applicants must agree to (1) submit an evaluative report to the NDLA executive board upon completion of the program for publication in the NDLA newsletter, (2) participate in the leadership of the NDLA executive board for one year (participation may include, but not be limited to, section chair, officer, committee chair, or committee work appointed by the NDLA president), (3) present a leadership program at the NDLA conference following participation in the leadership program or institute, (4) participate in the committee selection of the following year's recipient. No applicant may receive more than one grant per 24 months. A portion of expenses (dependent upon the NDLA budget) will be reimbursed upon completion of travel. A written contract between NDLA and the grant recipient will be entered into regarding completion of conditions.

**REQUIREMENTS AND RESTRICTIONS**
Vary by grant

**APPLICATION PROCEDURES**
**Submission Guidelines:** Application online

**Deadlines:** August

**CONTACT**
Lori K. West
Fargo Public Library
2801 32nd Ave. S.
Fargo, ND 58103
Phone: 701-476-5977
Fax: 701-476-5981
E-mail: lwest@cityoffargo.com

**GRANT-SPECIFIC WEBSITE**
www.ndla.info/profdev.htm

# North Dakota State Library

## Headquarters

604 E. Boulevard Ave., Dept. 250
Bismarck, ND 58505-0800
Phone: 800-472-2104 or 701-328-4622
www.library.nd.gov/

# Description

**Founded:** 1907

**Operating Locations:** North Dakota

Providing access to information for North Dakotans is the mission of the North Dakota State Library. The State Library specializes in state-of-the-art information services to libraries, state agencies, and the general public. The State Library assumes a leadership role in promoting the development of library service for all North Dakota residents.

# Grants Information

### GRANT TYPES
LSTA funds

### TYPICAL RECIPIENTS
North Dakota library and information science students

### GRANT VALUES
Highest Grant: $7,000
Lowest Grant: $1,000

### NAMED GRANTS

### LSTA TRAINING GRANT
The North Dakota State Library has established a training grant program to encourage North Dakotans to pursue a Master of Library and Information Science degree from an ALA-accredited school and to work in North Dakota.

North Dakota residents working on their ALA/MLIS degrees may apply for reimbursement grants when tuition, fees, and textbooks total a minimum of $1,000, up to a total of $7,000.

### REQUIREMENTS AND RESTRICTIONS
The applicant must be a resident of North Dakota at the time she/he is beginning the MLIS graduate program and be accepted into an ALA/MLIS program. Grant recipients must successfully complete their program as outlined by the graduate school in which they are enrolled. If a grant recipient withdraws from the program, she/he must return all grant money received from the State Library. Grant recipients must be employed in a North Dakota library within 9 months of receiving the MLIS degree and must work for 24 months in a full-time position in a North Dakota library. If these conditions are not met, recipients must return all of the money that has been paid to them from the State Library. The grant will be processed on a reimbursement basis, with the applicants submitting copies of invoices of tuition, fees, and/or textbooks paid; and a copy of the current transcript.

### APPLICATION PROCEDURES
**Submission Guidelines:** Application online. A complete application includes

- a completed application page agreeing to comply with the guidelines as outlined

- a letter of interest that includes progress in the program, goals for the program, why the applicant should be chosen for the grant, and career goals
- a current résumé
- two names and daytime telephone numbers of references who are current or previous supervisors or board members

Applications should be mailed to the address below.

**Decisions:** Applications will be reviewed within 1 month of receipt.

**CONTACT**
North Dakota State Library
604 E. Boulevard Ave.
Bismarck, ND 58505-0800
Phone: 800-472-2104 or 701-328-2492

**GRANT-SPECIFIC WEBSITE**
www.library.nd.gov/librarian.html

# OCLC Online Computer Library Center Inc.

## Headquarters

6565 Kilgour Pl.
Dublin, OH 43017-3395
Phone: 614-764-6000
www.oclc.org

## Description

**Founded:** 1967

**Operating Locations:** Ohio, Washington, China, Canada, Germany

Founded in 1967, OCLC Online Computer Library Center is a nonprofit, membership, computer library service and research organization dedicated to the public purposes of furthering access to the world's information and reducing the rate of rise of library costs. More than 71,000 libraries in 112 countries and territories around the world use OCLC services to locate, acquire, catalog, lend, and preserve library materials. Researchers, students, faculty, scholars, professional librarians, and other information seekers use OCLC services to obtain bibliographic, abstract, and full-text information when and where they need it.

## Financial Summary

Assets: $175,166,436
Gifts Received: $3,489,419
Total Giving: $125,894

## Grants Information

**GRANT TYPES**
Research

**TYPICAL RECIPIENTS**
Full-time academic faculty (or equivalent) in schools of library and information science

## GRANT VALUES

Total Dollar Amount of Grants: $125,894
Highest Grant: $15,000
Number of Grants: 1

## NAMED GRANTS

## OCLC/ALISE LIBRARY AND INFORMATION SCIENCE RESEARCH GRANT PROGRAM (LISRGP)

Recognizing the importance of research to the advancement of librarianship and information science, OCLC Research and the Association for Library and Information Science Education (ALISE) annually collaborate to offer the Library and Information Science Research Grant Program. The overall goal is to promote independent research, particularly work helping to integrate new technologies that offer innovative approaches, and research that contributes to a better understanding of the information environment and user expectations and behaviors. Grant awards range up to $15,000 and support one-year research projects. Research related, but not limited, to the following areas is encouraged:

- impact of digital technology on libraries, museums, and archives
- social media, learning, and information-seeking behavior
- new developments in knowledge organization (metadata, social tagging, linked data, etc.)

Full-time academic faculty in schools of library and information science or related fields are eligible to apply. OCLC and ALISE encourage international proposals and collaborative projects. To aid new researchers, priority will be given when possible to proposals from junior faculty and applicants who have not previously received LISRGP funds.

## REQUIREMENTS AND RESTRICTIONS

Reviewers consider the following criteria, among others, when evaluating proposals:

- Does the proposal meet the formal criteria as laid out in the Call for Proposals? Proposals not meeting formal criteria will not be further evaluated and will not be funded. This includes length of proposal, margin and font-size specifications, presence of requested signatures, eligibility of requesting institution, presence of budget, and description of role of all investigators.
- Is the project clearly described, the problem well defined, and are the research objectives clearly stated?
- Is there sufficient review of literature?
- Is the proposed methodology appropriate and are the investigative procedures clearly explained?
- What is the significance of the proposed research to either the library and information science community as a whole or to OCLC specifically?
- Are sufficient resources available? Do the people proposing the research

appear capable of conducting the research? Is institutional commitment to support the project apparent?

## APPLICATION PROCEDURES

**Submission Guidelines:** Proposals must be signed by the principal investigator, by the dean/director (or equivalent) of the school, and by an authorized official of the university. A complete application should include

- the OCLC/ALISE LISRGP proposal cover page
- a research proposal
- a detailed budget in U.S. dollars
- additional supporting materials such as curricula vitae of project staff, bibliography, project schedule, letters of support

Applications should be submitted online through this website: www.oclc.org/research/grants/alise.aspx.

**Deadlines:** September 15

**Decisions:** December

## CONTACT
www.oclc.org/research/feedback/form. asp?project = Grants

## GRANT-SPECIFIC WEBSITE
www.oclc.org/research/grants/

# State Library of Ohio

## Headquarters

274 E. First Ave., Suite 100
Columbus, OH 43201-3692
Phone: 614-644-7061
www.library.ohio.gov

## Description

**Founded:** 1817

**Operating Locations:** Ohio

The State Library of Ohio is a state agency that serves state government and all types of libraries. The library's vision is to lead in ensuring the delivery of all information and library services to all Ohio residents, anywhere, anytime. The library will realize its vision by leading and partnering in the development of library services throughout Ohio, promoting and enabling resource sharing among libraries and library networks, providing access to information for Ohio's state government, and providing specialized services to Ohio's residents.

## Grants Information

### GRANT TYPES
LSTA funds

## TYPICAL RECIPIENTS

Public, school, academic, research, and special libraries

## GRANT VALUES

NA

## NAMED GRANTS

### LSTA FULL GRANTS AND MINIGRANTS

The LSTA Full Grant and Minigrant programs provide funds to be used for items and activities that will assist a library in meeting one of the two broad-based purposes of LSTA: (1) technological innovation and electronic linkages, and (2) services to the underserved. Grant proposals should fall into one of the following categories:

- Technological innovation: projects that incorporate the use of new technologies or use current technology in different ways to improve access, services, or support to library customers
- Automation: to allow libraries that wish to automate to convert their card catalog and join a consortium and participate in statewide resource sharing
- Targeted populations: to provide services to targeted populations including, but not limited to, people of diverse geographic, cultural, and socioeconomic backgrounds; individuals with disabilities; persons with limited functional literacy and information skills; and those individuals having difficulty using a library
- Services to youth: to provide services to youth, ages birth through 18, with a particular emphasis on youth in poverty and those children from families with incomes below the poverty line
- Training: to provide technology literacy training on all levels to the public
- Library entrepreneurship: to develop new solutions or alternatives to library issues from which all libraries can learn and benefit and, if appropriate, replicate. Projects must meet library users' needs in a fresh way, have the breadth to become a platform for related services, increase the library's value to the community, and offer an advantage over current services or processes.

The State Library is especially interested in those proposals that demonstrate library cooperation and partnerships in achieving any of the above areas.

**Requirements and Restrictions:** LSTA funds are intended to be used as seed money, not for ongoing operational costs. A library or consortium may submit more than one proposal, but only one proposal per institution will be funded. A cash match of 25 percent of the total project cost is required from the institution (in-kind contributions do not qualify).

**Grant Values:** Typical Range of Grants, $50,000–$150,000 for Full Grants; Highest Grant, $24,000 for Minigrants

**Deadlines:** Full Grants, April; Minigrants, October

**Grant-Specific Website:** www.library .ohio.gov/lpd/lsta-full-grants; www. library.ohio.gov/lpd/lsta-minigrants

## LSTA Special Grants: Choose to Read Ohio

Special grant cycles are initiated when a unique or specific need has been identified in the library community which can be addressed through LSTA dollars. The limit on the amount of federal funds which can be requested and the funding period vary based on the special grant program. Most special grants are one-time opportunities.

The Choose to Read Ohio (CTRO) program, a project of the State Library, was initiated in 2009 and has one main goal: to encourage the reading of books together across Ohio communities. CTRO is a framework to spotlight Ohio authors and promote reading across the state. The State Library, in partnership with Ohioana Library, developed this initiative to encourage Ohioans of all ages to share literature by authors native to, residing in, or associated with Ohio.

The Choose to Read Ohio grant program focuses on the concept of

a community read wherein libraries promote reading the same book and participating in discussions or other activities around that shared experience. Each community has the opportunity to select from a title or titles on the CTRO list and tailor its approach in a somewhat different manner, but all will be building a community of readers and an appreciation of Ohio authors and literature.

**Requirements and Restrictions:** Funds may be used for purchasing copies of the selected title in various formats, purchasing additional materials supporting the theme of the chosen book, marketing and promotion of the program, author visits and honoraria for speakers, and costs associated with title tie-in activities. Food, prizes, and giveaways (aside from the selected book title) are nonallowable expenses for both federal and local matching funds. A cash match of 25 percent of the total project cost is required from the institution (in-kind contributions do not qualify).

In order to receive LSTA funds under this program, a library must be willing to share their titles as part of the statewide resource sharing initiative once their program is completed. Libraries receiving LSTA funds will be required to post information about their program on WebJunction Ohio and, if appropriate, to add content to the resource and discussion lists for their selected title.

**Grant Values:** Highest Grant, $10,000

**Submission Guidelines:** All proposals should be submitted electronically to mlodge@library.ohio.gov.

**Deadlines:** March and September

**Grant-Specific Website:** www.library. ohio.gov/lpd/choose-read-ohio-special-grant

## REQUIREMENTS AND RESTRICTIONS
Vary by grant

## APPLICATION PROCEDURES
**Submission Guidelines:** An original of the proposal should be sent to the address below. See the website for more details.

## CONTACT
LSTA Office
State Library of Ohio
274 E. First Ave., Suite 100
Columbus, OH 43201
Questions regarding the proposal process
should be addressed to
Missy Lodge
LSTA Program Coordinator
Phone: 800-686-1532 or 614-644-6914
E-mail: mlodge@library.ohio.gov

## GRANT-SPECIFIC WEBSITE
www.library.ohio.gov/lpd/general-lsta
-information

# Oregon State Library

## Headquarters

250 Winter St. NE
Salem, OR 97301-3950
Phone: 503-378-4243
www.oregon.gov/OSL/

## Description

**Founded:** 1905

**Operating Locations:** Oregon

The mission of the Oregon State Library is to provide quality information services to Oregon state government; to provide reading materials to blind and print-disabled Oregonians; and to provide leadership, grants, and other assistance to improve local library service for all Oregonians.

## Grants Information

### GRANT TYPES
LSTA funds, literacy

### TYPICAL RECIPIENTS
Public, academic, special, and school libraries; library cooperatives and consortia; organizations with tax-exempt, nonprofit status willing to serve as fiscal agent for a project to benefit one or more libraries

## GRANT VALUES

NA

## NAMED GRANTS

### LSTA COMPETITIVE GRANT

LSTA Competitive Grant funds can be used for technical studies, planning grants, service and technology development, and demonstration projects, as well as replication of outstanding projects. Grant projects do not need to be innovative, just new to the applicant. Competitive grants must address at least one purpose of the LSTA legislation as detailed in the Five-Year Plan. The LSTA Advisory Council stresses fully developed partnerships where possible in grant projects.

**Typical Recipients:** Any legally established public library, academic library, special library, school library, library cooperative, or library consortium, or any organization with tax-exempt, nonprofit status willing to serve as fiscal agent for a project to benefit one or more libraries

**Grant Values:** Total Dollar Amount of Grants, $1,023,701; Number of Grants, 20; Average Grant, $58,362; Highest Grant, $102,359; Lowest Grant, $5,525

**Past Grant Recipients:**

- Deschutes Public Library District (OR), Library Linx project, $36,380
- Lewis and Clark College (OR), Oregon Poetic Voices project, $34,150
- Multnomah County Library (OR), Kaboom! project, $52,793
- Multnomah County Library (OR), Preparing Black Children for Kindergarten: A Library Planning Grant, $45,901
- Oregon State University Libraries (OR), Oregon Digital Library Project, $69,373
- Sage Library System (OR), test and implement an open source integrated library system, $102,359

**Submission Guidelines:** Oregon uses a two-step grant application process. A three-page brief proposal is due in April. If the LSTA Advisory Council is interested, they will recommend that the State Library Board of Trustees invite the project to develop a full grant proposal, which is due in August. Applications are available online.

**Deadlines:** Brief proposal, April; full proposal, August

**Decisions:** Full proposal invitations, June; grant decisions, October

**Contact:** Ann Reed; Phone: 503-378-5027; E-mail: ann.reed@state.or.us; OR Mary Mayberry; Phone 503-378-2525; E-mail: mary.l.mayberry@state.or.us

**Grant-Specific Website:** http://oregon .gov/OSL/LD/LSTAcomp.shtml

### READY TO READ GRANT

Ready to Read Grant funds are to be used to establish, develop, or improve public library early literacy services for children from birth to five years of age and to provide the statewide summer reading program, as defined by rule of the Trustees of the State Library, for children from birth to 14 years of age.

**Typical Recipients:** All legally established public libraries in the state are eligible to apply.

**Grant Values:** Highest Grant, $76,000; Lowest Grant, $1,000

**Submission Guidelines:** Application online. Completed applications should be mailed to the address. Faxed applications will not be accepted.

**Deadlines:** August

**Contact:** Katie Anderson; Phone: 503-378-2528; E-mail: katie.anderson@state.or.us

**Grant-Specific Website:** http://oregon.gov/OSL/LD/youthsvcs/aboutready.shtml

### REQUIREMENTS AND RESTRICTIONS
Vary by grant

### APPLICATION PROCEDURES
Vary by grant

### CONTACT
Varies by grant

### GRANT-SPECIFIC WEBSITE
http://oregon.gov/OSL/LD/grantmainalt.shtml

# J. C. Penney Co.

## Headquarters

6501 Legacy Dr.
Plano, TX 75024
Phone: 972-431-2126
www.jcpenney.net

## Description

**Founded:** 1902

**Operating Locations:** Texas

**Type of Product/Service:** Department store

**In-Kind or Service Support:** Donated products for disaster relief only

# J. C. PENNEY CO. FUND

6501 Legacy Dr.
Plano, TX 75024
Phone: 972-431-2126
www.jcpenney.net/about/social_resp/default.aspx

**Foundation Information:** Corporate foundation of J.C. Penney Co., Inc.

## Financial Summary

Assets: $2,272,223
Total Giving: $1,494,023

# Grants Information

## GRANT TYPES
General support, matching, emergency

## TYPICAL RECIPIENTS
Arts and humanities, civic affairs, education, environment, health, religion, social services

## GRANT VALUES
Total Dollar Amount of Grants:
  $1,494,023

## PAST GRANT RECIPIENTS

*Library or School Related*
- Friends of Daugherty Public Library (IL), general support, $750
- Friends of the Glendora Library (CA), general support, $250
- Williston Community Library Foundation (ND), general support, $125
- Friends of the Mannheim Community Library (PA), general support, $250
- Timberglen Branch Library Friends (TX), general support, $100
- Utah University Extension (UT), general support, $500
- Adult Literacy Council (SC), general support, $250

*General*
- Ronald McDonald House Charities (WI), general support, $250
- Dallas Junior Hockey Association (TX), general support, $750

- Shelby Youth Sports (TN), general support, $500

## REQUIREMENTS AND RESTRICTIONS
NA

## APPLICATION PROCEDURES
NA

## CONTACT
Jodie Gibson
Phone: 972-431-1341

## GRANT-SPECIFIC WEBSITE
www.jcpenney.net/about/social_resp/
  default.aspx

# State Library of Pennsylvania

## Headquarters

Pennsylvania Department of Education,
Bureau of State Library
333 Market St.
Harrisburg, PA 17126-1745
Phone: 717-783-5968
www.pde.state.pa.us/portal/server.pt/
community/bureau_of_state_library/8811

## Description

**Founded:** 1816

**Operating Locations:** Pennsylvania

The State Library of Pennsylvania provides information for state government and citizens while collecting and preserving our written heritage through materials published for, by, and about Pennsylvania.

# Grants Information

### GRANT TYPES
LSTA funds

### TYPICAL RECIPIENTS
All types of libraries

### GRANT VALUES
NA

### NAMED GRANTS

### LSTA DIGITIZATION GRANT
The purpose of the LSTA Digitization Grant is to support the conversion of special materials to digital format for dissemination on the Internet. Digitization can provide increased access to collections through online image viewing and potentially through text searching, if optical character recognition (OCR) is applied to the resulting images (an additional charge). Grants will only be given to fund the digitization of materials that are of interest to the general public.

**Grant Values:** Highest Grant, $25,000 for single library applicants; $35,000 for collaborative projects

**Requirements and Restrictions:** If the following conditions are not met, the application will be ineligible: the project must be appropriate under the priorities of Commonwealth Libraries' LSTA Five-Year Plan; the library must meet the eligibility requirements of the application; and there must be no copyright restrictions preventing online access. Funding may not be used for construction/renovation, projects that have already begun, or operating expenses.

### LSTA K–12 LIBRARY COLLECTION DEVELOPMENT GRANT
LSTA K–12 Collection Development Grant funds are available for the purchase of library materials. Grants will be awarded to strengthen collections in science, social studies, or career education, or to address informational resource needs for English language learners or the physically disabled that also support the achievement of Pennsylvania's Academic Standards. Collections for English language learners or the physically disabled must also be in science, social studies, or career education.

**Grant Values:** Highest Grant, $5,000

**Requirements and Restrictions:** Each building within a school district to be considered must submit a separate application for its library. A collection assessment and development plan for the section of the library impacted by the new materials must be included in the proposal. A resource guide must be submitted with the final report. The guide must relate to the materials purchased with this grant, align to the Pennsylvania Academic Standards and Curriculum Framework, and identify both print and electronic resources for the grade level chosen. Libraries need to collaborate with classroom teachers to ensure the school library program is integral to the school curriculum. Evidence of collaboration will be required. More points will be awarded to proposals that show collaboration with special education teachers. Higher scores will be given to applications from school libraries that can document true cooperation with their local public libraries, and that demonstrate with statistics that over 5 percent of the total collection was weeded in the previous school year.

### LSTA MAJOR INNOVATION GRANT

LSTA Major Innovation Grants aid libraries in developing projects that can enhance library services statewide, that are both exemplary of better ways to serve, and that support the LSTA priorities.

**Grant Values:** Highest Grant, $50,000

**Requirements and Restrictions:** Size of service area will be taken into account when scoring the reasonableness

of the budget and making grant awards. Libraries in the Department of Corrections or in the Department of Public Welfare may apply for a group throughout the agency. Both single type and multitype library applications will be accepted.

### LSTA MINI INNOVATION "TRY IT" GRANT

LSTA Mini Innovation Grants are available to help libraries with projects that are both new to them and that support at least one of the LSTA priorities. Automation will not be funded.

**Grant Values:** Highest Grant, $5,000

**Requirements and Restrictions:** Size of service area will be taken into account when scoring the reasonableness of the budget and making grant awards. Individual institution libraries in the Department of Corrections or in the Department of Public Welfare, as well as other single institution libraries, may apply. Single-type library applications will be accepted.

### LSTA PUBLIC LIBRARY COLLECTION DEVELOPMENT GRANT

LSTA Public Library Collection Development Grants are available to support core consumer health/wellness or economic development collections, and are awarded to state-aided public libraries. Grant funds may be used for print, audio, or video materials. Electronic materials already provided on a statewide basis will not be funded. E-book purchases must be owned by the library.

**Grant Values:** Highest Grant, $5,000

**Requirements and Restrictions:** This grant will not fund materials for processing. More points will be awarded to first time applicants. Applicants must provide evidence of routine weeding to ensure currency of existing materials. Grantees will be expected to commit to maintaining a current collection of health/wellness or economic development materials.

## LSTA Technology Component Grant

LSTA Technology Component Grants are available to help public libraries purchase technology components that are necessary to link to a statewide database system.

**Grant Values:** Highest Grant, $5,000

**Requirements and Restrictions:** Grantees will be required to provide 70 percent of the project cost. Size of service area will be taken into account when scoring the reasonableness of the budget and making grant awards. Applications from individual public libraries will be accepted. Examples of fundable projects include public access computers, circulation computers, local

area network (LAN) and/or wide area network (WAN) connectivity to the Internet, and public wireless network access. This grant will not fund software, Apple equipment, self-check stations, or furniture.

**Contact:** If you do not have access to a local technology advisor and need further help in determining your technology needs, contact John Houser, Technology Coordinator; Phone: 215-534-6820; E-mail: houser@hslc.org.

## REQUIREMENTS AND RESTRICTIONS
Applicants must be located in the state of Pennsylvania. See grant guidelines online for additional requirements.

## APPLICATION PROCEDURES

**Submission Guidelines:** Applications must be completed online via the Pennsylvania Department of Education eGrant website below. Mail (do not fax) original copies (no correction fluid or pen/pencil corrections on the original) of the required letters and CIPA forms by the application deadline to the address below.

**Deadlines:** September

## CONTACT
LSTA Administrator
Pennsylvania Department of Education
Office of Commonwealth Libraries
Bureau of Library Development
333 Market St.

Harrisburg, PA 17126-1745
To reach the Pennsylvania Department
of Education Library Development
Grants and Contracting Manager
Phone: 717-783-5746
Fax: 717-787-2117
E-mail: ccardillo@state.pa.us
For assistance with the e-grant system
Phone: 717-783-6686
E-mail: ra-egrantshelp@state.pa.us

**GRANT-SPECIFIC WEBSITE**
www.pde.state.pa.us/portal/server.pt/
community/Library_Services_&_
Technology_Act/8738/
eGrant website: eGrants.ed.state.pa.us

# Peoples Bancorp Foundation

## Headquarters

138 Putnam St.
PO Box 738
Marietta, OH 45750
Phone: 740-374-6147

## Description

**Founded:** 2004

**Operating Locations:** Ohio

**Foundation Information:** Corporate
foundation of Peoples Bancorp, Inc.

## Financial Summary

Assets: $474,346
Gifts Received: $70,000
Total Giving: $190,425

## Grants Information

**GRANT TYPES**
General support, operating support,
scholarship

**TYPICAL RECIPIENTS**
Community investment and economic
development, youth and education,
human services programs that improve
the social needs of low- to moderate-
income communities and individuals,
arts and cultures

**GRANT VALUES**
Total Dollar Amount of Grants: $190,425
Number of Grants: 54
Average Grant: $1,000
Highest Grant: $25,000
Lowest Grant: $500
Typical Range of Grants: $1,000–$3,000

**PAST GRANT RECIPIENTS**
*Library or School Related*
- Friends of the Barlow Library (OH),
general operating fund, $1,000
- Ashland Community and Technical
College Foundation (KY), general
operating fund, $3,000
- Marietta College (OH), general
operating fund, $25,000

- Robert E. Evans Education Fund (OH), scholarships, $11,000
- Washington State Community College Foundation (OH), general operating fund, $2,000

*General*
- Highlands Museum and Discovery Center (KY), general operating fund, $1,000
- Huntington Area Development Council (WV), general operating fund, $2,000
- Colony Theater (OH), general operating fund, $5,000

**REQUIREMENTS AND RESTRICTIONS**
Applicants must be located in Ohio, West Virginia, or Kentucky.

**APPLICATION PROCEDURES**
**Submission Guidelines:** Send a letter of inquiry.

**CONTACT**
Kristi Close
Phone: 740-376-7128

**GRANT-SPECIFIC WEBSITE**
www.peoplesbancorp.com/community_
connections.html

# Perdue Farms

## Headquarters

31149 Old Ocean City Rd.
Salisbury, MD 21804
Phone: 410-543-3000
www.perdue.com

## Description

**Founded:** 1920

**Operating Locations:** Maryland

**Type of Product/Service:** Poultry farming

**Corporate Sponsorship:** Food donations to food pantries

# ARTHUR W. PERDUE FOUNDATION

c/o Foundation Source
501 Silverside Rd.
Wilmington, DE 19809
Phone: 800-839-1754
www.perdue.com/company/
commitments/contributions/

**Foundation Information:** Corporate foundation of Perdue Farms

# Financial Summary

Assets: $8,369,082
Total Giving: $489,815

# Grants Information

**GRANT TYPES**
General support, scholarship, capital

**TYPICAL RECIPIENTS**
Arts and humanities, civic affairs, education, health, social services

**GRANT VALUES**
Total Dollar Amount of Grants: $489,815

**PAST GRANT RECIPIENTS**

*Library or School Related*
- Milford District Free Public Library Commission (DE), building expansion campaign, $2,500
- Bridgeville Public Library (DE), capital building fund, $500
- Maine College of Art (ME), general support, $10,000
- Salisbury State University Foundation (MD), general support, $25,000
- United States Naval Academy Foundation (MD), scholarship, $10,000
- East Carolina University Foundation (NC), scholarship, $10,000

*General*
- Maryland 4-H Club Foundation (MD),

food safety education program, $10,000
- Dove Pointe Foundation (MD), purchase of playground equipment as part of capital campaign, $6,065
- Community Foundation (VA), general support, $10,000

**REQUIREMENTS AND RESTRICTIONS**
Applicants must have tax-exempt status. Grants will not be awarded to individual churches or religious denominations. The foundation considers requests from organizations based in the states of Alabama, Delaware, Georgia, Indiana, Kentucky, Maryland, North Carolina, South Carolina, Tennessee, and Virginia. Preference is given to programs in the communities in and around Perdue's major facilities.

**APPLICATION PROCEDURES**

**Submission Guidelines:** Guidelines and application form are available online.

**Deadlines:** Grant requests are reviewed quarterly. Requests should be sent at least 90 days in advance of when funds are needed.

**CONTACT**
William S. Hetherington
Phone: 410-543-3217

**GRANT-SPECIFIC WEBSITE**
www.perdue.com/company/
   commitments/contributions/

# Pfizer, Inc.

## Headquarters

235 E. 42nd St.
New York, NY 10017
www.pfizer.com

## Description

**Founded:** 1910

**Operating Locations:** New York

**Type of Product/Service:**
Pharmaceuticals

**In-Kind or Service Support:** Donation
of products to emergency relief;
volunteer programs to nonprofit
organizations with which the company's
employees and retirees are regularly
involved

**Corporate Sponsorship:** Arts and
cultural events

# PFIZER FOUNDATION

235 E. 42nd St.
New York, NY 10017
Phone: 212-733-4250
www.pfizer.com/responsibility/
**Foundation Information:** Corporate
foundation of Pfizer, Inc.

## Financial Summary

Assets: $210,342,315
Total Giving: $42,466,604

## Grants Information

### GRANT TYPES
General support, awards, matching,
emergency, conference attendance

### TYPICAL RECIPIENTS
Arts and humanities, civic affairs,
education, health, international, science,
social services

### GRANT VALUES
Total Dollar Amount of Grants:
$42,466,604

### PAST GRANT RECIPIENTS
*Library or School Related*
- Groton Public Library (CT), general
  support, $1,000
- AET Library Endowment (DC),
  general support, $1,000
- New York Public Library (NY),
  general support, $75,000
- Tenafly Public Library (NJ), general
  support, $1,000
- Foundation for Baltimore County
  Public Library (MD), general support,
  $500
- Library of Virginia Foundation (VA),
  general support, $300
- Letourneau University (TX), general
  support, $2,000

- Foundation for Lincoln Public Schools (NE), general support, $2,050
- University of Texas (TX), general support, $50,000
- Michigan State University (MI), support for FFA foundation, $1,000

## REQUIREMENTS AND RESTRICTIONS

Pfizer supports organizations in its operating communities. Pfizer does not support individuals, political causes or candidates, or organizations supported by United Way. Applicant organizations must be tax-exempt or nonprofit.

## APPLICATION PROCEDURES

**Submission Guidelines:** Organizations in communities in which Pfizer is located should contact the community relations representative at the site. Applicants should include background, history, and accomplishments of the organization and a brief description of the program for which funding is requested, including rationale, amount requested, specific objectives, and timetable.

## CONTACT

NA

## GRANT-SPECIFIC WEBSITE

www.pfizer.com/responsibility/
grants_contributions/grants_and_
contributions.jsp

# Public Library Association (PLA)

## Headquarters

50 E. Huron St.
Chicago, IL 60611
Phone: 800-545-2433, ext. 5752
www.pla.org

## Description

**Founded:** 1944

**Operating Locations:** Illinois

The Public Library Association (PLA), with more than 11,000 members, is one of the fastest growing divisions of the American Library Association, the oldest and largest library association in the world. PLA's core purpose is to strengthen public libraries and their contribution to the communities they serve. PLA is a member-driven organization that exists to provide a diverse program of communication, publication, advocacy, continuing education, and programming for its members and others interested in the advancement of public library service.

## Financial Summary

Total Giving: $64,000

# Grants Information

### GRANT TYPES
Collection development, conference attendance, scholarship

### TYPICAL RECIPIENTS
Public libraries and public librarians

### GRANT VALUES
Number of Grants: 4
Highest Grant: $8,000
Lowest Grant: $500

### NAMED GRANTS

### BAKER AND TAYLOR ENTERTAINMENT AUDIO MUSIC/ VIDEO PRODUCT AWARD
The Baker and Taylor Entertainment Audio Music / Video Product Award is designed to provide a public library the opportunity to build or expand a collection of either or both formats in whatever proportion the library chooses. The grant consists of $2,500 of audio music or video products. Sponsored by Baker and Taylor.

**Grant-Specific Website:** www.ala .org/ala/mgrps/divs/pla/plaawards/ btaudiomusicvideoproductaward/

### DEMCO NEW LEADERS TRAVEL GRANT
The DEMCO New Leaders Travel Grant is designed to enhance the professional development and improve the expertise of public librarians new to the field by making possible their attendance at major professional development activities. Plaques and travel grants of up to $1,500 per applicant are presented annually at the ALA Annual Conference. Eligible events are the PLA Spring Symposium workshops; PLA National Conferences; and other PLA events, such as preconferences, held in conjunction with ALA Annual Conference. Sponsored by DEMCO, Inc.

**Grant-Specific Website:** www.ala. org/ala/mgrps/divs/pla/plaawards/ demconewleadersgrant/

### ROMANCE WRITERS OF AMERICA LIBRARY GRANT
The Romance Writers of America Library Grant is designed to provide a public library the opportunity to build or expand its romance fiction collection and/or to host romance fiction programming. The grant consists of $4,500 to be used toward the purchase of books in print or audio format, author honoraria and travel expenses, and other applicable program expenses.

**Grant-Specific Website:** www.ala. org/ala/mgrps/divs/pla/plaawards/ romancewritersgrant/

### GROW YOUR OWN @ YOUR LIBRARY
This program was developed by PLA to address the education needs of public library staff working toward the ultimate

goal of obtaining a master's degree in library and information science. This program is intended to assist public library staff members who are working toward securing a library degree by awarding funds to the employing public library for reimbursement of employee course tuition costs at the undergraduate or graduate level. PLA recognizes that the institution is strategically positioned to best identify those employees with a commitment to librarianship, public libraries, and the institution/community.

PLA will provide up to nine public libraries with a lump sum of $8,000 each to be distributed to as many of their employees as they choose for the purpose of working toward obtaining an MLS degree. Of the total amount, $6,500 is to be used directly for payment of tuition at the undergraduate level or at an ALA-accredited library school graduate level, and $1,500 is to be used to support attendance for one or more of the selected scholarship recipients to attend a PLA-sponsored continuing education conference or event such as the PLA National Conference or PLA Spring Symposium.

One library from each of the nine PLDS size categories may be selected. The categories are

- Group 1: Service population of 1 million and over
- Group 2: Service population of 500,000–999,999
- Group 3: Service population of 250,000–499,999
- Group 4: Service population of 100,000–249,999
- Group 5: Service population of 50,000–99,999
- Group 6: Service population of 25,000–49,999
- Group 7: Service population of 10,000–24,999
- Group 8: Service population of 5,000–9,999
- Group 9: Service population under 5,000

Bachelor or master level courses taken between the February the library receives notification and accepts the scholarship and the March two years from the notification are eligible for tuition reimbursement under this program. The scholarships are awarded biennially if funding is available. The online application will be open September through November.

**Grant-Specific Website:** www.ala.org/ala/mgrps/divs/pla/plaawards/gyoinstscholarship/

## REQUIREMENTS AND RESTRICTIONS
Some grants require ALA and PLA membership. Other requirements vary by grant.

## APPLICATION PROCEDURES
**Submission Guidelines:** Application online

**Deadlines:** December

**Decisions:** February

### CONTACT
Julianna Kloeppel
Phone: 800-545-2433, ext. 5026, or 312-280-5026
E-mail: jkloeppel@ala.org

### GRANT-SPECIFIC WEBSITE
www.ala.org/ala/mgrps/divs/pla/plaawards/
Online application: www.ala.org/ala/mgrps/divs/pla/plaawards/apply/

# Charles L. Read Foundation

## Headquarters

111 Wohseepee Dr.
Bayside, NY 11706
Phone: 973-379-5850

## Description

**Founded:** 1956

**Operating Locations:** New York

**Foundation Information:** Private foundation

## Financial Summary

Assets: $2,696,170
Total Giving: $173,000

## Grants Information

### GRANT TYPES
General support

### TYPICAL RECIPIENTS
Arts and humanities, civic affairs, education, environment, health, religion, science, social services

### GRANT VALUES
Total Dollar Amount of Grants: $173,000
Number of Grants: 81
Average Grant: $2,100
Highest Grant: $32,000
Lowest Grant: $500
Typical Range of Grants: $1,000–$3,000

### PAST GRANT RECIPIENTS
*Library or School Related*
- Library of Chatham (NJ), general support, $2,000
- Louisa Adelia Read Memorial Library (NY), general support, $7,500
- Madison Public Library (NJ), general support, $1,000
- Hancock Central School (NY), trust and agency fund, $32,000
- Drew University (NJ), general support, $5,000
- Breckenridge Elementary PTSA (CO), general support, $2,500

*General*

- Deposit Community Theatre (NY), general support, $2,000
- Maine Maritime Museum (ME), general support, $1,500
- Tanglewood (MA), general support, $5,000
- Spice Handler Brain Tumor Research (NC), general support, $1,000

**REQUIREMENTS AND RESTRICTIONS**

Applicants must have tax-exempt status.

**APPLICATION PROCEDURES**

**Submission Guidelines:** Submit a brief résumé of activities for which the grant is desired, including latest financial statement and a copy of IRS tax-exemption letter.

**CONTACT**

Rodger K. Herrigel
249 Millburn Ave.
Millburn, NJ 07041-1735
Phone: 973-379-5850

**GRANT-SPECIFIC WEBSITE**

NA

# Reference and User Services Association (RUSA)

## Headquarters

50 E. Huron St.
Chicago, IL 60611
Phone: 800-545-2433, ext. 4395
www.ala.org/ala/mgrps/divs/rusa/index.cfm

## Description

**Founded:** 1956

**Operating Locations:** Illinois

The Reference and User Services Association (RUSA), a division of the American Library Association, is responsible for stimulating and supporting excellence in the delivery of general library services and materials to adults, and the provision of reference and information services, collection development, and resource sharing for all ages, in every type of library.

## Grants Information

**GRANT TYPES**

Research, conference attendance

## TYPICAL RECIPIENTS
Business librarians

## GRANT VALUES
Highest Grant: $5,000
Lowest Grant: $1,000

## NAMED GRANTS

### EMERALD RESEARCH GRANT AWARD
The Emerald Research Grant Award will be awarded to individuals seeking support to conduct research in business librarianship. The funds may be used at the discretion of the award recipient. Award recipient must be an ALA member; at least one member of a collaborative team must be an ALA member. Recipients may be asked to present their findings at a public BRASS event within two years of receiving the award (at the discretion of the BRASS executive committee). Recipients will also be required to acknowledge the Emerald Research Grant when publishing or presenting their research. Two $5,000 awards will be presented.

**Deadlines:** December

**Submission Guidelines:** Candidates must submit a detailed proposal outlining their proposed research project; methodology, scope, and timetable; how this project fits into the existing literature; and projected outcomes, including a statement outlining how this research will benefit the library profession. Research proposals should be sent to the committee chair, Todd Hines, by e-mail or mail to the address below.

**Contact:** Todd Hines, Princeton University, Firestone Library—SSRC, One Washington Road, Princeton, NJ 08544; Phone: 609-258-4459; E-mail: thines@princeton.edu

**Grant-Specific Website:** www.ala.org/ala/mgrps/divs/rusa/awards/emeraldgrant/

### GALE CENGAGE LEARNING STUDENT TRAVEL AWARD
The Gale Cengage Learning Student Travel Award provides $1,000 to a student enrolled in an ALA-accredited master's degree program to fund travel to and attendance at the ALA Annual Conference and a one-year membership in the Business Reference and Services Section (BRASS) of RUSA. Applicants should have demonstrated interest in a career as a business reference librarian, and potential to be a leader in the profession as demonstrated by activities that may include (but are not limited to) coursework, internships, jobs, special projects, and publications. In addition to attending the conference, the winner is required to participate in BRASS activities at ALA conference and to write a brief statement about conference experiences for RUSA Update.

**Deadlines:** January

**Grant-Specific Website:**
www.ala.org/ala/mgrps/divs/rusa/
awards/studenttravel/

## MORNINGSTAR PUBLIC LIBRARIAN SUPPORT AWARD

This annual award, sponsored by Morningstar, offers $1,000 in travel funds for ALA Annual Conference to a public librarian who has performed outstanding business reference service and who requires financial assistance to attend the conference. The winner must be a member of ALA, RUSA, and BRASS. The recipient shall have a demonstrated interest in pursuing a career as a business reference librarian and the potential to be a leader in the profession. In addition, he or she will be expected to participate in BRASS activities at the conference for which the award has been made and to write a short statement regarding his or her experience at the conference for publication following the event. Applicants will be evaluated based on the following: involvement in special projects; creation of a business website; outstanding service to the community; and publications or related activities.

**Guidelines:** Application online

**Deadlines:** December

**Grant-Specific Website:** www.ala.org/ala/mgrps/divs/rusa/awards/publibsupport/

## STARS-ATLAS SYSTEMS MENTORING AWARD

Sponsored by Atlas Systems, Inc., this award offers $1,000 to fund travel expenses associated with attending ALA Annual Conference. The recipient will be a library practitioner who is new to the field of interlibrary loan/document delivery or electronic reserves, and who has daily, hands-on involvement in the areas of borrowing, lending, document delivery, electronic reserves, material delivery, or resource sharing. This award is intended for persons who have been in the profession for less than two years, or who are newly employed in an interlibrary loan, resource sharing, or electronic reserves position and have little or no experience in that area. MLS or ALA membership is not required for this award. Preference will be given to those with greatest demonstrated need for the purposes of professional development, networking, education, and service to their local community. The STARS Education and Training Committee will assign a mentor to the recipient for the conference to help them navigate through the conference experience. The recipient is expected to participate in STARS events throughout the conference.

**Deadlines:** December

**Grant-Specific Website:** www.ala.org/ala/mgrps/divs/rusa/awards/mentoring/

**REQUIREMENTS AND RESTRICTIONS**
Vary by grant

**APPLICATION PROCEDURES**
**Submission Guidelines:** Applications online unless otherwise noted above.

**CONTACT**
Liz Markel
Phone: 800-545-2433, ext. 4398, or 312-280-4398
Fax: 312-280-5273
E-mail: lmarkel@ala.org

**GRANT-SPECIFIC WEBSITE**
www.ala.org/ala/mgrps/divs/rusa/awards/

# RGK Foundation

## Headquarters

1301 W. 25th St., no. 300
Austin, TX 78705
Phone: 512-474-9298
www.rgkfoundation.org

## Description

**Founded:** 1966

**Operating Locations:** Texas

**Foundation Information:** Private foundation established by Dr. George Kozmetsky and his wife Ronya Kozmetsky

## Financial Summary

Assets: $117,879,191
Total Giving: $6,767,949

## Grants Information

**GRANT TYPES**
General support, conference attendance, project, research, continuing support

**TYPICAL RECIPIENTS**
Arts and humanities, civic affairs, education, environment, health, religion, science, social services

**GRANT VALUES**
Total Dollar Amount of Grants: $6,767,949
Average Grant: $25,000
Highest Grant: $1,000,000
Lowest Grant: $5,000

**PAST GRANT RECIPIENTS**
*Library or School Related*
- Olympic High School (CA), fund to purchase equipment and materials for school's newly renovated science laboratory, $10,000
- Children's Literacy Initiative (GA, IL, NY), expand early literacy curriculum and teacher training in Atlanta, Chicago, and New York public schools, $210,000

*General*

- Assistance League of Southern California (CA), Children's Library Classroom Reference program, $20,000
- Outreach Productions (TX), Creative Learning through Literature program promoting library use and literacy, $5,000
- Los Angeles Operation Hope (CA), Banking on Our Future program providing free financial literacy education to youth in underserved communities, $20,000
- English at Work (TX), workplace language classes for English language learners in the health care industry, $10,000
- Educational Opportunities for Central Montana (MT), nursing skills lab at Central Montana Education Center, $25,000
- Communities in Schools of Alaska (AK), build and sustain statewide network to reduce school dropout rates, $25,000
- Laying the Foundation (TX), Advanced Placement and Pre–Advanced Placement teacher training, $174,500
- Campfire USA Balcones Council (TX), integrate literacy skills into outdoor education program for elementary, middle, and high school youth, $14,000

## REQUIREMENTS AND RESTRICTIONS

The foundation no longer accepts requests for international agencies or programs. Grants are made only to tax-exempt organizations. The foundation seldom awards grants for operating expenses, capital campaigns, or endowments or to individuals.

## APPLICATION PROCEDURES

**Submission Guidelines:** Submit an electronic letter of inquiry as directed on website.

**Decisions:** Applicant will receive acknowledgement of electronic letter of inquiry within 2 days to 2 weeks. Grant committee review usually takes at least 4 months.

## CONTACT

www.rgkfoundation.org/public/contact

## GRANT-SPECIFIC WEBSITE

www.rgkfoundation.org/public/guidelines

# State of Rhode Island Office of Library and Information Services

## Headquarters

One Capitol Hill
Providence, RI 02908-5803
Phone: 401-574-9300
www.olis.ri.gov

## Description

**Founded:** NA

**Operating Locations:** Rhode Island

The Office of Library and Information Services (OLIS) is the state library agency for Rhode Island. OLIS supports and strengthens library and information services in the state to ensure that all residents will benefit from free and convenient access to library and information resources and services. In addition, OLIS participates in planning and providing access to online government information for state agencies and the public.

## Grants Information

### GRANT TYPES
LSTA funds, library construction

### TYPICAL RECIPIENTS
All types of libraries

### GRANT VALUES
NA

### NAMED GRANTS

#### PUBLIC LIBRARY CONSTRUCTION REIMBURSEMENT
The State of Rhode Island, via the Office of Library and Information Services, provides grant-in-aid for the construction and capital improvement of any free public library in the state to provide better free library services to the public. Up to 50 percent of the eligible costs of public library construction and capital improvement projects may be reimbursed through this program.

**Contact:** Karen Mellor, Rhode Island Department of Administration, Office of Library and Information Services, One Capitol Hill, Providence, RI 02908; Phone: 401-574-9304; E-mail: Karen. Mellor@olis.ri.gov

**Grant-Specific Website:**
www.olis.ri.gov/grants/construction/

#### LSTA LIBRARY OF RHODE ISLAND GRANTS
OLIS award Library of Rhode Island (LORI) Grants supported through the federal Institute of Museum and Library Services and funded by the grants to states program under the Library

Services and Technology Act. An ad hoc committee of Library Board of RI reviews grant proposals and makes funding recommendations to OLIS. In addition to the prerequisites set forth by the LSTA, OLIS will give priority attention to proposals

- from groups of libraries and other nonprofit partners to create an infrastructure that would enable them to provide library services or programs for, to, or among the partners that could not be provided as well by a single partner alone
- that enhance and expand the functionality of LORI, by the addition of member libraries or by creating access to previously unavailable resources
- that enhance library capacity or performance in order for the library to comply with LORI standards and join LORI
- that develop and integrate social media into library collections and services
- that increase library collections with materials that can also be loaned as part of the statewide interlibrary network

In keeping with the LSTA, capital expenditures are not eligible for LORI Grants.

**Deadlines:** October

**Decisions:** November

**Contact:** Donna Longo DiMichele, Rhode Island Office of Library and Information Services, One Capitol Hill, Providence, RI 02908; Phone: 401-574-9303; E-mail: Donna.DiMichele@olis.ri.gov

**Grant-Specific Website:** www.olis.ri.gov/grants/lsta/

## REQUIREMENTS AND RESTRICTIONS
Vary by grant

## APPLICATION PROCEDURES
**Submission Guidelines:** Application online

## CONTACT
Varies by grant

## GRANT-SPECIFIC WEBSITE
www.olis.ri.gov/grants/

# Cele H. and William B. Rubin Family Fund

## Headquarters

c/o Ellen Gordon
32 Monadnock Rd.
Wellesley Hills, MA 02481
Phone: 781-235-4751

# Description

**Founded:** 1944

**Operating Locations:** Massachusetts

**Foundation Information:** Private foundation established by members of the Joseph Rubin family of the Sweets Company of America and Tootsie Roll Industries

# Financial Summary

Assets: $50,074,735
Gifts Received: $400,000
Total Giving: $3,117,212

# Grants Information

## GRANT TYPES
General support

## TYPICAL RECIPIENTS
Arts and humanities, civic affairs, education, environment, health, religion, science, social services

## GRANT VALUES
Total Dollar Amount of Grants:
    $3,117,212
Number of Grants: 87
Average Grant: $35,000
Highest Grant: $1,714,000
Lowest Grant: $50

## PAST GRANT RECIPIENTS

*Library or School Related*
- Wellesley Free Library (MA), general support, $1,500
- Buckingham, Browne and Nichols School (MA), general support, $50,000
- Fenwick High School (IL), general support, $9,000
- Vassar College (NY), general support, $5,000
- Saint Joseph College (CT), general support, $150
- Northwestern University, Kellogg Graduate School (IL), general support, $7,500
- Harvard Medical School (MA), general support, $510,000
- University of Michigan Medical Center (MI), general support, $510,000

*General*
- Morton Arboretum (IL), general support, $1,000
- Boston Symphony Orchestra (MA), general support, $500

## REQUIREMENTS AND RESTRICTIONS
NA

## APPLICATION PROCEDURES

**Submission Guidelines:** Call or send a letter of inquiry. No specific forms are required.

**CONTACT**
Ellen R. Gordon
Phone: 781-235-1075

**GRANT-SPECIFIC WEBSITE**
NA

# Sage Foundation

## Headquarters

PO Box 1919
Brighton, MI 48116
Phone: 810-227-7660

## Description

**Founded:** 1955

**Operating Locations:** Michigan

**Foundation Information:** Private foundation

## Financial Summary

Assets: $44,148,824
Total Giving: $2,284,150

## Grants Information

**GRANT TYPES**
Capital, endowment, general support, continuing support

**TYPICAL RECIPIENTS**
Arts and humanities, civic affairs, education, health, religion, science, social services

**GRANT VALUES**
Total Dollar Amount of Grants:
$2,284,150

**PAST GRANT RECIPIENTS**

*Library or School Related*
- Chicago Public Library Foundation (IL), general support, $15,000
- Recording for the Blind and Dyslexic (MI), general support, $6,000
- Cumberland College (KY), general support, $10,000
- University of Michigan Law School (MI), tuition scholarships, $10,000
- College Fund/UNCF (MI), general support, $12,500

*General*
- Detroit Educational Television (MI), general support, $5,000
- Hope Foundation for Autism and Epilepsy Research (IL), general support, $5,000
- Misericordia Heart of Mercy (IL), general support, $10,000
- Michigan Eye Bank (MI), general support, $10,000
- Steppenwolf Theatre Company (IL), Steppenwolf Young Adults program, $30,000
- Lincoln Center for the Performing

Arts (NY), programs and services for people with disabilities, $5,000

## REQUIREMENTS AND RESTRICTIONS

Applicants must have tax-exempt status.

## APPLICATION PROCEDURES

**Submission Guidelines:** Applicants should send a grant request letter, including

- amount of grant requested
- what the applicant intends to accomplish
- how the applicant will meet the stated objectives
- how the applicant will evaluate results
- name of applicant's contact person
- proof of tax-exempt status

## CONTACT

Melissa Sage Fadim, President/Secretary

## GRANT-SPECIFIC WEBSITE

NA

# S&T Bancorp

## Headquarters

PO Box 190
Indiana, PA 15701
Phone: 724-349-1800
www.stbank.com

## Description

**Founded:** 1902

**Operating Locations:** Pennsylvania

**Type of Product/Service:** Commercial banking services

# S&T BANCORP CHARITABLE FOUNDATION

c/o S&T Trust Dept.
PO Box 220
Indiana, PA 15701
Phone: 724-465-1443
**Foundation Information:** Corporate foundation of S&T Bancorp

## Financial Summary

Assets: $181,699
Gifts Received: $297,884
Total Giving: $546,903

## Grants Information

### GRANT TYPES

General support, capital, scholarship

### TYPICAL RECIPIENTS

Arts and humanities, civic affairs, education, health, religion, science, social services

## GRANT VALUES

Total Dollar Amount of Grants: $546,903

Number of Grants: 143

Average Grant: $3,800

Highest Grant: $100,000

Lowest Grant: $500

## PAST GRANT RECIPIENTS

*Library or School Related*

- Blairsville Library Foundation (PA), general support, $1,000
- Delmont Public Library (PA), summer reading program, $500
- Homer City Public Library (PA), general support, $500
- Indiana Free Library (PA), general support, $1,500
- Mengle Memorial Library (PA), capital campaign, $2,000
- Murrysville Community Library (PA), addition to collection, $1,000
- New Bethlehem Public Library (PA), general support, $1,000
- Norwin Public Library (PA), capital campaign, $10,000
- Rebecca M. Arthurs Library (PA), general support, $3,250

*General*

- Greater Pittsburgh Literacy Council (PA), general support, $2,000
- Westmoreland Cultural Trust (PA), general support, $5,000

## REQUIREMENTS AND RESTRICTIONS

Awards will be restricted to within the marketing area of the bank.

## APPLICATION PROCEDURES

**Submission Guidelines:** Submit a letter of inquiry with the amount and purpose of the funding.

## CONTACT

James C. Miller

Phone: 724-465-1443

## GRANT-SPECIFIC WEBSITE

NA

# Sarkeys Foundation

## Headquarters

530 E. Main St.

Norman, OK 73071

Phone: 405-364-3703

www.sarkeys.org

## Description

**Founded:** 1962

**Operating Locations:** Oklahoma

**Foundation Information:** Private foundation established by S. J. Sarkeys

## Financial Summary

Assets: $73,045,159

Total Giving: $2,902,475

# Grants Information

## GRANT TYPES
General support, capital, endowment, matching

## TYPICAL RECIPIENTS
Arts and humanities, civic affairs, education, environment, health, international, science, social services

## GRANT VALUES
Total Dollar Amount of Grants:
$2,902,475
Number of Grants: 82
Average Grant: $35,000
Highest Grant: $250,000
Lowest Grant: $250
Typical Range of Grants: $20,000–
$50,000

## PAST GRANT RECIPIENTS

*Library or School Related*
- Chickasaw Regional Library (OK), funding to complete construction, $30,000
- Friends of the Hulbert Library (OK), flooring and shelving for new library, $40,000
- Pioneer Multi-County Library System (OK), funding for board retreat, $2,000
- Isabel Library (OK), capital campaign, $35,000
- Rogers State University Foundation (OK), capital campaign, $50,000

*General*
- Hospice of Green County (OK), funding for purchase of educational materials for training library, $21,543
- Tulsa Boy's Home (OK), after-school care program, $25,000
- Stillwater Children's Museum (OK), support for a program coordinator, $21,124
- Regional Food Bank of Oklahoma (OK), capital campaign and Food4Kids program, $200,000
- Lyric Theatre of Oklahoma (OK), building renovation, $50,000

## REQUIREMENTS AND RESTRICTIONS
Grants are generally conferred on organizations in Oklahoma. Applicants must be tax-exempt organizations under the IRS tax code 501(c)(3). Proposals will not be accepted for local programs financed from community resources, hospitals, operating expenses, individuals, permanent financing of a program, or start-up funding for new organizations.

## APPLICATION PROCEDURES

**Submission Guidelines:** Application online. Print completed online form and mail with required attachments to foundation address above. The foundation does not accept faxed or e-mailed proposals.

**Deadlines:** Grant proposals are considered at trustee meetings in April and October. Proposals will be accepted from December 15 through February 1 for inclusion on the April agenda and from June 1 through August 1 for inclusion on the October agenda.

**CONTACT**
Susan Frantz, Diana Hartley, or Linda
    English Weeks
Phone: 405-364-3703

**GRANT-SPECIFIC WEBSITE**
www.sarkeys.org/pages/grant_making

# Scott Fetzer Co.

## Headquarters

865 Bassett Rd.
Westlake, OH 44145

## Description

**Founded:** 1914

**Operating Locations:** Ohio

**Type of Product/Service:** A diversified manufacturer of consumer, commercial, and industrial products that is an operating company for a group of more than 20 businesses

# SCOTT AND FETZER FOUNDATION

28800 Clemens Rd.
Westlake, OH 44145
Phone: 440-892-3000
**Foundation Information:** Corporate foundation of Scott Fetzer Co.

## Financial Summary

Assets: $308,924
Total Giving: $143,175

## Grants Information

**GRANT TYPES**
General support

**TYPICAL RECIPIENTS**
Arts and humanities, civic affairs, education, environment, health, religion, science, social services

**GRANT VALUES**
Total Dollar Amount of Grants: $143,175
Number of Grants: 54
Average Grant: $2,600
Highest Grant: $20,000
Lowest Grant: $25

**PAST GRANT RECIPIENTS**

*Library or School Related*
- Catholic Library Association (MA), general support, $1,500

- Canadian Library Association (Ontario), general support, $2,500
- Cleveland State University (OH), general support, $3,000
- University of Notre Dame (IN), general support, $1,500
- The Ohio Foundation of Independent Colleges (OH), general support, $1,000

*General*
- Direct Selling Education Foundation (DC), general support, $20,000
- Southwest Community Health Fund (OH), Tiara fund-raiser, $8,500
- Home Depot Foundation (GA), general support, $2,800
- Second Harvest Food Bank (TN), general support, $1,500
- American Welding Society Foundation (FL), general support, $5,000

## REQUIREMENTS AND RESTRICTIONS
Applicants must have tax-exempt status.

## APPLICATION PROCEDURES

**Submission Guidelines:** Send a letter outlining request and including a federal ID number.

## CONTACT
Edie DeSantis
Phone: 440-892-3000

## GRANT-SPECIFIC WEBSITE
NA

# Snapdragon Book Foundation

## Headquarters

2133 Bering Dr.
Houston, TX 77057
Phone: 770-597-7499
E-mail: info@ snapdragonbookfoundation.org
www.snapdragonbookfoundation.org

## Description

**Founded:** 2008

**Operating Locations:** Texas

**Foundation Information:** Private foundation established by Anne Knickerbocker

## Financial Summary

Assets: $155,796
Gifts Received: $155,940

## Grants Information

**GRANT TYPES**
Library improvement

**TYPICAL RECIPIENTS**
School libraries

## GRANT VALUES

Highest Grant: $15,000

Lowest Grant: $800

## PAST GRANT RECIPIENTS

*Library or School Related*

- West Denver Preparatory Charter School (CO), funds to add books to a new location and to serve 6th-grade expansion
- Coney Island Preparatory Public Charter School (NY), funds for a new library
- Excel Academy Charter School (DC), funds to add books to library of first all-girls public school in Washington, D.C.
- Excel Academy Charter School (MA), funds for a DEAR library expansion
- Marist High School (NJ), funds to develop a women's history and an Asian American history program
- High School of Economics and Finance (NY), funds to add global history biographies and Spanish-speaking-country books

## REQUIREMENTS AND RESTRICTIONS

Grants are limited to school libraries.

## APPLICATION PROCEDURES

**Submission Guidelines:** Application online

**Deadlines:** April

## CONTACT

Stacy Birdsell

Phone: 914-374-5358

E-mail: stacy@
  snapdragonbookfoundation.org

## GRANT-SPECIFIC WEBSITE

www.snapdragonbookfoundation.org/
  index/Apply.html

# John Ben Snow Foundation

## Headquarters

50 Presidential Plaza
Syracuse, NY 13202
Phone: 315-471-5256
E-mail: johnbensnow@verizon.net
www.johnbensnow.com/jbsf

## Description

**Founded:** 1948

**Operating Locations:** New York

**Foundation Information:** Private foundation established by John Ben Snow

## Financial Summary

Assets: $6,015,941
Total Giving: $343,650

# Grants Information

## GRANT TYPES
Capital, general support, project, matching

## TYPICAL RECIPIENTS
Arts and humanities, civic affairs, education, environment, health, social services

## GRANT VALUES
Total Dollar Amount of Grants: $343,650
Number of Grants: 39
Average Grant: $8,800
Highest Grant: $25,000
Lowest Grant: $800
Typical Range of Grants: $5,000–$15,000

## PAST GRANT RECIPIENTS

*Library or School Related*
- Edith B. Ford Memorial Library (NY), accessibility and fire safety projects, $10,000
- Tully Free Library (NY), handicapped-accessible automatic doors, $4,000
- Cayuga Community College Foundation (NY), upgrade science lab at Fulton campus, $15,000
- Learning Disabilities Association of CNY (NY), life- and job-skills program, $5,000
- OnPoint for College (NY), program for at-risk students to attend college, $25,000

*General*
- Cortland Area Communities That Care Coalition (NY), Family Reading Partnership program, $10,000
- Handweaving Museum and Art Center (NY), restoration and expansion of pottery studio, $10,000
- Friends of Oswego County Hospice (NY), support for children at Camp Rainbow of Hope, $5,000
- Syracuse Symphony Orchestra (NY), support for youth programming, $15,000
- Unity Acres (NY), install energy efficient windows, $4,000

## REQUIREMENTS AND RESTRICTIONS
Applicants must be located in New York or the eastern United States. The foundation will not accept proposals from individuals or from for-profit organizations. The foundation does not encourage proposals from religious organizations of proposals for endowments, contingency funding, or debt reduction.

## APPLICATION PROCEDURES

**Submission Guidelines:** Submit an initial letter of inquiry, including

- the background of the organization
- a description of the proposed project detailing the time frame and anticipated outcomes
- a high-level project budget

If the proposal meets the foundation's guidelines, a grant application will be sent. The grant application should include

- an executive summary (not to exceed one page)
- a detailed project budget, including itemized expenses and sources of income
- a list of the board of directors, including names and board positions held
- a copy of the organization's tax-exemption letter from the IRS
- the most recent audited financial statement
- current budget

**Deadlines:** Initial letter of inquiry, January 1; grant application, April 1

**Decisions:** July 1

**CONTACT**
Jonathan Snow
Phone: 315-471-5256

**GRANT-SPECIFIC WEBSITE**
www.johnbensnow.com/jbsfgp.html

# Society of American Archivists (SAA)

## Headquarters

17 N. State St., Suite 1425
Chicago, IL 60602-3315
Phone: 312-606-0722
www.archivists.org

## Description

**Founded:** 1936

**Operating Locations:** Illinois

Founded in 1936, the Society of American Archivists (SAA) is North America's oldest and largest national archival professional association. SAA's mission is to serve the educational and informational needs of more than 5,000 individual and institutional members and to provide leadership to ensure the identification, preservation, and use of records of historical value.

## Financial Summary

Assets: $579,467
Gifts Received: $23,625
Total Giving: $22,294

# Grants Information

## GRANT TYPES
Conference attendance

## TYPICAL RECIPIENTS
Archivists, students in graduate archival programs

## GRANT VALUES
Total Dollar Amount of Grants: $1,000
Average Grant: $500
Highest Grant: $450
Lowest Grant: $189

## NAMED GRANTS

### OLIVER WENDELL HOLMES TRAVEL AWARD
Established in 1979 and modified in 1991, the Oliver Wendell Holmes Travel Award enables overseas archivists who are already in the United States or Canada for training to augment their experience by traveling to the SAA annual meeting. Only archivists who reside outside the United States may apply. The award consists of a certificate and a cash award. The income of the prize fund for each year is divided between or among award recipients.

### DONALD PETERSON STUDENT SCHOLARSHIP AWARD
Established in 2005, the Donald Peterson Student Scholarship Award supports students and recent graduates from graduate archival programs within North America to attend SAA's annual meeting. The goal of the scholarship is to stimulate greater participation in the activities of the association by students and recent graduates. This participation must include either a presentation of research during the annual meeting or active participation in an SAA-sponsored committee, section, or round table. The award consists of up to $1,000 in support of registration, travel, and accommodation expenses associated with the SAA annual meeting. Applicants must be SAA members.

### HAROLD T. PINKETT MINORITY STUDENT AWARD
Established in 1993, the Harold T. Pinkett Minority Student Award recognizes and acknowledges minority undergraduate and graduate students, such as those of African, Asian, Latino, or Native American descent, who, through scholastic and personal achievement, manifest an interest in becoming professional archivists and active members of the Society of American Archivists. The award provides full complimentary registration to the SAA annual meeting and related expenses for hotel and travel for attending the meeting.

## REQUIREMENTS AND RESTRICTIONS
Vary by grant

## APPLICATION PROCEDURES

**Submission Guidelines:** Application online

**Deadlines:** February 28

**Decisions:** Awards are presented during a ceremony held in late summer at the SAA annual meeting.

**CONTACT**
Chair, Awards Committee
E-mail: info@archivists.org

**GRANT-SPECIFIC WEBSITE**
www2.archivists.org/recognition

# South Arts

## Headquarters

1800 Peachtree St. NW, Suite 808
Atlanta, GA 30309
Phone: 404-874-7244
www.southarts.org

## Description

**Founded:** 1975

**Operating Locations:** Georgia

South Arts strengthens the South through advancing excellence in the arts, connecting the arts to key state and national policies and nurturing a vibrant quality of life.

## Grants Information

**GRANT TYPES**
Project

**TYPICAL RECIPIENTS**
Nonprofit and governmental organizations

**GRANT VALUES**
Highest Grant: $2,500
Lowest Grant: $250

**NAMED GRANTS**

**LITERARY ARTS TOURING GRANT**
Offered in partnership with the National Endowment for the Arts, the Literary Arts Touring Grant gives organizations the opportunity to receive fee support to present writers who reside outside of the presenter's state. Support is awarded to literary projects that contain both a public reading and an educational component such as a writing workshop. The project can include single or multiple writers involved in an event. The grant will fund 50 percent of the writers' fees, up to a total of $2,500.

**REQUIREMENTS AND RESTRICTIONS**
Only nonprofit and governmental organizations in South Arts' nine-state region are eligible to apply. These states include Alabama, Florida, Georgia, Kentucky, Louisiana, Mississippi, North Carolina, South Carolina, and Tennessee. New applicants are encouraged to contact the program director to discuss eligibility prior to submitting an application.

## APPLICATION PROCEDURES

**Submission Guidelines:** Applicants must submit an application online on the South Arts eGrant.net System found at the website below. In addition to the application, the following materials must be submitted online:

- signed letter of intent or contract between the writer(s) and the presenting organization
- guest writer list for multiple writers (if applicable)
- proof of government status (if applicable)

The remaining required materials must be mailed to the South Arts office:

- writer(s)' résumé/biography and list of published works
- a sample of the writer(s)' work
- reviews of writer(s)' work (optional)
- self-addressed, stamped postcard for acknowledgement of support materials (optional)

Mailed, faxed, and incomplete applications will not be accepted.

**Deadlines:** May

### CONTACT
Nikki Estes
Phone: 404-874-7244, ext. 16
E-mail: nestes@southarts.org

### GRANT-SPECIFIC WEBSITE
www.southarts.org/site/c.
guIYLaMRJxE/b.1303445/k.E308/
Overview.htm

South Arts eGrant.net System: http://
southarts.egrant.net/login.
aspx?PIID=147&OID=61

# South Carolina State Library

## Headquarters

PO Box 11469
Columbia, SC 29211
Phone: 803-734-8666
www.statelibrary.sc.gov

## Description

**Founded:** 1929

**Operating Locations:** South Carolina

The South Carolina State Library optimizes South Carolina's investment in library and information services by supporting good governance for South Carolinians through the provision of research and information services to elected officials and state government personnel; providing equal access to information for all South Carolinians; ensuring collaboration and cooperation among information providers and cultural institutions; defining standards for libraries and librarianship that promote professionalism and excellence among library personnel statewide;

providing and promoting superior library and information services through research, development, and implementation of leading edge practices; and advocating for innovation and learning in order to create a better informed and more highly skilled South Carolina citizenry.

# Grants Information

### GRANT TYPES
LSTA funds, literacy

### TYPICAL RECIPIENTS
South Carolina public libraries and full-time library staff

### GRANT VALUES
NA

### NAMED GRANTS

### LSTA COMPETITIVE GRANT
LSTA competitive grants are awarded to South Carolina public libraries for qualifying projects up to $50,000; applications for larger projects will be considered. All LSTA-funded projects must meet at least one of the federal LSTA purposes and one of the state priorities outlined in the LSTA Five-Year State Plan for South Carolina. Preferred proposals will have one or more of the following characteristics: project is innovative and provides a "proof of concept" or a model for other libraries

to emulate; project includes a partnering arrangement with another community organization or service provider; library is a first-time applicant or has rarely applied for LSTA funding in the past.

**Typical Recipients:** South Carolina public libraries

**Submission Guidelines:** Submit a project proposal (forms available online). Successful proposals will be invited to submit a full application.

**Deadlines:** Project proposal, March; full application, May

**Decisions:** June

**Grant-Specific Website:** www.statelibrary.sc.gov/federal-aid-lsta

### LSTA CONFERENCE ATTENDANCE GRANT
Funds are available for library staff wishing to expand their professional knowledge by attending a professional conference such as the South Carolina Library Association conference, the PLA national conference, or the ALA Annual Conference. Reimbursement of related expenses is available for conference attendance that allows librarians to develop, expand, deliver, or promote services and programs that are related to the six federal LSTA purposes.

**Typical Recipients:** The county library is the applicant for this grant (not the participating employee). Only full-time library staff may receive grants under this program. Only first-time conference attendees are eligible.

**Requirements and Restrictions:**
Library directors are not eligible for grants. Each applicant library may seek a grant on behalf of one employee for one conference in the fiscal year. Exception: Up to three employees may apply to attend SCLA; the limit of $750 per county library remains in place. The grant application must be completed and signed by the library director. LSTA funds will cover only normal conference registration/fees, travel, and hotel (no meals, preconference fees, or other expenses).

**Grant-Specific Website:**
www.statelibrary.sc.gov/lsta-conference
-attendance-grants

## LSTA TUITION ASSISTANCE GRANT

Funds are available for library staff seeking a master's degree in librarianship. Reimbursement of tuition is available for coursework that prepares librarians to develop, expand, deliver, or promote services and programs that are related to the six federal LSTA purposes.

**Typical Recipients:** Only full-time library staff may receive reimbursement under this program. The library is the applicant for this grant (not the participating employee). The employee must be enrolled in a master's program at an accredited, ALA-approved school of librarianship.

**Requirements and Restrictions:**
This LSTA program is not intended to provide assistance for generic library coursework. General introductory librarianship courses, and coursework in other areas of librarianship not directly applicable to the six LSTA purposes, cannot be reimbursed. Only coursework in preparation for the MLIS is reimbursable under this grant (no Ph.D., B.S., or certificate programs are eligible). Participant must have successfully completed at least 9 hours of prior coursework in library and information studies before applying for this award. The grant application must be completed and signed by the library director. A separate section of the application is completed and signed by the employee. The employee must provide proof of completion of at least 9 hours of coursework in the librarianship program. The participating employee must provide proof of having received passing grades in all prior coursework for the librarianship degree. Each applicant library may seek a grant on behalf of no more than two employees for one course each per semester. Grants are available on a first come, first served basis, determined by the date applications are received at the State Library.

**Submission Guidelines:** A photocopy of the institution's description of the intended coursework must be attached to the application.

**Grant-Specific Website:**
www.statelibrary.sc.gov/lsta-tuition
-assistance-grants

## AWE EARLY LITERACY STATIONS GRANT

This project seeks to increase the ability of young children (ages 2–5) to use simple computer programs that convey basic literacy concepts via the AWE Early Literacy Workstations. Each of five participating libraries will receive one touch-screen Early Literacy Station.

**Typical Recipients:** This grant opportunity is open to public libraries that have not yet purchased an AWE Early Literacy Station.

**Requirements and Restrictions:** Participating libraries must commit to conducting at least one program for families before the end of the grant period, consisting of the following components: a short talk on the importance of parents reading to children, a tour of the library, an opportunity to register for a library card, and a demonstration of the use of the Early Literacy Station. No cash award is associated with this project. No matching funds need to be demonstrated by the library in the application; the local match is considered to be the time devoted to the project by library staff.

**Deadlines:** April

**Grant-Specific Website:** www.
statelibrary.sc.gov/awe-early-literacy-
stations-mini-grant-for-sc-public-libraries

### REQUIREMENTS AND RESTRICTIONS

Applicants must be located in the state of South Carolina. All LSTA grants require a 34 percent match of cash and/ or in-kind contributions.

### APPLICATION PROCEDURES

**Submission Guidelines:** Unless otherwise noted above, return the completed application (available online) with original signatures and accompanying documents to the address below. Faxed applications will not be accepted.

### CONTACT

Kathy Sheppard
LSTA Coordinator
South Carolina State Library
1430 Senate Street
Columbia, SC 29201
Phone: 803-734-8653
Fax: 803-734-8676
E-mail: ksheppard@statelibrary.sc.gov

### GRANT-SPECIFIC WEBSITE

www.statelibrary.sc.gov/federal-aid-lsta

# South Dakota Library Association (SDLA)

## Headquarters

28363 472nd Ave.
Worthing, SD 57077
Phone: 605-372-0235
www.sdlibraryassociation.org

## Description

**Founded:** 1906

**Operating Locations:** South Dakota

The South Dakota Library Association (SDLA) is a statewide organization representing libraries, library employees, library trustees, and library supporters. SDLA provides leadership and educational opportunities and supports its members in meeting the challenges of providing quality library service to all South Dakotans.

## Grants Information

### GRANT TYPES
Professional development, conference attendance, scholarship

### TYPICAL RECIPIENTS
South Dakota librarians

### GRANT VALUES
Number of Grants: 6
Highest Grant: $500

### NAMED GRANTS

#### PROFESSIONAL DEVELOPMENT GRANT
Professional Development Grants are available to assist SDLA members with the costs of attending conferences, workshops, or other professional learning opportunities. The $450 grants are designed for those who are already established in the area of librarianship.

**Deadlines:** March and September

#### SCHOLARSHIP
Two scholarships of up to $500 each are available to assist SDLA members with the costs of professional education in the field of librarianship.

**Deadlines:** May

#### CONFERENCE SCHOLARSHIP
Two conference scholarships of up to $450 are available to defray costs of registration, travel, and hotel expenses associated with attendance at the annual SDLA conference, plus costs of a substitute at the home library if needed.

**Deadlines:** August

### REQUIREMENTS AND RESTRICTIONS
Applicants must be located in the state of South Dakota and be members

of SDLA. No applicant may receive more than one grant per 12 months. Applicants are eligible to receive only one conference grant every five years.

## APPLICATION PROCEDURES

**Submission Guidelines:** Application online. Return one electronic copy or three paper copies of the application form and supporting documentation to the address below.

## CONTACT

Mary Kraljic
HM Briggs Library
Box 2115
SDSU
Brookings, SD 57007-1098
E-mail: mary.kraljic@sdstate.edu,

## GRANT-SPECIFIC WEBSITE

http://sdla.affiniscape.com/
    displaycommon.cfm?an = 5

# Seth Sprague Educational and Charitable Foundation

## Headquarters

Bank of America
114 W. 47th St.
New York, NY 10036

## Description

**Founded:** 1941

**Operating Locations:** New York

**Foundation Information:** Private foundation established by Seth Sprague

## Financial Summary

Assets: $54,777,638
Total Giving: $3,100,000

## Grants Information

### GRANT TYPES

General support, operating support, project, research, seed money

### TYPICAL RECIPIENTS

Arts and humanities, civic affairs, education, environment, health, religion, science, social services

### GRANT VALUES

Total Dollar Amount of Grants:
    $3,100,000

### PAST GRANT RECIPIENTS

*Library or School Related*
- Westport Library Association (CT), general support, $25,000
- Friends of Solana Beach Library (CA), general support, $5,000
- Children's Literacy Initiative (PA), general support, $7,500

- Cornell University (NY), general support, $70,000

*General*
- Lower East Side Tenement Museum (NY), general support, $5,000
- Metropolitan Opera (NY), general support, $10,000
- Women in Need (NY), general support, $3,500
- The Bone Marrow Foundation (NY), general support, $5,000
- Foundation for Landscape Studies (NY), general support, $5,000

**APPLICATION PROCEDURES**
**Submission Guidelines:** Send a letter of inquiry.

**CONTACT**
Bank of America
114 W. 47th St.
New York, NY 10036

**GRANT-SPECIFIC WEBSITE**
NA

# Starr Foundation

## Headquarters

399 Park Ave., 17th fl.
New York, NY 10022
Phone: 212-909-3600
www.starrfoundation.org

## Description

**Founded:** 1955

**Operating Locations:** New York

**Foundation Information:** Private foundation established by Cornelius Vander Starr

## Financial Summary

Assets: $1,201,239,493
Total Giving: $169,909,034

## Grants Information

**GRANT TYPES**
General support, capital, emergency, endowment, project, scholarship

**TYPICAL RECIPIENTS**
Arts and humanities, civic affairs, education, environment, health, religion, science, social services

**GRANT VALUES**
Total Dollar Amount of Grants:
    $169,909,034

**PAST GRANT RECIPIENTS**
*Library or School Related*
- Brooklyn Public Library (NY), general support, $125,000
- Brewster Public Library (NY), scholarship, $5,000
- New York Public Library (NY), endowment, integrated library system,

renovation of children's rooms in branches, $800,000
- Queens Library Foundation (NY), general support, $125,000
- Literacy, Inc. (NY), Teen Tutor Reading Partner program, $25,000
- Northwestern University (IL), scholarship, $50,000
- Johns Hopkins University (DC), general support, $2,500,000
- George Jackson Academy (NY), general support, $100,000

*General*
- Partnership for After School Education, Inc. (NY), general support, $100,000
- Facing History and Ourselves National Foundation, Inc. (MA), general support, $25,000
- Give2Asia (CA), China earthquake relief and recovery, $1,020,000

**REQUIREMENTS AND RESTRICTIONS**
Applicants must have tax-exempt status. Grants to individuals are limited to ongoing scholarship programs. In general, the foundation will not fund organizations that spend more than 25 percent of their annual expenses on administration and fund-raising.

**APPLICATION PROCEDURES**
**Submission Guidelines:** The foundation no longer accepts unsolicited proposals.

**CONTACT**
Phone: 212-909-3600

**GRANT-SPECIFIC WEBSITE**
www.starrfoundation.org

# Steele-Reese Foundation

## Headquarters

c/o J.P. Morgan
PO Box 6089
Newark, DE 19714
Phone: 212-464-2588
www.steele-reese.org

## Description

**Founded:** 1955

**Operating Locations:** Delaware

**Foundation Information:** Private foundation established by Eleanor Steele Reese

## Financial Summary

Assets: $37,507,765
Total Giving: $2,458,406

## Grants Information

**GRANT TYPES**
General support, endowment, scholarship

## TYPICAL RECIPIENTS

Arts and humanities, civic affairs, education, environment, health, religion, science, social services

## GRANT VALUES

Total Dollar Amount of Grants:
  $2,458,406
Number of Grants: 71
Average Grant: $3,500
Highest Grant: $100,000
Lowest Grant: $5,000

## PAST GRANT RECIPIENTS

*Library or School Related*
- Pierpont Morgan Library (NY), general support, $50,000
- Menifee County Public Library (KY), general support, $20,000
- Lees-McRae College (NC), general support, $50,000
- Olive Hill Adult Learning Center (KY), general support, $15,000
- Idaho State University Native American Business Administration Program (ID), general support, $50,000

*General*
- American Indian Business Leaders (MT), general support, $30,000
- Big Sky Institute of the Advancement of Nonprofits (MT), general support, $56,000
- Bitterroot Ecological Awareness Resources, Inc. (MT), general support, $33,000
- Community Foundation of Western North Carolina (NC), general support, $25,000

## REQUIREMENTS AND RESTRICTIONS

The foundation makes grants to charitable organizations operating in the western states of Idaho and Montana, and in the southern Appalachian mountain region of eastern Kentucky.

## APPLICATION PROCEDURES

**Submission Guidelines:** Application online

**Deadlines:** March 1

## CONTACT

Kentucky organizations should contact
Judy Owens
Steele-Reese Foundation
2613 Clubside Ct.
Lexington, KY 40513
Phone: 859-313-5225
E-mail: jkowensjd@aol.com
Idaho and Montana organizations should
  contact
Linda Tracy
Steele-Reese Foundation
PO Box 8311
Missoula, MT 59807
Phone: 406-207-7984
E-mail: linda@steele-reese.org

## GRANT-SPECIFIC WEBSITE

www.steele-reese.org

# S. Mark Taper Foundation

## Headquarters

12011 San Vicente Blvd.
Los Angeles, CA 90049
Phone: 310-476-5413
www.smtfoundation.org

## Description

**Founded:** 1989

**Operating Locations:** California

**Foundation Information:** Private foundation established by S. Mark Taper

## Financial Summary

Assets: $93,218,232
Total Giving: $6,314,410

## Grants Information

### GRANT TYPES
General support

### TYPICAL RECIPIENTS
Arts and humanities, civic affairs, education, environment, health, religion, science, social services

### GRANT VALUES
Total Dollar Amount of Grants:
$6,314,410

### PAST GRANT RECIPIENTS

*Library or School Related*
- Reach Out and Read (MA), general support, $5,000
- United through Reading (CA), general support, $10,000
- Marin Primary and Middle School (CA), general support, $10,000
- Gabriella Axelrad Education Foundation (CA), general support, $30,000
- New Community Jewish High School (CA), general support, $10,000
- Access Books (CA), general support, $334,000
- California State University Pomona (CA), Ennis Cosby Child and Family Services Friendmobile, $24,000

*General*
- Audubon Center at Debs Park (CA), general support, $25,000
- California Dental Association Foundation (CA), general support, $30,000
- East Valley Community Health Center (CA), general support, $100,000
- Friends of Ballona Wetlands (CA), general support, $25,000
- Los Angeles Museum of the Holocaust (CA), general support, $100,000

## REQUIREMENTS AND RESTRICTIONS

The S. Mark Taper Foundation will consider a letter of inquiry for any program or organization in Southern California. Applicants must be certified as tax exempt under Section 501(c)(3) of the Internal Revenue Code.

## APPLICATION PROCEDURES

**Submission Guidelines:** Submit a letter of inquiry, including

- specific amount of funding requested and what the funding is for
- basic organizational, brief historical, and any relevant program information
- how or why an S. Mark Taper Foundation grant would benefit your organization
- primary contact person's name, title, mailing address, e-mail address, and telephone number, and the organization's website address
- list of current board members, including affiliations
- IRS determination letter indicating 501(c)(3) status
- organization budget (including both revenue and expense) for the current fiscal year
- income statement/statement of activities (including both revenue and expense) for the most recently completed fiscal year

The letter must be signed by the organization's highest-ranking paid staff member. Additional information may be required for general operating support or program support requests (see the guidelines on the website). Mail the letter with attachments to the address below. Letters submitted by fax or e-mail will not be accepted. The foundation will send full applications to those applicants whose letters of inquiry are approved.

**Deadlines:** Letters of inquiry are accepted from December through February. Applications are mailed during April, May, and June.

**Decisions:** Decisions are made by the end of August, and organizations are notified if they are receiving a grant during August and September. Foundation grants are only paid during the month of December each year.

## CONTACT

Adrienne Wittenberg
Grants Director
S. Mark Taper Foundation
12011 San Vicente Blvd., Suite 400
Los Angeles, CA 90049
Phone: 310-476-5413
Fax: 310-471-4993
E-mail: questions@smtfoundation.org

## GRANT-SPECIFIC WEBSITE

www.smtfoundation.org

# Target Corp.

## Headquarters

1000 Nicollet Mall
Minneapolis, MN 55403
www.target.com

## Description

**Founded:** 1902

**Operating Locations:** Minnesota

**Type of Product/Service:** Retail

**In-Kind or Service Support:** Volunteers from Target stores and distribution centers through a partnership with First Book donate books as well as time to organize, clean, and brighten local libraries. With the support of nonprofit Heart of America, Target volunteers perform a complete School Library Makeover for libraries with the greatest need (see http://sites. target.com/site/en/company/page. jsp?contentId=WCMP04-039414).

**Corporate Sponsorship:** Arts and cultural events, music festivals, "Day of Giving" in spring

## Financial Summary

Assets: $10,815,374

Gifts Received: $8,195,000
Total Giving: $9,750,000

## Grants Information

**GRANT TYPES**
Education, literacy, arts

**TYPICAL RECIPIENTS**
Arts and humanities, education, health, science, social services

**GRANT VALUES**
Total Dollar Amount of Grants:
   $9,750,000
Number of Grants: 183
Average Grant: $53,000
Highest Grant: $1,225,000
Lowest Grant: $5,000
Typical Range of Grants: $25,000–
   $50,000

**NAMED GRANTS**

**ART AND CULTURE IN SCHOOLS GRANTS**
Music, art, dance, drama and visual arts are all part of the well-rounded education kids deserve. Through grants, Target helps schools bring more arts and culture into the classroom, enabling them to expand their creativity and their horizons. Grant applications are typically accepted between March 1 and April 30 each year, with grant notifications delivered in September. Grants are in the amount of $2,000.

## EARLY CHILDHOOD READING GRANTS

Reading is essential to a child's learning process. Target awards grants to schools, libraries, and nonprofit organizations to support programs such as after-school reading events and weekend book clubs. Grant applications are typically accepted between March 1 and April 30 each year, with grant notifications delivered in September. Grants are in the amount of $2,000.

## TARGET FIELD TRIP GRANTS

Learning opportunities extend far beyond the classroom. But schools are finding it more and more difficult to bring students to museums, historical sites, and cultural organizations. These $700 Field Trip Grants help give children these unique, firsthand learning experiences. Since launching the program in 2007, Target has awarded $9.76 million in grants—providing 1.2 million students in all 50 states with the opportunity to enhance their studies in the arts, math, science, and social studies. As part of the program, each Target store will award three Target Field Trip Grants to K–12 schools nationwide. Grant applications are typically accepted between August 1 and September 30 each year, with grant notifications delivered in January.

## TARGET FOUNDATION ARTS GRANTS

These Target Foundation general operating grants are awarded to programs and organizations that provide accessible and affordable arts and cultural experiences to the Twin Cities community. Target Foundation welcomes applications from organizations in the seven-county Minneapolis–St. Paul metropolitan area that are classified 501(c)(3) by the IRS. Arts applications are accepted between January 1 and February 1.

## REQUIREMENTS AND RESTRICTIONS

Applicants must be federally tax exempt, section 501(c)(3) charitable organizations, schools, libraries, or public agencies. Target does not make grants to individuals, programs located outside Target communities, educational institutions for regular instructional programs, religious organizations for religious purposes, treatment programs such as substance or alcohol abuse, athletic teams or events, fund-raiser or gala events, advocacy or research groups, capital or building construction projects, or endowment campaigns.

## APPLICATION PROCEDURES

**Submission Guidelines:** Applicants must create an account and submit an online application via the grant-giving website. Mailed or e-mailed applications will not be accepted. After you submit your application, you will receive an e-mail confirmation. After an initial review, you may be contacted to provide additional information. Communications will occur via e-mail or letter. After Target reviews your application, you will receive notification indicating whether your grant request has been approved or declined.

### CONTACT
E-mail: Community.Relations@target. com

### GRANT-SPECIFIC WEBSITE
http://sites.target.com/site/en/ company/page.jsp?contentId =WCMP04-031767

# Tauck Foundation

## Headquarters

PO Box 5020
Norwalk, CT 06855-1445
Phone: 866-828-2536
www.tauckfoundation.org

## Description

**Founded:** 1994

**Operating Locations:** Connecticut

**Foundation Information:** Private foundation established by Arthur C. Tauck

## Financial Summary

Assets: $15,230,272
Gifts Received: $230,620
Total Giving: $358,422

## Grants Information

### GRANT TYPES
General support

### TYPICAL RECIPIENTS
Arts and humanities, civic affairs, education, environment, health, science, social services

### GRANT VALUES
Total Dollar Amount of Grants: $358,422

### PAST GRANT RECIPIENTS

*Library or School Related*
- Westport Public Library (CT), general support, $2,700
- Crested Butte Friends of the Library (CO), general support, $1,000
- Westover School (CT), general support, $2,500
- University of Pennsylvania (PA), general support, $2,000
- Dazzle School for the Performing Arts (NY), general support, $10,000

*General*
- Norwalk Hospital Foundation (CT), general support, $12,500
- Southwest Florida Symphony (FL), general support, $2,000

- Greater Ithaca Activity Center (NY), general support, $1,000
- Friends of the Children (WA), general support, $10,000

**REQUIREMENTS AND RESTRICTIONS**
The foundation's youth grants are intended to fund organizations and programs that provide high-quality experiential learning opportunities to youth during out-of-school-time hours and/or during the summer. The foundation supports programs intentionally designed to develop understanding and knowledge, social and life skills, and leadership potential through "hands-on" or interactive experiences. Preference is given to programs that serve economically disadvantaged or underserved youth and that target children ages 11–18.

**APPLICATION PROCEDURES**

**Submission Guidelines:** Applicant should send a letter of inquiry including

- a description of your organization and its mission, as well as the specific program or project for which you are requesting funding. Please clarify whether the program/project is established and ongoing, newly or recently initiated, or proposed.
- an explanation of how the proposed program meets the Tauck Foundation's funding guidelines and priorities

- the total annual budget of the organization, as well as the overall budget of the proposed program/project. Please indicate the amount of funding you anticipate requesting from the Tauck Foundation.
- the name, title, address, phone, and e-mail of the contact person to whom any questions regarding the letter of intent can be addressed

All letters of inquiry should be e-mailed (ideally in PDF format), faxed or mailed to the address below.

**Deadlines:** December, February, and May

**CONTACT**
Eden Werring
Executive Director
The Tauck Foundation
P.O. Box 5020
Norwalk, CT 06856
Fax: 203-286-1340
E-mail: eden@tauckfoundation.org

**GRANT-SPECIFIC WEBSITE**
www.tauckfoundation.org

# Temple-Inland, Inc.

## Headquarters

1300 S. Mopac Expy., Floor 3N
Austin, TX 78746

Phone: 512-434-5800
www.templeinland.com

# Description

**Founded:** 1983

**Operating Locations:** Texas

**Type of Product/Service:** Corrugated board, building supplies

---

# TEMPLE-INLAND FOUNDATION

1300 S. Mopac Expy., Floor 3N
Austin, TX 78746
Phone: 512-434-2542
www.templeinland.com
**Foundation Information:** Corporate foundation of Temple-Inland, Inc.

## Financial Summary

Assets: $155,617
Gifts Received: $2,919,714
Total Giving: $2,903,924

## Grants Information

### GRANT TYPES
General support, employee matching

### TYPICAL RECIPIENTS
Arts and humanities, civic affairs, education, environment, health, science, social services

### GRANT VALUES
Total Dollar Amount of Grants:
   $2,903,924
Highest Grant: $60,000
Lowest Grant: $30

### PAST GRANT RECIPIENTS

*Library or School Related*
- Buena Park Library (CA), general support, $2,000
- Buna Public Library (TX), general support, $1,000
- TLL Temple Memorial Library (TX), general support, $49,575
- Friends of the Glendale Public Library (CA), general support, $2,000
- Friends of the Washington Parish Library (LA), general support, $1,000
- Rome-Floyd County Public Library (GA), general support, $600
- Greater Orange Area Literacy Service (TX), general support, $750
- Humphreys County Literacy Council (TN), general support, $800
- Friends of the Library, Collier County (FL), general support, $250
- Carmel Clay Public Library Foundation (IN), general support, $300

### REQUIREMENTS AND RESTRICTIONS
Applicants must have tax-exempt status.

### APPLICATION PROCEDURES

**Submission Guidelines:** Applicant should call to request an application form. Applicant should submit a completed application form, a description of the organization, amount requested, purpose of funds sought, recently audited financial statements, and proof of tax-exempt status.

**CONTACT**
Karen Lee
Phone: 512-434-3160

**GRANT-SPECIFIC WEBSITE**
www.templeinland.com/OurMission/
CorporateCitizenship/social.asp

# Tennessee State Library and Archives (TSLA)

## Headquarters

403 Seventh Ave. N.
Nashville, TN 37243
Phone: 615-253-3470
www.tennessee.gov/tsla/

## Description

**Founded:** NA

**Operating Locations:** Tennessee

The Tennessee State Library and Archives (TSLA) collects and preserves books and records of historical, documentary, and reference value, and promotes library and archival development throughout the state.

## Grants Information

**GRANT TYPES**
LSTA funds

**TYPICAL RECIPIENTS**
Tennessee libraries and county and municipal governments

**GRANT VALUES**
NA

**NAMED GRANTS**

**LSTA TECHNOLOGY GRANTS**
Competitive Technology Grants are available to eligible public libraries that can provide an equal amount of local funding for purchase of computer hardware, software, fax machines, and other library technology.

**Requirements and Restrictions:** Each library applying for a technology grant must match the federal funds with an equal or greater amount of local funds. Grant requests must be for a minimum of $500.

**Submission Guidelines:** Mail completed application (available online) to the address below.

**Deadlines:** November

**Contact:** Jack Stacy, Bibliographic Services Coordinator, Tennessee State Library and Archives, 403 Seventh Ave. N., Nashville, TN 37243-0312; E-mail: jack.stacy@tn.gov

**Grant-Specific Website:** www.tennessee.gov/tsla/lps/grants/grants.htm

## LSTA DIRECT SERVICE GRANTS FOR LIBRARY SERVICES TO THE DISADVANTAGED

Competitive Direct Service Grants for Library Services to the Disadvantaged are available biennially to eligible public libraries. Libraries that plan to use the grant as start-up funding for new projects or programs, rather than a continuation or diversification of existing projects or programs, will be given preference. However, applications showing significant change to out-dated, existing library programs will also be considered. Examples of projects to be funded include job-training centers in libraries and community building through video games.

**Grant Values:** Highest Grant, $7,500; Lowest Grant, $5,000

**Submission Guidelines:** Mail completed application (available online) to the address below.

**Deadlines:** February

**Contact:** Tennessee State Library

and Archives, 403 Seventh Ave. N., Nashville, TN 37243-0312

**Grant-Specific Website:** www.tennessee.gov/tsla/lps/grants/grants.htm

## DIRECT GRANTS TO LOCAL GOVERNMENT ARCHIVES

TSLA administers state grant funds to encourage the development of local archives. Each year, $50,000 is made available for some 10–15 program improvement grants to local government archives. The amount of funding available is most effectively concentrated on projects that get records up off the floor, off wooden shelves, out of acidic containers, cleaned and flattened, and under effective control so that records can be found when a member of the public wishes to examine them. Restoration of bound record books of permanent records also falls into the "rescue mission" criteria; however, the cost per item is high ($1,200–$1,800 per volume), and applicants are encouraged to focus their efforts on projects that will help to salvage and preserve larger quantities of records.

**Typical Recipients:** County and municipal governments

**Grant Values:** Highest Grant, $5,000

**Requirements and Restrictions:** To be eligible for a grant, a county must show that it has an active public records commission that includes at least the required statutory members, ex officio and appointed, and the county must certify that the public records commission meets at least twice a year as required by law. A county/municipality must show a clear, existing budget commitment and legislative appropriation to establish and/or sustain a formal archives and/or records office supervised by a county-appointed archivist or records officer.

**Submission Guidelines:** Mail completed application (available online) to the address below.

**Deadlines:** August

**Contact:** Jami Awalt, Archives Development Program, Tennessee State Library and Archives, 403 Seventh Ave. N., Nashville, TN 37243-0312; Phone: 615-253-3470; Fax: 615-532-5315; E-mail: jami.awalt@tn.gov

**Grant-Specific Website:** www.tn.gov/tsla/aps/grants/

## REQUIREMENTS AND RESTRICTIONS
Vary by grant

## APPLICATION PROCEDURES
Vary by grant

## CONTACT
Varies by grant

## GRANT-SPECIFIC WEBSITE
Varies by grant

# Texas State Library and Archives Commission (TSLAC)

## Headquarters

1201 Brazos St.
PO Box 12927
Austin, TX 78711-2927
Phone: 512-463-5455
www.tsl.state.tx.us

## Description

**Founded:** 1909

**Operating Locations:** Texas

The mission of the Texas State Library and Archives Commission (TSLAC) is to preserve the record of government for public scrutiny, to secure and make accessible historically significant records and other valuable resources, to meet the reading needs of Texans with disabilities, to build and sustain statewide partnerships to improve library programs and services, and to enhance the capacity for achievement of individuals and institutions with whom we work.

## Grants Information

### GRANT TYPES
LSTA funds, literacy, cultural preservation

## TYPICAL RECIPIENTS

Major resource library systems, regional library systems, libraries that are members of the TexShare Library Consortium or Texas Library System; nonprofit organizations; public school libraries

## GRANT VALUES

NA

## NAMED GRANTS

### LSTA COMPETITIVE COOPERATION GRANTS

LSTA Competitive Cooperation Grants provide funds for programs that promote cooperative services for learning and access to information. Programs involving collaboration are encouraged. Programs must emphasize improved services by the library to its customers. Programs may be in the following categories: (1) Expand services for learning and access to information and educational resources in a variety of formats; (2) Develop library services that provide all users access to information through local, state, regional, national, and international electronic networks; (3) Provide electronic and other linkages between and among all types of libraries; or (4) Develop public and private partnerships with other agencies and community-based organizations.

**Typical Recipients:** Major resource library systems, regional library systems, and libraries that are members of the TexShare Library Consortium or Texas Library System are eligible to apply for funds. Nonprofit organizations may be awarded funds for projects that involve a number of TexShare or Texas Library System member libraries, as well as other types of libraries or organizations. Public school libraries that are not members of the Texas Library System may participate as partners in grants led by eligible entities.

**Grant Values:** Total Dollar Amount of Grants, $300,000; Highest Grant, $75,000

**Grant-Specific Website:** www.tsl.state.tx.us/ld/funding/lsta/

### LSTA COMPETITIVE SPECIAL PROJECTS GRANTS

LSTA Competitive Special Projects Grants provide funds for programs that expand library services to all members of the library's community. It enables libraries to develop programs for populations with special needs. Programs involving collaboration are encouraged. Programs must emphasize improved services by the library to its customers. Programs may be in one of the following categories: (1) Target library services to individuals of diverse geographic, cultural, and socioeconomic backgrounds, to individuals with disabilities, and to individuals with limited functional literacy or information skills; (2) Target library and information services to persons having difficulty using a library and to underserved urban and rural communities, including children from families below the poverty line.

**Typical Recipients:** Major resource library systems, regional library systems, and libraries that are members of the TexShare Library Consortium or Texas Library System are eligible to apply for funds. Nonprofit organizations may be awarded funds for projects that involve a number of TexShare or Texas Library System member libraries, as well as other types of libraries or organizations. Public school libraries that are not members of the Texas Library System may participate as partners in grants led by eligible entities.

**Grant Values:** Total Dollar Amount of Grants, $300,000; Highest Grant, $75,000

**Grant-Specific Website:** www.tsl.state.tx.us/ld/funding/lsta/

## TEXAS READS GRANTS
The Texas Reads Grant funds public library programs to promote reading and literacy within local communities. Programs may be targeted to the entire community or to a segment of the community. Programs involving collaboration with other community organizations are encouraged. The agency may designate specific funding

priorities for each grant cycle in response to identified needs. If this occurs, staff will provide details of funding priorities and scoring implications to applicants and to the peer review panel.

**Typical Recipients:** Public libraries and local public library systems, through their governing authority (city, county, corporation, or district) are eligible to apply for grants.

**Grant Values:** Total Dollar Amount of Grants, $10,000; Highest Grant, $3,000

**Grant-Specific Website:** www.tsl.state.tx.us/ld/funding/#txReads

## TEXTREASURES GRANT
The TexTreasures grant program provides assistance and encouragement to libraries to provide access to their special or unique holdings, and to make information about these holdings available to all Texans. Applicants may propose projects designed to increase accessibility through a wide range of activities such as cataloging, indexing, or digitizing local materials with statewide significance.

**Typical Recipients:** Libraries that are members of the TexShare Library Consortium, or nonprofit organizations that are applying on behalf of TexShare members, are eligible to apply for funds. These funds are awarded to eligible applicants, but may be used with all types of libraries or with nonprofit organizations that participate as partners in the grant project.

**Grant Values:** Total Dollar Amount of Grants, $150,000; Highest Grant, $20,000 for a single institution or $25,000 for collaborative projects

**Contact:** Jennifer Peters, Library Development Division, Texas State Library and Archives Commission, PO Box 12927, Austin, TX 78711-2927; Phone: 512-463-5527; E-mail: jpeters@tsl.state.tx.us; OR TexShare Coordinator, Library Resource Sharing Division, Texas State Library and Archives Commission, PO Box 12927, Austin, TX 78711-2927; Phone: 512-463-0188; E-mail: texshare@tsl.state.tx.us

**Grant-Specific Website:** www.tsl.state.tx.us/texshare/textreasurespage.html

## REQUIREMENTS AND RESTRICTIONS

Applicants must be located in the state of Texas. Applicants must be members of the Texas Library System for the fiscal year the grant contracts are issued. The Texas State Library and Archives Commission requests that all applicants discuss their project with TSLAC staff before they begin developing a proposal.

## APPLICATION PROCEDURES

**Submission Guidelines:** TSLAC uses a Grant Management System (GMS) that enables applicants to apply for grants electronically through a web portal. In order to apply for the grant, you must obtain a user name and password for GMS. You will then be able to access and fill out the application. Signature pages (Application for State/Federal Support form, CIPA form, and letters of support) must be sent via fax, e-mail, or mail to the address below. Applications lacking signature pages will be deemed incomplete and not considered for funding. Step-by-step GMS instructions can be found at www.tsl.state.tx.us/ld/funding/lsta/gmsmanual.pdf

**Deadlines:** February

**Decisions:** August

## CONTACT

Jennifer Peters
Library Development Division
Texas State Library and Archives
    Commission
PO Box 12927
Austin, TX 78711
Phone: 512-463-5527
Fax: 512-463-8800
E-mail: jpeters@tsl.state.tx.us

## GRANT-SPECIFIC WEBSITE

www.tsl.state.tx.us/ld/funding/
Grant management system: https://gms.tsl.state.tx.us
Grant management system manual: www.tsl.state.tx.us/ld/funding/lsta/gmsmanual.pdf

# Timken Foundation of Canton

## Headquarters

200 Market Ave. N.
Canton, OH 44702
Phone: 330-452-1144

## Description

**Founded:** 1934

**Operating Locations:** Ohio

**Foundation Information:** Private foundation established by Henry H. Timken

## Financial Summary

Assets: $175,181,915
Total Giving: $10,284,257

## Grants Information

### GRANT TYPES
General support, operating support, capital, scholarship

### TYPICAL RECIPIENTS
Arts and humanities, civic affairs, education, environmental, health, religion, social services

### GRANT VALUES
Total Dollar Amount of Grants:
$10,284,257

### PAST GRANT RECIPIENTS

*Library or School Related*
- Lebanon Public Libraries Foundation (NH), construction of new library in West Lebanon, $150,000
- Friends of the Canal Fulton Public Library (OH), installation of new security system, $10,000
- Stark County District Library (OH), three self-check machines, $66,731
- Union County Carnegie Library (SC), renovation and reorganization of space in library, $140,000
- University of Akron Foundation (OH), construction of new engineering building, $1,600,000

*General*
- Lighthouse Ministries of Canton (OH), computer technology for neighborhood-based after-school initiative, $8,000
- Cheshire Medical Center (NH), construct and equip center for training nurses, $50,100
- Mesa Community Action Network (AZ), new kitchen and dining facilities for homeless center, $50,000
- Graceworks Lutheran Services (OH), renovation of private office to serve clients, $8,000
- Arizona Museum for Youth Friends (AZ), renovation, $20,000

- Monadnock Family Services (NH), purchase building in which adult care center operates, $50,000

### REQUIREMENTS AND RESTRICTIONS
Applicants must be tax exempt under IRS guidelines.

### APPLICATION PROCEDURES
**Submission Guidelines:** No specific form is required. Applicant must submit verification of tax-exempt status.

### CONTACT
Nancy Knudsen
Phone: 330-452-1144

### GRANT-SPECIFIC WEBSITE
NA

# Tisch Foundation

## Headquarters

655 Madison Ave., 19th fl.
New York, NY 10065
Phone: 212-521-2943

## Description

**Founded:** 1959

**Operating Locations:** New York

**Foundation Information:** Private foundation

## Financial Summary

Assets: $49,443,378
Total Giving: $12,876,139

## Grants Information

### GRANT TYPES
General support, operating support, capital, project, research

### TYPICAL RECIPIENTS
Arts and humanities, civic affairs, education, environment, health, international, religion, social services

### GRANT VALUES
Total Dollar Amount of Grants:
    $12,876,139
Number of Grants: 116
Average Grant: $11,000
Highest Grant: $2,701,000
Lowest Grant: $25

### PAST GRANT RECIPIENTS

*Library or School Related*
- Brooklyn Public Library (NY), general support, $50,000
- New York Public Library (NY), general support, $50,000
- Reading Reform Foundation of New York (NY), general support, $2,500
- University of Michigan (MI), general support, $200,000
- Skidmore College (NY), general support, $1,562,000

- Tufts University (MA), general support, $100,000

*General*
- Doctors Without Borders (NY), general support, $25,015
- National Football Foundation and College Hall of Fame, Inc. (NJ), general support, $10,000
- Elizabeth Glaser Pediatric AIDS Foundation (CA), general support, $48,600
- Michael Feinstein Foundation for the Education and Preservation of the Great American Songbook (IN), general support, $1,500
- National Museum of American Jewish History (PA), general support, $375,000

## REQUIREMENTS AND RESTRICTIONS
Grants are not made to individuals. Endowment funds, scholarships, fellowships, and matching funds are not supported.

## APPLICATION PROCEDURES
NA

## CONTACT
NA

## GRANT-SPECIFIC WEBSITE
NA

# C. W. Titus Foundation

## Headquarters

427 S. Boston Ave.
Tulsa, OK 74103
Phone: 918-582-8095

## Description

**Founded:** 1969

**Operating Locations:** Oklahoma

**Foundation Information:** Private foundation

## Financial Summary

Assets: $39,493,890
Total Giving: $1,949,100

## Grants Information

### GRANT TYPES
General support, project, research

### TYPICAL RECIPIENTS
Arts and humanities, civic affairs, education, health, religion, social services

### GRANT VALUES
Total Dollar Amount of Grants:
    $1,949,100

Number of Grants: 65
Average Grant: $30,00
Highest Grant: $250,000
Lowest Grant: $1,000

## PAST GRANT RECIPIENTS

*Library or School Related*

- Friends of Salina Library (OK), children's library, $35,000
- Friends of Springfield Greene County Public Library Foundation (MO), general support, $125,000
- Crosstown Learning Center (OK), general support, $5,000

*General*

- Tulsa Speech and Hearing Association (OK), general support, $10,000
- Philbrook Museum of Art (OK), general support, $40,000
- Oklahoma Special Olympics (OK), general support, $5,000
- Hospice of Greene County (OK), general support, $10,000
- Joplin Humane Society (MO), building of new shelter, $100,000
- Children's Mercy Hospital (MO), Children's Cancer Center, $50,000
- Development Center of the Ozarks (MO), capital campaign, $52,000

## REQUIREMENTS AND RESTRICTIONS

Applicants must be located in the states of Oklahoma or Missouri.

## APPLICATION PROCEDURES

**Submission Guidelines:** The foundation has no formal grant application procedure or special form.

**CONTACT**
Timothy Reynolds
Phone: 918-582-8095

**GRANT-SPECIFIC WEBSITE**
NA

# J. Edwin Treakle Foundation

## Headquarters

PO Box 1157
Gloucester, VA 23061
Phone: 804-693-0881

## Description

**Founded:** 1973

**Operating Locations:** Virginia

**Foundation Information:** Private foundation established by J. Edwin Treakle

## Financial Summary

Assets: $5,505,688
Total Giving: $405,000

## Grants Information

**GRANT TYPES**
Capital, general support, continuing support, research

## TYPICAL RECIPIENTS

Arts and humanities, civic affairs, education, environment, health, religion, science, social services

## GRANT VALUES

Total Dollar Amount of Grants: $405,000
Number of Grants: 71
Average Grant: $5,700
Highest Grant: $50,000
Lowest Grant: $500

## PAST GRANT RECIPIENTS

*Library or School Related*
- Gloucester Library Board of Trustees (VA), purchase of books and library materials, $23,000
- Friends of Matthews Memorial Library (VA), books, periodicals, DVDs, and children's summer program, $23,000
- Middlesex County Public Library (VA), patron computers, $500
- Rappahannock Community College Educational Foundation (VA), books for library, $8,000
- Reading Is Fundamental (VA), books, $2,000
- Literacy Volunteers of Gloucester, Inc. (VA), materials for daytime program, $2,000
- Gloucester County Public Schools Foundations (VA), minigrants to teachers, teacher awards, and school needs, $1,000
- Bay School (VA), art program for senior citizens, $2,000

- Christopher Newport University (VA), books for leadership study collection, $2,000

*General*
- HeadStart Community Foundation (VA), AEDs for public schools, $3,000
- Matthews Maritime Foundation (VA), educational materials for children's boating safety program, $1,000

## REQUIREMENTS AND RESTRICTIONS

Applicants must be located in the state of Virginia. Preference is given to local and educational organizations.

## APPLICATION PROCEDURES

**Submission Guidelines:** Write to foundation for an application form.

**Deadlines:** January 1 to April 30

## CONTACT

John Warren Cooke
Phone: 804-693-0881

## GRANT-SPECIFIC WEBSITE

NA

# Trimix Foundation

## Headquarters

50 Park Row W.
Providence, RI 02903
Phone: 401-274-9200

# Description

**Founded:** 1997

**Operating Locations:** Rhode Island

**Foundation Information:** Private foundation

# Financial Summary

Assets: $8,819,312
Total Giving: $490,155

# Grants Information

**GRANT TYPES**
General support

**TYPICAL RECIPIENTS**
Arts and humanities, civic affairs, education, environment, health, religion, social services

**GRANT VALUES**
Total Dollar Amount of Grants: $490,155
Number of Grants: 60
Average Grant: $8,200
Highest Grant: $65,000
Lowest Grant: $60

**PAST GRANT RECIPIENTS**
*Library or School Related*
- East Greenwich Free Library (RI), general support, $125
- Volunteers in Providence Schools (RI), Battle of the Books program, $1,500
- Union College (NY), annual fund, $5,000

*General*
- Dorcas Place Adult and Family Learning Center (RI), learning resource center/computer lab, $40,000
- Rhode Islanders Sponsoring Education (RI), general support, $1,000
- Young Voices (RI), urban youth programs, $11,500
- Rhode Island Family Shelter (RI), general support, $11,000
- Washington Park Citizens Association (RI), free/reduced-cost child care, $5,000
- Family Service of Rhode Island (RI), educational advocate program, $15,000

**REQUIREMENTS AND RESTRICTIONS**
Applicants must be located in the states of Massachusetts, New York, or Rhode Island.

**APPLICATION PROCEDURES**
**Submission Guidelines:** Applications should be written requests on letterhead and should provide information regarding qualified charitable status and intended use of grant.

**CONTACT**
Gail S. Mixer

**GRANT-SPECIFIC WEBSITE**
NA

# Unilever United States

## Headquarters

390 Park Ave.
New York, NY 10022
www.unilever.com

## Description

**Founded:** 1978

**Operating Locations:** New York

**Type of Product/Service:** Foods, personal care products

# UNILEVER UNITED STATES FOUNDATION

c/o UNUS Tax Dept.
800 Sylvan Ave.
Englewood Cliffs, NJ 07632
Phone: 201-567-8000
www.unileverusa.com/sustainability/
**Foundation Information:** Corporate foundation of Unilever United States

## Financial Summary

Assets: $159,606
Gifts Received: $3,955,258
Total Giving: $4,588,739

## Grants Information

**GRANT TYPES**
General support, matching

**TYPICAL RECIPIENTS**
Arts and humanities, civic affairs, education, environment, health, science, social services

**GRANT VALUES**
Total Dollar Amount of Grants:
    $4,588,739

**PAST GRANT RECIPIENTS**

*Library or School Related*
- Allentown Public Library Association (PA), general support, $400
- Friends of the Trumbull Library (CT), general support, $2,000
- Brewster Ladies Library Association (MA), general support, $100
- New York Public Library (NY), general support, $204
- Mt Sinai School of Medicine of New York University (NY), general support, $10,000
- Pennsylvania State University (PA), general support, $5,830
- Morristown-Beard School (NJ), general support, $7,500
- Immaculata College (PA), general support, $5,000

**REQUIREMENTS AND RESTRICTIONS**
Applicants must have tax-exempt status.

The foundation does not award grants to individuals, political parties, capital fund campaigns, sectarian religious organizations, or veterans groups for social events.

## APPLICATION PROCEDURES
**Submission Guidelines:** Submit a letter or proposal on letterhead signed by the chief executive officer, including the grant's purpose, background information about the organization, the most recent annual budget, a copy of the current operating budget, and proof of tax-exempt status.

## CONTACT
Deirdre Gann
Phone: 201-894-2236

## GRANT-SPECIFIC WEBSITE
NA

# Urban Libraries Council (ULC)

## Headquarters

125 S. Wacker Dr.
Chicago, IL 60606-4477
Phone: 312-676-0999
www.urbanlibraries.org

## Description

**Founded:** 1971

**Operating Locations:** Illinois

For more than 30 years the Urban Libraries Council (ULC) has worked to strengthen public libraries as an essential part of urban life. A membership organization of North America's premier public library systems and the corporations that serve them, ULC serves as a forum for sharing best practices resulting from targeted research, education, and future forecasting. ULC's programs are acclaimed for inspiring new organizational models that invigorate urban libraries and enrich the areas surrounding them. An alliance of more than 180 premier public libraries and corporations, ULC believes that by sharing strengths, libraries are better able to serve as cornerstones of vibrant communities, deliver innovative programs to educate and enlighten, and build local economies. ULC members support one another through idea sharing, research, and programs and industry-change initiatives, tailored to the needs of our communities and aimed at preparing libraries to serve the next generation of learners.

## Grants Information

### GRANT TYPES
Professional development

### TYPICAL RECIPIENTS
Senior-level managers or library directors from ULC member libraries

## GRANT VALUES

Total Dollar Amount of Grants: $5,000
Number of Grants: 1
Average Grant: $5,000

## NAMED GRANTS

### JOEY RODGER LEADERSHIP AWARD

The Joey Rodger Leadership Award grants up to $5,000 annually for senior-level library administrators to participate in a leadership program or other development opportunity. Leadership development is a key initiative of ULC's effort to build its members' organizational strength. The Joey Rodger award, one of three annual awards available to ULC members, was established in 2004 to honor Eleanor Jo "Joey" Rodger, who led ULC from 1992 to 2004. Past recipients have used the award for leadership training at the John F. Kennedy School of Government at Harvard and the Executive Education Program of the Brookings Institution.

## REQUIREMENTS AND RESTRICTIONS

Applicants must be located in North America and must be ULC members.

## APPLICATION PROCEDURES

**Submission Guidelines:** Complete an award application.

**Deadlines:** March

**Decisions:** May

## CONTACT

Veronda J. Pitchford
Phone: 312.676-0958
Fax: 312-676-0950
E-mail: vjpitchford@urbanlibraries.org

## GRANT-SPECIFIC WEBSITE

http://urbanlibraries.org/
    displaycommon.cfm?an = 13

# U.S. Department of Agriculture (USDA)

## Headquarters

1400 Independence Ave. SW
Washington, DC 20250-0700
Phone: 202-720-2791
www.usda.gov/wps/portal/usda/
usdahome/

## Description

**Founded:** 1862

**Operating Locations:** District of Columbia

The U.S. Department of Agriculture (USDA) provides leadership on food, agriculture, natural resources, and related issues based on sound public policy, the best available science, and efficient management.

# Grants Information

## GRANT TYPES
Library improvement

## TYPICAL RECIPIENTS
Municipal and county governments, special-purpose districts, nonprofit corporations, tribal governments

## GRANT VALUES
Total Dollar Amount of Grants:
$100,000,000
Highest Grant: $500,000

## NAMED GRANTS

### AMERICAN RECOVERY AND REINVESTMENT ACT FUNDING FOR RURAL LIBRARIES
The American Recovery and Reinvestment Act Funding for Rural Libraries is a grant or loan opportunity for libraries serving communities of 20,000 and fewer. Community Facilities Grants will help give rural communities the opportunity to improve their library facilities, enhance educational opportunities, and improve economic conditions in America's rural communities. Funds may be used to construct, enlarge, or improve public libraries. This can include costs to acquire land needed for a facility, pay necessary professional fees, and purchase equipment required for a facility's operation. Funds can be used to purchase shelving, furniture, computers, audiovisual equipment, distance learning equipment, and bookmobiles.

## REQUIREMENTS AND RESTRICTIONS
NA

## APPLICATION PROCEDURES

**Submission Guidelines:** Applications are handled by USDA Rural Development field offices. Field staff can provide application materials and current program information and assist in the preparation of an application. Interested applicants may also contact the USDA Rural Development Community Programs Division.

## CONTACT
Phone: 202-720-1490
Fax: 202-690-0471

## GRANT-SPECIFIC WEBSITE
www.rurdev.usda.gov/rhs/

# Utah State Library

## Headquarters

250 North, 1950 West, Suite A
Salt Lake City, UT 84116-7901
Phone: 801-715-6777
http://library.utah.gov/

# Description

**Founded:** 1957

**Operating Locations:** Utah

The Utah State Library works to develop, advance, and promote library services and equal access to information and library resources to all Utah residents.

# Grants Information

## GRANT TYPES
Library construction, library improvement, professional development

## TYPICAL RECIPIENTS
Utah libraries

## GRANT VALUES
NA

## NAMED GRANTS

### CAPITAL FACILITIES GRANT
Capital Facilities Grants provide funding for new construction, preservation, restoration, and renovation.

**Requirements and Restrictions:** Applicants must be located in the state of Utah. Prioritization will be based on the following criteria: goals of application, public benefit of project, and strategic value of partnerships.

**Submission Guidelines:** All applications must be submitted electronically via the Department of Community and Culture (DCC) and its division web portals.

**Deadlines:** June

**Contact:** Steve Matthews; Phone: 800-662-9150, ext. 722, or 801-715-6722; E-mail: smatthews@utah.gov

**Grant-Specific Website:** http://library.utah.gov/grants/capfacilities/

### COMMUNITY LIBRARY ENHANCEMENT FUND (CLEF)
Community Library Enhancement Fund grants may be used for any library purpose that improves library services to the community. Funds may be used for the following three areas: collection development (such as children's materials, video materials, online resources, materials in another language, special new collections, enhanced current collections), technology that directly affects the public (such as public access computing, library catalogs, online resources, technology training, Wi-Fi), community outreach (such as services for seniors, teens, migrants, head starts, outreach to those who don't use the library). The funds may not be used as a match for LSTA competitive grant applications and may not replace local funding.

**Typical Recipients:** All Utah public libraries that fulfill the requirements for state library certification are eligible to apply.

**Requirements and Restrictions:** Applicants must be located in the state of Utah. Recipients are required to complete an annual online report of expenditures under this grant.

**Contact:** Sara Wever, Grants Coordinator; Phone: 800-662-5540, ext. 732, or 801-715-6732; E-mail: swever@utah.gov

**Grant-Specific Website:** http://library.utah.gov/grants/clef/

## UPLIFT ORGANIZATION RESOURCE GRANT

The UPLIFT Organization Resource Grant is available to formal library organizations for specialized library training. It allows organizations to upgrade the skills of library staff, trustees, and supporters by addressing local needs. Library board members, volunteers, advocates, and other supporters may be included in the training as appropriate.

**Typical Recipients:** Formal library organizations eligible for state and federal funding

**Grant Values:** Highest Grant, $3,000

**Requirements and Restrictions:** Applicants must be located in the state of Utah. Allowable costs include trainer fees and travel, room rental in nonlibrary facility if required, and duplication/purchase of training materials.

**Submission Guidelines:** The applicant must submit an original, signed application form and two photocopies by mail, and a digital (e-mailed) copy of the completed application, and all supporting materials. Originals should be mailed to the address below.

**Deadlines:** February, June, and October

**Decisions:** Utah State Library notifies applicants of decisions within 30 days of the review dates and sends out contracts for signature.

**Contact:** Colleen Eggett, Training Coordinator, Utah State Library Division, 250 North 1950 West, Suite A, Salt Lake City, UT 84116-7901; Phone: 800-662-9150, ext. 776, or 801-715-6776; E-mail: ceggett@utah.gov

**Grant-Specific Website:** http://library.utah.gov/grants/uplift/resource.html

**REQUIREMENTS AND RESTRICTIONS**
Vary by grant

**APPLICATION PROCEDURES**
Vary by grant

**CONTACT**
Varies by grant

**GRANT-SPECIFIC WEBSITE**
Varies by grant

# Wayne and Gladys Valley Foundation

## Headquarters

1939 Harrison St.
Oakland, CA 94612
Phone: 510-466-6060

## Description

**Founded:** 1977

**Operating Locations:** California

**Foundation Information:** Private foundation established by F. Wayne Valley and Gladys Valley

## Financial Summary

Assets: $510,651,317
Gifts Received: $125,136
Total Giving: $36,730,869

## Grants Information

### GRANT TYPES
General support, capital, research, scholarship, matching

### TYPICAL RECIPIENTS
Arts and humanities, civic affairs, education, environment, health, religion, science, social services

### GRANT VALUES
Total Dollar Amount of Grants:
$36,730,869

### PAST GRANT RECIPIENTS

*Library or School Related*
- Santa Clara University (CA), construction of new library, $3,000,000
- Walnut Creek Library Foundation (CA), construction of new library, $500,000
- New Teacher Project (NY), support for new Practitioner Teacher program, $75,000
- Oakland Small Autonomous Schools Foundation (CA), support for After School Collaboratives, $100,000
- Teach for America (CA), general support, $250,000

*General*
- Oakland Museum of California Foundation (CA), renovation of museum's galleries and building, $1,875,000
- Business United in Investing, Lending and Development (CA), expansion of BUILD program into four schools in Oakland/Emeryville, $25,000
- Blind Babies Foundation (CA), general support for Off to a Good Start program, $25,000
- Down Syndrome Connection of the Bay Area (CA), general operating support, $25,000

- Military Outreach Ministry (CA), general support, $50,000
- Myelin Repair Foundation (CA), general support for repair therapies for multiple sclerosis patients, $700,000

## REQUIREMENTS AND RESTRICTIONS

None, although the foundation is interested in organizations serving California. No grants are made to organizations located in or serving areas outside of the United States.

## APPLICATION PROCEDURES

**Submission Guidelines:** Review the guidelines of the foundation, available on the website. The application letter should be concise and include the following:

- description and very brief history of the applicant organization: a short narrative on the success of the organization, including overall financial stability
- description of the project
- statement of the purpose and goals of the project
- number of people that will benefit from the project
- references to outside sources, materials, and research, if any, that have demonstrated a need for the proposed project
- time frame in which the project will be undertaken and proof of a well-thought-out business plan

- documentation of the planning process of the project for which funds are sought
- amount of funds requested from the foundation
- total cost of the project
- other sources of funds for the project, including the current status of other funding requests
- name(s) of person(s) in direct charge of project with brief biographical information, including comments on qualifications and commitment of personnel
- how progress and success of the project will be measured
- income and expense budget for the project, including projected sources of revenues
- list of the board of directors and their business or professional affiliations
- IRS Letter of Determination of 501(c)(3) and public charity status, State of California Exemption Letter from the Franchise Tax Board, and letter from chief financial officer of the applicant stating that tax-exempt and public charity status has not been revoked or modified
- copy of the most recent audited financial statement of the applicant (if the applicant ended with an operating deficit in any of the last four fiscal years, an explanation of the reason and corrective action taken to remedy the loss)

- copy of the most recent fiscal year's entire filed IRS form 990 of the applicant, including all schedules

## CONTACT
Michael D. Desler, Executive Director
Wayne and Gladys Valley Foundation
1939 Harrison Street, Suite 510
Oakland, CA 94612-3532
Phone: 510-466-6060
E-mail: info@wgvalley.org

## GRANT-SPECIFIC WEBSITE
http://foundationcenter.org/
    grantmaker/wgvalley/rules.html

# Verizon Foundation

## Headquarters

One Verizon Way
Basking Ridge, NJ 07920
Phone: 800-360-7955
http://foundation.verizon.com/index.html

## Description

**Founded:** 2000

**Operating Locations:** New Jersey

**Foundation Information:** Corporate foundation of Verizon Communications, Inc.

## Financial Summary

Assets: $241,741,456

## Grants Information

### GRANT TYPES
General support

### TYPICAL RECIPIENTS
Education, literacy, domestic violence prevention, technology for healthcare and healthcare accessibility

### GRANT VALUES
Total Dollar Amount of Grants:
    $68,000,000
Highest Grant: $716,000
Lowest Grant: $15
Typical Range of Grants: $5,000–
    $10,000

### PAST GRANT RECIPIENTS

*Library or School Related*
- Allegheny County Library Association (PA), $5,000
- Ames Free Library of Easton (MA), $7,500
- Anne Arundel County Public Library Foundation (MD), $13,750
- Bedford Hills Free Library (NY), $2,500
- City of Richmond Public Library Foundation (VA), $8,500
- Pikes Peak Library District Foundation (CO), $150

## REQUIREMENTS AND RESTRICTIONS

The Verizon Foundation does not fund private foundations—only tax-exempt IRS-qualified 501(c)(3) public charities. The Verizon Foundation provides one cash grant per calendar year to eligible nonprofit organizations. Organizations that have received a grant from the Verizon Foundation in the last three consecutive years may reapply after a one-year hiatus.

## APPLICATION PROCEDURES

**Submission Guidelines:** Application online

**Deadlines:** Applications may be submitted January through October.

## CONTACT

Phone: 800-360-7955

Fax: 908-630-2660

E-mail: Verizon.Foundation@Verizon. com

## GRANT-SPECIFIC WEBSITE

http://foundation.verizon.com/grant/

# The Library of Virginia

## Headquarters

800 E. Broad St.
Richmond, VA 23219
Phone: 804-692-3500
www.lva.virginia.gov

## Description

**Founded:** 1823

**Operating Locations:** Virginia

The Library of Virginia houses the most comprehensive collection of materials on Virginia government, history, and culture available anywhere. The library's printed, manuscript, map, and photographic collections attract researchers from across the country and the world, while the library's websites provide collection-based content and access to our digital collections to those at great distances who are not able to travel to Richmond. In addition to managing and preserving its collections, the library supplies research and reference assistance to state officials; provides consulting services to state and local government agencies and to Virginia's public libraries; administers numerous federal, state, and local grant programs; publishes award-winning books on Virginia history; provides educational programs and resources on Virginia history and culture for students and teachers; and offers the public a wide array of exhibitions, lectures, book signings, and other programs.

## Grants Information

### GRANT TYPES
Library support

### TYPICAL RECIPIENTS
Virginia libraries

### GRANT VALUES
Highest Grant: $250,000

### PAST GRANT RECIPIENTS
NA

### REQUIREMENTS AND RESTRICTIONS
Applicants must be located in the state of Virginia. State funds may be used for books and materials, salary, equipment, supplies, contractual services, fellowship, and other expenses directly related to making services accessible or available to the library's clientele. Ineligible expenses include postage, membership fees, insurance, utilities, telephone charges, bookmobile operation and maintenance, and all forms of travel. A local match of 40 percent is required.

### APPLICATION PROCEDURES
**Submission Guidelines:** Send a letter of application to the address below, along with the following documents:

- charter
- resolution
- bylaws
- list of trustees
- five-year plan and annual revision
- policy statements
- financial statements/Bibliostat annual report
- certified budget of local income
- operating expenditures

**Deadlines:** June

### CONTACT
The Library of Virginia
Library Development and Networking Division
800 E. Broad St.
Richmond, VA 23219-8000

### GRANT-SPECIFIC WEBSITE
www.lva.virginia.gov/lib-edu/LDND/state-aid/

# Volunteer USA Foundation

## Headquarters

516 N. Adams St.
Tallahassee, FL 32301

Phone: 850-562-5300
www.volunteerusafoundation.org

# Description

**Founded:** 2007

**Operating Locations:** Florida

**Foundation Information:** Private foundation

# Financial Summary

Assets: $3,050,076
Total Giving: $2,442,450

# Grants Information

**GRANT TYPES**
Literacy, family literacy, mentoring

**TYPICAL RECIPIENTS**
Community-based organizations, volunteer literacy organizations, public nonprofit agencies, libraries, schools

**GRANT VALUES**
Highest Grant: $70,000
Lowest Grant: $1,000

**PAST GRANT RECIPIENTS**
*Library or School Related*
- Brevard Schools Foundation (FL), mentoring/education program, $12,000
- Calhoun County Public Library (FL), mentoring/education program, $30,295

- Florida International University (FL), mentoring/education program, $63,450
- Polk County Schools (FL), mentoring/education program, $5,000

*General*
- Alliance for Families with Deaf Children (FL), mentoring/education program, $101,148
- Hispanic Unity of Florida (FL), mentoring/education program, $50,946

**REQUIREMENTS AND RESTRICTIONS**
Programs requesting grants must be in the southern United States; priority is given to programs in Florida, Tennessee, Georgia, and Louisiana. Programs must have nonprofit tax-exempt status and serve families and/or children with hearing impairments.

**APPLICATION PROCEDURES**

**Submission Guidelines:** Applications must state the purposes of the organization, number of clients served, and publications issued. Nonprofit organizations and nonexempt charitable trusts must enter amount of grants and allocations to others.

**CONTACT**
Literacy Mentoring Program
Teecy Matthews
Phone: 352-237-6685

E-mail: teecy.matthews@
    volunteerusafund.org
Family Literacy Program
Michael Thompson
Phone: 850-562-5300
e-mail: Michael.Thompson@
    volunteerusafund.org

**GRANT-SPECIFIC WEBSITE**
NA

# Wallace Foundation

## Headquarters

5 Penn Plaza, 7th fl.
New York, NY 10001
Phone: 212-251-9700
www.wallacefoundation.org

## Description

**Founded:** 1986

**Operating Locations:** New York

**Foundation Information:** Private foundation established by DeWitt and Lila Wallace (founders of *Reader's Digest*)

## Financial Summary

Assets: $1,115,216,051
Total Giving: $62,745,480

## Grants Information

**GRANT TYPES**
General support, multiyear continuing support

**TYPICAL RECIPIENTS**
Arts and humanities, civic affairs, education, environment, health, international, religion, science, social services

**GRANT VALUES**
Total Dollar Amount of Grants:
    $67,545,091

**PAST GRANT RECIPIENTS**

*Library or School Related*
- Harvard University (MA), support study to determine effective ways of developing out-of-school programs for middle and high school youth, $610,000
- Philadelphia Education Fund (PA), support arts integration into instruction and expose children to art in and out of school, $400,000
- Greater New Orleans After School Partnership (LA), support for summer programs, $450,000

*General*
- Chicago's Department of Children and Youth Services (IL), support After School Matters program, $3,000,000
- Corporation of Fine Arts Museums (CA), support for testing and

maintaining effective participation-building programs and create learning networks, $175,000
- Minneapolis Institute of Arts (MN), support for testing and maintaining effective participation-building programs and create learning networks, $150,000

## REQUIREMENTS AND RESTRICTIONS

The foundation supports effective ideas and practices in five major initiatives: school leadership, after-school programming, summer and extended learning time, arts education, and audience development for the arts. The foundation does not award grants for religious or fraternal organizations, international programs, conferences, historical restoration, health, medical or social service programs, environmental/conservation programs, capital campaigns, emergency funds or deficit financing, private foundations, or individuals.

## APPLICATION PROCEDURES

**Submission Guidelines:** Send an e-mail query describing the project, the organization, the estimated total for the project, and the portion requiring funding to the e-mail address below. If interested, the foundation will request a full proposal after screening the initial e-mail.

## CONTACT

Phone: 212-251-9700
E-mail: grantrequest@
   wallacefoundation.org

## GRANT-SPECIFIC WEBSITE

www.wallacefoundation.org/
   GrantsPrograms/GrantApproach/
   Pages/FundingGuidelines.aspx

# George R. Wallace Foundation

## Headquarters

c/o Goodwin Procter LLP
Exchange Pl.
Boston, MA 02109
Phone: 617-570-1735

## Description

**Founded:** 1965

**Operating Locations:** Massachusetts

**Foundation Information:** Private foundation

## Financial Summary

Assets: $7,954,814
Total Giving: $384,714

# Grants Information

## GRANT TYPES
General support, capital, endowment

## TYPICAL RECIPIENTS
Arts and humanities, civic affairs, education, environment, health, religion, science, social services

## GRANT VALUES
Total Dollar Amount of Grants: $384,714
Number of Grants: 5
Average Grant: $65,000
Highest Grant: $100,000
Lowest Grant: $20,000

## PAST GRANT RECIPIENTS

*Library or School Related*
- Leominster Public Library (MA), general support, $20,000
- Fitchburg State College (MA), general support, $100,000
- Epiphany School (MA), general support, $25,000
- Fitchburg High School (MA), Crocker Field restoration, $39,000

*General*
- Chewonki Foundation (ME), general support, $35,714

## REQUIREMENTS AND RESTRICTIONS
NA

## APPLICATION PROCEDURES
**Submission Guidelines:** Send a letter of inquiry to ask for application guidelines.

## CONTACT
Lucia Thompson
Phone: 617-570-1355

## GRANT-SPECIFIC WEBSITE
NA

# Walmart Foundation

## Headquarters

702 SW Eighth St.
Bentonville, AR 72716
Phone: 800-530-9925 or 479-273-8510
www.walmartfoundation.org

## Description

**Founded:** 1982

**Operating Locations:** Arkansas

**Foundation Information:** Corporate foundation of Walmart

## Financial Summary

Assets: $4,402,583
Total Giving: $530,000

# Grants Information

## GRANT TYPES
General support, employee matching, scholarship, programs

## TYPICAL RECIPIENTS
Arts and humanities, civic affairs, education, health, social services

## GRANT VALUES
Average Grant: $5,000
Highest Grant: $5,000,000
Lowest Grant: $250
Typical Range of Grants: $100–5,000

## PAST GRANT RECIPIENTS

*Library or School Related*
- Fayetteville Public Library Foundation (AR), $25,000
- Chatham Area Public Library District (IL), $10,000
- California State Library Foundation (CA), $10,000
- American Council on Education (DC), $2,500,000
- West Boylston Middle High School (MA), $10,000
- American Indian College Fund (CO), $10,000

*General*
- YouthBuild USA (MA), $5,000,000

## REQUIREMENTS AND RESTRICTIONS
The Walmart Foundation supports initiatives focused on enhancing opportunities in four main focus areas: education, workforce development/ economic opportunity, environmental sustainability, health and wellness. Applicants can apply for grants through the State Giving Program or the National Giving Program.

The foundation does not support cultural performances, film and video projects, or faith-based organizations whose projects benefit entirely their members or adherents. Grants are not given to individuals (except for scholarships) or for research, endowments, capital campaigns, conferences, travel, or fund-raising events.

## APPLICATION PROCEDURES

**Submission Guidelines:** Application online

**Deadlines:** Vary by program

## CONTACT
NA

## GRANT-SPECIFIC WEBSITE
State Giving Program: http://walmartstores.com/CommunityGiving/8168.aspx?p = 8979
National Giving Program: http://walmartstores.com/CommunityGiving/8782.aspx?p = 8979

# Andy Warhol Foundation for the Visual Arts

## Headquarters

65 Bleecker St.
New York, NY 10012
Phone: 212-387-7555
www.warholfoundation.org

## Description

**Founded:** 1987

**Operating Locations:** New York

**Foundation Information:** Private foundation established by Andy Warhol

## Financial Summary

Assets: $395,237,215
Total Giving: $13,401,970

## Grants Information

### GRANT TYPES
General support, operating support, project, fellowship, matching

### TYPICAL RECIPIENTS
Arts and humanities, civic affairs, education, environment, health, international, religion

### GRANT VALUES
Total Dollar Amount of Grants:
$13,401,970
Number of Grants: 129
Average Grant: $103,000
Highest Grant: $1,000,000
Lowest Grant: $5,000

### PAST GRANT RECIPIENTS

*General*
- Art Resources Transfer, Inc. (NY), support library program in underserved communities, $75,000
- Blue Star Contemporary Art Center (TX), support exhibition programs, $75,000
- McColl Center for Visual Art (NC), support artist-in-residence program, $80,000
- Museum of Contemporary Art Detroit (MI), support publications and exhibitions, $60,000
- Public Knowledge Washington DC (DC), support advocacy for intellectual property law and communications policy, $30,000
- Warhol Initiative (NY), library provisions, $40,000

### REQUIREMENTS AND RESTRICTIONS
Applicants must have tax-exempt status. No grants are made to individuals. The foundation awards one grant, the Wynn Kramarsky Freedom of Artistic Expression Award (named in honor of a former board chair), to recognize

the work of organizations with a deep commitment to preserving and defending the First Amendment rights of artists.

## APPLICATION PROCEDURES

**Submission Guidelines:** A full proposal for funding should include the following:

- a letter of approximately three pages describing the activity for which funds are being requested; if applying for the first time, give a brief description of the organization's mission, purpose, and goals.
- a project budget
- a copy of the organization's 501(c)3 ruling from the IRS

Please do not send any additional material with your proposal. Proposals may be submitted either by mail or by e-mail. Please select only one method of application and send only one copy. If submitting by e-mail, attach all materials as Word documents, Excel documents, or PDFs. Notification of receipt will be sent in the mail.

**Deadlines:** Postmark deadlines for proposals are March 1 and September 1.

**Decisions:** July 1 and January 1

## CONTACT

Rachel Bers, Acting Program Director
The Andy Warhol Foundation for the
     Visual Arts
65 Bleecker St., 7th fl.

New York, NY 10012
E-mail: deadline@warholfoundation.org

## GRANT-SPECIFIC WEBSITE

www.warholfoundation.org/grant/
     overview.html

# Washington Library Association (WLA)

## Headquarters

23607 Hwy. 99, Suite 2-C
Edmonds, WA 98026
Phone: 425-967-0739
http://wla.org

## Description

**Founded:** NA

**Operating Locations:** Washington

Washington's citizens rely upon libraries to further their education, enhance their skills in the workplace, fully function in today's global society, and enrich and enjoy their daily lives. The Washington Library Association, with a membership of over 1,300 individuals and 39 institutions, provides the leadership needed to develop, improve, and promote library services to all Washington residents.

# Grants Information

## GRANT TYPES
Travel, conference attendance

## TYPICAL RECIPIENTS
WLA members

## GRANT VALUES
Highest Grant: $500

## NAMED GRANTS

### TRAVEL GRANTS
The Washington Library Association funds Travel Grants for the professional development of its members. Grants of up to $500 per year per individual may be used for any travel expenses connected with participation in continuing education events and activities outside Washington State. Examples of CE events and activities include
- attendance at meetings of professional associations, as an officer or member
- attendance at a library-related conference for the purpose of presenting a program
- travel for the purpose of continuing education, such as language study in a country outside the United States
- participation in a program of library and library employee enhancement through people-to-people contact

Reimbursement is made after the travel is completed, based on actual receipts and submission of an expense report.

**Deadlines:** April 30, August 31, and December 31

**Contact:** Mary Ross, WLA Continuing Education Coordinator; E-mail: mbucherross@earthlink.net

**Grant-Specific Website:** http://wla.org/training/grants/travel-grants/

### CONFERENCE ATTENDANCE GRANTS
The Conference Attendance Grant funds up to $400 per recipient to defray the expense of attending the WLA annual conference. Any member of WLA is eligible to apply for a WLA Conference Attendance Grant. Some grants may be made to specific categories of applicants. Preference is given to applicants who are first-time conference attendees.

**Deadlines:** June

**Contact:** E-mail: karen@wla.org

**Grant-Specific Website:** http://wla.org/training/grants/conference-grants/

## REQUIREMENTS AND RESTRICTIONS
Applicants must be located in the state of Washington and be members of WLA.

## APPLICATION PROCEDURES
**Submission Guidelines:** Application online

## CONTACT
Phone: 425-967-0739
Fax: 425-771-9588

**GRANT-SPECIFIC WEBSITE**
Varies by grant

# Washington State Library

## Headquarters

6880 Capitol Blvd.
Tumwater, WA 98501-5513
Phone: 360-704-5200
www.sos.wa.gov/library/

## Description

**Founded:** 1889

**Operating Locations:** Washington

Ensures that Washingtonians have access to the information they need today and to the history of Washington for tomorrow. It strives to collect, preserve, and make accessible to Washingtonians materials on the government, history, culture, and natural resources of the state; provide leadership and coordination of services to all libraries in the state of Washington; support the information needs of residents in state institutions and of the visually impaired; and serve as the primary source in the region for published information from the federal government.

## Grants Information

**GRANT TYPES**
LSTA funds, continuing education

**TYPICAL RECIPIENTS**
Washington libraries and librarians

**GRANT VALUES**
NA

**NAMED GRANTS**

**CONTINUING EDUCATION GRANTS**
Funds are available to individual library staff or libraries who need financial assistance to attend or receive instruction or provide a workshop.

**Typical Recipients:** Librarians and library staff, libraries

**Grant Values:** Highest Grant, $1,000 per year for individuals, with a maximum of $750 per event; $3,000 per year for organizations

**Requirements and Restrictions:** Funds cannot be used for the following: activities that do not comply with at least one of the six federal priorities; activities that do not directly lead to the development and delivery of programs and services to the end user; attendance at general library conferences; training of which the sole aim is the improvement of management or supervisory skills or improvement of library operations; applications from and training for trustees, friends of libraries, and library foundation staff; out-of-country travel, unless the event is in British Columbia or Alberta, Canada, and has a direct connection to the Washington library community and is not a general conference. Applicants must be able to make at least a 25 percent match.

**Submission Guidelines:** Application online. Applications should be mailed to the address below. Faxed or e-mailed applications cannot be accepted.

**Deadlines:** All applications must be postmarked at least 30 days prior to the start date of the CE event (preferably 3 months before).

**Decisions:** Within 2 weeks of applying.

**Contact:** CE Grant Program, Washington State Library, PO Box 42460, Olympia, WA 98504; Phone: 360-570-5571 or 360-704-5246

**Grant-Specific Website:** www.sos.wa.gov/library/libraries/training/continuEd.aspx

## INFORMATION TECHNOLOGY CONTINUING EDUCATION GRANTS (ITCE)

Information Technology Continuing Education Grants were created to provide up-to-date training for the library community. LSTA funds will offset 50 percent of registration fees for the technical training of library and IT support staff.

**Typical Recipients:** Staff members of LSTA-qualified libraries and IT staff who directly support these libraries a minimum of 10 hours per week

**Grant Values:** Highest Grant, $2,000 per year per individual; $4,000 total per year per library system

**Requirements and Restrictions:** Technical training is limited to specific technical classes and other specialized courses not normally available to the library IT community. Initiative funds are focused on building basic IT competence and providing training opportunities. Upon approval by the Washington State Library, participants may register for the class and will be invoiced by the vendor for 50 percent of the registration costs. The remaining 50 percent of registration fees will be invoiced directly to WSL for payment.

**Submission Guidelines:** Application online. Mail form to the address below. Applications may be faxed, but an original must be sent by mail also.

**Deadlines:** Signed originals should be submitted no later than 30 days prior to the training session.

**Contact:** IT Continuing Education, Washington State Library, PO Box 42460, Olympia, WA 98504; Phone: 360-570-5579; Fax: 360-586-7575

**Grant-Specific Website:** www.sos.wa.gov/library/libraries/grants/itce.aspx

## LSTA—WASHINGTON RURAL HERITAGE GRANT

The purpose of this grant is to provide funds to small and rural public libraries to encourage the development of long-term sustainable digitization programs at these libraries through the creation of an initial digital collection published as part of the Washington Rural Heritage collection. Collaborative partnerships among libraries, museums, schools, and other community organizations are encouraged, though not required. Funds may be used to purchase equipment to digitize material or software to optimize digital files; train staff and/or volunteers to digitize, research, and/or catalog items; pay salary of staff and/or contract services to digitize and/or research and catalog items.

**Typical Recipients:** Public libraries or public library systems that serve a population of 25,000 or less, or individual branches that serve in an area whose population is 25,000 or less. A maximum of two branches from one public library system will be considered for an award.

**Grant Values:** Total Dollar Amount of Grants, $50,000; Number of Grants, 5; Highest Grant, $10,000

**Requirements and Restrictions:** It is not required that your library or staff already have experience in digitization projects; Washington Rural Heritage staff will coordinate and/or provide training in the following: developing and managing digital projects, copyright issues for digital projects, digital imaging, metadata creation, use of digital repository software.

**Submission Guidelines:** Application online. An application consists of three components: a single-sided, signed original; a paper copy; and an electronic copy saved on a disk or CD or sent via e-mail. Mail applications to the address below. Faxed applications will not be accepted.

**Deadlines:** April

**Contact:** Grants Program, Washington State Library, PO Box 42460, Olympia, WA 98504-2460; Phone: 360-704-5248 or 360-704-5246. *Hand-delivered applications should go to* Grants Program, Washington State Library, 6880 Capitol Blvd. S., Tumwater, WA 98501-5513.

**Grant-Specific Website:** www.sos.wa.gov/library/libraries/grants/grants.aspx

## LSTA—SUPPORTING STUDENT SUCCESS COMPETITIVE GRANT

Washington schools are required to report on their implementation of Social Studies Classroom Based Assessment (CBA) as a result of the Revised Code of Washington (RCW)

28A.230.095. The Supporting Student Success project focuses on the library's role in supporting the CBA research process. The purpose of this grant cycle is to provide grant funds to develop collaborative partnerships among libraries, learners, and schools. Grant-funded collaborative partnerships are intended to increase students' information and research skills and to support successful completion of Social Studies CBAs. Funds may be used to help libraries initiate new services or enhance existing services.

**Typical Recipients:** LSTA-eligible public libraries and public school libraries; collaborative partnerships consisting of a minimum of one public library and one school

**Grant Values:** Total Dollar Amount of Grants, $140,000; Number of Grants, 4–8; Highest Grant, $35,000

**Requirements and Restrictions:** Schools that have a school library must have the library involved in the collaboration. Schools without a library may be a partner but not an applicant. Funds may not be used for food and other refreshments, purchase of computers or to pay for direct costs associated with accessing the Internet, advertising and promotion of libraries in general, prizes and other incentives, overhead expenses, administrative and indirect costs. The purchase of technology/software may not exceed 50 percent of the total grant funds requested.

**Submission Guidelines:** Application online. An application consists of three components: a single-sided, signed original; a paper copy; and an electronic copy saved on a disk or CD or sent via e-mail. Mail applications to the address below. Faxed applications will not be accepted.

**Deadlines:** April

**Contact:** Grants Program, Washington State Library, PO Box 42460, Olympia, WA 98504-2460; Phone: 360-704-5248 or 360-704-5246. *Hand-delivered applications should go to* Grants Program, Washington State Library, 6880 Capitol Blvd. S., Tumwater, WA 98501-5513.

**Grant-Specific Website:** www.sos.wa.gov/library/libraries/grants/grants.aspx

## LSTA—CONNECTING LIBRARIES THROUGH RESOURCE SHARING

The purpose of the Connecting Libraries through Resource Sharing (CLRS) grant cycle is to encourage cooperation among public libraries in counties where inter-local agreements to share materials do not exist, by providing grant funds for collection development with materials to be rotated between partnering libraries. Funds will be awarded equally among partners with a maximum award of $715 dollars per library, including $500 for collection development, up to $140 for travel to attend two required meetings, and up to $75 for processing materials.

**Grant Values:** Total Dollar Amount of Grants, $5,000; Highest Grant, $715 per library

**Submission Guidelines:** Application online. An application consists of three components: a single-sided, signed original; a paper copy; and an electronic copy saved on a disk or CD or sent via e-mail. Mail applications to the address below. Faxed applications will not be accepted.

**Deadlines:** April

**Contact:** Grants Program, Washington State Library, PO Box 42460, Olympia, WA 98504-2460; Phone: 360-704-5248 or 360-704-5246. *Hand-delivered applications should go to* Grants Program, Washington State Library, 6880 Capitol Blvd. S., Tumwater, WA 98501-5513.

**Grant-Specific Website:** www.sos.wa.gov/library/libraries/grants/grants.aspx

### TRANSFORMING LIFE AFTER 50

The Transforming Life After 50 initiative is designed to help libraries better serve and engage midlife adults by positioning libraries as catalysts, resources, meeting places, and partners in creating opportunities for midlife adults to learn, teach, lead, build skills, prepare for new careers, and become civically engaged. To encourage Washington libraries to support this initiative, small grants are being made available to support programming and services for adults over 50 in the library. Programming and/or services should focus on one or more of the following topics: community partnerships, health, financial security, or work and volunteerism. Libraries are not required to have a community partner; however, partnerships would make for stronger applications.

**Typical Recipients:** Academic, public, and tribal libraries that serve adults over the age of 50

**Grant Values:** Total Dollar Amount of Grants, $25,000; Number of Grants, 5; Highest Grant, $5,000

**Submission Guidelines:** Application online. An application consists of three components: a single-sided, signed original; a paper copy; and an electronic copy saved on a disk or CD or sent via e-mail. Mail applications to the address below. Faxed applications will not be accepted.

**Deadlines:** September

**Contact:** Grants Program, Washington State Library, PO Box 42460, Olympia, WA 98504-2460; Phone: 360-704-5248 or 360-704-5246. *Hand-delivered applications should go to* Grants Program, Washington State Library, 6880 Capitol Blvd. S., Tumwater, WA 98501-5513.

**Grant-Specific Website:**
www.sos.wa.gov/library/libraries/
grants/grants.aspx

## REQUIREMENTS AND RESTRICTIONS
Applicants must be located in the state
of Washington.

## APPLICATION PROCEDURES
**Submission Guidelines:** Applications
available online unless otherwise noted
above

## CONTACT
Anne Yarbrough
LSTA Grants Manager
Washington State Library
PO Box 42460
Olympia, WA 98504-2460
Phone: 360-704-5246
E-mail: anne.yarbrough@sos.wa.gov

## GRANT-SPECIFIC WEBSITE
www.sos.wa.gov/library/libraries/
   grants/

# Widgeon Foundation

## Headquarters

PO Box 278
Wye Mills, MD 21679
Phone: 410-822-7707

## Description

**Founded:** 1961

**Operating Locations:** Maryland

**Foundation Information:** Private
foundation established by Elizabeth H.
Robinson

## Financial Summary

Assets: $3,198,277
Total Giving: $299,065

## Grants Information

### GRANT TYPES
General support

### TYPICAL RECIPIENTS
Arts and humanities, civic affairs,
education, environment, health,
international, religion, social services

### GRANT VALUES
Total Dollar Amount of Grants: $299,065
Number of Grants: 37
Average Grant: $8,000
Highest Grant: $50,000
Lowest Grant: $1,000

### PAST GRANT RECIPIENTS

*Library or School Related*
- Room to Read Foundation (CA),
  general support, $5,000

- Easton Montessori School (MD), general support, $8,000
- Smithsonian Institution (DC), general support, $50,000
- Virginia Tech Foundation, Inc. (VA), general support, $13,215
- Washington College (MD), general support, $14,000
- University of Texas (TX), general support, $47,000

*General*
- Wintergreen Volunteer Fire Department (VA), general support, $1,000
- St. Jude's Children's Research Hospital (TN), general support, $4,000
- Ronald McDonald House Charities (VA), general support, $4,000
- Shady Grove WMCA (VA), general support, $1,000

## REQUIREMENTS AND RESTRICTIONS

The foundation makes grants to organizations located in Maryland, Virginia, and Pennsylvania. Funding emphasis is on educational, religious, environmental, and medical organizations.

## APPLICATION PROCEDURES

**Submission Guidelines:** Applicant should send a written statement including name, activities, financial statement, and purpose of funds.

**CONTACT**
Richard Robinson
PO Box 278
Wye Mills, MD 21679
Phone: 410-822-7707

**GRANT-SPECIFIC WEBSITE**
NA

# E. L. Wiegand Foundation

## Headquarters

165 W. Liberty St.
Reno, NV 89501
Phone: 775-333-0310

## Description

**Founded:** 1982

**Operating Locations:** Nevada

**Foundation Information:** Private foundation established by Edwin L. Wiegand

## Financial Summary

Assets: $108,481,822
Total Giving: $4,181,621

# Grants Information

## GRANT TYPES
General support, project

## TYPICAL RECIPIENTS
Arts and humanities, civic affairs, education, health, international, religion, science, social services

## GRANT VALUES
Total Dollar Amount of Grants:
$4,181,621
Number of Grants: 42
Average Grant: $99,000
Highest Grant: $500,000
Lowest Grant: $500

## PAST GRANT RECIPIENTS

*Library or School Related*
- St. Viator School (NV), library/media center, $200,000
- Carroll College (MT), undergraduate research center, $522,125
- St. Albert the Great School (NV), science laboratory, $500,000
- Mills College (CA), performance project for dance students, $14,000
- St. George Parish School (WA), technology upgrade, $104,829

*General*
- American Council on Science and Health (NY), technology upgrade, $69,477
- Loyola University Medical Center (IL), pediatric oncology lounge and treatment center, $350,000
- White Pine Museum (NV), building repairs/restoration, $80,000

## REQUIREMENTS AND RESTRICTIONS
Nevada, Oregon, Washington, Idaho, Utah, Arizona, Washington DC, and New York

Institutions must be in existence a minimum of five years. The foundation will not make grants to government agencies or to charitable institutions that derive significant support from public tax funds or the United Way. Proposals for endowments, debt reduction, ordinary operations, general fund-raising, emergency funding, direct or indirect loans, media productions, or individuals will not be considered.

## APPLICATION PROCEDURES

**Submission Guidelines:** Applicants should contact the foundation for an informational booklet outlining the grant criteria. After reviewing the booklet, applicants should submit a letter of inquiry briefly describing the organization and the proposed request. The applicant will receive a numbered Application for Grant form if staff review warrants further consideration of the proposed grant by the foundation. Applicant then completes the application form and returns it to the foundation.

## CONTACT

Kristen Avansino
Phone: 775-333-0310

## GRANT-SPECIFIC WEBSITE

NA

# Wild Ones Natural Landscapers, Ltd.

## Headquarters

PO Box 1274
Appleton, WI 54912
Phone: 877-394-9453
www.for-wild.org

## Description

**Founded:** 1990

**Operating Locations:** Wisconsin

Wild Ones is a not-for-profit environmental education and advocacy organization that promotes environmentally sound landscaping practices to preserve biodiversity through the preservation, restoration, and establishment of native plant communities.

## Grants Information

### GRANT TYPES

Project

### TYPICAL RECIPIENTS

Nonprofit organizations

### GRANT VALUES

Typical Range of Grants: $100–$500

### NAMED GRANTS

#### LORRIE OTTO SEEDS FOR EDUCATION GRANT PROGRAM

The Lorrie Otto Seeds for Education Grant Program gives small monetary grants to schools, nature centers, and other not-for-profit places of learning in the United States with a site available for a stewardship project. Successful nonschool applicants often are a partnership between a youth group (scouts, 4-H, etc.) and a site owner. Libraries, government agencies, and places of worship are eligible, subject to youth participation.

### REQUIREMENTS AND RESTRICTIONS

Project goals should focus on the enhancement and development of an appreciation for nature using native plants. Projects must emphasize involvement of students and volunteers and increase the educational value of the site. Creativity in design is encouraged, but must show complete and thoughtful planning. The use of and teaching about native plants and the native plant community is mandatory, and they must be appropriate to the local ecoregion and the site conditions.

## APPLICATION PROCEDURES

**Submission Guidelines:** Applications must be completed using the fillable PDF application form found on the grant-giving website and submitted via e-mail. Any applications submitted in any other format will not be accepted.

**Deadlines:** October

**Decisions:** February

## CONTACT
E-mail: sfedirector@for-wild.org

## GRANT-SPECIFIC WEBSITE
www.for-wild.org/seedmony.html

# E. F. Wildermuth Foundation

## Headquarters

1014 Dublin Rd.
Columbus, OH 43215
Phone: 614-487-0040

## Description

**Founded:** 1960

**Operating Locations:** Ohio

**Foundation Information:** Private foundation

## Financial Summary

Assets: $5,085,406
Total Giving: $282,034

## Grants Information

### GRANT TYPES
General support

### TYPICAL RECIPIENTS
Arts and humanities, civic affairs, education, health, religion, social services

### GRANT VALUES
Total Dollar Amount of Grants: $282,034
Number of Grants: 15
Average Grant: $18,000
Highest Grant: $66,034
Lowest Grant: $1,500

### PAST GRANT RECIPIENTS
*Library or School Related*
- Ohioana Library (OH), general support, $3,000
- Indiana University (IN), general support, $10,000
- Illinois College of Optometry (IL), general support, $15,000
- University of Illinois Foundation (IL), general support, $4,000
- Ohio State University, College of Optometry (OH), general support, $50,000
- Pennsylvania College of Optometry (PA), general support, $50,000

*General*

- Fairfield Heritage Association (OH), general support, $3,000
- Preventing Blindness (OH), general support, $5,000
- Children's Hospital (OH), general support, $7,500
- ACT Community Theatre (IL), general support, $1,500
- Twin City Ballet (IL), general support, $2,000
- Wildermuth Memorial Church (OH), general support, $66,034

## REQUIREMENTS AND RESTRICTIONS

Applicants must have tax-exempt status and be located in Ohio or its contiguous states.

## APPLICATION PROCEDURES

**Submission Guidelines:** Applicant should send a letter stating background of organization, purpose of requested grant, amount requested, and proof of tax-exempt status.

**Deadlines:** July 31

## CONTACT

Robert W. Lee
Phone: 614-487-0040

## GRANT-SPECIFIC WEBSITE

NA

# Anne Potter Wilson Foundation

## Headquarters

c/o Nationsbank of Tennessee
231 S. LaSalle St.
Chicago, IL 60697

## Description

**Founded:** 1996

**Operating Locations:** Tennessee

**Foundation Information:** Private foundation

## Financial Summary

Assets: $18,936,585
Total Giving: $1,215,000

## Grants Information

### GRANT TYPES

General support

### TYPICAL RECIPIENTS

Arts and humanities, civic affairs, education, religion, social services

### GRANT VALUES

Total Dollar Amount of Grants:
$1,215,000

Number of Grants: 20
Average Grant: $60,000
Highest Grant: $455,000
Lowest Grant: $5,000

## PAST GRANT RECIPIENTS

*Library or School Related*
- Justin Potter Library (TN), general support, $100,000
- Intercollegiate Studies (DE), general support, $25,000
- Watkins College (TN), general support, $50,000
- Vanderbilt University (TN), general support, $455,000
- Fund for American Studies (DC), general support, $5,000
- Montgomery Bell Academy (TN), general support, $85,000

*General*
- Cystic Fibrosis Foundation (TN), general support, $5,000
- Barrier Islands Park Society (FL), general support, $25,000
- Family Action Council of Tennessee (TN), general support, $25,000
- Nashville Symphony Orchestra (TN), general support, $50,000
- Oasis Center (TN), general support, $25,000

## REQUIREMENTS AND RESTRICTIONS
Applicants must have tax-exempt status.

## APPLICATION PROCEDURES
**Submission Guidelines:** Applicants should submit letter of request describing organization's qualification or status and a copy of its tax-exempt determination letter.

## CONTACT
Peter T. Dirksen
Bank of America Plaza
414 Union St.
Nashville, TN 37219-1697
Phone: 615-749-3653

## GRANT-SPECIFIC WEBSITE
NA

# H. W. Wilson Foundation

## Headquarters

950 University Ave.
Bronx, NY 10452
Phone: 718-588-8400

## Description

**Founded:** 1954

**Operating Locations:** New York

**Foundation Information:** Private foundation established by H. W. Wilson

## Financial Summary

Assets: $11,546,772
Total Giving: $775,916

## Grants Information

### GRANT TYPES
Research, general support, scholarship

### TYPICAL RECIPIENTS
Arts and humanities, civic affairs, education, environment, health, international, religion, science, social services

### GRANT VALUES
Total Dollar Amount of Grants: $775,916

### PAST GRANT RECIPIENTS

*Library or School Related*
- Westchester Library System (NY), general support, $7,500
- New York Public Library (NY), general support, $15,000
- Special Libraries Association (VA), general support, $5,000
- Metropolitan Museum of Art Library (NY), general support, $7,500
- American Library Association (IL), general support, $20,000
- Standford Free Library (NY), general support, $10,000

### REQUIREMENTS AND RESTRICTIONS
NA

### APPLICATION PROCEDURES
**Submission Guidelines:** Applicant should send a description of the library and proposed use of the grant.

### CONTACT
William Stanton
Phone: 718-588-8400

### GRANT-SPECIFIC WEBSITE
NA

# Wisconsin Department of Public Instruction, Division for Libraries, Technology, and Community Learning

## Headquarters

125 S. Webster St.
PO Box 7841
Madison, WI 53707-7841
Phone: 608-266-3390
http://dpi.wi.gov/dltcl/

## Description

**Founded:** NA

**Operating Locations:** Wisconsin

The Department of Public Instruction's Division for Libraries, Technology, and Community Learning (DLTCL) serves the lifelong learning and information needs of all Wisconsin citizens, from preschoolers to senior citizens.

## Grants Information

### GRANT TYPES
LSTA funds

### TYPICAL RECIPIENTS
Wisconsin libraries

### GRANT VALUES
NA

### PAST GRANT RECIPIENTS
NA

### REQUIREMENTS AND RESTRICTIONS
LSTA grant criteria, priorities, and categories are established annually. Applicants must be located in the state of Wisconsin.

### APPLICATION PROCEDURES

**Submission Guidelines:** Complete application online and mail to the address below.

**Deadlines:** September

### CONTACT
Wisconsin Department of Public
   Instruction

Attn: LSTA Program Coordinator
Division for Libraries, Technology, and
   Community Learning
PO Box 7841
Madison, WI 53707-7841
Phone: 608-266-2413

### GRANT-SPECIFIC WEBSITE
http://dpi.wi.gov/pld/lsta.html

# Wyoming Community Foundation

## Headquarters

313 S. Second St.
Laramie, WY 82070
Phone: 307-721-8300
www.wycf.org

## Description

**Founded:** 1989

**Operating Locations:** Wyoming

The Wyoming Community Foundation is a nonprofit charitable 501(c)(3) organization that was created for the people of Wyoming. With assets over $60 million, the Community Foundation has developed into a valuable philanthropic resource for Wyoming.

# Grants Information

**GRANT TYPES**
General support, continuing education

**TYPICAL RECIPIENTS**
Publicly accessible libraries and community college libraries and their employees, nonprofit organizations

**GRANT VALUES**
Typical Range of Grants: $500–$5,000

**NAMED GRANTS**

## McMurry Library Grants
McMurry Library Grants are awarded from the McMurry Library Donor Advised Endowment Fund. These grants are intended to support Wyoming's publicly accessible libraries and community college libraries. Requested funds should support one of the following categories: improving patron access to library books and materials, collection development, and/or ensuring long-term financial stability through technical assistance and publications.

## McMurry Continuing Staff Education Grants
McMurry Continuing Staff Education Grants are awarded from the McMurry Library Donor Advised Endowment Fund. These grants are available to benefit professional and paraprofessional employees at Wyoming's publicly accessible libraries and community college libraries. Grants of up to $1,500 are available annually to support (1) coursework for certification or completion of degree in a library-related subject area; (2) attendance at conferences, workshops, and seminars in library-related subject areas; (3) general courses that may not be directly library related but will allow a library employee to do his or her job more effectively. In order to be eligible for CSE grants individuals must be employed at the same library for a minimum period of 12 months.

**Deadlines:** End of January, March, May, July, September, and November

**Submission Guidelines:** Application online

**Contact:** Jamie Markus; Phone: 307-777-5914; E-mail: jamie.markus@wyo.gov

**Grant-Specific Website:** www-wsl.state.wy.us/mcmurry/indivgrants.html

## WYCF Competitive Grants
WYCF Competitive Grants are awarded throughout Wyoming from WYCF Unrestricted, Geographic, Field of Interest, and Donor Advised Funds. Awards generally range in amounts between $500 and $5,000; grants of greater or lesser amounts may be considered. Eligible organizations include nonprofit organizations exempt from federal taxation under Section

501(c)(3) of the Internal Revenue Code and, on occasion, public/governmental agencies. Grants are not made to individuals. Proposals may be submitted in the areas of arts and culture, conservation and natural resources, education, civic projects, and health and human services.

The foundation focuses its competitive grant making around the theme of community building; priority is given to projects or organizations that promote

- strengthening the capacity of nonprofit organizations to do their work
- leveraging dollars received from the WYCF to obtain additional or future funding
- collaborating with other nonprofits or programs to enhance services without duplication
- raising the effectiveness of an organization or particular service to a higher level
- focusing on or addressing an identified community issue

**REQUIREMENTS AND RESTRICTIONS**
Applicants must be located in the state of Wyoming.

**APPLICATION PROCEDURES**
**Submission Guidelines:** Application online

**Deadlines:** March 1, July 1, and November 1

**CONTACT**
NA

**GRANT-SPECIFIC WEBSITE**
www.wycf.org/grants/

# Young Adult Library Services Association (YALSA)

## Headquarters

50 E. Huron St.
Chicago, IL 60611
Phone: 800-545-2433, ext. 4390
www.ala.org/yalsa/

## Description

**Founded:** 1957

**Operating Locations:** Illinois

The mission of the Young Adult Library Services Association (YALSA), a division of the American Library Association, is to advocate, promote, and strengthen service to young adults as part of the continuum of total library service, and to support those who provide service to this population.

## Grants Information

**GRANT TYPES**
Travel, library improvement, research

## TYPICAL RECIPIENTS

Young adult librarians

## GRANT VALUES

Total Dollar Amount of Grants: $7,000
Number of Grants: 5
Average Grant: $1,166
Highest Grant: $2,000
Lowest Grant: $1,000

## NAMED GRANTS

### BAKER AND TAYLOR/ YALSA CONFERENCE GRANT

This grant is awarded annually to two librarians who work directly with young adults in a public or school library. Each winner receives $1,000 to enable them to attend ALA Annual Conference for the first time. One grant is given to a school librarian and one grant is given to a public librarian. Applicants must have one to ten years of experience working with teenagers.

### BWI/YALSA COLLECTION DEVELOPMENT GRANT

This grant awards $1,000 for collection development to two YALSA members who represent a public library, and who work directly with young adults ages 12–18.

### ABC-CLIO/GREENWOOD PUBLISHING/YALSA SERVICE TO YOUNG ADULTS ACHIEVEMENT AWARD

This biannual grant of $2,000 recognizes the national contributions of a YALSA member who has demonstrated unique and sustained devotion to young adult services in two or more of the following areas: promoting literature or programming for young adults, conducting and publishing research about young adults, mentoring other professionals in the field, or for notable efforts in the work of the Young Adult Library Services Association. The purpose of the cash award will be to enable the recipient to further his or her good work in the field of young adult librarianship.

### FRANCES HENNE/YALSA/VOYA (VOICE OF YOUTH ADVOCATES) RESEARCH GRANT

This annual grant of $1,000 is to provide seed money for small-scale projects that will encourage research that responds to YALSA's research agenda.

**Submission Guidelines:** A proposal of one to two pages, and one page of biographical information, should be submitted and must include the following:

- title
- objectives
- problem statement/questions to be answered
- methodology, including how data will be collected and analyzed
- significance of the project, in light of previous research
- projected time line

- statement of how the money will be used
- brief biographical data on the researcher on a separate sheet, with contact information including e-mail, as well as the researcher's ALA membership number

## GREAT BOOKS GIVEAWAY COMPETITION

Each year the YALSA office receives approximately 1,200 newly published children's, young adult, and adult books, videos, CDs and audiocassettes for review. YALSA and the cooperating publishers annually offer one year's worth of review materials as a contribution to a library in need. The estimated value of this collection is $25,000.

### REQUIREMENTS AND RESTRICTIONS

Applicants must be YALSA members who work directly with young adults, or YALSA institutional members.

### APPLICATION PROCEDURES

**Submission Guidelines:** Unless otherwise noted above, applications are available online. Download and fill out application and e-mail to the address below.

**Deadlines:** December 1

**Decisions:** Most decisions will be announced at the midwinter meeting.

### CONTACT

Nichole Gilbert
Phone: 800-545-2433, ext. 4387, or 312-280-4387
E-mail: ngilbert@ala.org

### GRANT-SPECIFIC WEBSITE

www.ala.org/ala/mgrps/divs/yalsa/
awardsandgrants/yalsaawardsgrants
.cfm

# GRANTORS BY TOTAL GRANT VALUE

# GRANTORS BY STATE

# NAMED GRANTS

## M

# PROFESSIONAL LIBRARY
# ORGANIZATION GRANTORS